Criminal Law and Criminal Procedure Law in the People's Republic of China

Criminal Law and Criminal Procedure Law in the People's Republic of China

Commentary and Legislation

By

Jianfu Chen

With the translation assistance of

Suiwa Ke

MARTINUS NIJHOFF PUBLISHERS

LEIDEN · BOSTON
2013

Library of Congress Cataloging-in-Publication Data

Chen, Jianfu, 1960-
Criminal law and criminal procedure law in the People's Republic of China : commentary and legislation / By Jianfu Chen ; with the translation assistance of Suiwa Ke.
pages cm
ISBN 978-90-04-23444-4 (hardback : alk. paper) -- ISBN 978-90-04-23445-1 (e-book) 1. Criminal law--China. 2. Criminal procedure--China. I. Ke, Suiwa. II. Title.
KNQ3800.C383 2013
345.51--dc23

2013012300

This publication has been typeset in the multilingual "Brill" typeface. With over 5,100 characters covering Latin, IPA, Greek, and Cyrillic, this typeface is especially suitable for use in the humanities. For more information, please see www.brill.com/brill-typeface.

ISBN 978-90-04-23444-4 (hardback)
ISBN 978-90-04-23445-1 (e-book)

This book is printed on acid-free paper.

CONTENTS

PART A

COMMENTARY

PART B

TRANSLATION

ACKNOWLEDGEMENT

The present publication has been prepared on the basis of an earlier publication, J. Chen & Suiwa Ke (eds.), *China's Criminal Laws – Commentary and Translation* (Singapore: CCH Asia Pte Limited, 2000), with the commentary and translation having been substantially revised and updated for the present edition.

The initial preparation and translation of the Criminal Law and Criminal Procedure Law of the PRC, both for the 2000 CCH edition and the present publication, was undertaken by Ms Suiwa Ke. The translation was then proofread and edited by Jianfu Chen, and further edited by Gabi Duigu. The translation was then finalised for publication by Jianfu Chen.

The author gratefully acknowledges the great and continuing assistance of Ms Suiwa Ke and Gabi Duigu. Without their assistance this publication would not have materialised.

The permission of CCH to use the 2000 published materials for the present publication is also gratefully acknowledged.

PART A

COMMENTARY

CHAPTER ONE

INTRODUCTION

Criminal law has always been a prominent branch of law in the Chinese legal system. Indeed, traditional Chinese law was commonly identified with criminal law, although this interpretation has now increasingly been recognised to be inaccurate. Modern legal reform too started with the reform of the criminal law.[1] In all communist legal reforms, developing the criminal law has always been a major part of the effort.

However, it took some 29 years for the communist authorities finally to produce a comprehensive criminal code.[2] It then took another 18 more years to bring the code closer to internationally accepted standards for criminal justice,[3] and since then the revised code has undergone numerous amendments.[4]

While the first comprehensive code on criminal procedural matters in the PRC was issued at the same time as the Criminal Law was promulgated in 1979,[5] conceptually the importance of procedure in administering law and justice was not appreciated until quite recently. It is therefore not surprising that when the Criminal Procedure Law (CPL) of the PRC was issued it became one of the pieces of legislation most criticised by both Chinese and Western scholars. Its comprehensive revision at the 4th Plenary Session of the 8th National People's Congress (NPC)[6] in 1996 thus signified a major development towards a deeper understanding of the notion of Rule of Law and justice. Although the revision of the CPL was

---

[1] See Chapter 1 on legal history in Jianfu Chen, *Chinese Law: Context and Transformation*, Leiden/Boston: Martinus Nijhoff Publishers (2008).

[2] The Criminal Law of the People's Republic of China was first adopted at the 2nd Plenary Session of the 5th National People's Congress (NPC) on 1 July 1979 and became effective on 1 January 1980.

[3] A comprehensive revision of the Criminal Law was adopted on 14 March 1997 at the Fifth Plenary Session of the 8th NPC.

[4] The last amendment took place in February 2011 (and was effective from 1 May 2011).

[5] The Criminal Procedure Law of the People's Republic of China was initially adopted by the 5th National People's Congress at its 2nd Plenary Session on 1 July 1979, effective from 1 January 1980.

[6] The Decision concerning the Revision of the Criminal Procedure Law was adopted by the 8th National People's Congress at its 4th Plenary Session on 17 March 1996.

only a moderate step towards improving the criminal justice system in China, and its outcome was mainly a result of major compromises between opposing views among scholars, officials and various forces in the Chinese legal system, the progress made in the 1996 revision, in the view of the present author, represented one of the most significant advances in the Chinese legal system since the establishment of the PRC in 1949.

In March 2012, the CPL was comprehensively revised again,[7] in yet another attempt to reform and improve the CPL and to bring its fundamental principles and working mechanisms closer to international standards, as embodied in the various international conventions.

This Commentary reviews the two codes and their development since 1979. It also analyses the basic principles now embodied in the present codes. The focus of this Commentary is on the codes since their comprehensive revisions in 1997/1996, which are analysed to highlight the major developments in the Chinese criminal justice system.

After the 1997 revision, the Criminal Law was re-promulgated, and the post-1997 development has taken the form of adopting independent amendments (8 Amendments in total, each of which revises numerous articles) without the Law being re-promulgated. For the purpose of this Commentary, the two versions of the Criminal Law (CL) are referred to as the 1979 Criminal Law and the 1997 Criminal Law respectively, with the latter incorporating revisions introduced by all Amendments adopted since 1997. In the case of the Criminal Procedure Law (CPL), the Law has been re-promulgated after each revision. Thus, for the convenience of discussion the original CPL and the 1996 and 2012 revised CPL will be referred to as the 1979 CPL, the 1996 CPL, and the 2012 CPL respectively.

[7] See Decision Concerning the Revision of the Criminal Procedure Law, adopted by the 11th National People's Congress at its 5th Plenary Session on 14 March 2012.

CHAPTER TWO

THE DEVELOPMENT OF THE CRIMINAL LAW IN THE PRC

II. 1. *The 1979 Criminal Law and Its Development*

The 1979 Criminal Law was one of the first major codes to be promulgated in post-Mao China.[8] Although supposed to be a comprehensive code along Continental European lines, it consisted of only very general, ideology-ridden, vague and ambiguous principles set out in 192 articles, with a strong Soviet influence.[9] This particular feature of the 1979 Criminal Law can best be understood from its drafting history.

The initial drafting work, aimed at producing some guiding principles for criminal law, was begun by the Legal Committee of the Central Government in 1950. The earliest draft, consisting of 157 articles and entitled Draft Outline of the Criminal Law of the PRC, was completed in July 1950.[10] As a result of the adoption of the 1954 Constitution and the establishment of the NPC, the drafting work was taken over by the Law Office of the NPC's Standing Committee in October 1954.[11] By June 1957 the Law

[8] Although there was no comprehensive criminal code, China was not without criminal law before 1979. Starting from the Instruction on Suppressing Counter-Revolutionary Activities (jointly issued by the Council of Government Administration and the Supreme People's Court in July 1950, later formally issued by the Central Government as the Regulations of the PRC on Punishing Counter-Revolution, in February 1951), there were various regulations on punishment for corruption, crimes undermining state currency and the crime of leaking state secrets. There were also various administrative rules, regulations and orders containing penal provisions. See Lan Quanpu, *Thirty Years of the Development of Law and Regulations in Our Country* (*Sanshi Nian Lai Woguo Fagui Yange Gaikuang*) (Beijing: Press of the Masses, 1982), at 55–65; and Jerome Alan Cohen, *The Criminal Process in the People's Republic of China, 1949–1963: An Introduction* (Cambridge, Massachusetts: Harvard University Press, 1968), ch.VI.

[9] The 1979 Law was a mixture of the Soviet Criminal Codes of 1926 and 1960 and China's own innovations. There was a second-hand German influence through the Soviet codes. See Harold J. Berman, Susan Cohen & Malcolm Russell, 'Comparison of the Chinese and Soviet Codes of Criminal Law and Procedure', (1982) (vol. 73, No.1) *Journal of Crim. L. & Criminology* 238.

[10] Zhang Youyu & Wang Shuwen, *Forty Years of Legal Science in China* (*Zhongguo Faxue Sishinian*) (Shanghai: Shanghai People's Press, 1989), at 216.

[11] Before this, the Legal Committee of the Central Government had finished another draft in 76 articles, entitled Guiding Principles of the Criminal Law of the PRC. See Zhang & Wang, *supra* note 10, at 217.

Office had completed its 22nd draft and submitted it to the NPC for deliberation. It was decided by the NPC that this draft, after the incorporation of suggestions made by representatives of the NPC, would be adopted for trial implementation. This did not happen, as the nation-wide political campaign of the Anti-rightist Movement was soon launched.[12] Efforts to draft a criminal law were resumed only in May 1962; rapid progress was apparently made and by 1963 the 33rd draft of the criminal law was completed and submitted to the Standing Committee of the Politburo of the Communist Party of China and to Mao Zedong for examination.[13] However, the drafting work was again to be interrupted by nation-wide political movements and not resumed until 1979.

In March 1979 the Legislative Affairs Committee (LAC) of the Standing Committee of the NPC (SCNPC) was established, and it decided to use the above-mentioned 33rd draft as its basis for drafting the code.[14] After a short period of just four months the Criminal Law was adopted by the NPC. Thus the 1979 Criminal Law was essentially a product of the 1950s and 1960s – a period when Chinese legal science was being established by borrowing heavily from Soviet scholarship and legal experience.[15] It is therefore not surprising that the 1979 Criminal Law embodied a strong Soviet influence, though it also reflected the then political policy of ensuring social stability, order and economic development.

Major deficiencies in the 1979 Criminal Law soon became apparent when implementation of the law began. To start with, provisions in the 1979 Criminal Law were soon found to be too general and lacking in precision for actual implementation. Secondly, various anti-crime

---

12 See Zhang & Wang, *supra* note 10, at 218; and Criminal Research Group, the Law Institute of the Chinese Academy of Social Sciences, *Lectures on the Criminal Law*, translated in (Vol. XIII, No.2, 1980) *Chinese Law and Government*, at 8.

13 *Lectures on the Criminal Law, supra* note 12, at 8–9.

14 Zhang & Wang, *supra* note 10, at 220; Peng Zhen, 'Explanations on the Draft Criminal Law and Draft Criminal Procedure Law', delivered to the 8th Meeting of the Standing Committee of the 5th NPC on 7 June 1979, in Peng Zhen, *On Political and Legal Work in New China* (*Lun Xinzhongguo De Zhengfa Gongzuo*) (Beijing: Press of the Central Committee's Documents, 1992), at 146.

15 In relation to criminal law science, the efforts of Chinese scholars in the first few years of the 1950s were concentrated on the study of Soviet criminal law theories, Soviet codes and the translation of Soviet codes and textbooks. It was natural that drafts of criminal law in the 1950s were largely modelled on the Soviet Code of 1926. Although Chinese scholars began to write their own textbooks on criminal law, these textbooks were then based on the Chinese criminal law drafts. Thus Soviet influence continued to spread through the Chinese textbooks on criminal law. See Zhang & Wang, *supra* note 10, at 216–218.

campaigns launched in China from the early 1980s required the imposition of severe punishments for targeted crimes (e.g. rape, murder, smuggling, drug trafficking etc.). Thirdly, the deepening economic reform also led to certain economic crimes that were not anticipated in the 1979 Criminal Law.[16]

To deal with the above deficiencies, major supplementation began to emerge. Barely a year and half after the implementation of the 1979 Criminal Law, the Decision Regarding the Handling of Offenders Undergoing Reform Through Labour and Persons Undergoing Rehabilitation Through Labour Who Escape or Commit New Crimes, and the Provisional Regulations on the Punishment of Crimes of Servicemen in Violation of Duty were issued by the SCNPC on 10 June 1981. Thereafter, numerous 'Decisions', 'Provisional Regulations' and 'Supplementary Provisions' were issued by the SCNPC, amending or supplementing the 1979 Law.[17] Many new offences were also created by various non-criminal statutes issued by the NPC, its Standing Committee, or even the State Council.[18] Clearly, the Criminal Law had become too fragmented and unsystematic. Further, certain supplementary provisions violated the principles of the 1979 Criminal Law. For instance, the 1982 Decision of the SCNPC on Severely Punishing Criminals Who Gravely Endanger the Economy and the 1983 Decision of the SCNPC on Severely Punishing Criminals Who Gravely Endanger the Public Security of the Society clearly had retroactive force,

16 See Wang Hanbin, 'Explanations on the Draft Revision of the Criminal Law of the PRC', delivered to the 5th Plenary Session of the 8th NPC on 6 March 1997, in Huang Taiyun and Teng Wei (eds.), *A Practical Guide and Interpretation of the Criminal Law of the PRC (Zhonghua Renmin Gongheguo Xingfa Shiyi Yu Shiyong Zhinan)* (Beijing: The Redflag Press, 1997), at 670.

17 By the time of the 1997 revision, 22 such Decisions, Provisional Regulations and Supplementary Provisions had been issued. See Wang Hanbin, *supra* note 16, at 670–80. For a list of these Decisions, Provisional Regulations and Supplementary Provisions see Ma Kechang & Ding Muying (eds.) *The Revision and Improvement of the Criminal Law (Xingfa De Xiugai Yu Wanshan)* (Beijing: Press of the People's Court, 1995), at 2–3.

18 By early 1995, more than 70 non-criminal statutes prescribing criminal punishment had been issued. For a summary of these provisions see Ma & Ding, *supra* note 17, at 2. By the time of the 1997 revision, more than 130 provisions contained in various non-criminal statutes had provided for criminal liability. See Wang Hanbin, *supra* note 16, at 671. These provisions created no fewer than 103 criminal offences. See Lin Yagang & Jia Yu, 'On the Character of Special Criminal Laws and Their Incorporation into the Criminal Code', in (no.1, 1997) *Peking University Law Journal (Zhongwai Faxue)* 79, at 80. Together with the supplementary provisions, no fewer than 230 offences had emerged since 1979. See Chen Xingliang, 'Dual Task for Criminal Revision: Change in Values and Adjustment of Structure', (no.1, 1997) *Peking University Law Journal (Zhongwai Faxue)* 55, at 60.

whereas the 1979 Criminal Law prohibited the retrospective application of the criminal law.[19]

Further, provisions on analogy, counter-revolutionary crimes and the death penalty attracted severe criticism from many intellectuals and human rights organisations.[20] Chinese scholars then began to question the wisdom of including provisions on analogy and counter-revolutionary crimes and the extensive application of the death penalty.[21]

Under these circumstances, the need comprehensively to revise the 1979 Criminal Law required little justification. Indeed, as soon as the 1979 Law came into effect some scholars had already called for the revision of the law.[22] According to Wang Hanbin, then Vice-Chairman of the SCNPC, the decision to revise the Law was made in 1982 and preliminary guidelines for the revision were established by the SCNPC in 1988.[23] However, specific revision work was mainly carried out by a Criminal Law Revision Group established in 1994 within the LAC of the SCNPC, consisting of scholars and practitioners.[24] This substantial work was completed in three years.[25]

Although various ideas for revising the 1979 Criminal Law were advanced by Chinese scholars, ranging from a complete overhaul to the rejection of any comprehensive revision,[26] the guidelines for the 1997 Revision apparently offered an easy path. First, the revision was to incorporate various Decisions and Supplementary Provisions issued by the SCNPC since 1979. Secondly, the revision was to ensure the continuity and

---

[19] See Article 9 of the 1979 Criminal Law.

[20] See e.g. Lawyers Committee for Human Rights, *Criminal Justice with Chinese Characteristics* (New York, 1993); and numerous reports by Amnesty International, Human Rights Watch, etc.

[21] See various volumes of the *China Law Yearbook* (published by the Press of China Law Yearbook, Beijing), which summarise major academic studies on various branches of law in China. These issues are to be further discussed below.

[22] As early as 1980 some scholars had already called for the revision of the 1979 Criminal Law. See Zhang Mingkai, 'On Properly Dealing with Several Relations in Revising the Criminal Law', (no.1, 1997) *Peking University Law Journal* (*Zhongwai Faxue*) 65, in his footnote 3, at 71.

[23] Wang Hanbin, *supra* note 16, at 670. The revision was often interrupted by various factors. See Ma Kechang, 'Strengthen the Reform Force, Revise and Perfect the Criminal Law', (no. 5, 1996) *Law Review* (*Faxue Pinglun*) 1, at 1.

[24] Cao Zidan & Hou Guoyun (eds.), *A Precise Interpretation of the Criminal Law of the PRC*, (*Zhonghua Renmin Gongheguo Xingfa Jingjie*) (Beijing: China University of Political Science and Law Press, 1997), at 1.

[25] Chinese officials have, however, insisted that the 1997 revision was the result of 15 years of drafting. See Wang Hanbin, *supra* note 16, at 671.

[26] See a collection of essays by 86 Chinese scholars: Ma & Ding, *supra* note 17.

stability of the Law; thus provisions without 'major' problems would not be revised. Thirdly, general and vague provisions were to be elaborated and clarified.[27] In short, the revision was to rationalise, systematise, clarify and elaborate the 1979 Criminal Law.

Following the major revision made to the Criminal Procedure Law (CPL) in 1996, a comprehensive revision of the Criminal Law was adopted in March 1997. The original law of 192 articles was then expanded to 452 articles in total. The categorisation of crimes was overhauled, with many new offences being created to meet the prevailing circumstances for the orderly development of a socialist market economy. Certain fundamental principles of justice, e.g. *nullum crimen, nulla poena sine lege* (and the consequent abolition of the provision on analogy), equality before the law, and proportionality were for the first time expressly incorporated into the criminal law.

Although the revision was heralded as 'a major and significant measure to improve the criminal law and criminal justice',[28] it was disappointing in many respects, as will be shown in the following analyses. It should also be pointed out here that the revised Criminal Law of 1997, although supposed to systematise and stabilise the criminal law, has since been amended or supplemented by the SCNPC no fewer than nine times, not including the various interpretations issued by the SCNPC, the Supreme People's Court and the Supreme People's Procuratorate. The following summary provides an overview of how extensively the 1997 Criminal Law has since been amended and supplemented:[29]

(1) Decision of the Standing Committee of the National People's Congress Decision on the Punishment of Crimes involving Fraudulent Purchasing, Evading, and Illegal Trading of Foreign Exchange (29 December 1998), amending Article 190, but also supplementing the 1997 Criminal Law;
(2) Amendment I (12 December 1999), aiming at strengthening the economic order by way of imposing heavier punishments for economic crimes by amending Articles 162 (1), 168, 174, 180, 181, 182, 185, & 225(3);

---

[27] See Wang Hanbin, *supra* note 16, at 671–672.

[28] *People's Daily* Commentator, 'A Major and Significant Measure to Improve the Criminal Law and Criminal Justice', *People's Daily* (*Renmin Ribao*) (internet edition), 4 April 1997.

[29] Unless otherwise indicated, any reference to the '1997 Criminal Law' is a reference to the Criminal Law as revised since 1997 including the latest revision, the 8th Amendment enacted in February 2011.

(3) Amendment II (31 August 2001), aiming at punishing the illegal occupation of and damage to forest land, by amending Article 342 only;
(4) Amendment III (29 December 2001), tightening provisions on terrorism and imposing more severe punishment on terrorist activities, by amending Articles 114, 115, 120, 125, 127, 191, and adding a new Article 291(1) ;
(5) Amendment IV (28 December 2002), aiming at cracking down on the manufacture and sale of fake and shoddy medical apparatus and the smuggling of waste, punishing the use of child labour and the dereliction of duty of judicial officials, protecting valuable trees and plants and their products, by amending Articles 145, 155, 344, 345, 399, and adding a new Article 244(1);
(6) Amendment V (28 May 2005), targeting credit card fraud, by amending Article 196 and adding a new Article 177(1) and a new item to Article 369;
(7) Amendment VI (29 June 2006), being one of the more significant amendments since 1997. It mainly concerns crimes endangering public security, crimes against enterprise administration order, crimes undermining financial management order, crimes of harming the interests of listed companies and investors, and commercial embezzlement. Heavier punishments are imposed on offenders and more severe criminal liabilities are incurred by persons in charge/in authority involved in such crimes. 18 articles were revised (134, 135, 139, 161, 162, 163, 164, 169, 175, 182, 185, 186, 187, 188, 191, 262, 303, 312, 399) and 8 sub-articles were added.
(8) Amendment VII (28 February 2009), amending eight Articles (i.e. Art 151, 180, 201, 225, 312, 337, 375, and 395) and adding three new Articles and four sub-articles, targeting mainly fraud in security trading, tax evasion, illegal operation of financial businesses, corruption among state functionaries, computer crimes, etc.
(9) Amendment VIII (25 Feb 2011), being the most significant amendment since 1997: (a) it removes the death penalty for 13 economic crimes, representing a 19% reduction in death penalties in the Code (from 68 crimes to 55 crimes); (b) it strengthens the penalties for organised crime (and also incorporates the 2002 Standing Committee's Interpretation of Article 294 (1) of the Code; (c) it improves the application of non-custodial penalties (including suspended sentences), including the introduction of a community correction system and more lenient penalties for minors and senior citizens.

Additionally, the *Decision of the Standing Committee of the NPC on Revision of Certain Laws* (PRC Chairman's Decree No 18, 27 August 2009) affects two Articles (namely Art 381 and Art 410), changing the wording 'requisition (*zhengyong*)' to "acquisition and requisition (*zhengshou* and *zhengyong*)". Further, the SCNPC continues to adopt decisions that supplement the 1997 Criminal Law.[30] Finally, the SCNPC has issued many interpretations of specific provisions of the Criminal Law.[31] And, of course, there are many interpretations issued by the Supreme People's Court and Supreme People's Procuratorate on the enforcement and implementation of the Criminal Law.

II. 2. *General Principles*

II.2.1. *An Overview*

Following the Continental style of the German model, the 1979 Criminal Law was divided into two parts: General Provisions (often also translated as General Principles, *zongze*) and Specific Provisions (*fenze*). The General Provisions define the purposes and scope of application of the Law as well as notions of crime and criminal liability. They also provide rules on sentencing, parole and statutory limitations. Specific Provisions define and elaborate various crimes and offences and their consequent penalties. This overall structure is retained in the 1997 Criminal Law.

The structure of the first part, the General Provisions, is intact, and the revisions in 1997 and since of this part appear to be minimal. However, the incorporation of some fundamental principles of justice into the General Provisions constitutes the most significant progress and development in criminal law since 1979.

---

[30] See eg Decision of the Standing Committee of the National People's Congress on the Banning of Heretic Organisations and the Prevention and Punishment of Heretic Activities (30 October 1999); and Decision of the Standing Committee of the National People's Congress on Certain Issues Concerning Anti-Terrorism Work (29 October 2011).

[31] These include interpretations on Article 93 (2) (29 April 2000); Articles (228, 342, 410 (31 August 2001); Article 384(1) (28 April 2002), Article 294 (1) (28 April 2002); Article 313 (29 August 2002); provisions on dereliction of duty (28 December 2002); on credit cards fraud (29 December 2004), on export receipts, tax receipts and other valuable receipts (29 December 2005); and on fossils (29 December 2005). See Law Database of the People's Congress of the NPC, available at http://www.npc.gov.cn (last accessed 22/11/12).

II.2.2. *Nullum Crimen, Nulla Poena Sine Lege and the Abolition of Analogy*

The 1979 Criminal Law did not expressly provide the principle of *nullum crimen, nulla poena sine lege*; instead, Article 79 allowed the application of the Law by analogy, subject to the approval of the Supreme People's Court.[32] Many Chinese scholars and officials have, however, insisted that *nullum crimen, nulla poena sine lege* or its 'spirit' is one of the basic principles of Chinese criminal law.[33] The existence of analogy was said to be supplementary to the Law and represented a flexible application of the 'old and rigid' principle of *nullum crimen, nulla poena sine lege.*[34]

This Chinese argument is, however, not convincing. As pointed out above, the 1979 Criminal Law was based on the 33rd draft from 1963, which itself was developed from various drafts completed in the 1950s and early 1960s. The principle of *nullum crimen, nulla poena sine lege* was severely criticised after the Judicial Reform Movement in 1952 as being one of the bourgeois legal principles that gave aid and comfort to landlords and counter-revolutionaries at the expense of the public interest and, as such, had to be rejected by socialist law.[35] The discussion on this principle did not resume until after the promulgation of the 1979 Law.[36]

The principle of *nullum crimen, nulla poena sine lege,* furthermore, is inconsistent with the use of analogy, which was an ancient legal institution in China. According to Shen Jiaben, the founding father of modern law reform in China, the practice of interpreting the law by analogy started in the Han Dynasty (206–8 B.C.) and was sanctioned by law in the Sui

---

[32] Article 79 of the 1979 Criminal Law provided that '[a] person who commits crimes not explicitly defined in the Specific Provisions of the criminal law may be convicted and sentenced, after the approval of the Supreme People's Court has been obtained, according to the most similar article in this Law.'

[33] See eg. Wang Henbin, *supra* note 16, at 672; Su Huiyu, *Criminal Law* (*Xingfa Xue*) (Beijing: China University of Political Science and Law Press, 1994), at 32; Lan Quanpu, *supra* note 8, at 69; Zhao Zhenjiang (ed.), *Forty Years of the Chinese Legal System* (*Zhongguo Fazhi Sishinian*) (Beijing: Beijing University Press, 1990), at 338; Huang & Teng, *supra* note 16, at 4; and Ma & Ding, *supra* note 17, 31–32.

[34] *Id.*

[35] Shao-chuan Leng, *Justice in Communist China: A Survey of the Judicial System of the Chinese People's Republic* (New York: Oceana Publications, Inc., 1967), at 42, 160 and 176; Cohen (1968), *supra* note 8, at 330.

[36] See List of Publications (1949–1985) in Gao Mingxuan (ed.), *A Summary of Criminal Law Research in the New China* (*Xinzhongguo Xingfa Yanjiu Zongshu*) (Henan: Henan People's Press, 1986), at 757–971.

Dynasty (589–618 A.D.).[37] However, as the conservatives who opposed the abolition of analogy argued, the practice had perhaps started much earlier.[38] Meijer apparently agreed that the argument based on the *Li Ji* and the *Book of History* by the conservatives was more accurate.[39] It is clear, in any case, that analogy was codified in the earliest extant written code, the Tang Code (*Tang Lü Shuyi*, first published in A.D.753).[40] The long history of the practice of analogy is thus said to have created an 'analogy complex' in the Chinese mentality.[41] The nature and the actual use of analogy in traditional China, namely to create new categories of crimes retrospectively, or simply to elaborate the 'most appropriate' punishment, is however disputed among scholars.[42]

Eventually, in spite of strong opposition from conservative forces,[43] analogy was formally abolished and the principle *nullum crimen, nulla poena sine lege* introduced into Chinese criminal law during the law reforms in the dying days of the Qing Dynasty.[44]

The Chinese communist justice system did not, however, accept this revision. The Statute of the Chinese Soviet Republic on the Punishment of Counter-Revolutionary Crimes – the first comprehensive legislation under

---

37 See Section IV of The Commissioner for the Revision of the Laws, Shen Jia-pen Presents by Memorial the Draft of the Criminal Law, in M.J. Meijer, *Introduction of Modern Criminal Law in China*, 2nd edition (Hong Kong: Lung Men Bookstore, 1967), at 195–196. A similar view is also held by some modern scholars. See for instance, Mary Buck, 'Justice for All: The Application of Law by Analogy in the Case of Zhou Fuqing', (no.2, 1993) 7 *J.Chinese L* 113, at 117.

38 See Meijer, *id*, at 94.

39 See Meijer, *supra* note 37, at 68.

40 See Buck, *supra* note 37, at 117.

41 Chen Xingliang, '*Nullum Creme Noena Peona Sine Lege* in Modern Times', (no.2, 1996) *Studies in Law* (*Faxue Yanjiu*) 11, at 40.

42 See Buck, *supra* note 37, at 117. One of the authorities on traditional Chinese penal law, Professor Geoffrey MacCormack, clearly holds the view that the reasoning by analogy employed by the imperial judicial officials was similar to statutory interpretation in the West and was not in conflict with the principle *nulla poena sine lege*. See Geoffrey MacCormack, *The Spirit of Traditional Chinese Law* (Athens & London: The University of Georgia Press, 1996), at 172–74.

43 See Meijer (1967), *supra* note 37, at 94.

44 Article 3 of the Chapter on Rights and Duties of the Subjects of the Principles of the Constitution (1908, never formally promulgated) for the first time in Chinese history provided that '[a] subject shall not be liable to arrest, imprisonment or punishment except as prescribed by law'. The New Criminal Law issued by the Qing government in 1910 for the first time formally provided in law the principle of *nullum crimen sine lege* (Article 10 thus contained the principle of 'no offence, no punishment without previous legal provision'. See Meijer (1967), *supra* note 37, at 71.) Article 1 of the Criminal Code of the KMT issued in 1935 provided the same. See Chen Xingliang, *supra* note 41, at 39. See also Ma & Ding, *supra* note 17, at 70.

communist rule defining criminal acts – explicitly revived the application of law by analogy.[45] The principle of analogy was reaffirmed by the first comprehensive criminal law in the PRC, the 1951 Regulations of the PRC on the Punishment of Counter-Revolutionary Crimes.[46]

The need for analogy in the communist criminal justice system was justified on the grounds of the temporary lack of comprehensive laws. Thus in the 1957 *Lectures on the General Principles of the Criminal Law of the PRC* edited by the Teaching and Research Office for Criminal Law of the Central Political-Legal Cadres' School, it was said that analogy would be abolished when the criminal law was established.[47] This moderate view on analogy was however to be severely criticised by 1958,[48] when the non-retroactivity of the criminal law, together with other fundamental principles of criminal justice, was systematically denounced.[49]

Abolition of analogy began to be seriously debated again only after 1988.[50] Central to the debate were differing interpretations of the three major issues: the legal position and the trend towards *nullum crimen, nulla poena sine lege* in the world's major legal systems; the possibility of the co-existence of this principle with analogy; and preference in cases of conflict between *nullum crimen, nulla poena sine lege* and analogy.[51] Those who argued for the abolition of analogy believed strongly that *nullum crimen, nulla poena sine lege* was a universal principle upheld in all major legal systems under the Rule of Law, that it and analogy were mutually exclusive and, thus, that the upholding of *nullum crimen, nulla poena sine lege*

---

45 See Article 38. An English translation of the Statute can be found in W.E. Butler (ed.), *The Legal System of the Chinese Soviet Republic 1931–1934* (New York: Transnational Publishers Inc., 1983), at 204–207.

46 Article 16. An English translation of the Regulations (translated as 'Act of the PRC for Punishment of Counterrevolutionaries') can be found in Shao-Chuan Leng & Hungdah Chiu, *Criminal Justice in Post-Mao China: Analysis and Documents* (Albany: State University of New York Press, 1985), at 177–182.

47 The Lectures are extracted in Cohen (1968), *supra* note 8, at 336. This view was perhaps influenced by developments in the Soviet Union, where the principle of analogy was a key part of the 1926 Russian Criminal Code, but was criticised in the late 1930s and finally discarded by the Soviet Union in 1958. See Berman, Cohen & Russell, *supra* note 9, at 249.

48 See Fan Ming, 'Some Opinions about *Lectures on the General Principles of Criminal Law of the PRC*', CFYC, 4:73 (1958), translated in Cohen (1968), *supra* note 8, at 339.

49 See Cohen (1968), *supra* note 8, at 15.

50 Ma & Ding, *supra* note 17, at 56. Up to the mid-1980s scholarly discussion on analogy mainly concentrated on the justification for and the proper use of analogy; there was only some isolated discussion on abolishing it. See Gao Mingxuan, *supra* note 36, at 126–37; and Zhao Bingzhi & Xiao Zhonghua, 'A Discussion on the Debate About the Abolition of Analogy in Criminal Law', (no.4, 1996) *Jurists* (*Faxue Jia*) 54.

51 Zhao & Xiao, *id*, at 57.

necessarily required the abolition of analogy in criminal law.[52] Opponents were not convinced by these arguments, believing that the impossibility of making a perfect criminal code necessarily required the application of the law by analogy. They also believed that *nullum crimen, nulla poena sine lege* was not a principle in Common law countries and that its importance had decreased in all other countries.[53]

The final decision to abolish analogy was perhaps first of all influenced by the fact that the revised Criminal Law, after incorporating various supplements and decisions over the previous 18 years, would become relatively comprehensive and the coverage of the Law would be greatly expanded. Secondly, Article 79 on analogy in the 1979 Law had rarely been used by courts. Thus it was deemed possible to abolish analogy and to incorporate *nullum crimen, nulla poena sine lege* into the revised law.[54]

Article 3 of the 1997 Criminal Law now provides that '[a]ll criminal acts expressly stipulated by law as crimes shall be determined as such and punished according to the law; acts not expressly defined by law as criminal shall not be judged so and shall not be punished.'

II.2.3. *Equality Before the Law and Marxism-Leninism-Mao Zedong Thought as a Guiding Ideology for Criminal Law*

Article 4 of the 1979 Criminal Procedure Law, which was promulgated at the same time as the 1979 Criminal Law, provided that '[a]ll citizens are equal in the application of the Law. No privilege whatsoever is permissible before the Law.' This principle of 'equality before the law' was not, however, set out in the 1979 Criminal Law.

The omission of this principle was perhaps attributable to the upholding of Marxism-Leninism-Mao Zedong Thought as the guiding ideology for criminal law,[55] which strongly emphasised the class nature of law. Under this ideology, criminal law was an important weapon for class

52 See e.g. Zhao & Xiao, *supra* note 50; Hu Yunteng, 'Abolition of Analogy and the Scientific Nature of Criminal Law', (no.5, 1995) *Studies in Law* (*Faxue Yanjiu*) 55; and Chen Xingliang, *supra* note 41.

53 See Hou Guoyun, '*Nullum Crimen, Nulla Poena Sine Lege* in a Market Economy and the Value of Criminal Analogy', (no.3, 1995) *Studies in Law* (*Faxue Yanjiu*) 61; Hou Guoyun, 'On the Retention or Abolition of Analogy', in Ma & Ding, *supra* note 17, at 56–68.

54 Wang Hanbin, *supra* note 16, at 672. According to Chinese scholars, in the 18 years of implementation of the 1979 Criminal Law only just over 70 cases were decided by analogy, and most of them concerned minor offences. See Ma & Ding, *supra* note 17, at 7; Hou Guoyun, *supra* note 53, at 64.

55 See Article 1 of the 1979 Criminal Law.

struggle, aimed primarily at attacking 'counter-revolutionaries and other criminals who seriously undermined social order and socialist construction'.[56] According to Mao's theory on correctly handling two kinds of social contradictions, i.e. those between enemies and the people and those among the people,[57] criminals were mainly enemies of the state who must be dealt with severely by criminal law. The 'people', though they might also be punished by the criminal law, had to be treated differently from the 'enemies'.[58] Under this ideology, it was not surprising that equality before the law was repudiated as an anti-Party bourgeois concept in the late 1950s and during the Cultural Revolution.[59]

Equality before the law as a legal principle re-emerged in the post-Mao era. However, there were also heated debates in the late 1970s and early 1980s as to whether equality before the law meant only equality in the application of the law or also included the making of law. Further, the major concern of upholding the principle was to prevent privilege being accorded to officials of all ranks; that is, law was to attack 'tigers and flies' alike. The emphasis was not so much on protection as on punishment.[60] Thus the principle was not included in the substantive law (the Criminal Law) but was incorporated into procedural law (the Criminal Procedure Law) or organic laws (the Organic Laws of the Court and the Procuratorate).[61] The debate in the late 1970s and early 1980s also led to the reinstatement of the equality principle in the 1982 Constitution.[62]

Article 4 of the 1997 Criminal Law now provides that '[a]ll are equal in the application of law. No privilege whatsoever is permissible beyond the law.' As with the previous equality provisions in other laws, the emphasis is on the application of law and on the elimination of official privileges.[63]

---

56 See discussions in Cohen (1968), *supra* note 8, at 71–96.

57 For Mao's theory see his thesis on Problems Relating to the Correct Handling of Contradictions Among the People, translated in Cohen (1968), *supra* note 8, at 83–88.

58 Lan Quanpu (1982), *supra* note 8, at 70–71.

59 See Leng & Chiu, *supra* note 46, at 104.

60 See the collection of papers debating the principle: Office for Research Materials, Law Institute of the Chinese Academy of Social Science (ed.), *On Equality Before the Law* (*Lun Falü Mianqian Renren Pingdeng*) (Beijing: Publishing House of Law, 1981). See further discussions in Leng and Chiu, *supra* note 46, at 104–108.

61 See Article 5 of the Organic Law of the Courts and Article 8 of the Organic Law of the People's Procuratorates. All these laws were adopted at the same session of the NPC during which the Criminal Law was also adopted.

62 See Article 33 of the 1982 Constitution.

63 See interpretations by scholars in China: Huang & Teng, *supra* note 16, at 4–5; and Cao & Hou, *supra* note 24, at 5–6.

It is also important to note that Marxism-Leninism-Mao Zedong Thought as a guiding principle of criminal law has now been formally dropped, which presumably means the final burying of the class nature of the criminal law.[64]

II.2.4. *Proportionality* (*Zuixing Xiang Shiying*)

One of the guiding principles incorporated in the 1979 Criminal Law was the policy of combining punishment with leniency,[65] which meant 'leniency to those who confess and severity to those who resist' in the determination of sentences.[66] However, the Law did not provide specific aggravating and mitigating circumstances to guide the court in sentence determination. This was to allow law enforcement to be adapted to the needs of the political situation at the time.[67] As with the concerns regarding equality before the law, such a policy can provide, and did provide, loopholes in the law for officials in power to escape legal sanctions or avoid severe punishment.[68] Further, the emphasis on confession was also potentially in conflict with the presumption of innocence.[69]

As was the fate of Marxism-Leninism-Mao Zedong Thought as a guiding principle, the principle of combining punishment with leniency was also abolished by the 1997 revision. Article 5 of the 1997 Criminal Law now provides that 'the severity or leniency of punishment shall be proportionate to the crime committed by the criminal and the consequent criminal liability [prescribed by law].' This is what Chinese scholars refer to as the principle of proportionality (*zuixing xiang shiying yuanze*).

The Chinese principle of proportionality is fundamentally based on the theory developed by the 18th century Italian scholar Cesare Beccaria in his seminal work *On Crimes and Punishments*.[70] The incorporation of this

---

64 Chinese scholars have, however, insisted that, since the Four Fundamental Principles are constitutional principles, the Criminal Law issued under the Constitution would logically still include this principle. See Huang & Tend, *supra* note 16, at 1; and Cao & Hou, *supra* note 24, at 3–4.

65 See Article 1 of the 1979 Criminal Law.

66 See Leng & Chiu, *supra* note 46, at 129.

67 Ibid.

68 Zhang Jun, 'The Three Basic Principles of the Criminal Law', *People's Daily* (*Renmin Ribao*) (overseas edition), 26 April 1997, internet edition.

69 The presumption of innocence was partially incorporated into the Criminal Procedure Law when it was revised in 1996. See Article 7 of the 1996 Criminal Procedure Law. See also discussions below on criminal procedure law.

70 See Hu Xuexiang, 'The Problems in the Principle of Proportionality and Their Solutions', (no.3, 1994) *Law Review* (*Faxue Pinglun*) 18; Liao Zengyun, 'Basic Principles that

principle, according to explanations given to the NPC by Wang Hanbin, is to make sure that serious crimes are punished heavily and minor crimes leniently. It is also to make sure that there will be a balance between various provisions of the Law in punishing crimes.[71] Thus, this principle encompasses the following aspects: First, the principle of proportionality is the basis for the General Provisions in dealing with issues of preparation to commit a crime, attempted crimes, incomplete crimes, joint offence, recidivism, and voluntary surrender. Secondly, the Specific Provisions of the Law are to have a balanced approach in defining punishments for criminal offences according to the seriousness of the crime. Thirdly, the nature of the crime and its social harm will be the main factors in the judicial determination of punishment.[72] This last point is important; it means that the principle of proportionality in China at present is not purely a reflection of the backward-looking philosophy of retributive justice (*lex talionis, 'an eye for an eye; a tooth for a tooth'*). The traditional forward-looking utilitarian views on justice, such as the educational function of the criminal law, are not discarded. Indeed, Article 57 of the 1979 Criminal Law is retained without any revision. This article requires that in individual sentence determination, courts shall consider the facts of a crime, its nature and circumstances, as well as its harm to society.[73] This article, however, gives judges great latitude in imposing punishment. To achieve the intended purpose of avoiding the misuse of leniency, the 1997 Law now further elaborates a number of articles dealing with aggravating and, in particular, mitigating circumstances. Thus Article 63 specifically provides that the imposition of punishment below the minimum punishment prescribed by the law must be approved by the Supreme People's Court.[74]

Should Be Clearly Adopted in Our Criminal Law', (no.1, 1990) *Legal Science in China* (*Zhongguo Faxue*) 54; Chen Xingliang, 'On the Development and Improvement of Our Criminal Law', (no.3, 1989) *Legal Science in China* (*Zhongguo Faxue*) 53; Li Shaoping & Deng Xiuming, 'Some Theoretical Considerations on Improving the Law on Crimes and Punishments', (no.1, 1996) *Modern Law Science* (*Xiandai Faxue*) 9; and Hu Xuexiang, 'Improving the Legislative Structure on Punishment', (no.2, 1996) *Modern Law Science* (*Xiandai Faxue*) 124. For Beccaria's theory on proportionality, see Cesare Beccaria, *On Crimes and Punishments*, translated by Henry Paolucci (Indianapolis/New York: The Bodds-Merrili Co. Inc., 1963). For a more recent translation by Richard Davies, Virginia Cox and Richard Bellamy see Richard Bellamy (ed.), *Beccaria On Crimes and Punishments and Other Writings* (Cambridge: Cambridge University Press, 1995).

[71] See Wang Hanbin, *supra* note 16 at 672.

[72] Huang & Teng, *supra* note 16 at 5–6.

[73] Article 57 is renumbered as Article 61 in the 1997 Criminal Law.

[74] Under Article 59 of the 1979 Criminal Law this was to be approved by the judicial committee of a people's court. Article 63 of the 1997 Criminal Law was further revised in

Article 67 now defines voluntary surrender as not only voluntary surrender to the authority after committing a crime, but also includes the truthful confession of crimes committed. Further, any criminal suspects, criminal defendants or convicted criminals who voluntarily and truthfully confess to crimes not yet discovered by the judicial authorities will also be treated leniently.[75] A new addition in 1997, Article 68, provides lenient punishment for offenders who provide information or other assistance to investigatory organisations in solving crimes committed by other people.

Despite the above improvement in the criminal law in dealing with severity and leniency of punishment, the 1997 Criminal Law continues to be very weak in terms of elaborate and detailed provisions on aggravating and mitigating circumstances. The frequent use in the Criminal Law of such vague terms as 'minor', 'relatively minor', 'serious', 'relatively serious' and 'particularly serious' without definition provides little useful guidance for sentencing in practice. Thus a proper application of the principle of proportionality is a crucial point in the actual operation of the Criminal Law. Further, the immediate practical effect of incorporating some fundamental principles is doubtful. For instance, the abolition of principles of upholding Marxism-Leninism-Mao Zedong Thought as the guiding ideology and of combining punishment with leniency as sentencing policy meant that the legal foundation for Yanda ('anti-crimes') campaigns had been removed, but Yanda continued well after the revision of the criminal law in 1997.[76] Clearer indications emerged only more recently. The annual work reports presented by the Supreme People's Court and the Supreme People's Procuratorate to the National People's Congress in March 2007 seemed to suggest that the Yanda anti-crime policy will now be abandoned in judicial work and, in its place, the legal requirement that 'the severity or leniency of punishment shall be proportionate to the crime committed by the criminal and the consequent criminal liability [prescribed by law]' as adopted in the 1997 Criminal Law will be strictly

2011 to provide more detailed guidance for cases where more than one scope of penalties is available.

[75] Article 67 is a revised version of Article 63 of the 1979 Criminal Law. This article was further revised in 2011. It now includes the provision that confession by one suspected of crimes, though not qualified as voluntary surrender, may be treated as a mitigating factor in imposing punishment.

[76] For a comprehensive study on Yanda up to 2006 see Susan Trevaskes, *Courts and Criminal Justice in Contemporary China* (Plymouth, UK: Lexington Books, 2007).

implemented.[77] These reports thus give the clearest indication that China may finally abolish politico-legal campaigns in administering criminal justice.[78] And if this is the case, we may finally see the practical effect of the fundamental principles as embodied in the 1997 Criminal Law.

II.2.5. *'White Collar' Crime – 'Unit Criminality'* (*Danwei Fanzui*)

Imposing criminal liability upon corporations is almost exclusively a tradition of the Common law.[79] Corporate criminal liability has mainly been advocated in the mid 20th century in European Continental countries as a means of controlling the excesses of increasingly powerful economic entities.[80] The development of the criminal liability of corporations as legal persons in all legal systems, however, has followed a long and winding path. The difficulties associated with corporate criminal liability are apparent. To start with, a corporation as an abstraction is conceptually without its own mind; thus there are difficulties in locating *mens rea* in imposing criminal liability. Further, it has no physical existence of its own. Thirdly, most forms of criminal punishment, such as incarceration, are clearly inapplicable to a corporation. Finally, the principle of *ultra vires* in corporation law certainly does not help in developing a theory of corporate criminal liability. However, for all practical purposes these difficulties are now largely overcome in both Civil and Common law jurisdictions.[81]

The Chinese legal system is no exception. When the Criminal Law was enacted in 1979 it did not expressly provide for, nor absolutely exclude, the criminal responsibility of a legal person. Some provisions seemed to hold

---

[77] See 'China rejects "strike hard" anti-crime policy for a more balanced approach', available: http://english.people.com.cn/200703/14/eng20070314_357516.html (last accessed 5/03/13).

[78] The 2001 Yanda campaign is so far the last reported nationwide Yanda campaign in post-Mao China. See Dai Yuzhong, 'Thirty Years of Chinese Criminal Justice', available at http://law.ruc.edu.cn/cyflpl/ShowArticle.asp?ArticleID=20164 (last accessed 27/8/12).

[79] L.H. Leigh, *The Criminal Liability of Corporations in English Law* (London: London School of Economics and Political Science, 1969), at 1.

[80] L.H. Leigh, 'The Criminal Liability of Corporations and Other Groups: A Comparative View', (1982) 80 *Michigan Law Review* 1508, at 1508.

[81] See further discussions in Leigh (1969), *supra* note 79; Leigh (1982), *supra* note 80; Elkins, 'Corporations and the Criminal Law: An Uneasy Alliance', (1976) 65 *Ky.L.J.* 73; 'Developments in the Law – Corporate Crimes: Regulating Corporate Behaviours through Criminal Sanctions', (1979) 92 *Harvard Law Review* 1227; and Leonard Orland, 'Reflections on Corporate Crime: Law in Search of Theory and Scholarship', (1980) 17 *American Criminal Law Review* 501.

only the individual liable;[82] others tended to hold both the legal person and the individual liable.[83] However, the prevailing criminal law theory at that time did not seem to lend much support to arguments for corporate criminal liability.[84] This was because, according to Chinese theory, crimes could only be committed with consciousness, and legal persons themselves could not commit any intentional criminal activities. Any such criminal activities could be committed only by the natural persons who constitute the legal person, and thus only these natural persons should be responsible for crimes committed by themselves.[85]

However, the emergence of economic crimes committed by enterprises as a result of economic reforms began to change judicial attitudes and practice towards corporate criminality. In 1985 the Resolutions of the Supreme People's Court and the Supreme People's Procuratorate Concerning Certain Questions on the Practical Application of the Law in the Present Adjudication of Cases of Economic Crimes (Trial Implementation) expressly affirmed the criminal liability of legal persons guilty of certain economic crimes.[86] For instance, the Resolutions provided that, if any state organ, association, institution, enterprise or collective economic entity was engaged in smuggling, illicit speculation, seeking illegal profits and bribery, criminal liability would be imposed on the person in charge of the legal person and on the person directly involved in the crime, and the property of the legal person involved in the crime would be confiscated.[87] Furthermore, two articles (Articles 49 and 110) of the General Principles of Civil Law seem to indicate that crimes may be

[82] For instance, Article 131 provided that: 'The rights of the person, the democratic rights and the other rights of citizens are to be protected and are not to be unlawfully infringed by any person or any organ. When the circumstances of unlawful infringement are serious, those persons directly responsible are to be given criminal sanctions'.

[83] For instance, Article 121 provided that: 'Those directly responsible for violating tax laws and regulations, evading taxes or resisting taxes, if the circumstances are serious, in addition to making up the tax due and paying any fine possibly imposed in accordance with the tax laws and regulations, are to be sentenced to not more than three years of fixed-term imprisonment or criminal detention'. This article did not specify the subject of crime (i.e. who commits the crime). If it was a legal person which violates tax laws, it seemed that the criminal punishment of imposing fines might apply to the legal person itself.

[84] See Yang Chuanxi, et al, *General Principles of Criminal Law* (Beijing: Beijing University Press, 1981), at 139–140; and *Chinese Encyclopaedia – Law* (*Zhongguo Dabaike Quanshu – Faxue*) (Beijing/Shanghai: The Chinese Encyclopaedia Press, 1984), at 128.

[85] Yang Chuanxi, ibid., at 141.

[86] See section 2(2) of the Resolutions of the Supreme People's Court and the Supreme People's Procuratorate Concerning Certain Questions on the Practical Application of the Law in the Present Adjudication of Cases of Economic Crimes (Trial Implementation).

[87] Ibid.

committed by legal persons and criminal liability may be imposed on legal persons in accordance with law.[88] However, the wording of these provisions is still very vague.

In 1987 the Customs Law of the People's Republic of China was adopted by the SCNPC. Article 47 (3) of the Customs Law states that '[w]here an enterprise, an undertaking, an organ or a social organisation is guilty of smuggling, the judicial organ shall pursue the criminal liability of the person in charge of the respective unit and the person directly answerable for the offence and shall impose a fine on the unit and confiscate the smuggled goods and articles, the means of transport used to carry them and the illegal incomes obtained therefrom'. This provision is interpreted by some Chinese scholars as meaning that Chinese legislation for the first time expressly adopted the so-called 'dual punishment' principle.[89] This legislative approach was later followed by two other pieces of legislation adopted by the SCNPC: Article 9 of the Supplementary Rules of the SCNPC on the Severe Punishment of Corruption and Bribery Offences (1988) provided that '[a]ny enterprise, institution, authority or body that offers rebates and handling charges to a state functionary, member of staff of a collective economic body or any other person holding public office for unlawful advantages in breach of state regulations shall be fined where severity justifies it. The officer-in-charge directly responsible and other persons directly responsible shall be sentenced to imprisonment or criminal detention of not more than five years…', and Article 5 of the Supplementary Rules of the SCNPC on the Punishment of Smuggling (1988) stated that '[a]ny enterprise, institution, state authority, or association that engages in the smuggling of goods and articles specified in Articles 1 to 3 of the present Rules shall be fined; the directly responsible officer-in-charge and other directly responsible persons shall be punished in accordance with the provisions of the present Rules governing

---

[88] Article 49 states that: 'Should any one of the following circumstances apply to an enterprise legal person, it shall assume liability and, in addition, its legal representative may be subject to administrative sanction or a fine; if a crime is constituted, criminal liability shall be investigated and determined according to the law: …'. Article 110 states that: 'If it is necessary to investigate and determine administrative liability with regard to a citizen or legal person bearing civil liability, such administrative liability shall be investigated and determined. If a criminal offence is constituted, the criminal liability of the citizen or of the legal representative of the legal person shall be investigated and determined'.

[89] See Zhu Huaron & Lin Jianhua, 'On Our Legislation and Perfecting the Legislation Concerning Crimes Committed by Legal Persons', (no.5, 1988) *Journal of China University of Political Science and Law* (*Zhengfa Luntan*) 26; Yang Chunxi, 'Legislative Improvement on Corporate Criminality', (no.5, 1995) *Legal Science in China* (*Zhongguo Faxue*) 35.

smuggling offences committed by individuals'. By 1997, no fewer than 13 Decisions and Supplementary Provisions had provided corporate criminality.[90] However, there was no law regarding the general concept of crimes committed by legal persons, nor general guidelines for the criminality of legal persons. There were also no procedural rules concerning prosecuting legal persons. It was still unclear whether a legal person, in general, could be a defendant in criminal procedures.

Along with the legislative and judicial developments came the challenge to the traditional criminal theory that denied corporate criminal liability. In around 1982 some scholars began to advocate corporate criminality.[91] At that point two theories, 'affirmative theory' (*Kending Shuo*) and 'negative theory' (*Fouding Shuo*) in the Chinese terminology, existed in opposition to each other.[92]

Generally, the 'negative theory' offered little new; it concentrated on the difficulties of imposing criminal liability on legal persons.[93] Scholars of the 'affirmative theory' school argued that the decision-making organ of a legal person was just like that of the human brain, and thus decisions made by the organ reflected the intention and the will of the legal person.[94] It was further argued that, if legal persons could perform intentional civil legal actions, there was no reason why a legal person could not perform criminal activities with consciousness and be held liable for those criminal actions.[95] Further, scholars in this group argued that since the decision-making power was in the hands of the decision-making organ of the legal person, which generally made its decisions on the basis of majority voting, it would be wrong to punish the person in charge of the legal person (such as the director or manager) for the activities committed by the legal person through the legal person's decision, which the person in

[90] Lin Yagang & Jia Yu, 'On the Characters of Special Criminal Laws and Their Incorporation into the Criminal Code', (no.1, 1997) *Peking University Law Journal* (*Zhongwai Faxue*) 79, at 81.

[91] According to Chinese scholars, the challenge first appeared in 1982, and intensified in 1984 when the Party decided that enterprises should become legal persons, and economic crimes were more frequently committed by enterprises and other economic entities. See Zhu & Lin, *supra* note 89 at 25; and Gao Mingxuan, *supra* note 36 at 199.

[92] Gao Mingxuan, *supra* note 36 at 199.

[93] Gao Mingxuan, *supra* note 36 at 206–213; Ma Junju, *On the Institution of Legal Person* (*Faren Zhidu Tonglun*) (Wuhan: Wuhan University Press, 1988), at 299; Chen Zhixian, 'On Criminal Law Issues Concerning Legal Persons', (no.6, 1986) *Political Science and Law* (*Zhengzhi Yu Falu*), at 41; Zhao Bingzhi, 'Certain Considerations as to Why Legal Persons Cannot Become Subjects of Crime', (no.5, 1989), *Studies in Law* (*Faxue Yanjiu*) 57.

[94] Gao Mingxuan, *supra* note 36, at 202.

[95] Chen Zhixian, *supra* note 93, at 41.

charge might actually have voted against.[96] Also, if the person in charge, as an innocent person, was not punished, and nor was the legal person, then the result would be that a crime would be left unpunished.[97] If a crime was left unpunished, it was further argued by the scholars in this group, the criminal law's purpose of preventing crime would be circumvented.[98] Only punishment imposed on legal persons could prevent them from committing crimes and serve the educational purposes of the criminal law.[99] Regarding punishments for crimes committed by legal persons, these scholars argued that both the person in charge (the person participating in decision-making or directly performing the criminal actions) and the legal person should be held liable and be punished.[100] They argued that some provisions for supplementary punishment such as fines and confiscation of property were most appropriate for legal persons.[101]

Although in the mid-1980s only a few scholars argued for corporate criminal liability, legal literature in the PRC had by the late 1980s shifted attention to discussions on improving current criminal legislation.[102]

---

96 Ibid., at 42.

97 *Id.*

98 Chen Zhixian, *supra* note 93, at 43.

99 See Gao Mingxuan, *supra* note 36, at 204.

100 Ibid., at 204–205. Chinese scholars in this group called this kind of punishment the 'principle of dual punishment' (*Liangfa Yuanze*), i.e. both the legal person and the individual should be punished.

101 Ibid., at 205. Punishments in the 1979 Criminal Law were divided into principal punishments and supplementary punishment. Principal punishments include Control; Criminal Detention; Fixed-term Imprisonment; Life Imprisonment; and the Death Penalty. The types of supplementary punishments were Fines; Deprivation of Political Rights; and Confiscation of Property. Under the Law, supplementary punishment may also be applied independently. See, Articles 27, 28, and 29 of the 1979 Criminal Law.

102 See Shu Yongbao & Chen Yonglu, 'Causes of and Counter-measures Towards Crimes by Legal Persons', (no.2, 1989) *Political Science and Law* (*Zhengzhi Yu Falu*), at 63; Zhao Junru & Li Shenglong, 'Discussions on Legislation on Crimes by Legal Persons', (no.3, 1989) *Modern Law Science* (*Xiandai Faxue*), at 55–58; Zhou Yuan, 'Suggestion on Legislation on Duality of Liability of Crimes by Legal Persons', (no.1, 1990) *Modern Law Science* (*Xiandai Faxue*), at 54–57; Cuei Qingsen, 'On Crimes by Legal Persons', (no.5, 1990) *Studies in Law* (*Faxue Yanjiu*), at 14–22; Li Mingliang, 'Personal Opinions on Methods of Legislating on Crimes by Legal Persons', (no.2, 1991) *Modern Law Science* (*Xiandai Faxue*), at 61–62; Zhang Wen, et al, 'A Further Study on Several Questions regarding Corporate Criminality', (no.1, 1994) *Legal Science in China* (*Zhongguo Faxue*) 57; Li Xihui, 'Some Considerations on Restructuring Criminal Legislation on Corporate Crimes', (no.1, 1994) *Journal of China University of Political Science and Law* (*Zhengfa Luntan*) 16; and Ma & Ding, *supra* note 17, at 74–82.

This seems to suggest that there was then consensus among Chinese jurists on affirming the criminal liability of legal persons.

Among various legislative proposals advanced by advocates for corporate criminal liability, three main ideas can be identified. First, there was the proposal that the General Part of the Criminal Law be amended to provide expressly for the criminality of legal persons and that individual acts and regulations be made to provide for specific crimes and punishments.[103] The second group suggested that the Criminal Law be wholly amended to provide both for the criminal liability of legal persons in general, and for specific crimes and punishments in detail.[104] The third opinion advocated the making of a special code on the criminal liability of legal persons which would provide general principles of criminal liability of legal persons and guidelines for the imposition of punishments upon them.[105]

A major development in the 1997 Revision has been the adoption of corporate criminal liability as advocated by the 'affirmative school'. A new section entitled 'Unit Crimes' (*Danwei Fanzui*), is now found in Chapter One of the General Part. Article 30 of the 1997 Criminal Law now provides that '[c]ompanies, enterprises, institutions, state organs and social organisations when committing acts endangering the society shall assume criminal liability when prescribed by the law.' Article 31 further provides that '[w]hen a unit commits a crime, it shall be fined. At the same time, the person in charge of the unit and other directly responsible persons shall be liable to be punished by the criminal law unless otherwise provided by the Specific Provisions of the Law or by other laws.' In the Specific Provisions of the 1997 Criminal Law there are more than 80 articles prescribing unit criminal liability.[106] It should be pointed out that the 1997 Criminal Law uses the term 'Unit Crime' instead of 'corporate crime'. The reason is that many organisations are not necessarily corporations but may nevertheless commit a criminal offence; thus the term 'Unit' is designed to encompass not only companies, but also other unincorporated organisations.[107]

---

103 Zhao & Li, *supra* note 102.

104 Zhou Yuan, *supra* note 102; and Cuei Qingsen, *supra* note 102.

105 Li Mingliang, *supra* note 102.

106 Based on my own calculation.

107 Liu Shengrong, 'Corporate Crimes or Unit Crimes', (no.6, 1992) *Legal Science in China* (*Zhongguo Faxue*) 77; Cao & Hou, *supra* note 24, at 31–32.

II.2.6. *Territorial and Extraterritorial Application*

The Criminal Law is applicable to offences committed by any person (Chinese or foreigner alike), including offences committed aboard ships or aircraft of the PRC if either the commission or the effect takes place within the territory of the PRC.[108] However, the criminal responsibility of foreigners who enjoy diplomatic privileges and immunity will be resolved through diplomatic channels.[109] Further, flexible implementation of the Law in minority autonomous regions is allowed.[110] Finally, the Law is not applicable in Hong Kong or Macau unless otherwise declared by the NPC in accordance with emergency powers stipulated in the Basic Laws of Hong Kong and Macau.

The Chinese Criminal Law has always maintained its extraterritoriality. Under the 1979 Criminal Law an offence committed by a Chinese national outside China would not be punished by the Criminal Law if the act was not punishable by the law of the place where it was committed or if the minimum punishment under the Chinese law was imprisonment for less than three years, unless the Chinese national committed a more serious offence (e.g. counter-revolutionary crimes) as specified in Article 4.[111] The revised law has now greatly expanded the extraterritorial application. The 1997 Criminal Law now applies to all offences committed outside China by a Chinese national if the maximum punishment under Chinese law is imprisonment for three years or more.[112] Further, any offences committed by Chinese state personnel or military personnel are covered by the Criminal Law.[113] The expansion of the extraterritorial application has, at least initially, been targeted at the increasing number of Chinese students and business people now studying or working abroad.[114]

---

108 Article 6 of the 1997 Criminal Law.

109 Article 11 of the 1997 Criminal Law.

110 Article 90 of the 1997 Criminal Law.

111 See Articles 4 & 5 of the 1979 Criminal Law.

112 Article 7. This provision clearly is not one that could easily be enforced. However, there have been reports that China actually enforces it. For instance, in mid-August 2012, a joint operation by Chinese and Angolan police raided Chinese 'criminal gangs' (committing crimes against Chinese citizens in Angola) in Angola, arrested 37 suspects and took them back to China for trial. See '37 suspects involved in violent crimes in Angola sent back to China', available at http://news.xinhuanet.com/english/china/2012–08/25/c_131807401.htm (last accessed 5/03/13).

113 See Article 7 of the 1997 Criminal Law. 'State personnel', under Article 93 of the 1997 Criminal Law, includes all state personnel working in state-owned companies, enterprises and institutions as well as those assigned by the state to work in non-state-owned companies, enterprises, institutions and social organisations.

114 See Huang & Teng, *supra* note 16, at 8.

The extraterritorial application to foreigners committing offences against China outside the country has remained the same; that is, the law is applicable if an offence is committed by a foreigner against China or a Chinese national and the minimum punishment prescribed by the law is imprisonment for not less than three years, unless the act is not punishable by the law of the place where it is committed.[115] Further, even if an offence has been tried by a foreign state, the extraterritorial application of the law remains. However, if the offender has been punished by a foreign state, the punishment may be entirely waived or partially mitigated.[116] This provision clearly rejects the principle of double jeopardy as far as crimes committed outside China are concerned.[117]

In terms of retroactivity, the 1997 Criminal Law re-affirms the principle of non-retroactivity; that is, that offences committed before the revision shall be pursued by the previous law, but if the new law does not consider the act an offence, or provides a lighter punishment, the revised Law shall be applied.[118]

II. 3. *Crime and Punishment*

II.3.1. *An Overview*

The Chinese Criminal Law defines as criminal any act which endangers state sovereignty and territorial integrity and security, splits the state, jeopardises the political powers of the people's democratic dictatorship and socialist system, undermines social and economic orders, encroaches upon state property, collective property of the working masses or the privately owned property of citizens, infringes the personal, democratic and other rights of citizens or any other act which endangers society and is punishable according to law as a criminal offence, except those offences which are obviously of a minor nature and whose harm is negligible.[119] Following this definition and according to Chinese jurisprudence, there are three basic criteria for determining criminality. First, a criminal offence is an act that endangers society. Secondly, such an act violates

[115] Article 8 of the 1997 Criminal Law.

[116] Article 10 of the 1997 Criminal Law.

[117] See Cao & Hou, *supra* note 24, at 11.

[118] See Article 12 of the 1997 Criminal Law.

[119] See Article 13 of the 1997 Criminal Law. The original Article 10 of the 1979 Criminal Law has been revised to abolish the more ideological terms (eg. 'socialist revolution' and 'proletariat dictatorship' etc.) and to emphasise the protection of economic order.

the criminal law. Thirdly, such an act is punishable by the criminal law.[120] The Chinese law also requires the existence of *mens rea* (either intention or criminal negligence); an act which results in harmful consequences due to irresistible or unforeseeable factors rather than due to intention or negligence is not a criminal offence.[121]

These provisions defining the concept of crime have not been substantially revised; nor have the original eight types of crimes stipulated in the 1979 Criminal Law been substantially amended or supplemented. Thus the 1997 Criminal Law now contains ten types (in ten chapters) of crime:

(1) Crime endangering state security;
(2) Crime endangering public safety;
(3) Crime undermining the socialist market economic order;
(4) Crime infringing the personal rights or democratic rights of citizens;
(5) Crime encroaching upon property;
(6) Crime disrupting social administration order;
(7) Crime endangering the interests of national defence;
(8) Crime of embezzlement and bribery;
(9) Crime of malfeasance (dereliction of duty); and
(10) Crime in violation of military duties.[122]

In comparison with the 1979 Criminal Law, the structure of the Law in stipulating crime has not significantly changed, but the Specific Provisions of the Criminal Law for these crimes have been substantially expanded through the incorporation of various decisions and

---

[120] See Leng & Chiu, *supra* note 46, at 124; Cao & Hou, *supra* note 24, at 15; Huang & Teng, *supra* note 16, at 15; and *Lectures on the Criminal Law, supra* note 12, at 23–24. This concept of criminality is identical to that articulated in the 1950s. See also Cohen (1968), *supra* note 8, at 328–334.

[121] See Articles 14–16 of the 1997 Criminal Law.

[122] According to the classification of the Supreme People's Procuratorate, these ten crimes in the initially revised Criminal Law of 1997 included 414 criminal offences. See Supreme People's Procuratorate Opinion on the Names of Offences in the Specific Provisions of the Criminal law, issued on 25 December 1997. A copy of the Opinion (including the specific classifications) is available in *China Law Yearbook 1998* (*Zhongguo Falü Nianjian 1998*) (Beijing: China Law Yearbook Press, 1998), at 692–699. Because of the continuing revisions made to the 1997 Criminal Law, the classification of offences has been amended five times jointly by the Supreme People's Court and the Supreme People's Procuratorate. At present, the Criminal Law (as revised) contains a total of 451 offences. For a complete list of the offences see http://www.chinalawyer.cc/xingfa/20100831202210_369003.html (last accessed 27/8/12). See also http://club.148com.com/?uid-56839-action-viewspace-itemid-57712 (last accessed 27/8/12).

supplementary provisions issued by the NPC between 1979 and 1997 and amendments since 1997. Thus, 'crime undermining the socialist market economic order' is further divided into eight sections dealing with eight sub-divisions of the crime, while 'crime disrupting social order and its administration' is subdivided into nine sections. Further, 'crime against marriage or the family' is now incorporated into 'crime infringing on the personal rights or democratic rights of citizens'. At the same time the 'crime of bribery and embezzlement' has been separated from malfeasance and become an independent category of crime. Finally, and of symbolic significance, 'counter-revolutionary crime' is now renamed 'crime against state security'. 'Crime endangering the interests of national defence' and 'crime in violation of military duties' form a new category in the criminal law by incorporation of the NPC's earlier decisions.

Criminal punishment has remained the same since the initial enactment of the 1979 Criminal Law. There are five types of 'principal punishment' (*zhuxing*):

(1) Control and Surveillance (Control, *guanzhi*) (from three months to two years);[123]
(2) Criminal detention (*juyi*) (from one month to six months);[124]
(3) Fixed term imprisonment (from six months to 15 years and up to 25 years when the death penalty is commuted to a fixed term or in cases of combined punishment for more than one crime);[125]
(4) Life imprisonment;
(5) The death penalty.

In addition, there are three types of 'supplementary punishment' (*fujia xing*):

(1) Fines (there is no specified monetary limit);
(2) Deprivation of political rights (including right to election, freedom of speech and press, the right of protest, the right to hold a position in state organs, and the right to hold a leading position in a state-owned

---

123 Article 38 of the 1997 Criminal Law. 'Guanzhi' is sometimes translated as 'Public Surveillance', but often referred to as 'Control' in legal literature. In this Commentary, we continue to use the word 'Control' so as to be consistent with other publications on Chinese law.

124 Article 42 of the 1997 Criminal Law.

125 Articles 45, 50 & 69 of the 1997 Criminal Law.

company, enterprise, institution or people's organisation, for one to five years, but with permanent deprivation for those sentenced to death or life imprisonment);[126]

(3) Confiscation of property.

These supplementary punishments may also be imposed independently of the principal punishment.

In addition to the above types of punishment, deportation may be applied as an independent or supplementary penalty to a foreigner who commits a crime.[127] Further, the convicted criminal may also be required to compensate for the economic losses of their victims.[128] Finally, the court has the discretionary power to exempt a convicted person from criminal punishment where the crime is minor and does not require punishment. But in such a case the offender may be reprimanded or ordered to make a statement of repentance or formal apology, or to pay compensation for losses, or be subjected to administrative penalties or sanctions by the competent authority.[129]

Among these principal and supplementary types of punishment, the death penalty has been the most controversial form of punishment for decades, and has been finally subject to some major reforms since 2006.[130]

In the 2011 reform (the 8th Amendment) of the 1997 Criminal Law, control as a penalty was also subject to some significant reforms.

'Control' as a form of punishment was initially developed as a measure for controlling counter-revolutionaries in the PRC.[131] Before the enactment of the Criminal Law in 1979, it was often used imprecisely. Thus, when the Criminal Law was being drafted, there were debates about whether *guanzhi* should be incorporated into the Criminal Law as a form of punishment.[132] During the 1997 revision many scholars again debated whether control should be abolished altogether.[133] Instead, the

126 Articles 54–55 of the 1997 Criminal Law.

127 Article 35 of the 1997 Criminal Law.

128 Article 36 of the 1997 Criminal Law.

129 Article 37 of the 1997 Criminal Law.

130 The death penalty will be discussed further below.

131 See Cohen (1968), *supra* note 8, ch.V.

132 See Gu Angran, *Socialist legal System and Legislative Work* (*Shehui Zhuyi Fazhi He Lifa Gongzuo*) (Beijing: China University of Political Science and Law Press, 1989), at 190–191.

133 See Ma & Ding, *supra* note 16, 32 & 42; Cao Zidan, 'On the Basis for the Existence of *Guanzhi* in Our Country', (no.1, 1990) *Legal Science in China* (*Zhongguo Faxue*) 61; Jiang Lihua, 'On the Retention and Improvement of *Guanzhi* as a Punishment', (no.1, 1990)

1997 revision elaborated the restrictions imposed on a person sentenced to control, including the deprivation of the right to freedom of speech and press, to freedom of assembly, association, procession and demonstration, unless otherwise permitted by the executing organ, and restrictions on movement and activities, as well as relocation.[134]

Finally in 2011, two major reforms were introduced into the Criminal Law in relation to control – prohibition orders and community corrections.

In 2003 a notice, entitled Notice on Trial Implementation of Community Corrections, was jointly issued by the Supreme People's Court, Supreme People's Procuratorate, the Ministry of Public Security, and the Ministry of Justice. This Notice formally kick-started the introduction of community correction into the Chinese justice system. The Notice designated the Ministry of Justice as the leader in organising the trial implementation, and the principal functions in the administration of the community correction service fell to the Ministry of Justice.[135] Initially, the trial was conducted in the cities of Beijing, Tianjin, Shanghai, and Jiangsu, Zhejiang and Shandong provinces.[136] In January 2005, a further joint notice was issued, expanding the trial implementation to 12 provinces.[137] Finally, in 2009, community corrections were implemented nationwide.[138] Thus a national network of community corrections was established in China for those sentenced to control, or other convicted offenders to whom the application of incarceration is not appropriate or not necessary.[139] The

---

Legal Science in China (*Zhongguo Faxue*) 66; and Cao Jianglun & Liu Defa, 'A Suggestion to Abolish *Guanzhi* as a Punishment in Our Criminal Law', (no.1, 1990) *Legal Science in China* (*Zhongguo Faxue*) 71.

134 Article 39 of the 1997 Criminal Law.

135 A set of Interim Measures on Community Corrections by Judicial Administrative Organs was issued by the Ministry of Justice on 9 May 2004. On 10 January 2012 the Implementing Measures for Community Corrections were jointly issued by the Supreme People's Court, Supreme People's Procuratorate, the Ministry of Public Security, and the Ministry of Justice. Article 2 of the Measures stipulates that the judicial administration authorities are responsible for the administration and implementation of community correction work.

136 See Item 4 of the Notice.

137 See Notice on Expanding the Areas for Trial Implementation of Community Corrections, jointly issued by the Supreme People's Court, Supreme People's Procuratorate, the Ministry of Public Security, and the Ministry of Justice, *sifa* (2005) No. 3, 20 January 2005.

138 See Opinion on Nationwide Trial Implementation of Community Corrections, *sifatong* (2009) No.169, jointly issued by the Supreme People's Court, Supreme People's Procuratorate, the Ministry of Public Security, and the Ministry of Justice on 2 September 2009.

139 See Item 1 of the 2003 Notice.

development in this trial has been very rapid: by June 2010, community corrections had been implemented in 31 provinces, 226 municipalities, 1,572 counties, and 19,500 towns, involving 494,000 convicted offenders in total.[140]

With the rapid development of community corrections in China, the 8th Amendment of the Criminal Law (2011) formally revised Article 38 of the 1997 Criminal Law, stipulating that 'criminals sentenced to control shall be subject to community correction pursuant to the law.' This revision also formally removes the police from the administration of control as a criminal penalty.[141]

While the effect of the reform involved in the introduction of community correction has been in some sense to reduce the severity of control as a criminal punishment, the second reform of the introduction of prohibition orders has in fact led to further restrictions being imposed on persons under a control order. Under Article 38 of the Criminal Law (as revised in 2011), a person sentenced to control may be prohibited from engaging in specified activities, entering into specified areas, or contacting specified persons – often referred to as the 'three prohibitions'. This mechanism for the courts to issue prohibition orders (*Jinling*) during criminal processes provides an entirely new discretionary power to courts by the 8th Amendment of the Criminal Law (2011). It is therefore unclear how the courts might exercise this discretionary power in their sentencing work.

II.3.2. *Counter-Revolutionary Crimes and Crimes against State Security*

'Counter-revolution' had been the primary targeted crime in the Chinese communist justice system for a long time before the 1997 revision of the Criminal Law. The provisions on 'counter-revolution' in the 1979 Criminal Law were vague and sweeping, reminiscent of the 1926 Russian Criminal Code.[142] In particular, Article 90 of the 1979 Criminal Law contained a catch-all provision which defined 'crimes of counter-revolution' as '[a]ll acts endangering the People's Republic of China committed with the goal of overthrowing the political power of the dictatorship of the proletariat and the socialist system.' Although this provision itself did not stipulate

[140] See 'Seven Years of Trial Implementation of Community Correction Has Received Nearly Half a Million Convicted Offenders', *China Youth Daily*, 19 August 2010, available at http://legal.people.com.cn/GB/12482491.html (last accessed 29/8/12).

[141] The police however retain the power to punish those who violate the prohibition orders issued by a court (para 4 of Article 38 of the 1997 Criminal Law).

[142] Berman, Cohen & Russell, *supra* note 9, at 252–253.

specific penalties, the 1979 Law contained 12 articles specifying punishment for various kinds of 'counter-revolutionary crimes'. Indeed, 'counter-revolution' attracted the most severe punishment prescribed in the 1979 Criminal Law. Sixty per cent of the provisions prescribing the death penalty, 45% of the provisions imposing life imprisonment, and 37% of the provisions stipulating imprisonment for ten or more years concerned the crime of counter-revolution.[143]

Although many of the subcategories of 'counter-revolutionary crimes' may be seen as acts endangering social order and security, such as causing explosions, setting fires etc. (Article 100 of the 1979 Criminal Law), many other 'counter-revolutionary' acts were clearly aimed at political activities, such as organising or leading 'counter-revolutionary' groups (Article 98 of the 1979 Criminal Law), and propagandising for and inciting the overthrow of the political power of the dictatorship of the proletariat and the socialist system (Article 102 of the 1979 Criminal Law). Indeed, the essential element of all 'counter-revolutionary' crimes was the aim of 'counter-revolution', which was clearly a political rather than a legal concept. As such it is not surprising that provisions on 'counter-revolutionary' crimes attracted much criticism both within China and abroad. For this reason socialist countries, such as North Korea, Vietnam and the former Soviet Union, all replaced 'counter-revolutionary crimes' with 'crimes against the state' or some similar category many years ago.[144]

In China, discussions on redefining 'counter-revolutionary crimes' began in the mid-1980s. One of the views emerging from these discussions on abolishing this category was the recognition that the concept blurred legal acts and political views and, thus, created difficulties in judicial practice. Further, it was argued that if 'counter-revolutionary crime' was not redefined as an ordinary crime, China would not be able to pursue criminals who had escaped abroad. It was also recognised that the concept of 'counter-revolution' would not be compatible with the practice of 'One Country Two Systems' – a policy meant to be implemented for unification with Hong Kong, Macau and Taiwan.[145] The first specific sign of the

143 Lan Quanpu, *supra* note 8, at 73.

144 As early as 1958 the Soviet Union had discarded the concept of 'counter-revolutionary crimes'. See Bermen, Cohen & Russell, *supra* note 9, at 252.

145 See Cao & Hou, *supra* note 24, at 87; Ma & Ding, *supra* note 17, at 8; 'Criminal Law Called to Revise', (24–30 April 1989) *Beijing Review* 7; Cao Zidan & Hou Guoyun, 'On Redefining "Counter-revolutionary Crimes" "Crimes Endangering State Security"', (no.2, 1991) *Legal Science in China (Zhongguo Faxue)* 9; Zhang & Wang, *supra* note 10, at 242–243; Gao Mingxuan, Zhao Bingzhi & Wang Yong, 'A Review of the Criminal Legislation in the

introduction of the concept of crimes against state security as a substitute for counter-revolution emerged in February 1993 in the promulgation of the Law on State Security. The Law was intended to curb domestic and foreign activities that pose security threats, but it did not use the term 'counter-revolution' itself.[146]

The 1997 revision and developments since then have, however, been a major disappointment. 'Counter-revolutionary crime' was indeed redefined as 'crime endangering state security' and all reference to the term 'counter-revolution' was deleted from the Law.[147] Essentially, however, the 1997 revision was a matter of renaming, restructuring and supplementing, as the majority of the previous provisions on 'counter-revolutionary crimes' have been retained.[148] Thus acts of inciting the overthrow of political power and the socialist system continue to be a major crime in the revised Law.[149] The ambiguous provision on the crime of colluding with foreign states in plotting to harm the sovereignty, territorial integrity and security of the state remains; so does the vague provision on the crime of stealing, secretly gathering or providing state secrets and intelligence for foreign organisations or foreigners.[150] The 1997 revision also added a provision to make it a crime for state personnel to desert their posts and escape to foreign countries to engage in activities endangering state security.[151] Apparently, this provision is aimed at those who were sent to work or study abroad and then decided to stay by, for example, applying for refugee status in a foreign country. In China's own words, these provisions are aimed at acts of joint efforts to westernise China.[152]

Past Ten Years and Prospect', (no.2, 1989) *Legal Science in China* (*Zhongguo Faxue*) 66; and Zhang Sihan, 'On Crimes Endangering State Security', *People's Daily* (*Renmin Ribao*) (overseas edition), 14 June 1997, internet edition. See also Lawyers Committee for Human Rights, *supra* note 20, at 79; Albert H.Y. Chen, *An Introduction to the Legal System of the PRC* (Singapore: LexisNexis/Butterworths Asia, 1992), at 188.

146 See Lawyers' Committee for Human Rights, *supra* note 20, at 80.

147 See Chapter One of the Specific Provisions of the revised Criminal Law. As discussed in Chapter 3 in Chen, *supra* note 1, similar words were also removed from the Constitution through the 1999 Constitution Revision.

148 Although the total number of provisions in the Chapter on Crimes Endangering State Security has been reduced from 15 to 12 articles, this reduction has been achieved only by removing some provisions to chapters on crime endangering public security and crime against social order and administration. See Wang Hanbin, *supra* note 16, at 675. Since 1997, only two articles (Articles 107 & 109) have undergone some minor revision (in 2011)

149 See Article 105 of the 1997 Criminal Law.

150 Article 102 and Article 111 of the 1997 Criminal Law.

151 Article 109 of the 1997 Criminal Law, which underwent a minor revision in 2011.

152 Zhang Sihan, *supra* note 145.

The punishment for these crimes continues to be very harsh. The majority of the 12 crimes endangering state security can attract the death penalty.[153] In addition, confiscation of property is applicable to all 12 crimes endangering state security.[154]

II.3.3. *Crimes Endangering Public Security and Social Order*

Crimes endangering public security are those acts that endanger the lives of the general public and damage public property and facilities.[155] Reflecting the traditional idea of collective rights over individual rights, crimes endangering public security have always been seen as the most dangerous form of crime among the 'ordinary crimes'.[156] It is not surprising that immediately after the provisions on crimes endangering state security come the provisions on crimes endangering public security.

In response to the continuing increase in crimes and the rising incidence of certain serious crimes (such as the hijacking of aeroplanes, organised crime, and terrorism) at the time,[157] Chapter Two was extensively expanded during the 1997 revision; in fact, the total number of provisions was more than doubled (from 11 to 26 articles) with 15 new offences being created. It now contains 47 offences in total after the 8th Amendment in 2011. In addition to the previous offences (such as setting fires, breaching dykes, causing explosions, and sabotage) against public lives (that is, offences which are not aimed at a particular person or persons), public property (such as factories, farms, mines etc.) and facilities (such as public transport facilities, power stations and public communications facilities), the 1997 revision created the following new offences: organising, leading and actively participating in terrorist activities (Article 120);[158] hijacking air traffic facilities (Article 121);[159] hijacking

[153] See Article 113 of the 1997 Criminal Law.

[154] See Article 113 of the 1997 Criminal Law.

[155] See Li Guangcan (ed.), *On Criminal Law of the People's Republic of China* (*Zhonghua Renmin Gonghe Guo Xingfa Lun*), vol. 2 (Changchun: Jilin People's Press, 1981), at 98–101; Cao & Hou (1997), *supra* note 24, at 97.

[156] Li Guangcan, *id*, at 98. The term 'ordinary crimes' is used by Chinese scholars to contrast with 'counter-revolutionary crimes'.

[157] See Chu Huaizhi, 'The Contradiction between Crimes and Punishments and the Reform of the Criminal Law', (no.5, 1994) *Legal Science in China* (*Zhongguo Faxue*) 107. As pointed out earlier, provisions on terrorism were further revised in 2001.

[158] This Article was amended in 2001 by the 3rd Amendment to the Criminal Law adopted on 29 December 2001. The 3rd Amendment also added a new article, Article 120 (1).

[159] This article incorporates the Standing Committee Decision on Severe Punishment on Hijacking Air Traffic Facilities of 28 December 1992.

boats and vehicles (Article 122); using violence on aeroplanes to endanger the safety of air traffic (Article 123); illegally selling weaponry (Article 126); illegally owning, possessing and lending weaponry (Article 128); failure to report the loss of weaponry promptly (Article 129); illegally taking weaponry, knives, explosive and poisoning materials into public places or onto public transport facilities (Article 130); violation by transport personnel of traffic regulations and the causing by them of major accidents (Articles 131–133);[160] failure to rectify safety problems thus causing major accidents in work sites (Article 135);[161] negligence in the building industry (including designing, building and supervision) (Article 137); failure to take measures for the safety of schools and educational facilities (Article 138);[162] and failure to take action for fire safety after being instructed to do so (Article 139).[163]

In the post-Mao era maintaining social stability and order has been one of the top priorities for the leadership; it is part of the effort to create a social environment conducive to economic development. Again, many *ad hoc* legislative responses to specific situations had led to the creation of a large number of individual statutes and of penal provisions in other statutes, supplementing the original Chapter 6 of the 1979 Criminal Law on crimes against social order and its administration. Chapter 6 on Crimes Hindering Social Administration of the 1997 Criminal Law now absorbs all these provisions, and has thus now become the longest and most complicated chapter in the whole Criminal Law. Altogether, after the 1997 revision, Chapter 6 proscribed 116 offences in 91 articles, with 63 offences being new creations of the 1997 revision.[164] With the continuing revision, Chapter 6 now contains 125 offences in total. It should be pointed out that, in addition to the penal provisions in Chapter 6, there is also the 2005 Law concerning Punishment in the Administration of Social Order (replacing the Regulations concerning Punishment in the Administration of Social

160 Through the 8th Amendment, a new article, Article 133 (1), was added to the Criminal Law, making illegal car racing on public roads and driving while intoxicated criminal offences.

161 This Article incorporates Article 92 of the Labour Law (1994). It was further amended by the 6th Amendment to the Criminal Law, adopted 29 June 2006. The 6th Amendment also added a new article, Article 135 (1), to the Law, making major accidents in large scale mass activities criminal offences.

162 This Article incorporates Article 73 of the Law on Education (1995).

163 The 6th Amendment to the Criminal Law, adopted 29 June 2006 also added a new article, Article 139 (1), to the Law. Under Article 139 (1), failure to report or providing a false report of major safety accidents is a criminal offence.

164 Cao & Hou, *supra* note 24, at 262.

Order) which imposes administrative penalties for minor acts in violation of the social order and its administration.

Chapter Six now deals with penalties for all acts which violate the social order and its administration; that is, acts endangering stability, peace and order in the proper operation and running of state organisations, enterprises and institutions, and the proper order for scientific research and teaching.[165] It is divided into nine sections. Section One deals with violations of public order. In addition to the previously proscribed crimes of obstructing state personnel in the carrying out of their functions, hooliganism and gambling, it now also includes two previously 'counter-revolutionary' crimes, namely inciting the masses to resist or to sabotage the implementation of laws and decrees, and organising and using superstitious sects and secret organisations in violation of the law. It also creates a number of new offences, including the illegal production and sale and purchase of police uniforms and car number plates; the illegal production, sale and use of espionage equipment; computer offences; stealing and violating dead bodies; and offences in violation of demonstration and assembly laws.

Section Two contains a new subcategory of crime (Crime hindering judicial functions),[166] created by the 1997 revision. This section collects various provisions in the 1979 Criminal Law and further prohibits all acts hindering the performance of judicial powers, including the violation of orders in court proceedings, attacking judicial personnel and violation of prison order. Despite the continuing difficulties in enforcing court orders in civil and commercial law, and the controversies relating to Article 206 on lawyers' liability in criminal cases, none of the provisions in this Section have been affected by any of the revisions since 1997. Section Three on Crimes Violating Border Administration again collects together various provisions dealing with the violation of border administration as well as the Supplementary Provisions on Severe Punishment of Organising and Transporting People to Illegally Cross the Border.[167] Section Four penalises acts violating the administration of cultural relics, historical records and

[165] Cao & Hou, *supra* note 24, at 262.

[166] The 1979 Criminal Law dealt with a number of offences relating to the performance of judicial functions, such as perjury (Article 148), refusal to execute court judgments or orders (Article 157), escape from detention or prison (Articles 96 and 160). Scholars had argued for the establishment of a separate section on crimes hindering judicial functions for a number of years before the 1997 revision. See Zhang & Wang *supra* note 10, at 243.

[167] The Supplementary Provision was issued by the Standing Committee on 5 March 1994.

places of historical interest. Section Five deals with acts endangering public health. Except for Article 332, which deals with the violation of border health and quarantine regulations,[168] this Section collects together penal provisions from various statutes, such as the Law on the Prevention of Infectious Diseases,[169] Border Health Quarantine Law,[170] Measures for Dealing With Medical Accidents,[171] Administrative Regulations on Blood Products,[172] and the Quarantine Law on the Import and Export of Animals and Plants.[173] Section Six penalises violations of environmental protection and natural resource administration. Again this section collects together various penal provisions in the original Criminal Law as well as individual statutes. Section Seven on the Trafficking in and Production of Drugs retains the original provisions in the 1979 Criminal Law and incorporates the Decision on Prohibition of Drugs.[174] Section Eight deals with crimes relating to prostitution. It incorporates the original provisions of the 1979 Criminal Law as well as the Decision on the Prohibition of Prostitution.[175] The final section incorporates the Decision on the Punishment of the Smuggling, Production, Sale and Circulation of Pornographic Materials.[176]

Clearly the various newly enacted offences in relation to public security and social order have been created on an *ad hoc* basis, and many of them were created in 1997 as legislative responses to major incidents that had occurred in China in the first 20 years of reform.

II.3.4. *Crimes Undermining the Socialist Market Order and Economic Crimes*

Economic development has since 1978 remained a top priority for the post-Mao leadership. Crimes against such development are thus treated seriously and punished heavily. As economic policy has been considerably relaxed since 1979,[177] many kinds of economic activities that

[168] Originally Article 178.
[169] Issued on 21 February 1989 by the Standing Committee.
[170] Issued 2 December 1986 by the Standing Committee.
[171] Issued by the State Council on 29 June 1987.
[172] Issued by the State Council in January 1997.
[173] Issued on 30 October 1991.
[174] The Decision was issued by the Standing Committee on 28 December 1990.
[175] The Decision was issued by the Standing Committee on 4 September 1991.
[176] The Decision was issued by the Standing Committee on 28 December 1990.
[177] See Chapter 2. See also Jianfu Chen, *From Administrative Authorisation of Private Law: A Comparative Perspective of the Developing Civil Law in the People's Republic of China* (Dordrech/Boston/London: Martinus Nijhoff Publishers, 1995), ch. 3.

were non-existent (e.g. private enterprises, share markets, real estate, insurance and the futures market etc) have now been permitted, leading to a rise in crimes that were not anticipated in the original 1979 Criminal Law. Further, the dual system, that is the co-existence of a market economy with the continuing control by the government authorities of many forms of economic activity (such as the existence of licence and approval systems) has also led to a drastic increase in many types of economic crime and corruption. Thus some scholars argued that the main task of the criminal law should switch from targeting 'counter-revolutionary' crimes to economic crimes.[178] The government response was the issuing of many individual statutes on an *ad hoc* basis, to supplement the 1979 Criminal Law. The 1997 Revision of crimes against the socialist market order and other economic crimes was designed to incorporate these individual statutes and other penal provisions in various ordinary statutes issued by the NPC and its Standing Committee.

When the 1979 Criminal Law was revised in 1997, Chapter Three was divided into eight sections containing 92 articles with 89 offences. It now contains 109 offences in total. Section One deals with the production and sale of fake and substandard products. This section initially mainly incorporated the Standing Committee's Decision on the Punishment of the Production and Sale of Fake and Substandard Products,[179] but several provisions have been revised by the 4th and 8th Amendments to the Criminal Law, adopted in 2002 and 2011. Section Two deals with crimes of smuggling, with its provisions mainly coming from the Supplementary Provisions on the Punishment of Smuggling Crimes[180] and the Decision on the Punishment of the Smuggling, Production, Sale and Circulation of Pornographic Materials,[181] but with some provisions having now been revised by the 4th, 7th and 8th Amendments to the Criminal Law, adopted in 2002, 2009 and 2011 respectively. Section Three on Crimes Undermining Company and Enterprise Administrative Orders is a relatively new creation. The provisions were first created by the Standing Committee's Decision on the Punishment of Crimes in Violation of Company Law which was issued on 28 February 1995 after the Company Law was adopted

[178] See Gao, Zhao & Wang, *supra* note 145, at 72.
[179] Issued on 2 July 1993.
[180] Issued by the Standing Committee of the NPC on 21 January 1988.
[181] Issued by the Standing Committee of the NPC on 28 December 1990.

on 29 December 1993. The 1997 Revision was mainly based on the above Decision, but it also created a number of offences,[182] some of which were then further revised by the 1st, 6th and 8th Amendments to the Criminal Law, adopted in 1999, 2006 and 2011 respectively. Section Four deals with crimes undermining financial administrative order. The original 1979 Criminal Law proscribed counterfeiting or trafficking in counterfeit national currency (Article 122) and counterfeiting cheques, share certificates or valuable securities (Article 123). These provisions were supplemented by the above-mentioned supplementary provisions on smuggling crimes, and by decisions on crimes against company law. Most importantly, they were supplemented by the Decision on the Punishment of Crimes Undermining Financial Order.[183] The 1997 Criminal Law incorporates all these decisions and supplementary provisions as well as further proscribing other crimes in the financial market, such as fraud in bank loans (Article 175), insider trading (Article 180), fabricating and circulating false information about exchange markets (Article 181), etc.[184] Section Five specifically deals with financial fraud. Again, its 1997 provisions were mainly derived from the Decision on the Punishment of Crimes Undermining Financial Order, and further revised by the 7th and 8th Amendments. Section Six prohibits acts endangering the collection and administration of taxes. Apart from Articles 201 and 202, which were revised from the original Article 121, provisions in this section come from the Supplementary Provisions on Punishing the Evasion and Refusal of Taxes[185] and the Decision on the Punishment of the Fabricating, Counterfeiting and Illegal Sale of Value-added Tax Receipts,[186] and were further revised by the 7th and 8th Amendments. Section Seven punishes the violation of intellectual property by incorporating the Supplementary Provision on the Punishment of Counterfeiting Registered Patents[187] and the Decision on Punishing Crimes in Violating Copyright.[188] It further

182 These include Articles 164–169.

183 Issued by the Standing Committee of the NPC on 30 June 1995.

184 Once again, this Section has now been revised many times by the 1st, 3rd, 4th, 5th, 6th, and 7th, Amendments to the Criminal Law since 1997, as well as the SCNPC Decision on the Punishment of Crimes involving Fraudulent Purchasing, Evading, and Illegal Trading of Foreign Exchange.

185 Issued by the Standing Committee of the NPC on 4 September 1992.

186 Issued by the Standing Committee of the NPC on 30 October 1995.

187 Issued by the Standing Committee of the NPC on 23 February 1993.

188 Issued by the Standing Committee of the NPC on 5 July 1994.

penalises the betrayal of trade secrets.[189] Section Eight prescribes punishment for violation of the market order. This section contains 13 crimes, the majority of which are new creations of the 1997 revision, though some provisions were revised by the 7th and 8th Amendments.

Further, to demonstrate the government's determination to eliminate corruption, this is now dealt with in a separate chapter, Chapter Eight. The new chapter now expands the original two provisions (Articles 155 and 185) to 16 articles,[190] largely through the incorporation of the Supplementary Provisions on the Punishment of Corruption.[191]

Encroachment on property as an economic crime is also separately dealt with in Chapter Five. This chapter also creates some new offences (e.g. illegal use of telecommunication facilities owned by others) and incorporates provisions from other statutes (e.g. Decisions on the Punishment of Crimes in Violation of Company Law). It was most recently revised by the 8th Amendment.

Clearly, the provisions on economic crimes have undergone some rather significant revisions in the last few years since the revised Criminal Law was adopted in 1997.

II.3.5. *Crimes Endangering Personal Rights and Democratic Rights*

'Crimes endangering personal rights and democratic rights' refers to the violation of personal security, other associated rights (e.g. reputation and dignity), and democratic rights guaranteed by the Constitution (e.g. the right to election, right of appeal, freedom of correspondence, etc.).[192] Chapter Four in the 1997 Criminal Law incorporates provisions from Chapter Four in the original 1979 Criminal Law, some provisions in the original Chapter Eight and the Decision on Severely Punishing the Selling and Kidnapping of Women and Children (4 September 1991) issued by the Standing Committee. This Chapter, now containing 42 offences in total, covers murder and manslaughter, causing bodily injury, rape (including all sexual intercourse with girls under 14) and molesting or humiliating women by means of violence or threats, illegal detention or deprivation of

189 Article 219. This is a new creation in the 1997 revision, which further supplements the provision on trading secrets first provided in the Law of the PRC Against Unfair Competition (1993).

190 Article 388 (1) was added by the 7th Amendment to the 1997 Criminal Law.

191 Issued by the Standing Committee on 21 January 1988.

192 Cao & Hou, *supra* note 24, at 216.

personal freedom, kidnapping, selling or buying women and children, falsely accusing or framing another person with the intention to cause the person to be convicted of a crime, forced labour in violation of labour laws, illegal searching of another person or residence, insulting or defaming another person, the use of torture by judicial and prison officials, inciting racial hatred or discrimination and insulting minority nationals in publications, illegal deprivation of freedom of religion and serious violation of minority customs, serious violation of freedom of correspondence, abusing power and using public office for private gain, carrying out retaliation and frame-ups against complainants, activities endangering elections, interference in freedom of marriage, bigamy, and domestic violence. Through the 6th and 7th Amendments, it also penalises the selling or illegal supply of personal information, organising, by means of violence or coercion, handicapped persons or children under the age of 14 to beg, and organising minors to undertake activities violating the social administration order.

The notable improvement in this chapter is the clarification of ambiguous provisions (such as those on hooliganism), and the further supplementation of provisions in detailed form, thus making the provisions more precise and easier to implement.

II.3.6. *Dereliction of Duty*

Chapter Nine deals with dereliction of duty by state personnel in their performance of state duties. It amends and expands the original Chapter Eight in the 1979 Criminal Law by incorporating various supplementary provisions issued by the Standing Committee, including the Supplementary Provisions on the Punishment of Crimes in Violation of Company Law, Decision on the Punishment of Fabricating, Counterfeiting and Illegal Sale of Value-added Tax Receipts, Decision on the Punishment of Production and Sale of Fake and Substandard Products, Supplementary Provisions on the Severe Punishment of Organising and Transporting People To Illegally Cross the Border, the Decision on Severely Punishing the Selling and Kidnapping of Women and Children, Decision on the Prohibition of Prostitution, and penal provisions of other statutes (e.g. Education Law and Law on the Protection of Cultural Relics). It has undergone revisions four times by way of the 4th, 6th and 8th Amendments to the 1997 Criminal Law, and it now contains a total of 37 offences.

II.3.7. *Crimes Undermining the Interests of National Defence and Military Duty*

Two new chapters were introduced into the Criminal Law on crimes undermining the interests of national defence (Chapter Seven) and military duty (Chapter Ten) by the 1997 revision.

Chapter Seven on crimes endangering the interests of national defence is completely new. It covers the use of violence to interfere with military personnel in carrying out their duties, causing damage to military facilities and installations, knowingly supplying substandard equipment to military forces, forcibly entering into and violating orders in military 'prohibited areas', impersonating military personnel, inciting the desertion of military personnel or knowingly employing military deserters, fraudulently supplying unqualified personnel to the army, illegally producing, selling and buying, or fabricating military marks and documents, supplying false information to the military during war, and refusal or intentional delay in fulfilling military purchase orders during war. Since 1997 it has been only slightly revised in 2009 by the 7th Amendment.

Crimes in violation of military duty, contained in Chapter 10 of the 1997 Criminal Law, are broadly defined as violations of duty by service personnel which endanger state military interests.[193]

Crimes in violation of military duty were first codified in the Interim Regulation on the Punishment of the Crimes of Servicemen in Violation of Duty.[194] The new Chapter Ten essentially incorporates and supplements this Interim Regulation, and it has remained the same since its enactment in 1997.

II. 4. *Administrative Sanctions v. Criminal Punishments*

One of the major problems in the Chinese criminal justice system is its artificial and arbitrary distinction between administrative sanctions and criminal punishments.[195] This distinction has caused many problems in human rights protection, as the imposition of administrative sanctions is

---

193 Article 420 of the revised Criminal Law.

194 Issued on 10 June 1981.

195 For a discussion on the various forms of administrative sanction see Randall Peerenboom, *China Modernizes: Threat to the West or Model for the Rest?* (New York: Oxford University Press, 2007), at 94–97.

out of the control of due process and beyond the supervision of the judiciary.

To be fair, it should be acknowledged that major efforts have been made to address this 'abnormal' practice in the last two decades or so, with mixed results. First, in 1996 the NPC adopted the Law on Administrative Penalties. Article 9 of the Law provides specifically that all restraints of personal freedom must be prescribed by law. Article 10 then adds that administrative rules and regulations can only prescribe penalties other than the restraint of personal freedoms. Again, in 2000 the NPC promulgated the Law on Law-making which establishes a detailed list of exclusive legislative powers, to be exercised only by the NPC and SCNPC. Under the Law, administrative authorities are barred from enacting regulations on such matters as those relating to crimes and criminal penalties, the deprivation of the political rights of citizens, coercive measures, and penalties which restrict personal freedom. These legislative developments lay down a framework to limit the power of the administrative authorities in imposing sanctions against personal freedom and liberties.

Secondly, in 2005 the Law concerning Punishment in the Administration of Social Order was adopted by the SCNPC. The Law repealed the Regulations concerning Punishment in the Administration of Social Order (initially issued in 1986, revised and re-promulgated in 1994). This Law then introduced into the national law framework a major form of administrative penalty and its administration for minor acts in violation of social order (though the mechanism continued to be administered by an administrative authority, namely the police).

Thirdly, two most notorious forms of administrative sanctions were abolished, one formally and the other in a rather twisted manner. In reforming the Criminal Procedure Law in 1996 and after much debate, Shelter and Investigation (*Shourong Shencha*) (ostensibly a pre-trial measure but serving effectively as a punishment) was formally abolished when the 1996 Criminal Procedure Law came into force on 1 January 1997.[196] Then there was the Detention and Repatriation mechanism established by the State Council Measures on Detention and Repatriation. In 2003 a university graduate named Sun Zhigang was detained in a Southern city in Guangdong Province under the Measures and was apparently beaten to death. Several scholars then petitioned the SCNPC to start a constitutional review of the Measures. However, the Measures were quickly repealed by

196 On the abolition of Shelter and Investigation see discussions in Section III.2.3 below.

the State Council, and this effectively abolished yet another administrative mechanism imposing detention by the administrative authorities, before any SCNPC procedure was actually activated.[197]

Other efforts to curb the power of the administrative authorities in imposing penalties restricting personal freedom and liberties have not so far been successful, and this is particularly true in relation to Re-education through Labour (*Laojiao*).[198]

The *Laojiao* system was first initiated by the Communist Party Central Committee in the 1950s as a measure to combine labour and education to deal with 'historical counter-revolutionaries' and other 'bad elements' in society.[199] It was then formally established by the State Council Decision Relating to *Laojiao* Problems and the Supplementary Provisions of the State Council on *Laojiao*,[200] both of which were approved by the SCNPC. For practical purposes, however, the most significant measures have been the Trial Implementation Measures on *Laojiao* (issued by the Ministry of Public Security on 21 January 1982 and endorsed by the State Council), the Provisions on Handling *Laojiao* Cases by Public Security Authorities (issued by the Ministry of Public Security on 12 April 2002), and Implementing Opinions on Further Strengthening and Improving the *Laojiao* Examination and Approval Work (issued by the Ministry of Public Security on 13 September 2005).

The initial State Council Decision of 1957 and the Supplementary Provision of 1979 define *Laojiao* as both a compulsory education-through-labour measure and a mechanism for arranging employment,[201] though in practice loss of personal freedom is implied. Measures and Provisions issued by the Ministry of Public Security have effectively changed the fundamental nature of *Laojiao*: under this regime of regulations by the Ministry of Public Security, *Laojiao* is used to detain people whose offence is not serious enough to warrant criminal punishment, yet too serious to be dealt with under the Regulations concerning Punishment in the Administration of Social Order (since upgraded to a Law). More recently,

---

197 For detailed discussion see Section 4.8 of Chapter 3, in Chen, *supra* note 1.

198 Another extremely controversial mechanism is '*Shuanggui*' that is administered by the Communist Party of China, not even by the administrative authorities. On *Shuanggui* see also discussions in Section 3.3 of Chapter 8, in Chen, *supra* note 1.

199 Instructions on Completely Wiping Out Hidden Counter-revolutionary Elements, issued by the Central Committee of the Party in 1955.

200 The Decision was issued in August 1957 and re-published in November 1979. The Supplementary Provisions were issued in November 1979.

201 See Item 2 of the 1957 Decision.

it has been widely used as a measure for 'maintaining social stability', and not infrequently used as a means to punish citizens who have made complaints against a government.[202] Although it is theoretically not a criminal penalty, a person could be detained for up to 4 years by a decision of a local *Laojiao* Administration Committee,[203] comprising representatives from the bureaus of civil administration, labour and justice, but in fact mainly administered by the local Public Security organs.[204] Clearly it is arbitrary to define such loss of freedom as an administrative sanction.

The legality of such an institution was openly questioned in 1996 when the NPC adopted the Law on Administrative Penalties. It clearly violates Articles 9 and 10 of the Law, as only the State Council is constitutionally empowered to issue administrative rules and regulations. Thus it was suggested that the *Laojiao* should either be abolished or be absorbed into the Criminal Law by establishing a new category of punishment, namely, police orders (similar to community based orders in the West).[205] Indeed, during the revision of the Criminal Law suggestions were also made by scholars to have the *Laojiao* system reformed or abolished.[206] These opinions were however ignored by the authorities, and the revision of the Criminal Law chose not to deal with the issue of *Laojiao* at all.

---

[202] See 'Legislative Efforts to Abolish Re-education through Labour Met Difficulties and the Nature of Re-education through Labour Has Deviated from Its Origin', available at http://www.tianzelaw.com.cn/ShowNews.asp?ID=971 (last accessed 27/8/12); and 'Legislation Is the Only Way to Reform Re-education through Labour', *Beijing News*, 18 February 2012, available at http://www.bjnews.com.cn/opinion/2012/08/18/217499.html (last accessed 30/8/12).

[203] See Article 2 of the State Council Supplementary Provision (1979). However, Article 13 of Implementing Opinions on Further Strengthening and Improving the *Laojiao* Examination and Approval Work (2005) reduced the maximum term to 2 years. Articles 7–10 of the Implementing Opinions also allow limited assistance by lawyers for the persons detained under *Laojiao*.

[204] This power was effectively given to itself by the Ministry of Public Security: See Article 2 of the Provisions on Handling *Laojiao* Cases by Public Security Authorities (2002). See further Tao Jigang, 'Some Thoughts on the Law on Re-education through Labour', (no.3, 1995) *Journal of the China University of People's Police* (*Zhongguo Renmin Jingcha Daxue Xuebao*) 12, at 12; Ma Kechang, *supra* note 23, at 7–8; 'Legislation Is the Only Way to Reform Re-education through Labour', *supra* note 202; and 'What Are the Difficulties in Reforming Re-education through Labour?', available at http://news.xinhuanet.com/politics/2012-09/06/c_112975742.htm (last accessed 6/9/12).

[205] Ma Kechang, *supra* note 23, at 7–8; Chen Xingliang, *supra* note 18, at 56–60.

[206] See e.g. Tao Jigang, *supra* note 204; Chen Xingliang, *supra* note 18, at 56–60.

The controversy did not however die down after the revision of the Criminal Law in 1997; in fact, the debate has intensified since then.[207] As mentioned above, the 2000 Law on Law-making clearly bars the State Council from enacting laws on matters such as penalties which restrict personal freedom. In fact, under the Law on Law-Making, the legality of the arbitrary distinction between administrative (e.g. re-education through labour) and criminal penalties as a whole is seriously challenged unless it is clearly authorised by the NPC or the SCNPC.

With pressures for reform, both from within and without, the SCNPC finally made a concrete move towards reforming the *Laojiao* in 2005.[208] In March 2005 the Legislative Affairs Committee of the SCNPC finally submitted a draft Law on Educational Correction of Unlawful Behaviour to the SCNPC; the latter then formally included the deliberation of the proposed law in its 2005 legislative plan.[209] Under the proposed scheme, the maximum incarceration period would be capped at 18 months and judicial remedies would also be made available. However, despite repeated announcements of the inclusion of the deliberation of such a law in the annual legislative plan of the SCNPC, this draft law has never been formally presented to the SCNP. More than eight years have since passed and the outcome of this proposed reform remains uncertain.[210]

---

[207] For a discussion of the recent controversy over *Laojiao* and different opinions on its reform see Peerenboom, *supra* note 195, at 209–210; 'Legislative Efforts to Abolish Re-education through Labour Met Difficulties and the Nature of Re-education through Labour Has Deviated from Its Origin', *supra* note 202; 'Legislation Is the Only Way to Reform the Re-education through Labour', *supra* note 202; and 'What Are the Difficulties in Reforming the Re-education through Labour?', *supra* note 204.

[208] Other reports suggest that the move was made as early as 2003. See 'Legislative Efforts to Abolish Re-education through Labour Met Difficulties and the Nature of Re-education through Labour Has Deviated from Its Origin', *supra* note 202.

[209] See 'Our Laojiao System Is Facing Reform towards Correction of Unlawful Behaviour', available http://news.xinhuanet.com/legal/2005-03/02/content_2636013.htm (last accessed 19/6/07). According to the SCNPC 2007 legislative plan, a first deliberation of the proposed law will be conducted in the October SCNPC session. See '2007 Legislative Plan and Supervision Plan', in http://npc.people.com.cn/GB/28320/41246/41337/5422052.html (last accessed 20/6/07).

[210] The last announcement was made in 2010 that the deliberation of this law was included in the 2010 annual legislative plan, but nothing has happened since then. Recent media reports however suggest that some trial operations by the Centre for Educational Correction of Unlawful Behaviour are now underway in four cities (Nanjing, Lanzhou, Zhengzhou and Jinan). See eg Zhuang Pinghui, 'Project hints at reform of mainland's re-education through labour policy', *South China Morning Post*, 4 September 2012, available at http://www.scmp.com/news/china/article/1028868/projects-hint-reform-mainlands-re-education-through-labour-policy (last accessed 5/9/12).

II. 5. *The Death Penalty*

Reflecting the idea of relying heavily on criminal punishment to maintain social stability and order, the death penalty was widely prescribed in imperial Chinese codes and frequently used in practice.[211] A reduction in the application of the death penalty thus became one of the major aspects of criminal law reform at the turn of the 20th century. The Qing reform managed to reduce capital offences from more than 800 in total to about 20.[212] The KMT governments continued the reform regarding the death penalty. The various criminal codes issued by different governments retained about 20 capital offences, most of which related to violent crimes.[213] Communist justice however began with a show of violence and frequent summary executions, especially against 'counter-revolutionaries'. This practice continued until well after the founding of the PRC as the campaign to eliminate 'counter-revolutionaries' continued, although Mao and the authorities did from time to time call for caution in the application of the death penalty.[214]

According to Peng Zhen the 1979 Criminal Law significantly reduced capital offences as originally contained in the previous drafts.[215] Even so, the 1979 Criminal Law prescribed 28 capital offences in 15 articles.[216] Chinese authorities obviously realised the severity of such a penalty, and thus the death penalty with a two-year suspension period was introduced from the very early period of the PRC's justice system.[217] At the same time a policy of cautious application was introduced.[218] However, this policy

---

[211] See Stephen B. Davis, 'The Death Penalty and Legal Reform in the PRC', (1987) 1 *Journal of Chinese Law* 303, at 306–308.

[212] See Ma & Ding, *supra* note 17, at 115; See also Meijer (1967), *supra* note 37, at 28–35.

[213] Ma & Ding, *supra* note 17, at 115–116.

[214] See Peng Zhen, *supra* note 14, at 151. See also Kang Yunshen, 'On Mao Zedong's Creative Contribution to the Marxist-Leninist Theory on the Death Penalty', (no.6, 1991) *Journal of China University of Political Science and Law* (*Zhengfa Luntan*) 29.

[215] Peng Zhen, *supra* note 14, at 151.

[216] Ma Kechang, *supra* note 23; and Lan Quanpu, *supra* note 8, at 73.

[217] The death penalty with a two-year suspension period is a unique innovation of the PRC; it is said that the idea came from Mao Zedong and formed an important contribution to the Chinese justice system. See Gao, Zhao & Wang, *supra* note 145, at 68; Zhang Youyu, 'Mao Zedong's Creative Contribution to the Development of Marxist Legal Theory', in China Law Society (ed.), *A Collection of Articles on Mao Zedong's Legal Theories* (*Mao Zedong Sixiang Faxue Lilun Lunwen Xuan*) (Beijing: Law Publishing House, 1985), at 25; 1979 *Lectures on Criminal Law, supra* note 12, at 34; Kang Yunshen, *supra* note 214, at 32. This policy of suspension for two years was first explained by the *People's Daily* on 1 June 1951. See Davis, *supra* note 211, at 314.

[218] Peng Zhen, *supra* note 14, at 151.

was rarely translated into practice; indeed, Decisions and Supplementary Provisions by the SCNPC promulgated during various anti-crime campaigns had by March 1997 increased the application of the death penalty to no fewer than 80 offences, contained in over 50 criminal law provisions.[219] Although this calculation is perhaps not accurate, and the more reliable number of offences liable to capital punishment would be just over 70,[220] the incorporation of all capital offences into the code would, as some scholars argued, make the Chinese Criminal Law a 'Death Penalty Code'.[221] As to the actual application, no one knows the exact number of death penalties handed down in China each year, as the number is treated as a 'state secret'. Western media often put the number as between 1,000 and 3,000.[222] In mid-March 2004, for the first time, Chinese media reported that some 10,000 people were sentenced to immediate execution every year in China, not including people sentenced to death with a two-year suspension.[223] This number of executions is not an official figure and has never been confirmed officially, but Amnesty International reports have consistently put the Chinese number at more than the combined total of execution in all other countries worldwide.[224] Occasionally, the Chinese practice amounts to almost a form of summary execution.[225]

---

219 Shen Deyong, 'Our Criminal Law Should Establish a "Limited Use" Principle on the Death Penalty', *Legal Science in China* (*Zhongguo Faxue*) 27, at 28; Xing Yan, 'Criminal Law Revision: Minor or Major Revision or No Revision At All', in (no.1, 1997) *Peking University Law Journal* (*Zhongwai Faxue*) 49, at 50.

220 See Zhenjie Zhou, 'The Death Penalty in China: Reforms and Its Future', initially published in Bulletin of Waseda University Research Institute, 2011, PDF version available at www.waseda.jp/wias/achievement/bulletin/data/z_zhou_2011.pdf (last accessed 28/8/12), at 32.

221 Chu Huazhi, 'Criminal Law Revision and Criminal Law Policy', in (no.1, 1997) *Peking University Law Journal* (*Zhongwai Faxue*) 49, at 53.

222 See Lawyers Committee for Human Rights, *supra* note 20, at 82; 'Death penalty pressure', *The Australian*, 9 September 1998, at 10.

223 See '41 deputies suggested that the Supreme People's Court should re-centralise the approval power over the death penalty', originally published in the *Zhongguo Qingnian Bao* (*China Youth Daily*), and re-published in the *Renmin Ribao*, 16 March 2004, website edition: http://www.people.com.cn/GB/shehui/1060/2388561.html (last accessed 22/3/04).

224 See Figure 2, in Zhenjie Zhou, *supra* note 220, at 34.

225 One of the most notorious cases that has attracted international condemnation was that concerning workers Bian Hanwu, Xu Guoming and Yan Xuerong, who were arrested for allegedly setting fire to a train during demonstrations in Shanghai on 6 June 1989. They were charged on 11 June, sentenced to death on 14 June and executed on 21 June 1989 after an appeal on 20 June to the Shanghai High People's Court. The whole process took only two weeks. See Lawyers Committee for Human Rights, *supra* note 20, at 83–84.

If the death penalty has caused concern for the authorities, it has certainly been seen by scholars as one of the areas needing reform.[226] However, few Chinese scholars advocate the abolition of the death penalty,[227] the majority of them arguing for restrictions and restraint in its use and, ultimately, abolition in the future.[228] For these scholars, China's reputation and international trends are among the major considerations for restraint.[229] Although some of them advocate the gradual abolition of the death penalty, their targeted timetable has undermined their own argument.[230] Some have pointed out that, according to statistics from one province, 90% of death penalties were imposed for the crimes of murder, robbery, rape, serious bodily injuries and major theft, and that only ten offences seem frequently to have attracted the death penalty.[231] Some have further pointed to the huge discretion in imposing the death penalty. For instance, it has been pointed out that more than 20 offences attract penalties ranging from criminal detention to the death penalty.[232] Many of them clearly see the death penalty as an inappropriate form of punishment for economic crimes.[233]

However, the Chinese legislature has been slow in accepting these opinions. The policy on the death penalty in the 1997 revision was neither to

[226] See Ma & Ding, *supra* note 17, at 105–124; Cui Qingsen & Liao Zengyun, 'On Limited and Cautious Use of the Death Penalty', (no.2, 1989) *Studies in Law* (*Faxue Yanjiu*) 69; Gao, Zhao & Wang, *supra* note 145, at 75–76; Wang Fengzhi, 'Several Questions on the Abolition or Retention of the Death Penalty', (no.4, 1995) *Journal of China University of Political Science and Law* (*Zhengfa Luntan*) 23; Shen Deyong, *supra* note 219; Ma Kechang, *supra* note 23, at 5–7; Chen Xingliang, *supra* note 18, at 57–58; Zhang Mingkai, *supra* note 22; Jia Yu, 'Reduction of Capital Offence – An Important Aspect of Criminal Law Reform', (no.1, 1997) *Politics and Law* (*Zhengzhi Yu Falü*) 7. One of the most comprehensive studies on the death penalty in China is Hu Yunteng, *To Abolish or to Continue: A Theoretical Study on the Death Penalty* (*Quan yu Fei: Sixing Jiben Lilun Yanjiu*) (Beijing: China Procuratorial Press, 2000). A summary of this study in English is published in Hu Yunteng, 'Application of the Death Penalty in Chinese Judicial Practice', in Jianfu Chen, Jan Michiel Otto, & Yuwen Li (eds), *Implementation of Law in the PRC* (The Hague/London/New York: Kluwer Law International, 2002), at 247–276.

[227] See Zhenjie Zhou, *supra* note 220, at 38.

[228] See *supra* note 226; Ma & Ding, *supra* note 17, at 22–23; Hu Yunteng, *supra* note 226, at 264–266; Zhenjie Zhou, *supra* note 220, at 38–39.

[229] *Supra* note 226.

[230] For instance, one scholar argued that the death penalty should be gradually abolished, but that it would take about one hundred years to do so. See Ma & Ding, *supra* note 17, at 120. Other Chinese scholars claim that it would be safe to assume that China would not abolish the death penalty for at least 50 years. See Zhenjie Zhou, *supra* note 220, at 38.

[231] Chen Xingliang, *supra* note 18, at 57.

[232] Chu Huazhi, *supra* note 221, at 54.

[233] Ma & Ding, *supra* note 17, at 110; Cui & Liao, *supra* note 226, at 71; Ma Kechang, *supra* note 23, at 6.

reduce nor to increase the incidence of the death penalty.[234] This confirmed the fear of some scholars that the revised Criminal Law would look like a 'death penalty code': Among the 542 articles in the Criminal Law after the 1997 revision, 76 articles contained the death penalty.[235] Further, many of these articles dealt with more than one offence, and thus there were at least 68 offences in the 1997 revised criminal law that could attract the death penalty.[236] By any criterion, it was a major disappointment in the reform of criminal law.

As in the case of administrative sanctions, the death penalty debate continued in China after the 1997 revision of the Criminal Law,[237] and this has also led to some significant reform since 2006.

As mentioned above, there is a general consensus among academics and officials that the death penalty needs to be applied cautiously, whether its abolition is politically unrealistic or not.[238] However, the problem with the death penalty is not just that it is too common; its application lacks strict control. Under the original 1979 Criminal Law all death sentences had to be reviewed by the Supreme People's Court before they were actually carried out. However, the final review powers were delegated to High Courts at the provincial level by the Supreme People's Court in the 1980s during the 'anti-crimes campaigns'.[239] Under this delegated system, many

---

234 Wang Hanbin, *supra* note 16, at 679. The death penalty for people under 18 years was however reduced to life imprisonment in order to satisfy China's international obligation under the UN Convention on the Rights of the Child, which was ratified by the Standing Committee in November 1991.

235 Based on my own examination of and calculation on the revised Criminal Law.

236 See Hu Yunteng (2002), *supra* note 226, at 264. See also 'Explanation on the Draft 8th Amendment to the Criminal Law', delivered at the 16th Session of the Standing Committee of the 11th NPC, available at http://www.npc.gov.cn/npc/flcazqyj/2010-08/28/content_1592773.htm (last accessed 27 June 2011).

237 While strong academic support for a reduction in the use of the death penalty since 2000 was important in building momentum for change, public support joined the force when the Chinese media began, in 2005, to expose a series of wrongful convictions that involved the imposition of the death penalty and in which some wrongfully convicted persons had already been executed. Together with international pressures, these factors played an important role in pushing forward the reform of the death penalty. See more detailed analysis in Kandis Scott, 'Why Did China Reform Its Death Penalty', published in *Pacific Rim Law and Policy Journal* (2009), available at http://ssrn.comabstract=1446976 (last accessed 28/8/12).

238 The Chinese leadership has, however, made it rather clear that, while it supports the cautious use of the death penalty, it does not support its abolition. See Kandis Scott, *supra* note 237.

239 The delegation was made by means of eight Supreme People's Court Notices issued between 1980 and 1997. A list of these notices is appended to the Decision of the Supreme People's Court on the Relevant Issues concerning the Uniform Exercise

death penalty sentences were simply not reviewed in any meaningful sense. The reason is simple: most cases involving the death penalty were tried by an Intermediate Court in the first instance and appealed to a High Court. In this way, the High Court was both the appeal court and the court exercising the final review power. In March 2004 the Supreme People's Court finally indicated that it would reclaim the final review power over the death penalty.[240] In October 2006 the Organic Law of the People's Courts of the PRC was revised by the SCNPC, reinstating the review power of the Supreme People's Court. Thus in December 2006 the Supreme People's Court finally decided to reclaim this power,[241] with effect from 1 January 2007 when the revised Organic Law of the People's Courts of the PRC became effective. While this is only a small step towards reform of the death penalty in China, it is in fact, and has been proven to be, a life-saving measure under the current system.[242]

Since then, several major reforms have been undertaken by the Supreme People's Court to strengthen and limit the application of the death penalty,[243] including reforms to the trial procedures for death

---

of the Death Penalty Review Power, issued by the Supreme People's Court on 28 December 2006.

[240] See 'The Death Penalty Review Power at Provincial Level Should Be Given a "Sudden Death"', *Nanfang Weekend* (*Nanfang Zhoumo*), 14 October 2004, available in http://www.nanfangdaily.com.cn/zm/20041014/xw/tb/200410140001.asp (last accessed 18/10/04).

[241] Decision of the Supreme People's Court on the Relevant Issues concerning the Uniform Exercise of the Death Penalty Review Power, *supra* note 199.

[242] Under the delegated system the Supreme People's Court retained the review power over the death penalty for crimes against state security and for corruption. According to a Chinese source, between 10% and 20% of cases reviewed by the Supreme People's Court ended in changes in sentences. See 'How Far China Is from the Abolition of the Death Penalty', in http://news.xinhuannet.com/global/2004-06/01/Content_1502050htm (last accessed 1 June 2004). A more recent report, after the Supreme People's Court reclaimed its review power over all death penalty cases, claims that 15% of cases reviewed by the Supreme People's Court were not approved by the Court due to the problems of unclear facts, insufficient evidence, inappropriate application of law or violation of procedure law. See 'Several Insights on the Success of Death Penalty Review as 15% Cases were not Approved', *Legal Daily*, 21 March 2008, available at http://www.legaldaily.com.cn/0705/2008-03/21/content_819629.htm (last accessed 21/3/08). According to a prominent scholar, Professor Zhao Benzhi, in many provinces death sentences have been reduced by as much as 30% and in some provinces by 50% since 2007 when the Supreme People's Court reclaimed the review power. See 'Zhao Benzhi: Death Sentences Clearly Reduced after the Supreme People's Court Reclaimed Review Power', *Legal Daily*, 30 August 2012, available at http://www.legaldaily.com.cn/Frontier_of_law/content/2012-08/30/content_3808566.ht (last accessed 1/9/12).

[243] For more detailed discussions see Zhenjie Zhou, *supra* note 220; 'China's Death Penalty Reforms: An HRIC Issues Brief', available at hrichina.org/public/PDFs/CRF.2.2007/CRF-2007-2_Penalty.pdf (last accessed 28/8/12); and Kandis Scott, *supra* note 237.

penalty appeal cases, detailed rules on conducting the review of the death penalty, specific evidence rules for death penalty cases and the exclusion of illegal evidence, and many other *ad hoc* replies, rules and provisions.[244] Among these, the Provisions on Certain Issues concerning the Review of the Death Penalty set out the details of orders that the Supreme People's Court might issue after reviewing the cases.[245] The Review involved the review of facts, evidence, application of law, and legal procedures by trial courts. Most importantly, many of these judicial interpretations and provisions established a foundation for the revision of the Criminal Procedure Law in 2012.[246]

The most significant reform was undertaken by the 8th Amendment to the Criminal Law in 2010. For the first time since the enactment of the *Criminal Code* in 1979 the use of the death penalty has been systematically reduced, with the number of offences attracting capital punishment reduced from 68 to 55, representing a reduction of 19% in the total number of capital offences in Chinese Criminal Law.[247] As a result, the following non-violence crimes have now been removed from capital punishment: smuggling cultural relics (Art 151); smuggling precious metals (Art 151); smuggling precious and rare animals (Art 151); smuggling goods and objects subject to a large amount of tax (Item 1 of Art 153); fraud with financial bills, certificates and other financial instruments (Art 194); fraud in credit certificates (Art 195); fraud in special value-added tax invoices or other invoices fraudulently claiming export refunds or offsetting taxes (Art 205); forging or selling forged special invoices for value-added tax (Art 206); stealing public or private property or money (Art 264); teaching methods of committing crimes (Art 295); digging up and robbing ancient cultural ruins or tombs with historical, artistic or scientific value (Art 328); and digging up and stealing ancient human fossils and ancient vertebrate fossils with historical, artistic or scientific value (Art 328).

Additionally, pregnant women and those under the age of 18 years at the time of the crime may not be sentenced to death. Further, the death

---

244 For a collection of these rules see Special Topic on the Death Penalty, Sichuan Criminal Lawyers, available at http://www.scxsls.com/ZtList_217.htm (last accessed 28/8/12).

245 The Provision was issued as *Fashi* (2007) No.4, issued on 27 February 2007 and effective from 28 February 2007.

246 See detailed discussions on CPL below.

247 See Explanations on the Eighth Amendment to the Criminal Law, available from http://www.npc.gov.cn/huiyi/cwh/1116/2010-8/28/content_1593165.htm, (last accessed on 27/6/11).

penalty may not be applied to persons aged 75 or above at the time of the crime (unless particularly brutal methods are used in causing another's death).[248]

On the other hand, for those who have been sentenced to death with a two-year suspension of execution and whose death penalty is later commuted to life imprisonment and further reduced to fixed-term imprisonment, the minimum period of imprisonment will be 25 years,[249] raised from the original 15–20 years.

Whether the 2011 reform of the Criminal Law in relation to the death penalty will lead to any significant reduction in the use of the death penalty in China is still an open question,[250] as the 13 offences had rarely attracted the death penalty. This reform is however important in building momentum for further reform in this area.

---

248 Article 49 of the 1997 Criminal Law. The non-applicability of the death penalty to persons aged 75 or more was added by the 8th Amendment to the Criminal Law in 2011.

249 Article 50 of the 1997 Criminal Law.

250 Zhenjie Zhou, *supra* note 220, at 37.

CHAPTER THREE

THE DEVELOPMENT OF THE CRIMINAL PROCEDURE LAW IN THE PRC

III. 1. *The 1979 CPL*

The 1979 CPL, based on drafts prepared in the mid-1950s and early 1960s,[251] was one of the first seven major laws enacted in post-Mao China.[252] The purpose of its enactment was two-fold: to elaborate the constitutional provisions regarding the division of powers and responsibilities among the people's courts, the people's procuratorates and the public security organs; and to provide working procedures for criminal adjudication. Although the 1979 CPL was supposed to be a comprehensive code, its provisions were short, vague and, in many instances, ambiguous. Its deficiencies, both on its face and in its actual practice, were soon to become apparent and thus to attract severe criticism, particularly from Western human rights organisations.[253] Fundamentally, many important 'due process' principles, such as the presumption of innocence, the right to silence, rules against self-incrimination, judicial independence, adequate right to legal counsel, etc, were absent from the CPL; many other

[251] In particular it was based on a draft prepared in 1963. See Wang Guo'ou, Wang Yizhen & Wang Cunhou (eds.), *An Outline of the Criminal Procedure Law* (*Xingshi Susongfa Gailun*) (Beijing: Beijing University Press, 1981), at 50–52; and Peng Zhen, 'Explanations on the Drafts of the Seven Laws', delivered to the Second Plenary Session of the Fifth NPC on 26 June 1979, in Peng Zhen, *On Political and Judicial Work in the New China* (*Lun Xinzhongguo De Zhengfa Gongzuo*) (Beijing: Press of the Chinese Communist Party Documents, 1992), at 157.

[252] The other six laws include a substantial criminal code, an organic law for local people's congresses and local governments, two organic laws for the people's courts and people's procuratorates respectively, and a law on Sino-foreign equity joint ventures.

[253] There were many reports of human rights violations in relation to criminal processes under the 1979 CPL in China by international human rights organisations. See e.g. Amnesty International (1991), *China – Punishment Without Crime: Administrative Detention* (ASA 17/27/91; Amnesty International, 1992), *Torture in China* (ASA 17/55/92, Amnesty International, 1996), *China: No One Is Safe*, ASA 17/01/96; Lawyers Committee for Human Rights, *supra* note 20; and *Reports of the Australian Human Rights Delegation to China*, First Report, July 1991 and Second Report, November 1992 (Canberra, Australian Government Publishing Service).

provisions of the 1979 CPL fell far short of minimum requirements for the administration of justice.[254]

This defective law was made even worse by many decisions of the Standing Committee of the NPC (SCNPC), issued during various anti-crime campaigns,[255] and by the inability or unwillingness of the law-enforcement authorities to act within the law. Indeed, no sooner had the 1979 CPL been implemented than the realisation arose of the inability of the judiciary to handle criminal cases according to the law. In February 1980 – one month after the CPL came into effect – the SCNPC authorised the standing committees at the provincial level to approve extensions of time limits for handling criminal cases as prescribed by the CPL.[256] Such authorisation was again granted by the SCNPC in September 1981 for handling criminal cases during the 1981–1983 period.[257] Thereafter no fewer than 20 revisions (in the form of Decisions and Supplementary Provisions) concerning criminal and criminal procedure matters were made by the SCNPC before the end of 1995.[258] Many of these provisions had serious

[254] By minimum requirements I mean those provisions embodied in the Universal Declaration of Human Rights (1948) and the International Covenant on Civil and Political Rights (ICCPR) (1966). Many of the principles in these two documents are elaborated in other UN Conventions, e.g. UN Convention Against Torture and Other Cruel, Inhuman or Degrading Treatment or Punishment, and principles adopted by various UN agencies and endorsed by the UN General Assembly, e.g. General Comments made by the UN Human Rights Committee under the ICCPR, the UN Body of Principles for the Protection of All Persons Under Any Form of Detention or Imprisonment, GA Resolution 43/179 (1988); Basic Principles on the Role of Lawyers, endorsed by the UN Resolution 45/121 (1990), Basic Principles on the Independence of the Judiciary, endorsed by the UN GA Resolution 40/146 (1985), and many more. Of course these are ideal and desired practices that are not necessarily satisfied in many countries.

[255] For discussions on the anti-crime campaigns see 'Note: Concept of Law in the Chinese Anti-Crime Campaign', (1985) 98 *Harvard Law Review* 1890; Deborah E. Townsend, 'The Concept of Law in Post-Mao China: A Case Study of Economic Crime', (1987–88) 24 *Stanford Journal of International Law* 227, and Susan Traveskes, *Courts and Criminal Justice in Contemporary China* (New York/Toronto: Lexington Books, 2007).

[256] See Decision of the Standing Committee of the NPC Regarding the Questions of Implementation of the Criminal Procedure Law (12 Feb. 1980). A copy of the Decision can be found in Huang Shengye (ed.), *A Lawyer's Handbook* (*Lüshi Shouce*) (Beijing: Press of the Economic Daily, 1996), at 1284.

[257] See further discussions in Shao-Chuan Leng & Hungdah Chiu, *Criminal Justice in Post-Mao China: Analysis and Documents* (Albany: State University of New York Press, 1985), at 87.

[258] Huang Taiyun, 'Major Reforms in the Criminal Processes – An Outline of the Major Revisions to the Criminal Procedure Law', (no. 2, 1996) *Legal Science in China* (*Zhongguo Faxue*) 29, at 30. Texts of these Decisions, Supplementary Provisions and many other judicial documents issued by the Supreme People's Court, the Supreme People's Procuratorate and the Ministry of Public Security concerning the implementation of the CPL can be found in Huang Shengye, *supra* note 256.

implications for the protection of human rights and the administration of justice in China.[259] Some of them, such as the Decision of the SCNPC on the Procedures for Rapid Adjudication of Cases Involving Criminal Elements Who Seriously Endanger Public Security (1983),[260] were criticised by Chinese scholars as being a blatant violation of the Chinese Constitution.[261]

With these supplementary provisions, many of them issued specifically for anti-crime campaigns with *ad hoc* policy orientation, the deficiencies of the CPL were no longer restricted to its vagueness and ambiguities, but also involved internal contradictions and confusion. This fact, together with the inability or unwillingness of the law-enforcement authorities to act within the law, meant that the practical consequences for society were serious abuses of human rights, including the widespread application of so-called administrative sanctions, prolonged detention without trial, and disregard for minimum procedural protection.[262] Thus fundamental concerns about human rights in China can easily be traced to the structure and functioning of the PRC's criminal justice system.[263]

Gellat, writing on behalf of the Lawyers Committee on Human Rights, provided the following overall assessment of the 1979 CPL and its implementation before the 1996 revision:

> The 1979 CPL is a detailed document that provides procedures for the criminal process which were completely absent during the PRC's first 30 years. Nevertheless, the procedure law contains numerous defects that on their face violate international standards of fair judicial process. In addition, the authorities frequently violate the provisions of the procedural law. They take advantage of ambiguities in the law or simply disregard legal protection existing in the formal criminal process. They also commonly circumvent such protection by use of administrative, 'non-criminal' sanctioning methods. These abuses occur perhaps most frequently and egregiously in political cases, but also in ordinary criminal cases.[264]

---

259 See *supra* note 253; and Leng & Chiu, *supra* note 257.

260 The Chinese text of the Decision can be found in *A Complete Collection of Laws of the PRC* (*Zhonghua Renmin Gonghe Guo Falü Quanshu*) (Jilin: Jilin People's Press, 1989), at 222; An English translation can be found in Leng & Chiu, *supra* note 257, at 232.

261 See Cui Min, 'A Summary of the Discussions on Revising and Perfecting the Criminal Procedure Law', (no.1, 1995) *Modern Law Science* (*Xiandai Faxue*) 92, at 96.

262 See discussions on specific topics below.

263 Lawyers Committee for Human Rights, *supra* note 20, at 1

264 *Id.* at 9–10.

III. 2. *Major Reforms in 1996 and 2012*

III.2.1. *An Overview*

To be fair, it should be noted that the 1979 CPL was a product of a particular historical time. First, the CPL was adopted before the promulgation of the 1982 Constitution, which provided some general principles for the administration of justice that were absent from the 1978 Constitution under which the CPL was drawn up. Further, the promulgation of the 1979 CPL coincided with the re-establishment of the law enforcement institutions, namely, the public security organs, the people's procuratorates and the courts, the latter two having been effectively 'smashed' during the so-called Cultural Revolution (1966–1976).[265] The inability of the law-enforcement authorities and the judicial organs to act in accordance with the law was to be expected, although the abuse of the criminal process is another matter. Finally, in the late 1970s, legal research and study had just resumed after the Cultural Revolution, as had the debates on certain fundamental 'due process' principles. The applicability of these principles in China was then, and to a significant extent still is, a hotly contested and unsettled issue.

With the development of legal research and the 'open door' policy which brought in foreign influences, Chinese scholars soon recognised the deficiencies in their law and began to argue for the inclusion of many Western criminal procedural principles in the CPL.[266] Many problems in the implementation of the CPL also came to the attention of scholars and officials.[267] Thus the issue of revising the CPL became a topic of academic discussion and official consideration.[268]

---

265 The People's Procuratoratees were officially abolished in 1969; their functions were assigned to the public security organs by the 1975 Constitution. See Zhao Zhenjiang (ed.), *Forty Years of the Chinese Legal System* (*Zhongguo Fazhi Sishinian*) (Beijing: Beijing University Press, 1990), at 368.

266 For a summary of major debates see Chen Guangzhong, 'Forty Years of the Chinese Criminal Procedure Science', *Journal of the China University of Political Science and Law* (*Zhengfa Luntan*), Pt I in no.4, 1989, at 5–14, Pt. II in no.5, 1989, at 1–8. The whole article was reprinted in Zhang Youyu & Wang Shuwen (eds.), *Forty Years of the PRC's Legal Science* (*Zhongguo Faxue Sishinian*) (Shanghai: Shanghai People's Publishing House, 1989), at 251–287. These debates will be further reviewed in the following discussions on the specific issues.

267 One Chinese scholar described the problems in the criminal process in the following way: '[t]hose [laws] that have been published are not implemented; and those not published are enforced'; 'those who see the patients do not give prescriptions and those who give prescriptions do not see the patients – the separation of hearing from decision'. See Zhao Zhenjiang, *supra* note 265, at 380–384.

268 As early as mid-1985, the Legislative Affairs Committee (LAC) of the SCNPC had indicated that the revision of the CPL was already under consideration. See Gu Angran,

The first formal forum to discuss the revision of the CPL was held in Beijing in January 1991, organised by the LAC of the SCNPC. A report on the forum was prepared and submitted to the Central Committee of the Communist Party of China. Several seminars among Chinese scholars were later held in various locations. In September 1993 it was officially announced by the Director of the LAC, Mr. Gu Angran, that a formal decision had been made by the SCNPC to include the revision of the CPL on the Legislative Agenda of the NPC.[269] Thereafter, the LAC formally entrusted the drafting work to Professor Chen Guangzhong of the China University of Political Science and Law, who then organised a group of scholars and PhD students to carry out the drafting work.[270] This work was efficiently completed in about six months.[271] Thereafter many more symposiums were held to discuss the revision of the CPL, organised either by scholars or by the LAC. In October 1995 the LAC issued a draft Bill and Explanations on Several Major Issues Concerning the Revision of the CPL. These two documents then formed the basis for further academic discussion.[272] At the same time the draft Bill was twice submitted to the SCNPC for deliberation.[273] Thus it can be said that the 1996 revision of the CPL was a product of major joint efforts by scholars and law-makers.

The 1996 revision was a major one: 70 of the original 164 articles were revised, 2 articles abolished and 63 articles added to the CPL, thus making

---

'Some Major Issues in the Drafting of Criminal and Criminal Procedure Laws – a speech delivered to the training class for law-making cadres, May 1985', in Gu Angran, *The Socialist Legal System and Legislative Work* (*Shehui Zhuyi Fazhi He Lifa Gongzuo*) (Beijing: China University of Political Science and Law Press, 1989), at 206. One of the major academic gatherings to discuss the 'perfecting' of the CPL was the 1986 Guangzhou Conference, at which over 100 procedure law specialists came together to discuss a wide range of issues concerning the improvement of the CPL. See Zhao Zhenjiang, *supra* note 265, at 373–375.

269 Cui Min, *supra* note 261, at 92.

270 This was said to be the first time that the drafting of law had been entrusted to scholars in China. Ibid.

271 Cui Min, *supra* note 261, at 92.

272 Major issues discussed by academics were: (1) the overall desirability of the draft Bill; (2) requirements for approval of arrest; (3) the scope of criminal investigation by the people's procuratorates; (4) the scope of private prosecution; (5) exemption from prosecution; (6) the time at which lawyers and other defenders should be allowed to enter into the criminal process; (7) the procedures for court trials; (8) the status and procedural rights of crime victims; (9) time limits for the handling of cases; (10) the means of investigation by the people's procuratorates; and (11) the review of death penalty cases. See Wei Tong, 'A Report of the Discussions on the Revision of the CPL', (no.1, 1996) *Journal of the China University of Political Science and Law* (*Zhengfa Luntan*) 89, at 89.

273 Gu Angran, 'Explanations on the Revision of the Criminal Procedure Law of the PRC', delivered at the 4th Plenary Session of the 8th NPC on March 12, 1996, in (no.3, 1996) *Gazette of the Standing Committee of National People's Congress of the PRC* (*Zhonghua Renmin Gongheguo Quanguo Renmin Daibiao Dahui Changwu Weiyuanhui Gongbao*), at 85.

the CPL much more comprehensive and precise. The significance of the revision lies, however, not in the total number of articles revised, but in that, to some extent, certain fundamental 'due process' principles were incorporated into the CPL for the first time when the revision was officially adopted by the NPC in 1996.

As will be discussed below, the 1996 reform was significant, but incomplete. Further, practical difficulties soon emerged, as expected, especially in the areas of the role of the lawyer in criminal processes, and the protection of his/her rights as incorporated in the 1996 CPL.[274] At the same time academic studies on the CPL were becoming increasingly sophisticated and focused on both particular aspects of the law and on specific practical issues.[275] These studies helped law-makers and law enforcement forces to understand better not only the operation of the Law, but also the specific difficulties and problems in law and in practice. Thus, law-makers seemed to accept that the various compromises made in 1996 in revising the 1979 CPL were part of the cause of the generally unsatisfactory operation of the Law, and in October 2003 the SCNPC formally decided to start a new round of revision by including the task in its five-year legislative plan.[276] This then prompted Professor Chen Guangzhong, who was pivotal to the 1996 CPL reform, to establish an expert group to start a new expert draft. In 2006, after three years of work, this group produced its expert draft in 450 articles.[277] While Professor Chen emphasised that any revision had to be undertaken within the current constitutional framework and had to aim at retaining the existing structure of the CPL, the expert draft nevertheless stresses human rights protection in criminal procedures, the absorption

[274] See, for instance, Human Rights Watch, *"Walking on Thin Ice": Control, Intimidation and Harassment of Lawyers in China,* April 2008, available at http://www.hrw.org (last accessed 26 March 2012); Mike McConville (ed), *Criminal Justice in China: An Empirical Enquiry* (UK: Edward Edgar Publishing Limited, 2011).

[275] See eg Chen Guangzhong (ed), *The Procedure on Criminal Re-trial and the Protection of Human Rights* (*Xingshi Zaishen Chengxu yu Renquan Baozhang*) (Beijing: Beijing University Press, 2005); Xiong Qiuhong, *The Changing Science of Criminal Procedural Law* (*Zhuanbianzhong De Xingshisusong Faxue*) (Beijing: Beijing University Press, 2004); and Xiang Zexuan, Wu Xiaocheng, Luo Rui, *On Legal Supervision and Remedies of Criminal Procedural Law* (*Falü Jiandu Yu Xingshi Susong Jiujilun*) (Beijing: Beijing University Press, 2005).

[276] See Yao Dongqing, 'Insight into the Revision of the Criminal Procedure Law', *China Economic Weekly* (*Zhongguo Jingji Zhoukan*), 26 March 2012, at 27–29.

[277] The Draft (in a bilingual format) and its accompanying explanations are published as Chen Guangzhong (ed), *Expert Draft on Further Revision of the Criminal Procedural Law of the PRC and Its Explanations* (*Zhonghua Renmin Gongheguo Xingshi Susong Fa Zaixiugai Zhuanjia Jianyigao Yu Lunzheng*) (Beijing: China Legal System Press, 2006).

of international criminal justice principles as found in international treaties (including the two covenants on human rights) that China has signed or ratified, the resolution of practical difficulties and problems, and the balancing of procedural justice with substantive justice.[278] Their proposed draft doubled the existing provisions, from 225 to 450 articles. According to the 2007 SCNPC legislative plan, a first discussion of the CPL draft revision would be conducted during the October 2007 SCNPC session.[279] If the revision had been conducted along the lines suggested by the expert group we should have seen some significant improvements in the CPL, which would have come closer to internationally accepted standards for criminal justice. However, major disagreements between academics and law enforcement agencies (especially the Public Security authorities (the Police)) and power struggles between the Police and the Procuratorate in relation to their powers and roles in the criminal processes, ensured that the revision was not going to be completed within the Five-Year Legislative Plan and, indeed, revision work was suspended in 2007.[280]

Efforts to resume the revision work were made in 2009 when the SCNPC formally instructed the LAC of the SCNPC to start the drafting of the revision.[281] According to Professor Chen Guangzhong, an important factor pushing forward the resumption of the work was the issue by the Party of the Certain Opinions on Deepening the Reform of the Judicial System and Its Working Mechanisms in 2008. These Opinions contained many elements of judicial reform that also required the reform of the Criminal Procedure Law.[282]

There was clearly great enthusiasm among academics and lawyers for the further reform of the CPL. Not surprisingly, in addition to the various drafts issued by the LAC of the SCNPC for public or internal discussion, four "unofficial" drafts were also issued, three by different groups of academics and one by practising lawyers.[283] The reform also attracted major international attention,[284] as well as interest and debate among the

[278] See 'Underlying Principles for the Further Revision of the Criminal Procedure Law', in Chen Guangzhong, *id*, at 1–16.

[279] See '2007 Legislative Plan and Supervision Plan', in http://npc.people.com.cn/GB/28320/41246/41337/5422052.html (last accessed 20/6/07).

[280] See Yao Dongqing, *supra* note 276, at 24.

[281] See Yao Dongqing, *supra* note 276, at 29.

[282] See Yao Dongqing, *supra* note 276, at 24.

[283] See Yao Dongqing, *supra* note 276, at 24.

[284] See eg. Amnesty International, 'Bringing China's Criminal Procedure Law in Line with International Standards: Memorandum to the National People's Congress of the

general population.[285] The process was a reasonably democratic one, but the result is once again a compromise between academics, law-makers and law enforcement agencies.[286]

The final version of the draft was adopted on 14 March 2012 by the 11th NPC at its 5th Session, and the revised law became effective on 1 January 2013. The 2012 revision is once again a major reform: more than half of the provisions in the 1996 CPL have been revised,[287] with four major chapters/sections having been added to the CPL. On the whole, the 2012 revision continues the reform started in the 1996 with mixed results, and remains unfinished business.

III.2.2. *Ideological Shift*

Chinese law almost always starts with a provision setting out the fundamental principles underlying the enactment of the law. Article 1 of the original 1979 CPL provided that the CPL, 'taking Marxism-Leninism-Mao Zedong Thought as its guide and the Constitution as its basis, is formulated in the light of the actual circumstances and concrete experiences of the people of all China's nationalities in carrying out the people's democratic dictatorship, led by the proletariat and based on the worker-peasant alliance, that is, the dictatorship of the proletariat, and for the practical purpose of attacking the enemy and protecting the people.' Clearly, it reflected the understanding, at the time, of law as a weapon for class struggle. This article was revised in 1996, and then provided that the CPL 'is formulated in accordance with the Constitution, in order to ensure the proper enforcement of the Criminal Law, to punish crimes, to protect people, to safeguard national security and public safety, and to maintain a socialist social order.'[288] This revision indicates an ideological shift, from class struggle to maintaining law and order.

PRC by Amnesty International', March 2012, ASA 17/007/2012; Project Group on the Revision of the CPL, *CPL Revision Proposals and Their Reasoning – Centred on the Rights Protection of the Accused* (*Xingshi Susongfa Xiugai Jianyigao yu Lunzheng – yi beizhikongren de quanli baohu wei hexin*), December 2008, being a project sponsored by the Danish Human Rights Institute (document on personal file).

285 The LAC of the SCNPC published its draft for public discussion in August 2011 and attracted 78,000 responses from the general public by October of the same year. See Yao Dongqing, *supra* note 276, at 29.

286 See Yao Dongqing, *supra* note 276; and 'Some Aspects of the Revised CPL Seen as Backward Steps: Experts Claim They Are the Results of Compromise', http://www.legaldaily.com.cn/index_article/content/2011-09/09/content_2942365.htm?node=5955 (last accessed 10/9/11).

287 See Yao Dongqing, *supra* note 276, at 31.

288 This provision remains unchanged in the 2012 reform.

In March 2004, the 1982 Constitution was revised for the fourth time, and the revised Constitution declares that the State respects and protects human rights.[289] This declaration soon led to calls from deputies to the NPC, academics, lawyers and organisations for the inclusion of human rights protection in revising the CPL.[290] While efforts were made to improve human rights protection in criminal processes, the call for an explicit declaration of human rights protection in the CPL encountered considerable resistance. The official line was that Article 1 already contained the phrase 'protecting the people' and therefore there was no need to add a new provision on human rights protection.[291] Thus neither the draft issued for public consultation in October 2011, nor the second draft for deliberation by the SCNPC in December 2011, contained any direct reference to human rights protection. A compromise was reached only in the final draft submitted to the full NPC for deliberation and adoption:[292] instead of declaring human rights protection in Article 1, the revised Article 2 now adds the protection and respect of human rights as one of the tasks of the CPL. While some Chinese scholars were not totally satisfied because this human rights protection provision is not set out in Article 1 as an underlying principle for the CPL,[293] it is nevertheless a significant conceptual advance for the CPL. The real test of its significance lies in future practice – will the human rights protection provision be able to guide the operation and enforcement of the CPL in the future?

III.2.3. *Preliminary Detention, 'Shelter and Investigation', and 'Shuanggui'*

The CPL divides the criminal processes into three stages:[294] pre-trial, trial and appeal, and execution. The pre-trial stage includes three steps: filing a case (*li'an*), investigation, and institution of prosecution. These three

289 Para 3, Article 33 of the revised Constitution.

290 See Liu Wenfeng (ed), *The New Criminal Procedure Law: Interpreting the New and Revised Provisions and Their Legislative Grounds* (*Xin Xingshi Susongfa: Xinzeng Xingai Tiaowen Jingjie yu Lifa Liyou*), Beijing: Press of the People's Court (2012), at 93.

291 See 'Legal Experts Interpret the Revision of the Criminal Procedure Law: Many Important Aspects still Not Addressed, available from http://news.sina.com.cn/c/sd/2012-03-15/145824120642.shtml (last accessed 3 August 2012).

292 See 'Legal Experts Interpret the Revision of the Criminal Procedure Law: Many Important Aspects still Not Revised', *id.*

293 See Yao Dongqing, *supra* note 276, at 27–28; and 'Legal Experts Interpret the Revision of the Criminal Procedure Law: Many Important Aspects still Not Revised', *id.*

294 This structure was retained after the 1996 and 2012 revisions, though the 2012 revision adds four more special procedures to the CPL. See III.2.8 below.

pre-trial steps concern mainly two principal acts: detention and arrest,[295] and investigation, and are to be carried out by the public security organs and the people's procuratorates.

The Chinese pre-trial process under the 1979 CPL was very different from that in the West; it was a process during which the investigatory organs were supposed to have completed investigation of the defendant's alleged crime, and complete and reliable evidence should have been collected.[296] In order for the investigatory organs to complete the above tasks, the 1979 CPL provided very generous time limits for each of the investigation stages. A public security organ might first detain an active criminal or a major suspect in any of the following circumstances: (a) if he/she was in the process of preparing to commit a crime, was committing a crime or was discovered immediately after committing a crime; (b) if he/she was identified as having committed a crime by the victim or by an eye witness at the scene; (c) if he/she was discovered to have criminal evidence on his/her person or at his/her residence; (d) if, after committing the crime, he/she attempted to commit suicide or to escape or was a fugitive; (e) if he/she might possibly destroy or falsify evidence or collude with others to devise a consistent story; (f) if his/her identity was unclear and there was strong suspicion that he/she was a person who went from place to place committing crimes; or (g) if he/she was carrying on 'beating, smashing and looting' and gravely undermining work, production or the social order.[297]

If a public security organ considered it necessary to arrest the detained person, it was required, within three days after detention, to submit a request to the people's procuratorate for review and approval. Under special circumstances, the time for requesting review and approval might be extended by from one to four days. The people's procuratorate was to make its decision whether or not to approve the arrest within three days after receiving the application for approval of arrest from the public security organ.[298] If the requested arrest was not approved, the detained person

---

[295] The CPL distinguishes two kinds of detention, detention (*juliu*) and arrest (*daibu*). The former refers to preliminary apprehension of a suspect by the public security organs and the latter to formal arrest with approval of the procuratorate. See Articles 39 & 41 of the 1979 CPL (now Articles 78–80 of the 2012 CPL).

[296] See Article 100 of the 1979 CPL.

[297] Article 41 of the 1979 CPL. See also Article 6 of the Detention and Arrest Regulations of the PRC (1979). These Regulations were abolished when the 1996 CPL took effect on 1 January 1997.

[298] Article 48 of the 1979 CPL. See also Article 8 of the Detention and Arrest Regulations of the PRC (1979).

had to be released immediately.[299] If the above procedure was not followed by the public security organ or by the people's procuratorate, the detained person or his/her family had the right to demand release, and the detained person had to be released immediately.[300] Under these provisions, the maximum period of detention before formal arrest could not exceed ten days. Once the suspect was arrested, the period for holding a defendant in custody during investigation might not exceed two months. Where the circumstances of a case were complex and the case could not be concluded before the expiry of the period, the period might be extended by one month with the approval of the people's procuratorate at the next level up.[301] In the event of an especially major or complex case that still could not be concluded after the extension, the Supreme People's Procuratorate was to request the NPC's Standing Committee to approve postponement of the hearing of the case.[302] After the expiry of the above time limits, the people's procuratorate was to make a decision to initiate a public prosecution, to exempt the person from prosecution or to quash the case, if the investigation was carried out by the procuratorate.[303] If the investigation was carried out by a public security organ, the public security organ was, upon the expiry of the above time limits, to draft an opinion recommending prosecution or one recommending exemption from prosecution and send this together with the materials in the case file and the evidence to a people's procuratorate at the same level for review and decision.[304] Upon receiving the case transferred from the public security organ, the decision to initiate a prosecution or to exempt from prosecution was to be made by the people's procuratorate within one month. In major or complex cases there might be an extension of one and a half months.[305] Cases where supplementary investigation was required were to be completed within one month.[306]

Clearly, the maximum duration of detention before trial as provided by the 1979 CPL was a far cry from any international standard for preliminary detention. However, even this over-generous allowance, with the possibility of indefinite detention for major and especially serious cases,

---

299 Article 48 of the 1979 CPL.
300 Ibid.
301 Article 92 of the 1979 CPL.
302 Ibid. Here a legal loophole apparently existed for indefinite detention before a trial.
303 Article 93 of the 1979 CPL.
304 *Id.*
305 Article 97 of the 1979 CPL.
306 Article 99 of the 1979 CPL.

was extended during the so-called 'Rapid Adjudication of Cases Seriously Endangering Public Orders' campaigns in the 1980s. According to Item 1 of the Supplementary Provisions Regarding the Question of the Time Limits for Handling Criminal Cases,[307] the time limit for holding a defendant in custody during investigation as stipulated in the first paragraph of Article 92 of the Criminal Procedure Law (i.e. two months plus an extension of one month) could be extended by two months with the approval or decision of the people's procuratorate at the level of the province, autonomous region or municipality. This extension, theoretically, only applied to cases of major criminal gangs or major and complex cases in which criminals went from place to place committing crimes. Also if, during investigation, a defendant was found to be associated with another major and serious crime, the supplementary investigation might be conducted with the approval or decision of the people's procuratorate. In such cases, the custody period might be recalculated.[308]

The matter was made much worse in practice by the Chinese 'ingenious' distinction between 'administrative' and 'criminal' sanctions. As discussed earlier, administrative sanctions are those penalties provided by administrative regulations and administered and executed by administrative organs.[309] Limited judicial supervision was only available after the promulgation of the Administrative Litigation Law in 1989 and the Administrative Penalties Law in 1996. The most notorious and widely used form of administrative sanction was the so-called 'Shelter and Investigation' provision (*Shourong Shencha*).

'Shelter and Investigation' was first established in 1961 and intended as a form of preventive detention, not as a punishment,[310] and was an alternative measure widely used by the public security organs to detain people and thus to bypass the procedures for arrest and detention as provided in the Arrest and Detention Regulations (abolished in 1997) and the 1979 CPL.[311] However its precise legal nature was unclear and it was a very controversial institution for many years.[312]

---

307 Issued by the SCNPC in July 1984. A copy of the Chinese text can be found in *A Complete Collection of Laws of the PRC, supra* note 260, at 223.

308 Item 3 Supplementary Provisions Regarding the Question of the Time Limits for Handling Criminal Cases, *id.*

309 See discussions in II.4 above.

310 Amnesty International (1991), *supra* note 253, at 6–7.

311 In every large and medium-sized city in China there were several 'Shelter and Investigation' Centres and, each year, hundreds of thousands of people were detained under this institution. See Amnesty International (1991), *supra* note 253, at 6.

312 See *id.*, at 5–14.

Several serious problems were identified by Chinese scholars. Chen Weidong, of the Department of Law of the People's (Renmin) University, and Zhang Tao, of the Law Institute of the Chinese Academy of Social Sciences, for instance, provided excellent analyses of the theoretical and practical problems associated with the institution of 'Shelter and Investigation'.[313] First, with regard to the nature of 'Shelter and Investigation', they examined various relevant documents on the subject and then concluded that, in its form, 'Shelter and Investigation' was an administrative measure of investigation of a coercive nature, but in its nature it was used to combat criminal activities committed by minor offenders, or other criminal activities, in order to deal with cases of suspects where it was not possible to clarify major criminal acts and obtain the necessary evidence within the time limits laid down for criminal detention in the CPL. It was thus obviously inappropriate to define such extended 'criminal detention' as being of an 'administrative' nature.[314] Secondly, and again relying on those documents, they believed that the scope of application and the legal authority for such application were unclear.[315] Finally, they outlined several major problems in the use of 'Shelter and Investigation', which included its widespread use, detention exceeding time limits, poor management of the system, and unlawful practices of investigation involved in its application.[316] Despite all these 'shortcomings', Chen and Zhang, however, believed that 'Shelter and Investigation' should continue to be available to the public security organs, but that the system should be improved through legislation. They insisted that as 'Shelter and Investigation' was used before the start of criminal proceedings it had nothing to do with criminal procedure law. They further asserted that 'Shelter and Investigation' filled a gap between punishment in order to maintain public order and coercive measures in criminal proceedings and, therefore, naturally should be regulated by the State Council and implemented by public security organs.[317]

---

313 Chen Weidong and Zhang Tao, 'Research into Several Problems with Shelter and Investigation', (no.2, 1992) *Legal Science in China* (*Zhongguo Faxue*) 82; and Chen Weidong and Zhang Tao, 'A Further Talk on Why Shelter and Investigation Should Not Be Abolished', (no.3, 1993) *Legal Science in China* (*Zhongguo Faxue*) 113.

314 The following documents were discussed by the authors: the 1985 Notice on the Strict Control of the Use of Shelter and Investigation (issued by the Ministry of Public Security); Relevant Situations concerning Shelter and Investigation (issued by the Ministry of Public Security); and A Reply to Several Questions Concerning Propaganda of Shelter and Investigation (issuing authority not specified). None of these documents was made public.

315 Chen & Zhang (1992), *supra* note 313, at 82–83.

316 *Id.*, at 83.

317 Chen & Zhang (1993), *supra* note 313, at 113–114. See also Cheng Rongbing, 'Coercive Measures and Shelter and Investigation', (no.5, 1994) *Legal Science in China* (*Zhongguo Faxue*) 38.

Scholars who opposed the use of such an extra-legal form of sanction also questioned its nature and its legal basis, its constitutionality and legality, its scope of operation and its abuse in practice, but put more emphasis on the importance of the protection of individual rights. Wang Xinxin of the Department of Law of the People's University, for example, declared:

> Under various regulations issued by the State Council and the Ministry of Public Security, 'Shelter and Investigation' applies to those who roam around committing crimes or criminal suspects, when investigation into their crimes and the collection of evidence have not been completed. In the cases of criminal suspects without necessary evidence, the deprivation of personal freedom by 'Shelter and Investigation' in order to complete investigation is a violation of the fundamental principles of the Constitution and criminal procedure law. In its nature, it is a presumption of guilt. Furthermore, such practice shifts the burden of investigation within statutory limits from judicial organs to the suspects. Therefore provisions concerning criminal detention and arrest and for the protection of citizens' rights and statutory process and time limits are rendered meaningless by 'Shelter and Investigation'. 'Shelter and Investigation' also deprives those who should not be detained of their personal freedom. Therefore the contents of 'Shelter and Investigation' are also in violation of the Constitution and criminal procedure law.[318]

Wang made it very clear that 'Shelter and Investigation' must be abolished because it was itself a serious violation of citizens' rights as provided for by the Constitution.'[319]

Whatever the nature of this extra-legal form of detention, the public security organs preferred the 'Shelter and Investigation' provision to the two mechanisms for detention as provided in the CPL.[320] Further, many Chinese scholars agreed on the explanation for the widespread use of this institution: the time limit provided for arrest by the CPL was too short to fulfil the task of clarifying the facts of a crime in order to have a suspect arrested.[321] Officials too, were concerned and openly admitted that such

[318] Wang Xinxin, 'Shelter and Investigation Should Be Abolished – A Discussion with Comrades Chen Weidong and Zhang Tao', (no.3, 1993) *Legal Science in China* (*Zhongguo Faxue*) 110, at 112.

[319] *Id.*, at 110. In the same article, Wang also questioned the constitutional basis for the State Council to regulate matters concerning criminal procedural matters.

[320] This was the widespread practice termed by Chinese scholars as 'those (laws) that have been published are not implemented; and those not published are enforced'. See Zhao Zhenjiang, *supra* note 265, at 380.

[321] Cui Min, 'A Comment on the Major Changes to the Criminal Procedure Law', *Guangming Daily* (*Guangming Ribao*), 28 March 1996, at 6; see also Lawyers Committee for Human Rights, *supra* note 253, at 13–4.

an institution of prolonged detention administered solely by public security organs violated the CPL provisions and lacked supervision and control.[322] With this understanding it was not surprising that major reforms in the 1996 revision concerning preliminary detention involved re-defining the requirements for arrest, extending the duration for detention, and abolishing the practice of 'Shelter and Investigation'.

Under Article 40 of the 1979 CPL one of the requirements for the approvgal of an arrest was that 'major crime facts have been clarified'. This, as discussed above, was said to be one of the major reasons that caused the prolonged detention and the use of 'Shelter and Investigation'. Article 27 of the 1996 Decision concerning the Revision of the Criminal Procedure Law then changed the requirement to be that 'there is evidence of crime' (Article 60 of the 1996 CPL).[323] 'Clarification' of crime facts and adequacy of evidence are matters to be inquired into and dealt with during the trial process.[324] The revision also strengthens the preventive institutions, thus making detention and arrest the last means of coercive action. Hence Article 26 of the 1996 Decision added eight articles (Articles 51–58 of the 1996 CPL)[325] to the CPL to strengthen the procedures for obtaining a guarantor or a bond and thus awaiting trial out of custody, and allowing a suspect to live at home under surveillance. Further, the duration of preliminary detention by public security organs in major cases where the persons are suspected of going from place to place committing crimes, or repeating crimes or committing crimes in a group, was extended to 30 days, thus allowing the investigatory organs to have sufficient time to complete their investigation.[326] With these provisions in place, 'Shelter and Investigation' was then formally abolished.[327]

---

322 Gu Angran, *supra* note 273, at 86.

323 Article 60 underwent further revision in 2012; it is now Article 79 of the 2012 CPL. The revised provision now lists circumstances under which arrest must be carried out immediately. By doing so, the revised provision further relaxes the requirement for arrest under specific circumstances but, at the same time, also limits the discretionary power of the police to decide when to carry out arrest.

324 See discussions on trial process below.

325 These provisions, now Articles 65–78 of the 2012 CPL, underwent some significant revision in 2012. The 2012 revision further expands the scope for the use of bail (guarantors or bonds) and home surveillance, as well as strengthening the administration of these mechanisms.

326 Article 69 of the 1996 CPL. This provision has remained the same, but is renumbered as Article 89 in the 2012 CPL.

327 A few more words need to be added regarding the abolition of 'Shelter and Investigation': as discussed above, 'Shelter and Investigation' was not in fact a measure provided by the CPL; the revision of the CPL had thus not actually affected the operation of

If 'Shelter and Investigation' was widely used against 'ordinary' crime suspects only until 1996, another extra-legal mechanism, 'Shuanggui', continues to be applied by the Communist Party authorities to Party members suspected of certain crimes.

'Shuanggui' is a Party mechanism under which a Party cadre is ordered to appear at a 'specific time' in a 'specific place' to be investigated for, principally, corruption allegations.[328] Despite its mild language, 'Shuanggui' is in fact an extra-legal and secret detention mechanism operated by the Party Disciplinary Commissions without any legal regulation (though there have been Party regulations since 1994) or any judicial oversight. It is, strictly speaking, unconstitutional,[329] and clearly unlawful as, under Article 8 of the Chinese Law on Law-Making, only the NPC and its Standing Committee have the power to enact laws on such matters as the restriction of personal freedoms or the imposition of coercive measures. While the mechanism is very controversial in China, there is no sign that the Party has any intention of abolishing it in the foreseeable future.

III.2.4. *The Presumption of Innocence, the Right to Silence and Rules against Self-incrimination*

In the early 1980s, the presumption of innocence was defined in Chinese jurisprudence as 'one of the principles of criminal procedure law in some bourgeois countries, which means that a defendant should be deemed as an innocent person before he/she is found guilty in accordance with law.'[330] This principle, according to the *Encyclopaedia*, was initiated by the bourgeoisie during periods of revolution to oppose the feudalist presumption of guilt. It had thus played some positive and 'progressive' roles in the struggle against autocratic feudalism.[331] In short, it was a bourgeois principle which had once been progressive in the evolution of society. The ambiguity is apparent: as a bourgeois principle it should be rejected by a socialist legal system; yet, as it had played some positive and progressive roles, arguably it may still have some positive elements that a socialist

this form of administrative detention. The abolition of 'Shelter and Investigation' was therefore announced in the 'Explanations on the Revision of the CPL of the PRC', delivered by Gu Angran at the 4th Plenary Session of the 8th NPC, not in the Decision concerning the Revision of the Criminal Procedure Law. See *supra* note 273, at 86.

328 For a detailed analysis of 'Shuanggui' see Flora Sapio, 'Shuanggui and Extralegal Detention in China', 22 (2008) *China Information* 7.

329 Sapio, *id*, at 24.

330 *Chinese Encyclopaedia – Law, supra* note 84, at 625.

331 Ibid.

legal system could adopt. Indeed, this ambiguity permitted strenuous debates on the presumption of innocence in the 1950s and again since the 1980s.

Although Chinese scholars asserted that the presumption of guilt is a feudalist criminal practice, they were also able to locate many legal provisions from the ancient codes of law to support the assertion that certain elements of the presumption of innocence, in particular the emphasis on evidence and lenient treatment in cases of doubt, existed in traditional China.[332] However, it was not codified as a criminal procedure principle before the KMT Criminal Procedure Code (1935), a piece of legislation largely borrowed from Continental European and Japanese legal systems. That law, together with all KMT laws, was abolished when the PRC was founded in 1949. When serious legal efforts resumed after the adoption of the 1954 Constitution, academic debate began on many theoretical and practical issues, including the presumption of innocence. That debate was however short-lived, as the 1957 Anti-Rightist Movement was soon to denounce those who advocated bourgeois theories as 'rightists', and to silence all serious theoretical debate.[333]

Legal reform in the late 1970s created a more receptive environment for 'bourgeois' theories and practice, but the 1979 CPL did not adopt the doctrine. Instead, Article 4 of the 1979 CPL, reflecting the Party policy of 'seeking truth from facts', provided that in conducting criminal proceedings, the people's courts, the people's procuratorates and the public security organs must rely on the masses and 'must take facts as the basis, and law as the criterion.' This provision, according to Chinese officials, did not support or reject any 'presumption'.[334] In reality, people were presumed guilty until proved innocent.[335] Nevertheless an ambivalent attitude, although characterised by some Chinese scholars as 'empty talk',[336]

332 See e.g. Ning Hanling, 'On the Presumption of Innocence', in *Enquiring Into Legal Theories* (*Faxue Tanwei*) (Chongqing: Chongqing Press, 1986), at 99. This article was first published in (no.4, 1982) *Social Sciences in China* (*Zhongguo Shehui Kexue*).

333 For discussions on the debate in the 1950s see Timothy A. Gellat, 'The People's Republic of China and the Presumption of Innocence', (1982) 73 *The Journal of Criminal Law and Criminology* 259, esp. 267–281; and G.V. Thieme, 'The Debate on the Presumption of Innocence in the People's Republic of China', (1984) *Review of Socialist Law* 277, esp. 278–283. For a Chinese treatise on the debate, see Guo Daohui, Li Buyun, & Hao Tiechuan (eds), *A Record of Legal Debate in Contemporary China* (*Zhongguo Dangdai Faxue Zhengming Shilu*) (Changsha: Hunan People's Press, 1998).

334 See Lawyers Committee on Human Rights, *supra* note 20, at 14.

335 *Id.*, at 14.

336 *Id.*, at 14.

left room for academic debate. Thus, after more than twenty years of silence the debate on the presumption of innocence resumed in the 1980s.

The debate resumed even before the promulgation of the CPL in 1979. The *People's Daily* led the way by publishing an article advocating the inclusion of the presumption of innocence in the CPL which was then being drafted.[337] After this many academic articles were published on the topic, either advocating or rejecting the doctrine, or trying to find a third position on the controversial principle to accommodate some elements of the doctrine.[338]

The third position seeks to avoid the controversy of the wholesale adoption or total rejection of the doctrine. It advocates the critical adaptation of certain positive elements. Specifically, it argues for the limited adoption of the doctrine in the following sense: (1) no one should be deemed guilty until declared so by a court of law; (2) when a person cannot be proved guilty, he/she should be treated as innocent; (3) in doubtful cases, the law should be interpreted in favour of the accused.[339] This third position, characterised in Chinese as '*Zuiyi Congwu*' (presumption of innocence in doubtful cases) was proposed by some scholars as a compromise to be included in the 1996 revision of the CPL.[340]

The third position triumphed in the revision of the CPL. Article 7 of the 1996 Decision concerning the Revision of the Criminal Procedure Law added a new provision to the CPL, which states that '[n]o one shall be deemed guilty until a judgment has been passed by a people's court in

337 Tian Cai, 'A Question Worth Investigating', *People's Daily* (*Remin Ribao*), 17 February 1979, at 3. Ironically, the debate in the 1950s was also first silenced by the *People's Daily*, which accused those advocating the doctrine of using specious theory to help counter-revolutionaries and other criminals escape criminal responsibility. See Gellat, *supra* note 333, at 275.

338 For detailed discussions see Thieme, *supra* note 333; and Gellat, *supra* note 333; Chen Guangzhong (Pt II), *supra* note 266, at 2–3; Zhang Lingjie, Zhang Xun & Wang Mingyuan, 'On the Principle of the Presumption of Innocence', (no.4, 1991) *Studies in Law* (*Faxue Yanjiu*) 34; Chen Jianguo, 'The Principle of the Presumption of Innocence Should be Written into the Criminal Procedure Law', (no.5, 1994) *Legal Science in China* (*Zhongguo Faxue*) 35; and Fan Fenglin, 'Several Thoughts on the Presumption of Innocence', (no.5, 1994) *Legal Science in China* (*Zhongguo Faxue*) 36. For a concise summary of arguments for and against the doctrine, see Tian Cai, *supra* note 337, at 3, Guo, Li & Hao, *supra* note 333, 300–320.

339 Chen Guangzhong (Pt II), *supra* note 266, at 3. See further Tang Guanda, 'The Presumption of Innocence Should be Concretely Analysed', (no.1, 1980) *Studies in Law* (*Faxue Yanjiu*) 62; Liao Zengyun, 'Views on the Principle of Presumption of Innocence', (no.5, 1980) *Studies in Law* (*Faxue Yanjiu*) 32; Chen Guangzhong, 'The Principle of the Presumption of Innocence Should be Critically Adopted', (no.4, 1980) *Studies in Law* (*Faxue Yanjiu*) 34.

340 See Cui Min, *supra* note 261, at 94.

accordance with the law.' (Article 12 of the 1996 CPL).[341] This, according to Professor Chen Guangzhong who was in charge of drafting the revision, was designed deliberately to avoid the controversy of the doctrine.[342] Clearly, it is not a total endorsement of the presumption of innocence, but it is a significant improvement on the 1979 CPL provisions. Further, Article 34 of the 1996 Decision applies the new term 'criminal suspect' to all persons suspected of committing crimes, but before the institution of prosecution. The change of terminology reinforces the rejection of the presumption of guilt, but does not necessarily support the adoption of the presumption of innocence.

With this compromise arrangement in the revision it is not surprising that the principle of the presumption of innocence continues to be controversial in China. However, if the essence of this principle is to afford better protection to the accused against over-eager prosecutors or police officials who find it easier to intimidate the accused on the basis of a presumption of guilt,[343] then the practical significance of this revision depends on the reform of other aspects of the procedural law, such as the law on evidence and the trial process. Indeed, other reforms in the 1996 and 2012 reforms, to be discussed below, seem to strengthen the actual functions of this fundamental due process principle.

The right to silence is part and parcel of the principle of the presumption of innocence and so it is not surprising that the 1979 CPL contained no such right at all. The 1996 reform however did not introduce the right to silence into the CPL either. As can be expected, many, though not all, scholars called for the inclusion of such a right in the 2012 reform.[344] This issue however became one of the most contentious aspects of that reform, with all law enforcement agencies universally opposing such an inclusion, on the ground that such a right would affect the proper exercise of the major functions of the CPL – the investigation and punishment of crimes.[345] Also, certain restrictions on the right to silence imposed in

---

341 This provision remains the same after the 2012 revision of the CPL.

342 See Chen Guangzhong and Yan Duanzhu, *A Draft and its Explanation on the Revision of Criminal Procedure Law* (Beijing: China Fangzheng Press, 1995), at 107. See also Huang Taiyun, *supra* note 258, at 32.

343 Leng & Chiu, *supra* note 257, at 96.

344 See 'Legal Expert: The Police, the Procuratorate and the Court all oppose the inclusion of the right to silence', originally published in Jinghua Daily, 19 November 2011, available at http://news.163.com/11/0919/03/7E9J1APG00014AED.html (last accessed 15/8/12).

345 See 'Legal Expert: The Police, the Procuratorate and the Court all oppose the inclusion of the right to silence', *id*; and Yao Dongqing, *supra* note 276, at 24–25.

western countries in their anti-terrorism laws were relied upon by opponents of the inclusion of this right.[346]

Advocates for the inclusion of the right to silence, however, managed to add a new provision to Article 43 (now Article 50 of the 2012 CPL), stating that 'no one shall be forced to prove his/her own guilt'. This effectively introduces a partial rule against self-incrimination. The effectiveness of such a provision is however doubtful, as Article 93 (now Article 118 of the 2012 CPL) requires the suspect to answer questions truthfully. The 2012 revision further adds to the Article that the suspect is to be notified that his/her confession of crimes could lead to lenient punishment under the law. The government has insisted that there is no conflict between the two provisions,[347] but many scholars disagree.[348]

III.2.5. *Exemption from Prosecution and the Decision not to Prosecute*

Article 101 of the 1979 CPL provided that '[i]n cases where, according to the provisions of the Criminal Law, it is not necessary to impose a sentence of criminal punishment or an exemption from criminal punishment may be granted, a people's procuratorate may grant Exemption from Prosecution (*Mianyu Qisu*).' For Exemption from Prosecution to be granted, three requirements had to be met: a) the crime facts were clear; b) the evidence was sufficient and certain; c) no criminal punishment was necessary or an exemption from criminal punishment might be allowed according to the Criminal Law.[349] This is what the Chinese scholars called the 'unique Chinese institution' of Exemption from Prosecution.[350] Its origin, according to a Chinese authority on CPL, could be traced back to the Decision on Dealing with Detained Japanese War Criminals From the Sino-Japan War, issued by the SCNPC on 25 April 1956, which for the first time granted the people's procuratorate the power to exempt people from prosecution.[351]

A decision by a people's procuratorate to exempt someone from prosecution was different from a decision not to prosecute. Article 104 of the

---

[346] See 'Legal Expert: The Police, the Procuratorate and the Court all oppose to the inclusion of the right to silence', *id*; and Yao Dongqing, *supra* note 276, at 24–25.

[347] See 'Press Conference on the Revision of the CPL', available at http://news.xinhaunet.com/politics/2012lh/2012-03/09/c_122810577.htm (last accessed 9/3/12).

[348] See 'Focusing on CPL Revision: Bright Spots and Controversial Issues', available at http://www.chnlawyer.net/ShowArticle.shtml?ID=2011926102738729.htm (last accessed 29/6/12).

[349] Wang, Wang & Wang, *supra* note 251, at 213–4.

[350] Chen Guangzhong (Pt II), *supra* note 266, at 5.

[351] Ibid.

1979 CPL provided that when any of the circumstances provided in Article 11 of the CPL applied, the people's procuratorate should make a decision not to prosecute. Circumstances provided in Article 11 included: (a) if the circumstances were clearly minor, the harm was not great, and the act was thus not deemed to be a crime; (b) if the period of limitation for prosecuting the crime had expired; (c) if an exemption from criminal punishment had been ordered in a special amnesty decree; (d) if, according to the Criminal Law, a crime was to be handled only upon complaint and there had been no complaint or the complaint had been withdrawn; (e) if the defendant was deceased; or (f) if other laws or decrees provided for exemption from investigation of criminal responsibility.

The difference between a decision to exempt someone from prosecution and a decision not to prosecute was that the person exempted from prosecution was guilty of a crime but was exempted from punishment, whereas in the latter case the person was not guilty of any crime, or the law would not pursue any criminal punishment on specific legal grounds.[352] The problem was therefore, as Gellat has pointed out, that the public prosecutor made a decision on guilt, usurping the role of the courts and acting before the suspect was legally entitled to counsel.[353] Further, in cases where the investigation was conducted by the procuracy, the people's procuratorate assumed all three functions of investigation, prosecution, and adjudication, which were clearly required by the CPL to be divided among the three law-enforcement organs: the public security, the procuratorate and the court.[354] Exemption from Prosecution also lacked supervision, which led to the abuse of that legal institution through the use of the device to exempt guilty persons from prosecution as a result of corruption, or to record an Exemption from Prosecution for innocent people.[355]

For these reasons, calls to abolish the practice had been made and debated in China for some time. The debate was heated but inconclusive.[356] Opponents of the abolition argument asserted that this practice

352 Wang, Wang & Wang, *supra* note 251, at 215.

353 Lawyers Committee for Human Rights, *supra* note 20, 21.

354 See Article 5 of the 1979 CPL.

355 See further Cui Min, *supra* note 321, at 6; Shi Huifang, 'An Opinion on Abolishing the Institution of Exemption from Prosecution', (no.1, 1995) *Journal of the China University of Political Science and Law (Zhengfa Luntan)* 33; and Lawyers Committee for Human Rights, *supra* note 20, 24–25.

356 Chen Guangzhong (Pt II), *supra* note 266, at 5. See further Xu Yichu, 'My Opinion on the Exemption from Prosecution', (no.3, 1989) *Studies in Law (Faxue Yanjiu)* 74; Song Yinghui & Wu Jie, 'A New Study into the Exemption from Prosecution', (no.1, 1992) *Studies*

was a reflection of the judicial policy of 'combining punishment with leniency (*Chengban Yü Kuanda Xiangjiehe*)'; it was only an exercise of discretionary power by the procuratorate; and it was economically efficient.[357] As in the debate on the presumption of innocence, a compromise solution was proposed during the revision process. This solution was to abolish the Exemption from Prosecution provision, but at the same time to expand the scope of decisions not to prosecute.[358] Again the compromise solution was adopted. Articles 58–61 of the 1996 Decision concerning the Revision of the Criminal Procedure Law abolished Exemption from Prosecution. The scope of decisions not to prosecute under Article 104 of the 1979 CPL was expanded to include cases 'where the circumstances of crime are minor and, according to the Criminal Law, it is not necessary to impose a sentence of criminal punishment, or criminal liability is to be exempted.'[359]

The abolition was a step forward, but the compromise solution was not without some fundamental problems. The major problems with Exemption from Prosecution identified by the SCNPC included, first, that its practice violated the principles of Rule of Law, as a person could be found guilty without adjudication by a court; and, secondly, that some innocent persons could be given a decision of Exemption from Prosecution, which then violated the lawful rights of the persons concerned, while some who deserved criminal punishment could be exempted from prosecution.[360] Under the new provision a person whom the procuratorate decided not to prosecute could nevertheless be regarded as being guilty of a minor crime, and this guilty verdict was not delivered by a court. Further, the phrase 'the circumstances of crime are minor' would in practice be subject to interpretation. There was then no guarantee that 'persons who deserve criminal punishment' would not escape prosecution. Thus the actual operation of the new provision could easily

---

in Law (*Faxue Yanjiu*) 24; Wang Mingyuan, 'Several Questions on the Exemption from Prosecution', (no.2, 1992) *Legal Science in China* (*Zhongguo Faxue*) 75; Shi Huifang, *supra* note 355; Wang Hongxiang, 'Upholding and Perfecting the Exemption from Prosecution', (no.5, 1994) *Legal Science in China* (*Zhongguo Faxue*) 42; Cui Min, 'Abolishing the Exemption from Prosecution', (no.5, 1994) *Legal Science in China* (*Zhongguo Faxue*) 44.

357 See Chen Guangzhong (Pt II), *supra* note 266, at 5; Cui Min, *supra* note 261, at 95; Huang Taiyun, *supra* note 258, at 36–37.

358 Huang Taiyun, *supra* note 258, at 37; and Cui Min, *supra* note 261, at 95.

359 Article 142 of the 1996 CPL (now Article 173 of the 2012 CPL). The 2012 revision adds the situation where there is no evidence of crime to the circumstances for a decision not to prosecute.

360 Gu Angran, *supra* note 273, at 89.

defeat the original intention of the revision of the law in this regard. It could also undermine the new provision on the presumption of innocence.

III.2.6. *Right to Counsel*

The 1982 Constitution provides an ambivalent right of defence. Article 125 states that '[a]ll cases handled by the people's courts, except for those involving special circumstances as specified by law, shall be heard in public. The accused has the right of defence.' It is unclear in the Chinese language (*youquan huode bianhu*) whether such a right of defence includes a right to counsel, although it does do so in practice. More importantly, it is unclear whether such a right is limited to trials in court or also allowed during pre-trial investigations. More detailed rules regarding the right of defence were provided in the CPL. Article 8 of the 1979 CPL repeated the above constitutional clause but further added that 'the people's courts have the duty to guarantee that defendants obtain defence.' The right to counsel – a lawyer, or relative or other citizen – was specifically provided for by Article 26 of the 1979 CPL. However, the 1979 CPL was again silent on whether the defendant had a right to counsel in pre-trial processes; it provided only that the court was required, seven days before the opening of the court session, to deliver to the defendant a copy of the bill of prosecution and to inform him/her that he/she might appoint a defender, or, when necessary, to designate a defender for the defendant (Article 110). Although a right to counsel before trial was not guaranteed by the law, it is difficult to see any technical barrier to a defender's participation in pre-trial investigations. Chinese scholars, however, interpreted Article 110 to mean that defenders were allowed to enter into the criminal process only seven days before the trial,[361] and this in fact became the usual practice prior to the 1996 reform of the CPL.[362]

The inadequate protection for timely access to a defence lawyer has long been of concern to Chinese scholars.[363] The issue was strongly

361 See e.g. Zhang Wei, 'Several Issues Regarding the Involvement of Lawyers in Criminal Procedure', (no.5, 1994) *Legal Science in China* (*Zhongguo Faxue*) 39, at 39; Chen Guangzhong & Xiong Qiuhong, 'Some Opinions on the Revision of the Criminal Procedure Law – Pt I', (no.4, 1995) *Legal Science in China* (*Zhongguo Faxue*) 91, at 92.

362 See Leng & Chiu, *supra* note 257, at 92; Lawyers Committee for Human Rights, *supra* note 20, at 29–30; and Zhang Tao & Chen Weidong, 'A Discussion of the Time for Defence Lawyers to Participate in the Criminal Process', (no.2, 1990) *Legal Science in China* (*Zhongguo Faxue*) 43, at 43.

363 See Chen Guangzhong (Pt I), *supra* note 266, at 13.

debated for many years,[364] but the controversial issue was not whether lawyers should be allowed earlier participation in the criminal process, but how much earlier they should be allowed in.[365] Not surprisingly, the major opposition to lawyers' early participation came from the investigatory organs. They argued that the early participation of lawyers in the criminal process would unduly interfere with investigatory conduct, particularly in secret investigations.[366] In response to this concern a compromise was proposed: lawyers should be allowed early participation, ideally, immediately after the first questioning of the accused by the public security, but such participation should be limited to providing legal assistance and collecting materials for the defence. Further, certain supervisory powers should be granted to the public security organs to control access to lawyers by defendants.[367]

Again, the SCNPC decided to accept the compromise solution. Article 41 of the 1996 Decision concerning the Revision of the Criminal Procedure Law added a new provision, as Article 96 of the 1996 CPL, which stated that '[a]fter the first questioning or the imposition of coercive measures, a criminal suspect has a right to appoint a lawyer to provide him/her with legal advice and to present petitions (*Shensu*) or complaints (*Konggao*) on his/her behalf. When a suspect is arrested the appointed lawyer may apply for bail (the obtaining of a guarantor and release from custody pending trial, *Qubao Houshen*) on his/her behalf. When the case involves state secrets, the appointment of a lawyer by the suspect must be approved by the investigatory organs.' This article further provides that '[t]he appointed lawyer has a right to ask for the names of the alleged crimes from the investigatory organ, and may interview the suspect under detention to acquaint himself/herself with the circumstances of the case. When interviewing the suspect under detention, the investigatory organ may, according to the circumstances and the needs of the case, have representatives present. When the case involves state secrets, the interview of a suspect by

---

364 Lawyers Committee for Human Rights, *supra* note 20, at 36.

365 See Chen Guangzhong (Pt I), *supra* note 266, at 13; Hong Bing, 'Major Measures to Perfect the Criminal Procedure System', (no.3, 1996) *Politics and Law* (*Zhangzhi Yu Falü*) 13, at 15; Huang Taiyun, *supra* note 258, at 34; Zhang & Chen, *supra* note 362, at 43; Zhang Wei, *supra* note 361, at 39.

366 Ibid.; and Lawyers Committee for Human Rights, *supra* note 20, at 36–7.

367 See e.g. Chen & Xiong, *supra* note 361 at 93; Li Baoyue, 'A Discussion on the Time When Lawyers Should Participate in the Criminal Process', (no.4, 1994), *Legal Science in China* (*Zhongguo Faxue*) 98, at 100; and Xu Yichu, 'Criminal Processes and Human Rights Protection', (no.2, 1996) *Studies in Law* (*Faxue Yanjiu*) 89, at 92.

a lawyer must be approved by the investigatory organ.'[368] To strengthen the right to defence counsel, Article 16 of the 1996 Decision added a new provision to Article 26 of the 1979 CPL as the new Article 33 of the 1996 revised CPL, which provided that '[i]n a case of public prosecution, a criminal suspect has the right to appoint a defence counsel when his/her case is transferred [to the people's procuratorate] for review and prosecution. The accused in cases of private prosecution may appoint a defence counsel at any time.'[369] This article also imposed an obligation on the people's procuratorate to inform the accused of his/her right to appoint a defence counsel in cases of public prosecution within three days of receiving the case from an investigatory organ, and on the people's court to do the same in cases of private prosecution within three days after it accepted the private prosecution. The rights of a defence lawyer were then provided in Article 36 of the 1996 CPL (revising Article 29 of the 1979 CPL): '[w]hen the people's procuratorate begins to review and prosecute a case, a defence lawyer may consult, extract and copy prosecution materials and other expert and technical assessment materials in relation to the case. He/she may also interview and correspond with the criminal suspect. Other defence counsel may also, with the permission of the people's procuratorate, consult, extract and copy prosecution materials and other expert and technical assessment materials in relation to the case, and interview and correspond with the criminal suspect.'[370] This article also provided similar rights for defence counsel after the court has accepted the case for adjudication. Two more articles (Articles 37 and 38 of the 1996 CPL) were added by the 1996 revision, which empowered the defence lawyer to collect relevant material from witnesses, crime victims and their relatives and other persons, and imposed an obligation on the defence lawyer not to help the crime suspect or the accused to conceal or destroy evidence or to obtain or alter evidence by threat or inducement, or to engage in any other activities interfering with judicial proceedings.[371]

The above provisions clearly tried to distinguish between the roles of defence lawyer during investigation and after prosecution, and to limit the scope of activities of the defence lawyer during investigation.

---

368 It should be pointed out that Article 96 was abolished during the 2012 reform when major reforms were undertaken to strengthen the right to counsel during investigation. See further discussion below.

369 This provision was further revised in 2012, see discussion below.

370 This provision was further revised in 2012, see discussion below.

371 Article 38 then became a major risk for lawyers in criminal defence. See discussion below.

The rationale, according to Chinese scholars, was to strike a balance between the protection of citizens' rights and the prevention of interference in criminal investigation.[372] However, a range of discretionary powers was granted to the investigatory organs, such as the presence of personnel from investigatory organs in interviews and the approval of the appointment of lawyers in cases involving 'state secrets'.

While the 1996 reform did to a certain extent strengthen the right to counsel and defence, the overall practical effect was described by Chinese scholars as 'one step forward two steps backward', reflected in the so-called 'three difficulties' and professional risks for lawyers.[373]

The 'three difficulties' for lawyers refers to the difficulty in meeting detainees, the difficulty in collecting evidence, and the difficulty in examining police/prosecution case files.[374] While Article 96 of the 1996 CPL allowed the defence lawyer to meet the detainee, local investigatory authorities often demanded that lawyers must apply for such a meeting in advance and approval was required. Further, excuses such as that 'the case involves state secrets', 'such a meeting will hamper investigation', 'the person-in-charge is away', 'the leader is away', 'it is too busy a time to make such an arrangement' etc, were used deliberately to delay such meetings. While Article 11 of the Provisions on Certain Issues relating to the Implementation of the Criminal Procedure Law[375] specifically required that such a meeting be arranged within 48 hours of a request for a meeting, it was extremely rare for such a meeting to be arranged within the time limit.[376] In relation to collecting evidence from the victims of crime, lawyers needed not only the consent of the victim but also the approval of the procuratorate or the court. And in relation to examining case files, lawyers were often provided only with a list of evidence, a list of witnesses, and photocopies or photos of the main evidence.[377]

The more serious problem facing lawyers was the possibility of themselves being prosecuted in the course of defending others under Article

[372] Huang Taiyun, *supra* note 258, at 35.

[373] Project Group on the Revision of the CPL, *supra* note 284, at 41.

[374] See Project Group on the Revision of the CPL, *supra* note 284, at 41.

[375] Jointly issued by the Supreme People's Court, Supreme People's Procuratorate, Ministry of Public Security, Ministry of State Security, Ministry of Justice and the Legislative Affairs Commission of the SCNPC on 19 January 1998.

[376] See Huang Taiyun, 'Interpreting the Revision of Criminal Procedure Law', in *People's Prosecution* (*Renmin Jiancha*) no.620 (April 2012), at 24–25.

[377] See Project Group on the Revision of the CPL, *supra* note 284, at 41.

306 of the 1997 Criminal Law[378] and Article 38 of the 1996 CPL.[379] According to a prominent criminal lawyer, Mr Tian Wenchang, since the implementation of the 1996 CPL, there were no fewer than 200 officially recorded cases where lawyers were prosecuted under Article 306 of the 1997 CL and Article 38 of the 1996 CPL and there would be many more that were not on the official record.[380] The reality is rather ugly, as Human Rights Watch reported in 2008:

> ... lawyers often face violence, intimidation, threats, surveillance, harassment, arbitrary detention, prosecution, and suspension or disbarment from practising law for pursuing their profession. This is particularly true in politically sensitive cases.[381]

According to a survey conducted by the Research Centre for Human Rights at Guangzhou University, 46% of lawyers believed that their work was restricted by the 'three difficulties', 37% of lawyers worried about professional risks in criminal defence cases, and 47% of lawyers believed that the limited impact they might have in criminal defence discouraged them from taking up criminal cases.[382] This then led to a situation where lawyers felt ashamed to be involved in criminal cases, as it was generally perceived among lawyers that only the less capable ones would take up such cases, and so most were reluctant to do so.[383] Even in a major city like Beijing, only around 2.5% of criminal cases actually involved representation by lawyers in 2011.[384]

Of course the causes leading to difficulties and professional risks for lawyers are complicated and deep-rooted in the politico-legal system, and

---

[378] Article 306 of the 1997 Criminal Law provides 'A defence counsel or litigation agent in a criminal proceeding, who destroys or forges evidence, assists the parties concerned to destroy or falsify evidence, or threatens or induces a witness to change his/her testimony to depart from the facts or to make false testimony, shall be sentenced to fixed-term imprisonment of not more than three (3) years or criminal detention; where the circumstances are serious, he/she shall be sentenced to fixed-term imprisonment of not less than three (3) years and not more than seven (7) years.'

[379] Article 38 of the 1996 CPL provides 'Defence lawyers or other defence counsel must not assist a criminal suspect or the accused to conceal, destroy or falsify evidence or to make a collusive confession, must not threaten or induce a witness to alter his/her testimony or commit perjury or adopt other acts to interfere with the activities of a judicial organ.'

[380] See Yao Dongqing, *supra* note 276, at 29.

[381] Human Rights Watch, *supra* note 274, at 3.

[382] Project Group on the Revision of the CPL, *supra* note 284, at 41.

[383] Yao Dongqing, *supra* note 276, at 28.

[384] See Yao Dongqing, *supra* note 276, at 28.

the CPL is only part of the problem.[385] Nevertheless, any improvement in the CPL would facilitate the actual exercise of the right to counsel and professional practice in criminal processes. Indeed, some improvements were made in the 2012 reform, though they were far from addressing all the problems identified by Chinese lawyers, human rights activists, and academics more generally.

The combined effect of articles 33 and 96, as explained above, meant that if a lawyer wished to meet a detainee during the investigation period but before the institution of prosecution, it was not clear in what capacity he/she could request such a meeting and, if such a meeting was granted, the lawyer's functions were limited. To address this problem, Article 33 was revised again in 2012, and now specifically allows a criminal suspect to appoint a lawyer as his/her defence counsel after the first interrogation by the investigatory organ or the imposition of coercive measure(s).[386] Article 96 of the 1996 CPL was abolished and a new article, Article 36 of the 2012 CPL, was added, clarifying the functions of the lawyer as defence counsel during the investigation period. This effectively means that lawyers as defence counsel now participate in the criminal process from the first interrogation by the investigation authorities; they no longer need to wait until the case has been transferred to the procuratorate. With this revision, Article 36 of the 1996 CPL has also been re-written, and now becomes Article 37. With the exception of cases involving a crime of endangering state security or a crime of engaging in terrorism, or a particularly serious crime of bribery, a lawyer, upon production of a practising certificate, a law firm certificate and a letter of an attorney or an official letter of a legal aid organ can now request a meeting with the detainee (including persons under house surveillance), and such meeting must be arranged no later than 48 hours after the request is made. Further, such meeting shall not be monitored by the investigatory authorities.[387] Finally, under the new Article 38, defence lawyers are now entitled to examine and photocopy all case file materials and, under the new Article 39, may request the procuratorate or the court to obtain the evidence materials that have been collected but not submitted by the public security organ or the people's procuratorate, which may prove the innocence of the accused

---

385 See Human Rights Watch, *supra* note 274, at 3. See also discussion in Chapter 4 on Legal Institutions, in Chen, *supra* note 1.

386 Under Article 73 of the 2012 CPL, Article 33 is also applicable to persons under house surveillance.

387 See Article 37 of the 2012 CPL. It should be pointed out that such a right to meet detainees had earlier been provided by the 1996 revised Law on Lawyers.

or the less serious nature of a crime. With these revised or added provisions, the right to counsel has now been significantly strengthened, if it is properly enforced.

However, there are two aspects that caused huge controversies during the 2012 reform but were not satisfactorily addressed by the revision.

First, under Article 64 of the 1996 CPL, relatives or the working unit of detained persons had to be notified of the place of and reasons for detention, unless such notification would affect the investigation or it was not possible to deliver the notice. This provision did not specify whether such a place of detention had to be a detention centre or another specified place, nor did it specify any circumstances under which such notice was not required. 'Secret' detention, forced confession by torture, and other forms of obtaining a confession or evidence illegally mostly occurred during this period.[388] A major revision of this article was undertaken, with the revised Article 64 (now Article 83) providing that a detained person must be transferred to a detention centre within 24 hours, and relatives must be informed of the detention within the same time limit, unless notification is impossible to deliver or where it involves a crime of endangering State security or terrorism and the notification would impede the investigation. In addition to this provision, a new article, Article 73, has been added to the 2012 CPL. This new article allows residential surveillance to be conducted in a designated residence, and where there is suspicion of a crime of endangering State security, a terrorism crime or a particularly serious crime of bribery, and the execution of residential surveillance at a domicile may impede the investigation, residential surveillance, upon approval from the people's procuratorate or the public security organ at the next highest level, may also be carried out at a designated residence. Further, relatives must be notified of such designated residential surveillance unless such notification is not possible. Together, Articles 73 and 83 create the possibility of secret detention and, not surprisingly, the two articles became the most controversial and contested issues during the 2012 revision. Proponents believe that the two articles represent a major improvement in the 1996 CPL, as the circumstances for 'secret' detention have been limited and specified, whereas the 1996 CPL could potentially be applied to, and in fact was used in practice, in any criminal case.[389] It is also suggested by some scholars that the allowance for such 'secret'

[388] Huang Taiyun, *supra* note 376, at 21.

[389] See Wu Danghong, 'Articles 73 and 83 of the New CPL Represent Progress', *People's Daily* (*Renmin Ribao*) (overseas edition), 15 March 2012, at 1.

residential surveillance may in fact bring 'shuanggui' into the legal process rather than, as it is now, being exercised outside the formal legal process.[390] Others, however, are not so sure, believing that such detention means that legal regulations applicable to detention centres would be bypassed and that forced confession and torture would continue to occur.[391] In any case, as pointed out by Chinese scholars, the potential for such 'secret' detention is huge, as the Chinese law is yet to define strictly what is a crime endangering state security, and how such an excuse might be challenged when police refuse to notify the relatives of detainees.[392]

The second issue was the question whether Article 38 of the 1996 CPL should be abolished. After some heated debate, Article 38 (now Article 42) was partially revised. Instead of applying to defence counsel only, Article 42 now applies to all persons involved in a case (presumably also to police) and, if a lawyer is charged with an offence under Article 306 of the Criminal Law, Article 42 now stipulates that the investigation must be undertaken by investigatory authorities not involved in the case in which the defence counsel was originally engaged. This revision provides some additional protection to lawyers, but continues to subject lawyers to potential prosecution.

III.2.7. *Evidence Rules*

The 1996 CPL contained only eight articles on evidence, which included material and documentary evidence, witness testimonies, victim statements, defendants' statements or explanations, conclusions from expert evaluations, records of inspection and examination, and audio-visual material. The Interpretation on Certain Issues relating to the Implementation of the Criminal Procedure Law of the PRC, issued by the Supreme People's Court on 2 September 1998, further elaborates, in 11 articles (Articles 52–62), the application rules for the CPL provisions on evidence. The CPL on evidence is thus highly underdeveloped and essentially simplistic, providing little useful guidance in practice. Practical rules are spread out in various judicial interpretations and provisions as well as some rules issued by law enforcement agencies such as the Ministry of

390 See 'Legal Expert: The Police, the Procuratorate and the Court all oppose to the inclusion of the right to silence', *supra* note 344.

391 'Legal Expert: The Police, the Procuratorate and the Court all oppose to the inclusion of the right to silence', *supra* note 344.

392 See 'Legal Experts Interpret the Revision of the Criminal Procedure Law: Many Important Aspects still Not Revised', *supra* note 291.

Public Security.[393] Together, they are incomplete, unsystematic, and often lacking in operational detail.[394] Despite continuing calls for the enactment of a comprehensive evidence law since 1998,[395] there is no sign that such a law is to be enacted soon.

In the absence of a sophisticated system of evidence law, and with reliance on confession (sometimes obtained by torture and other illegal means), wrongful conviction is almost inevitable.[396] Such cases have heightened the importance of evidence law and the need for further rules on evidence. On 12 June 2010 two sets of evidence rules were finally issued jointly by the Supreme People's Court, the Supreme People' Procuratorate, the Ministry of Public Security, the Ministry of State Security, and the Ministry of Justice: Provisions on Examining and Evaluating Evidence in Death Penalty Cases, and Provisions on the Exclusion of Illegally Obtained Evidence in Criminal Cases. While the first set of provisions targets death penalty cases, the Notice issuing the two sets of rules specifically provides that these rules will also be applied to other criminal cases by reference.

The 2012 CPL reform in relation to evidence then was aided by the above evidence rules, but focused only on several specific issues.

First, among the various types of evidence, the emphasis of the CPL is on material evidence gathered from investigation; oral statements are consequently given less weight than physical evidence. Further in gathering various types of evidence, the use of torture, threats, enticement, deceit or other illegal means is prohibited. Although the 1996 CPL did not specify the legal effect of evidence obtained by torture and other illegal means, the 1998 Supreme People's Court Interpretation on Certain Issues relating to the Implementation of the CPL (Article 61) makes it clear that such evidence must not be used in criminal cases. [397] In reality, these provisions did not change the practice of torture and other illegal practices,

---

393 See Zhang, Feng, Zhu, 'Thirty Years of Rule of Law in China – Evidence', available at http://www.chinalaw.org.cn/Column/Column_View.aspx?ColumnID=398&InfoID=1670 (last accessed 24/8/12).

394 See *id.*

395 See *id.*

396 From 2000 onward, a number of major wrongful conviction cases, including cases where a suspended death penalty was imposed, were exposed by the media. See Zhang, Feng, Zhu, *supra* note 393. For a more recent case see 'Murder convict set free after "victim" turns up', available at www.chinadaily.com.cn/china/2010-05/10/content_9826537.htm (last accessed 22/8/12).

397 The Provision is then elaborated in the 2010 Provisions on the Exclusion of Illegally Obtained Evidence in Criminal Cases.

as 'confession is taken to be king'.[398] The 2012 reform now adds 5 new articles (Articles 54–58) to the CPL, providing much more detailed rules to exclude illegal evidence obtained by torture or threat, or evidence obtained in breach of procedural rules. The revised Article 46 (now Article 53 of the 2012 CPL) further establishes the following criteria that define what would amount to accurate and sufficient evidence in criminal cases: (1) all facts used for determining guilt and sentence are supported by evidence; (2) all evidence on which the case is decided has been verified and proven to be true through procedures prescribed by law; and (3) based on an overall evaluation of the evidence, all facts are proven beyond reasonable doubt. Additionally, a new article (Article 49 of the 2012 CPL) now provides that the burden of proof is to be borne by the people's procuratorate or the private prosecutor in cases of private prosecution. These additional provisions represent, no doubt, some significant improvement of the law. Their practical effect, however, awaits future testing.[399]

Secondly, under Article 48 of the 1996 CPL, a person who has knowledge about a case has a duty to testify, with the exception of handicapped persons or minors. In reality, less than 1% of witnesses actually appear in court to testify and to be cross-examined.[400] This is described by Chinese scholars as the 'three strange phenomena': a witness will testify to police and prosecutors but not to courts; a witness will provide written evidence but not appear in court; and police do not appear in court to testify or to be cross-examined.[401] In response to these problems, two new articles (Articles 187 and 188) now make it compulsory for important witnesses (including police) and expert witnesses deemed necessary by the court to testify and to be cross-examined in court. Article 63 (a new addition to the 2012 CPL) also provides that the state shall pay the associated costs incurred by witnesses. Finally, a new article, Article 62, provides some special protection to witnesses in cases involving the crime of endangering

[398] See 'Respecting and Protecting Human Rights a Major Progress: Ten Major Bright Points in the CPL Reform', available at http://news.xinhuanet.com/politics/2012lh/2012-03/09/c_111625145.htm (last accessed 9/3/12). See also 'Focusing on CPL Revision: Bright Spots and Controversial Issues', *supra* note 348.

[399] According to Chinese scholars, during the two years of implementation of the 2010 Provisions on Exclusion of Illegal Evidence, there was rarely any case that actually excluded illegal evidence. See 'Legal Experts Interpret the Revision of the Criminal Procedure Law: Many Important Aspects still Not Revised', *supra* note 291.

[400] 'Chen Guangzhong: A Greater Step Will Ensure Better Revision', an interview by China Economic Weekly, in *China Economic Weekly* (*Zhongguo Jingji Zhoukan*), 26 March 2012, at 31.

[401] See Zhang, Feng, Zhu, *supra* note 393.

State security, terrorism crime, organised crime, drug related crimes, etc. Clearly, these new provisions provide both sticks and carrots for witnesses to appear in courts.

Thirdly, the 2012 CPL also expands the scope of evidence. Verification and investigative testing are specifically added to written records as evidence, and electronic data are also recognised as evidence.[402] Further, a new paragraph was inserted into the revised Article 45 (now Article 52), which provides that physical evidence, documentary evidence, audio and visual evidence, electronic data and other evidence collected by administrative organs in the course of administrative law enforcement or of handling a case may be used as evidence in criminal proceedings. This new addition is intended to improve the efficiency of investigation, at least in avoiding the repetition of the same investigation when a case is transferred from an administrative law enforcement agency to the police or the procuratorate. At the same, however, there are also doubts whether administrative law enforcement personnel have sufficient knowledge of criminal procedure law in relation to the proper collection of evidence.[403]

Finally, in addition to the maintenance of confidentiality of evidence involving state secrets, commercial confidentiality and personal privacy have now been accorded the same protection.[404]

III.2.8. *The Trial Process*

The trial process, both on paper and in practice, had been flawed since it was re-institutionalised by the 1979 CPL. Its problems ranged from the passive role for lawyers to lack of judicial independence, starting from the preliminary examination through to the passing of judgments. A Chinese scholar severely criticised the trial process thus:

> Many shortcomings of the criminal trial process have been documented. For instance, the practice of judges reviewing, examining and discussing the case based on materials supplied by the procuratorate before the trial has led to the prejudice of judges and the consequence of 'verdict first, trial second' (*Xian Ding Hou Shen*); the discussion and decision by the judicial committee and the practice of the first instance court seeking instructions from a higher court have caused the problems of 'trial judges not making decisions and decision-makers not trying the case' (*Shenzhe Bu Pan, Panzhe Bu*

[402] See Article 48 (revising Article 42 of the 1996 CPL).
[403] 'Focusing on CPL Revision: Bright Spots and Controversial Issues', *supra* note 348.
[404] See Article 52 of the 2012 CPL.

> *Shen*) and 'higher courts deciding and lower courts delivering' (*Shangpi Xiapan*); because judges are required to present evidence to prove the guilt of the accused there is the phenomenon of 'non-separation between adjudication and prosecution' (*Kong Shen Bu Fen*) and 'the *ultra vires* of adjudication' (*Shenpan Yuewei*), etc. All these practices weaken, or even diminish the function of defence, thus rendering court trial a formality only.[405]

Some Chinese scholars thus described the trial process as a process of legitimising the conclusion which had already been drawn before the trial.[406] This kind of practice led to the judicial reality of the presumption of guilt.[407]

These problems were deeply rooted in the fundamental political system (e.g. the lack of judicial independence) and the lack of an established legal tradition (e.g. the emphasis on substantive justice at the expense of procedural justice, the minimal role played by lawyers in society and in litigation). However, the majority of Chinese scholars blamed the inquisitorial system for causing such problems. According to them, the inquisitorial system China adopted was an 'extreme' one in which judges played an extremely active and powerful role both in preliminary examination and in the actual trial process.[408] Thus the major debate on reforming the trial process in 1996 was centred on the merits and shortcomings of the inquisitorial and adversarial systems and the comparison between the two.[409]

---

[405] Zhang Zhiming, 'A Further Thought on the Reform of the Trial Process', (no.4, 1995) *Studies in Law* (*Faxue Yanjiu*) 93, at 94–95. Similar criticisms were made by many other Chinese scholars. See e.g. Li Jianmin, 'Several Thoughts on the Reform of the Criminal Trial Process', (no.1, 1995) *Studies in Law* (*Faxue Yanjiu*) 84, at 85; Huang Taiyun, *supra* note 258, at 37; and Xie Youping, 'Ideal and Reality: A Comment on the Revised Criminal Procedure Law', (no.2, 1996) *Modern Law Science* (*Xiandao Faxue*) 9, at 10–11. The Chinese trial process had been equally severely, if not more so, criticised by Western scholars and human rights activists. See e.g. Leng and Chiu, *supra* note 257, ch.5; and Lawyers Committee for Human Rights, *supra* note 20, esp. 38–60.

[406] Chen Guangzhong & Xion Qiuhon, 'Some Opinions on the Revision of the Criminal Procedure Law – Pt II', (no.5, 1995) *Legal Science in China* (*Zhongguo Faxue*) 85, at 85; and Hong Bing, *supra* note 365, at 56.

[407] Li Xuekuan, 'Some Legal Considerations on the Functions of Defence Lawyer in Our Country', (no.6, 1995) *Legal Science in China* (*Zhongguo Faxue*) 90, at 94.

[408] See e.g. Xie Youping, *supra* note 405, at 11; and Zhang Zhiming, *supra* note 405, 94.

[409] See e.g. Chen Guangzhong, et al., 'The Market Economy and the Future of the Science of Criminal Procedure Law', (no.5, 1993) *Legal Science in China* (*Zhongguo Faxue*) 3; Li Jianmin, *supra* note 159; Zhang Zhiming, *supra* note 159; Wang Shaonan, 'Establishing a Direction for Trial Process Reform', (no.1, 1995) *Studies in Law* (*Faxue Yanjiu*) 77; Zhang Xiu, 'Choices for the Reform in the Trial Process for Public Prosecution Cases', (no.2, 1996) *Studies in Law* (*Faxue Yanjiu*) 96. See also an excellent summary of major debates on criminal procedure law: Wang Minyuan & Liu Donghua, 'A Comment on and Summary of the Study of Criminal Procedure Law', (no.1, 1996) *Studies in Law* (*Faxue Yanjiu*) 51, esp. 57–61.

Though there were scholars advocating the wholesale adoption of the adversarial system and others strongly resisting such a move, many scholars soon agreed that adopting certain elements from the adversarial system was an appropriate approach to reforming the trial process.[410] This approach was then adopted by the NPC in its 1996 reform, which was further strengthened by the 2012 revision in relation to the appearance of witnesses in court and the review of the death penalty.

Four major changes were made by the 1996 revision,[411] which was further strengthened by the 2012 revision. First, under Article 108 of the 1979 CPL a court would open a session and adjudicate on the case only if, after preliminary examination of the case initiated by the public prosecution, the court had decided that the facts of the crime were clear and the evidence was complete. If the principal facts were not clear and the evidence insufficient, the court might remand the case to the people's procuratorate for supplementary investigation. It was this requirement that led to the practice of 'verdict first, adjudication second'. In 1996, a new provision (Article 150 of the 1996 CPL) was added, providing that a court should open its session and adjudicate on the case if the bill of prosecution contained alleged crime facts, a list of the evidence, names of witnesses and copies or photos of the principal evidence. This provision thus substantially reduced the extent of preliminary examination by the court; the question of sufficiency of evidence was now a matter for debate and determination during a court session. In the 2012 revision, the requirement to include the list of the evidence, names of witnesses and copies or photos of the principal evidence was dropped altogether, further lowering the prosecution requirements for initiating a court session.[412] Further, supplementary investigation is now not to be initiated by a court; it is to be applied for by the procuratorate and to be approved by a court during a court session. The maximum period allowed for supplementary investigation is limited to one month.[413]

Secondly, the functions of the collegiate panel and the judicial committee were re-defined. Under the 1979 CPL, cases other than minor criminal matters were required to be adjudicated on by a collegiate panel consisting of judges and people's assessors.[414] However, judicial committees were

---

410 See e.g. Zhang Zhiming, *supra* note 405; Wang & Liu, *id*; Xie Youping, *supra* note 405; and Chen & Xiong (Pt II), *supra* note 406.

411 Gu Angran, *supra* note 273, at 88.

412 Article 150 of the 1996 CPL has now become Article 181.

413 See Articles 198–199 of the 2012 CPL (Articles 165–166 of the 1996 CPL).

414 Article 105 of the 1979 CPL.

also established at all levels of the people's court.[415] Their functions were vaguely defined as being 'to sum up judicial experience and to discuss important or difficult cases and other issues relating to judicial work.'[416] Under Article 107 of the 1979 CPL, all major and difficult cases were to be submitted to the judicial committee for discussion and decision, and the collegiate panel had to carry out the decisions of the committee. Other than this, the CPL was silent on the relationship between the collegiate panel and the judicial committee. In reality, many courts relied on the judicial committees to discuss and decide cases regardless of the importance of the cases concerned, and sometimes before a trial by a court.[417] Under Article 149 of the 1996 CPL,[418] after deliberation a collegiate panel had to deliver a judgment. Only when the collegiate panel decided that it was unable to make a decision in difficult, major or complex cases could it request the president of the court to transfer the case to the judicial committee for discussion and decision. In other words, cases would not be decided by a judicial committee before trial, and difficult, major or complex cases would no longer be automatically submitted to judicial committees for deliberation and decision. This provision was thus designed to resolve the problem of 'trial judges not making decisions and decision-makers not trying the case' (*Shenzhe Bu Pan, Panzhe Bu Shen*).[419]

Thirdly, instead of the trial judge presenting evidence to the court and questioning the witnesses, the revised CPL now required the prosecutors and defenders to present evidence to the court, and questioning and debating on the evidence and the alleged crime facts would be mainly left to the prosecutors and the defenders.[420] In short, the trial judges would take a much more passive role, concerning themselves mainly with the maintenance of court order and orderly debate, thus leaving much more room for meaningful defence. As already discussed above, the 2012 revision further strengthened the requirement for witnesses to appear in court and evidence to be contested and cross-examined.[421]

---

415 Article 11 of the Organic Law of the PRC (as revised). See also discussions in Chapter 4, in Chen, *supra* note 1.

416 Ibid.

417 China University of Political Science and Law (ed.), *Research into and Discussions on Theoretical and Practical Problems of Criminal Procedure* (Beijing: Law Publishing House, 1987) at 205–206.

418 Now Article 180 of the CPL.

419 Cui Min, *supra* note 321, at 6.

420 See Articles 186–194 of the 2012 CPL (revising Articles 155–161 of the 1996 CPL).

421 See Articles 187–188 (new addition by the 2012 revision), Articles 192–193 (revising Article 159–160 of the 1996 CPL).

Finally, a new summary procedure was established during the 1996 reform to deal with minor criminal offences.[422] This would allow the court to concentrate its human and other resources on the more adversarial proceedings which would certainly be more time-consuming and, perhaps, more expensive.

As already alluded to, the trial processes, though having undergone some fundamental reform in 1996, were subject to further reform in 2012.

First, application of the summary procedure for minor offences now requires the consent of all defendants in the case.[423] Such procedure may also be conducted by a collegiate bench, not necessarily by a sole judge.[424]

Secondly, in addition to the summary procedure for minor offences, four new special procedures, dealing with juvenile cases, reconciliation between parties, confiscation of illegal gains, and compulsory medical treatment for suspects with mental illness respectively, were introduced into the CPL.[425] These new procedures recognise special needs or the special nature of the cases, and their introduction has been mostly welcomed by scholars and practitioners.

Finally, with the reform in the area of the death penalty in the last few years, the 2012 reform further strengthens the review and approval process for cases involving the imposition of the death penalty by adding two articles (Articles 239 & 240) to the CPL. Article 239 now requires that, when reviewing the case of a death sentence, the Supreme People's Court must make an order on whether or not it approves the death sentence. Where it does not approve the death sentence, the Supreme People's Court may remit the case for a retrial or impose a new sentence. Article 240 stipulates that the Supreme People's Court must interrogate the accused and, where the defence lawyer makes such a request, hear the opinion of the defence lawyer. During the course of reviewing the case of a death sentence, the Supreme People's Procuratorate may inform the Supreme People's Court of its opinion.

---

422 Articles 174–179 of the 1996 CPL (now Article 208–215). These procedures are further regulated by the Certain Opinions on the Application of Summary Procedures in the Adjudication of Pubic Prosecution Cases, issued jointly by the Supreme People's Court, the Supreme People's Procuratorate and the Ministry of Justice on 14 March 2003. Since the summary procedures resemble plea bargaining, to a certain extent, and are generally seen as being inconsistent with an inquisitorial system, they have since become quite controversial. See Randall Peerenboom, *China Modernizes: Threat to the West or Model for the Rest?* (New York: Oxford University Press, 2007), at 204–208.

423 Articles 208 and 211 of the 2012 CPL.

424 Article 210 of the 2012 CPL.

425 See the new Part V of the 2012 CPL.

III. 3. *Other Developments*

There were also a number of other notable revisions in 1996 and 2012. First, the scope of cases to be directly investigated by the people's procuratorates has been narrowed.[426] Secondly, the status of crime victim has been defined and certain rights in the trial process are provided.[427] Further, the function of judicial supervision in criminal processes by the people's procuratorates is strengthened.[428] Finally, when the 1996 CPL came into effect on 1 January 1997 several sets of measures issued in the late 1970s and early 1980s were abolished.[429]

In the 2012 reform, despite initial resistance from the police and state security authorities,[430] a new section on technical measures for investigation was inserted as Section 8 in Chapter 2 in Part II of the CPL (Articles 148–152 of the 2012 CPL). These measures (eg electronic surveillance and covert investigation) have been used by the investigatory agencies for years, but they are only publicly acknowledge and regulated for the first time in the 2012 CPL reform. Evidence obtained through these measures can now be used as evidence in criminal litigation.[431] These measures may, however, only be used in limited circumstances, such as investigation into crimes endangering state security, terrorism, organised crime, major drug trafficking, major bribery and corruption cases.[432] While a strict approval procedure must be followed before undertaking such technical investigatory measures,[433] the CPL does not specify what authority will have the approval power. According to an insider to the 2012 CPL revision, law makers simply could not agree on which authority or authorities should be vested with such power and, as a result, this critical issue is left for future clarification by other laws.[434]

---

426 See Article 18 of the 1996 CPL, which remains the same in the 2012 CPL.

427 See Articles 37, 40–41, 82, 87–88, 145, & 182 of the 1996 CPL. These provisions remain the same after the 2012 revision, but are now re-numbered as Articles 41, 44–45, 106, 111–112, 176, & 218 respectively.

428 See Articles 8, 87, 112, & 169 of the 1996 CPL. These provisions remain the same after the 2012 revision, but are re-numbered as 8, 11, 137, & 203 respectively.

429 These included the 1979 Regulation on Detention and Arrest; the very much criticised Decision of the Standing Committee of the NPC on the Procedures for Rapid Adjudication of Cases Involving Criminal Elements Who Seriously Endanger Public Security (1983); and the Supplementary Provisions of the Standing Committee of the NPC Regarding the Question of the Time Limits for Handling Criminal Cases (1984).

430 See Yao Dongqing, *supra* note 276, at 26–27.

431 Article 152 of the 2012 CPL.

432 Article 148 of the 2012 CPL.

433 Article 148 of the 2012 CPL.

434 Huang Taiyun, *supra* note 376, at 37.

III.4. *The Missing Element in the CPL Reform*

A crucial issue relating to the quality of the criminal process has not yet been addressed, namely the issue of judicial independence – the 'most glaring deficiency in the PRC's trial process'.[435] Judicial independence has been a subject of debate in the PRC since the 1950s.[436] The 1954 Constitution – the first constitution in the PRC – provided that 'people's courts shall conduct adjudication independently and shall be subject only to the law'.[437] However, advocating judicial independence was denounced as Rightist thought and severely criticised in the late 1950s and during the Cultural Revolution. The 1975 and 1978 Constitutions thus abolished the 1954 provision. The present Constitution – the 1982 Constitution – stipulates an ambiguous principle: '[t]he people's courts shall, in accordance with the law, exercise judicial power independently and are not subject to interference by administrative organs, public organisations or individuals.'[438] On the other hand, the 1982 Constitution upholds the so-called Four Fundamental Principles, among which is the upholding of the leadership of the Communist Party. This constitutional arrangement, particularly when compared with the 1954 constitutional provision, seems to suggest that judicial independence, such as it is, is subject to Party leadership. Indeed, Party leadership over the judiciary has been constantly asserted in China.[439] Sometimes such leadership

---

435 Lawyers Committee for Human Rights, *supra* note 20, at 52.

436 Of course there was no discussion on this sensitive issue during the Cultural Revolution (1966–1976). For a discussion on the debate in the 1950s see Jerome Alan Cohen, 'The Chinese Communist Party and 'Judicial Independence': 1949–59', (1969) 82 *Harvard Law Review* 967. For discussions on the debate since the 1980s see Hikota Koguchi, 'Some Observations About 'Judicial Independence' in Post-Mao China', (1987) 7 *Boston College Third World Law Journal* 195; Margaret Y.K. Woo, 'Adjudication Supervision and Judicial Independence in the PRC', (1991) 39 *The American Journal of Comparative Law* 95; and Guo, Li & Hao, *supra* note 335. For an English translation of Chinese views in the 1950s and early 1980s see Liao Kuangsheng, 'Independent Administration of Justice' and the PRC Legal System', (Vol 16, 1983) *Chinese Law & Government* 123.

437 Article 78 of the 1954 Constitution. The same was also provided by Article 4 of the Organic Law of the People's Courts of the PRC (1954).

438 Article 126 of the 1982 Constitution. Article 4 of the 1979 Organic Law of the People's Courts of the PRC repeats the same.

439 For instance, the Certain Opinions of the Communist Party of China on Deepening the Reform of the Judicial System and Its Working Mechanisms (document on personal file), issued in 2008, makes it clear that such reform must always maintain Party leadership and socialist direction and must always take the cause of the Party, the interest of the people, and the Constitution as the utmost priorities. This Party leadership is most recently stated to be 'absolute'. See 'Zhou Yongkang: always maintain the absolute leadership of the Party in politico-legal work', Xinhua, 2 July 2011, available at http://news.xinhuanet.com/2011-07/02/c_121614063.htm (last accessed 21/7/11).

involves the requirement of Party approval for specific cases,[440] despite the fact that a review and approval system by Party committees was officially abolished in 1979.[441]

The 1979 CPL was silent on the issue of judicial independence. Scholars thus proposed, during the 1996 revision, that the 1954 constitutional provision be inserted into the CPL.[442] The NPC, however, opted to repeat the 1982 constitutional provision in the 1996 CPL.[443] No further reform was undertaken in the 2012 reform, which means that the issue of judicial independence is unresolved. Thus, there are good reasons to doubt the effect of the above-mentioned reforms of the trial process, as many of the problems identified by Chinese scholars are, in one way or another, linked with Party intervention in criminal adjudication, especially in politically sensitive cases and in rural areas.[444]

It should also be noted that even the Chinese version of judicial independence – adjudication by an independent institution – is a relatively new development in the modern legal history of China. There was no independent judiciary in traditional China; adjudication was part of administration. The first modern judicature system in a Continental European style, separate from administrative organs, was established only at the turn of the 20th century.[445] Although the old judicial system established by the Kuomintang Government was abolished in 1949, the new one continued to be based on the Continental European system. To mention this here is to remind readers that there is no legal tradition to back up the operation of a relatively independent judiciary in the PRC. The compromise revision of the CPL should be understood with this background in mind.

---

440 See Chen Guangzhong (Pt I), *supra* note 266, at 11–12; Bian Jianlin, 'Direct Contesting and the Reform of the Trial Process', (no.6, 1995) *Legal Science in China* (*Zhongguo Faxue*) 96, at 97.

441 Leng & Chiu, *supra* note 255, at 99. The Party Review and Approval System was abolished by the Instruction of the Central Committee of the Chinese Communist Party Concerning the Full Implementation of the Criminal Law and Criminal Procedure Law. For a full text in English see the Appendix in Hikota Koguchi, *supra* note 356, at 208–233.

442 Cui Min, *supra* note 261, at 94.

443 Article 5 of the 1996 CPL.

444 See more detailed discussions in Lawyers Committee for Human Rights, *supra* note 20, esp. at 52–61.

445 See discussions in Chapter 1, in Chen, *supra* note 1.

CHAPTER FOUR

CONCLUSION

Legal development in China since 1978 can always be assessed from two quite different perspectives: how far China has travelled towards a rule of law, and how much further it has to go to achieve this.

Comparing the 1979 Chinese Criminal Law with the Soviet Criminal Code of 1960, Berman and his colleagues noted a striking difference in the style of the two sets of codes, namely in the profuse moralism of the Chinese and the stern formalism of the Soviet code.[446] They believed that the Soviet codes at the time embodied the law of a revolution that had settled down, whereas the Chinese code embodied the law of a revolution that was still boiling.[447] Clearly, the Chinese Criminal Law as amended in 1997 and thereafter now represents a formalistic approach to crime and punishment. It also signals the stabilisation of a revolution.

However, the 1997 revision was also a major disappointment. Although the revision strove to deal with, and has been quite successful in dealing with, a number of technical deficiencies in the criminal justice system (e.g. the fragmentation of the criminal law, the vagueness and ambiguities of the provisions, and the imbalance in punishments among criminal offences), it failed to address some of the fundamental problems, chief among them being 'counter-revolutionary' crimes, the artificial distinction between administrative sanctions and criminal penalties, and the death penalty. The removal of counter-revolutionary crime as a legal category may be seen as a step forward. The retention of most of the counter-revolutionary crime provisions without the subjective label of 'counter-revolution' is however a major failure. One must be concerned whether in this way it actually legitimises the punishment of political crimes (e.g. advocacy for changing the socialist system) as they are now treated as 'ordinary' crimes.

The post-1997 reform of the Criminal Law is generally positive, and the reform of the death penalty since 2006 represents a major advance in the

446 Berman, Cohen & Russell, *supra* note 9, at 239.
447 Berman, Cohen & Russell, *supra* note 9, at 257.

Chinese criminal justice system. While the frequent revisions made to the 1997 Criminal Law continue the instrumentalist approach towards the criminal law as a means of ensuring social stability, the needs of which are perceived on an *ad hoc* basis at any particular time, the method of making systematic amendments to the Criminal Law, instead of separate supplementary laws, has ensured a reasonable degree of consistency in the law.

In the case of the criminal procedure law, with the revisions introduced between 1996 and 2012 there is little doubt that the quality of criminal processes should improve considerably. Its practical effect on upholding justice and protecting human rights and its future reform depend very much on reform outside the legal system per se, as Gellat has pointed out,

> changes in many areas beyond the legal arena will be required to bring about substantial improvements in the human rights situation in the PRC. An overarching concern is of course the subservience of the legal system to the arbitrary dictates of the Communist Party, a problem that cannot by any means be resolved solely by reforms within the legal system. Without fundamental political changes there can be no independent judiciary or an autonomous bar – key elements of the rule of law'.[448]

The practical significance of the recent CPL revisions will depend on the actual endeavour of law-enforcement agents and lawyers. As a Chinese scholar has rightly pointed out, 'a just law does not guarantee the justice of law.'[449] The adoption, even though only partially, of many of the Western practices, e.g. the presumption of innocence, early participation by lawyers, elements of the adversarial system, etc.,[450] requires a change in the approach and thinking of judicial personnel. The strengthening of the defence role in trials, the limitation of the powers of investigatory organs, and the more adversarial trial process demand higher judicial and professional standards. Effective measures must be found to prevent interference in judicial work, including interference from the Party and administrative organs.[451] The crucial concern will be whether lawyers will be able to limit the operation of the various qualifications and restrictions still existing in the CPL on the implementation of the fundamental 'due

---

448 Lawyers Committee for Human Rights, *supra* note 20, 85.

449 Xie Youping, *supra* note 405, at 1.

450 These principles have a rather short history in China; they were all first introduced into China during the Qing and KMT reforms and their initial introduction was extremely controversial. See also Li Chunlei, *A Study of the Transformation of the Criminal Procedure Law in Modern China* (1895–1928) (*Zhongguo Jindai Xingshi Susong Zhidu Biange Yanjiu 1895–1928*) (Beijing: Beijing University Press, 2004).

451 Xie Youping, *supra* note 405, at 13.

process' principles. Clearly, these qualifications and restrictions have the potential to be abused by the investigatory organs. In order to address the concerns that were raised when the CPL was under reform, the critical issue for lawyers is to argue strongly and forcefully that these qualifications and restrictions must remain strictly limited; they should not allow such qualifications and restrictions to be used as a back door or a loophole in the CPL to circumvent the fundamental 'due process' principles now incorporated in the law.

The implementation of the 1996 CPL were rather disappointing and there have been many difficulties, as explained above, such as the huge difficulties encountered by lawyers who genuinely want to pursue justice and fairness for defendants. As Peerenboom correctly points out, these difficulties are not ones that can easily be overcome by a revision of the law; they are political, economic and cultural.[452] Similarly, it has been commented that '[t]he Criminal Procedure Law is often seen as a mini constitution, which is closely related to the political system in our country. As such, we should not have an idealised expectation of its revision; any progress is an advance. In the absence of a major reform in the political system, all that can be done are technical adjustments of the Criminal Procedure Law.'[453] Technical these improvement may be, but eventually the accumulated effect of all these, and of future reforms,[454] may well change the nature of the law altogether.

In short, the reform of the Chinese criminal justice system is, by any criterion, far from being finished business,[455] but there are reasons to believe it will continue to improve incrementally and gradually.

---

452 See Peerenboom, *supra* note 422, at 199–204.

453 Xie Youping, Professor of Fudan University, quoted in 'Legal Experts Interpret the Revision of the Criminal Procedure Law: Many Important Aspects still Not Revised', *supra* note 291.

454 Though the CPL has just been revised, scholars are already talking about more revisions in the near future. See 'Legal Experts Interpret the Revision of the Criminal Procedure Law: Many Important Aspects still Not Revised', *supra* note 291; and 'If the CPL were to be revised, what revisions are required?, *China Economic Weekly* (*Zhongguo Jingji Zhoukan*), 26 March 2012, at 32.

455 Indeed, major reforms have continued since the adoption of the revised Criminal Law and Criminal Procedure Law in 2011 and 2012 respectively, focussing on practical issues. Thus, the Supreme People's Court and Supreme People's Procuratorate have accelerated their periodical review of judicial interpretations, with the latest batches of appealed judicial documents being published on 14 January 2013 and 4 January 2013 respectively. New practical guidelines have also been issued by the relevant authorities, including Procedural Provisions governing the Handling of Criminal Cases by Public Security Authorities (issued by the Ministry of Public Security on 13 December 2012, and effective on 1 January 2013), Rules on Criminal Procedure for People's Procuratorates (issued by the

Supreme People's Procuratorate on 22 November 2012, and effective on 1 January 2013), Interpretation on the Application of the Criminal Procedure Law (issued by the Supreme People's Court on 20 December 2012, and effective on 1 January 2013), and Provisions concerning Certain Issues in the Implementation of the Criminal Procedure Law (jointly issued by the Supreme People's Court, Supreme People's Procuratorate, Ministry of Public Security, Ministry of State Security, Ministry of Justice, and the Legislative Affairs Committee of the Standing Committee of the National People's Congress on 26 December 2012, and effective on 1 January 2013). These are all detailed practical rules, with the Supreme People's Court Interpretation being the longest judicial interpretation (548 articles in 24 chapters) ever issued by the Supreme People's Court in the history of the PRC.

PART B

TRANSLATION

I CRIMINAL LAW OF THE PEOPLE'S REPUBLIC OF CHINA

(Translator's Note: Unlike the practice in the revision of the Criminal Procedure Law, which underwent comprehensive revision twice and was re-promulgated after each revision, the Criminal Law since its re-promulgation in 1997 has taken the method of adopting separate Amendments on specific provisions, without having the revised law re-promulgated after each revision. This translation, based on the repromulgated Law of 1997, incorporates all Amendments, except the 1998 Decision on the Punishment of Crimes Involving Fraudulent Purchasing, Evasion and Illegal Trading of Foreign Exchange, which both revised and supplemented the 1997 Criminal Law. Since the Chinese Criminal Law upholds the principle of rejecting retrospective application, footnotes are added to indicate revisions introduced by specific Amendments.)

Adopted 1 July 1979 by the 2nd Plenary Session
of the 5th National People's Congress
Revised 14 March 1997 at the Fifth Plenary Session
of the Eighth National People's Congress Re-promulgated
by Presidential Order No 83 (8th NPC), 14 March 1997
Effective from 1 October 1997

Incorporating revisions introduced by
The "Decision on the Punishment of Crimes Involving Fraudulent
Purchasing, Evasion and Illegal Trading of Foreign Exchange"
(29 December 1998, effective on promulgation),
Amendment (I) (25 December 1999, effective on promulgation),[1]
Amendment (II) (31 August 2001, effective on promulgation),
Amendment (III) (29 December 2001, effective on promulgation),
Amendment (IV) (28 December 2002, effective on promulgation),
Amendment (V) (28 February 2005, effective on promulgation),
Amendment (VI) (29 June 2006, effective on promulgation),
Amendment (VII) (28 February 2009, effective on promulgation),

[1] The 25 December 1991 revision decision was adopted as an Amendment, without numbering. For consistency purposes, this Amendment is referred to as Amendment (I) in this translation as it often occurs in academic discussions.

The "Decision of the Standing Committee of the NPC on the Revision of Certain Laws" (27 August 2009, effective on promulgation), and Amendment (VIII) (25 February 2011, effective 1 May 2011)

TABLE OF CONTENTS

Part I

General Provisions

Chapter I

Tasks, General Principles and Scope of Application of the Criminal Law

Article 1 This Law is formulated in accordance with the Constitution, in the light of the practical experience of fighting against crime and in line with actual circumstances in our country, in order to punish crimes and protect the people.

Article 2 The tasks of the Criminal Law of the People's Republic of China are to use criminal punishment to fight against any criminal acts in order to protect state security, the political power of the people's democratic dictatorship and the socialist system; to protect state-owned property and property collectively owned by the working masses; to protect property privately owned by citizens; to protect the personal rights, democratic rights and other rights of citizens; to maintain social and economic order and to safeguard the smooth progress of the course of socialist construction.

Article 3 An act explicitly stipulated by law to be a criminal offence shall be prosecuted and punished in accordance with the law, and an act that is not explicitly stipulated by law to be a criminal offence shall not be convicted or punished.

Article 4 Whoever commits a crime shall be treated equally in the application of the law. No one is permitted to enjoy any privilege to transgress the law.

Article 5 The severity or leniency of punishment shall be proportionate to the crimes committed by the criminal and the consequent criminal liabilities prescribed by law.

Article 6 This Law applies to anyone who commits a crime within the territory of the People's Republic of China, unless otherwise specifically provided by law.

This Law applies also to anyone who commits a crime on a vessel or an aircraft of the People's Republic of China.

A crime is deemed to have been committed within the territory of the People's Republic of China, where either a criminal act or one of the consequences of a crime takes place within the territory of the People's Republic of China.

Article 7 This Law applies to citizens of the People's Republic of China who commit crimes specified in this Law outside the territory of the People's Republic of China; but those whose crimes are punishable by fixed-term imprisonment of less than three (3) years as stipulated by this Law may not be pursued with criminal liability.

This Law applies to state functionaries and servicepersons who commit crimes specified in this Law outside the territory of the People's Republic of China.

Article 8 This Law may apply to foreigners who commit crimes outside the territory of the People's Republic of China against the State of the People's Republic of China or its citizens, which are punishable by a fixed term of imprisonment of more than three (3) years as stipulated by this Law, unless the crimes are not punishable according to the laws of the places where they were committed.

Article 9 This Law is applicable to crimes stipulated in international treaties which the People's Republic of China has ratified or acceded to and under which the People's Republic of China exercises criminal jurisdiction within the scope of its obligations.

Article 10 Anyone who commits a crime outside the territory of the People's Republic of China for which he/she must bear criminal liability in accordance with this Law and for which he/she has been tried in a foreign country, may still be pursued subject to this Law. However, having received a criminal punishment in a foreign country, he/she may be exempted from punishment or given a mitigated punishment.

Article 11 Criminal liabilities of a foreigner who enjoys diplomatic privileges and immunities shall be resolved through diplomatic channels.

Article 12 Where an act committed after the founding of the People's Republic of China and before the implementation of this Law was not deemed a crime under the laws in force at that time, the laws in force at that time shall apply. Where an act was deemed a crime under the laws in force at that time and is subject to prosecution under the provisions of

Section 8 of the general provisions in Chapter IV of this Law, criminal liability shall be pursued according to the laws in force at that time, but if it is not deemed a crime, or has a lighter punishment imposed by this Law, this Law shall apply.

Prior to the implementation of this Law, all effective judgments rendered according to the laws in force at that time continue to be effective.

CHAPTER II

CRIMES

Section 1 Crimes and Criminal Liabilities

Article 13 Any act that endangers the sovereignty, territorial integrity and security, splits the State, subverts the political power of the people's democratic dictatorship and overthrows the socialist system, undermines the social and economic order, encroaches upon state-owned property, property collectively owned by the working masses or property privately owned by citizens, infringes upon the personal rights, democratic rights and other rights of citizens, or any other act that jeopardises the society, which shall be punished by criminal sanctions pursuant to the law, is a crime. But if the circumstances are obviously minor and the harm is not great, it is not deemed a crime.

Article 14 A crime committed by a person who has clear knowledge that his/her act will cause socially harmful consequences and who hopes for or knowingly allows such consequences to occur is an intentionally committed crime.

Intentionally committed crimes must be subject to criminal liabilities.

Article 15 A crime committed by a person who should have foreseen that his/her act may cause socially harmful consequences but who fails to do so because of his/her carelessness or who has foreseen the consequences but readily believes that they can be avoided, and therefore causes the occurrence of such consequences, is a negligently committed crime.

Negligently committed crimes are subject to criminal liabilities when the law so stipulates.

Article 16 An act that results in harmful consequences due to irresistible or unforeseeable causes rather than from intent or negligence, is not a crime.

Article 17 A person who has reached the age of 16 and commits a crime must bear criminal liability.

A person who has reached the age of 14 but not the age of 16 who commits a crime of intentional homicide, intentionally inflicting grave bodily harm or the death of another, rape, robbery, drug trafficking, arson, explosion, or poisoning, must bear criminal liability.

A person who has reached the age of 14 but not the age of 18 who commits a crime, shall be given a lighter or a mitigated punishment.

Where a person is not punished by criminal sanctions because of being under the age of 16, the head of his/her family or his/her guardian shall be ordered to subject him/her to discipline. Where it is necessary, he/she may also be taken in by the government for rehabilitation.

Article 17 (A)[2] A person who has reached the age of 75 may be given a lighter or mitigated punishment if he/she commits an intentional crime; or shall be given a lighter or mitigated punishment if he/she commits a negligent crime.

Article 18 A person with mental illness who causes harmful consequences at a time when he/she is unable to recognise or control his/her own conduct, upon verification and confirmation through legal process, shall not bear criminal liability; but his/her family members or guardian shall be ordered to subject him/her to strict surveillance and medical treatment. Where it is necessary, he/she may be compelled by the government to receive medical treatment.

A person with intermittent mental illness who commits a crime when he/she is in a normal mental state must bear criminal liability.

A person with mental illness who commits a crime when he/she has not yet completely lost the ability to recognise or control his/her conduct must bear criminal liability, but may be given a lighter or a mitigated punishment.

An intoxicated person who commits a crime must bear criminal liability.

Article 19 A deaf and mute or blind person who commits a crime may be given a lighter or mitigated punishment or be exempted from punishment.

---

2 This article was added on 25 February 2011 by Amendment (VIII).

Article 20 A person who takes action in order to stop an immediate unlawful infringement of the interest of the State, the public, or the personal rights, property rights or other rights of his/her own or another person, and causes harm to the unlawful perpetrator, is deemed to be acting in justifiable defence and shall not be subject to any criminal liability.

When acting in justifiable defence that results in exceeding the limits of necessity and causes major harm, the person shall bear criminal liability, but shall be given a mitigated punishment or be exempted from punishment.

Where a person takes action to defend against immediate physical assault, murder, robbery, rape, kidnap, or other violent crimes that seriously endanger personal safety, and causes injury or death to the unlawful perpetrator, his/her action shall not be deemed excessive defence and he/she shall not bear criminal liability.

Article 21 A person who has no choice but to take emergency action in order to avert an immediate danger to the State or the public interest or to the personal rights, property rights or other rights of the person or other persons, and causes damage, shall not bear criminal liability.

Where a person taking emergency action to avert danger exceeds the limits of necessity and causes unnecessary harm, he/she shall bear criminal liability, but shall be given a mitigated punishment or be exempted from punishment.

The provisions in the first Paragraph on the averting of danger to the actor personally do not apply to a person who takes specific responsibility by virtue of his/her post or profession.

Section 2 Preparation for a Crime, Attempted Crime and Discontinuation of a Crime

Article 22 Preparation for a crime refers to the preparation of instruments or the creation of conditions for the commission of a crime.

A person who prepares for a crime may be given a lighter or mitigated punishment or be exempted from punishment, with reference to punishment imposed on one who has committed a crime.

Article 23 An attempted crime refers to a case in which the offender is already in the action of committing a crime but is prevented from completing it because of factors independent of the criminal's will.

An offender in an attempted crime may be given a lighter or mitigated punishment, with reference to punishment imposed on one who has completed a crime.

Article 24 Discontinuation of a crime refers to a case in which the offender, in the process of committing a crime, voluntarily discontinues the crime or voluntarily and effectively prevents the occurrence of the consequences of the crime.

An offender who discontinues a crime shall, if no harm is done, be exempted from punishment or, if harm is caused, be given a mitigated punishment.

Section 3 Joint Crimes

Article 25 A joint crime refers to a crime committed intentionally by two or more persons jointly.

The action of two or more persons together negligently committing a crime is not deemed a joint crime; those who shall bear criminal liability shall be punished individually according to the crimes they have committed.

Article 26 An offender who organises and leads a criminal gang to engage in criminal activities or who plays a principal role in a joint crime is a ringleader.

A crime gang refers to a relatively well-established criminal organisation composed of three or more persons for the purpose of committing crimes together.

A principal offender who organises or leads a criminal gang shall be punished for all crimes committed by the gang.

A principal offender, other than those stipulated in the third Paragraph, shall be punished for all the crimes he/she participated in, organised or directed.

Article 27 An offender who plays a secondary or supplementary role in a joint crime is an accomplice.

An accomplice shall be given a lighter or mitigated punishment, or be exempted from punishment.

Article 28 A person who is coerced into participating in a crime shall, according to his/her circumstances in the crime, be given a mitigated punishment or be exempted from punishment.

Article 29 A person who instigates another to commit a crime shall be punished according to the role he/she plays in the joint crime. A person who instigates a person under the age of 18 to commit a crime shall be subject to a heavier punishment.

If the person instigated to commit a crime does not do so, the instigator may be given a lighter or mitigated punishment.

Section 4 Unit Crimes

Article 30 A company, enterprise, institution, organ or organisation committing an act which is harmful to the society shall, if the act is defined as a unit crime by the law, bear criminal liability.

Article 31 A unit committing a crime shall be punished with a fine, and the directly responsible person(s)-in-charge and any other directly responsible persons shall be punished by criminal penalty. Where provisions in the Specific Provisions of this Law or other laws provide otherwise, those provisions prevail.

CHAPTER III

PUNISHMENTS

Section 1 Types of Punishments

Article 32 Punishments are classified into principal punishments and supplementary punishments.

Article 33 The types of principal punishment are as follows:

(1) control and surveillance (*Guanzhi*);[3]
(2) criminal detention;
(3) fixed-term imprisonment;
(4) life imprisonment; and
(5) the death penalty.

Article 34 The types of supplementary punishment are as follows:

(1) fines;
(2) deprivation of political rights; and
(3) confiscation of property.

---

[3] *Guanzhi* is often translated as "Control" and, sometimes, as "Public Surveillance".

Supplementary punishments may also be imposed independently.

Article 35 Deportation may be imposed independently or additionally on a foreigner who commits a crime.

Article 36 Where a victim suffers economic loss as a result of a criminal act, the criminal shall, in addition to being subject to criminal sanctions in accordance with the law, be ordered to pay compensation for the economic loss relative to the circumstances.

Where a fine is concurrently imposed with an order for civil compensation but the convicted person's property is not sufficient to pay the compensation and fine, or the person is also sentenced to confiscation of property, he/she shall first discharge the liability for civil compensation to the victim.

Article 37 Where the circumstances of a crime are minor and criminal punishment is not necessary, the offender may be exempted from criminal sanctions but, depending on the circumstances of the case, he/she may be given an admonishment, be ordered to make a statement of repentance or an apology or to pay compensation for losses, or be subjected to administrative penalties or administrative discipline by the competent department.

Section 2 Control and Surveillance

Article 38[4] The term of control and surveillance shall be more than three months and less than two years.

A criminal sentenced to control and surveillance may also, in light of the circumstances of the crime, be ordered not to engage in certain activities, to enter certain areas or places or to contact certain persons during the term of serving his/her sentence.

Criminals sentenced to control and surveillance shall be subject to community correction pursuant to the law.

Violation of prohibition orders as provided in Paragraph 2 shall be penalised by the public security organ in accordance with the "Law of the People's Republic of China on Public Order Administration Punishments".

---

[4] This article was revised on 25 February 2011 by Amendment (VIII).

Article 39 A criminal sentenced to control and surveillance must observe the following rules during the term of serving his/her sentence:

(1) observing laws and administrative regulations and submitting him/her self to supervision;
(2) without the approval of the executing organ, not exercising the rights to freedom of speech, of the press, of assembly, of association, of procession and of demonstration;
(3) reporting his/her own activities in accordance with the rules of the executing organ;
(4) observing the rules on meeting with visitors set by the executing organ;
(5) reporting to the executing organ for approval of a change in residence or departure from the city or county he/she lives in.

A criminal sentenced to control and surveillance shall receive equal pay for equal work when engaging in labour.

Article 40 Upon the expiration of the term of the control and surveillance, the executing organ shall announce the termination of the control and surveillance to the criminal who is sentenced to control and surveillance and to the unit where the criminal works or the general public in the area where the criminal lives.

Article 41 The term of control and surveillance is calculated from the date on which the judgment begins to be executed. Where the criminal is held in custody before the execution of the sentence, one day in custody is calculated as two days for the term sentenced.

Section 3 Criminal Detention

Article 42 The term of criminal detention is more than one (1) month and less than six (6) months.

Article 43 A sentence of criminal detention of a criminal is to be executed by the public security organ in the vicinity.

During the period of execution, the criminal sentenced to criminal detention may visit his/her family for one to two (2) days each month; when engaging in labour, he/she may receive pay at the appropriate rate.

Article 44 The term of criminal detention is calculated from the date on which the sentence begins to be executed; where the criminal is held in custody before the execution of the judgment, one (1) day in custody is to be calculated as one (1) day for the term sentenced.

Section 4 Fixed-Term Imprisonment and Life Imprisonment

Article 45 The term of fixed-term imprisonment is more than six (6) months and less than 15 years, except for those cases provided for in Articles 50 and 69 of this Law.

Article 46 A criminal sentenced to fixed-term imprisonment or life imprisonment shall serve his/her sentence in prison or in another execution place; anyone who is able to work must perform labour and accept education and reform.

Article 47 The term of fixed-term imprisonment is calculated from the date on which the sentence begins to be executed; where the criminal is held in custody before the execution of the judgment, one (1) day in custody is to be calculated as one (1) day for the term sentenced.

Section 5 The Death Penalty

Article 48 The death penalty applies only to criminals who commit the most heinous crimes. Where the immediate execution of the death sentence is not deemed essential, a two-year suspension of execution may be announced at the same time as the death sentence.

Except for judgments rendered by the Supreme People's Court according to law, all death sentences must be submitted to the Supreme People's Court for verification and approval. Sentences of death with suspension of execution may be decided or verified and approved by a High People's Court.

Article 49[5] The death penalty shall not apply to a person who has not reached the age of 18 at the time of committing the crime or to a woman who is pregnant at the time of adjudication.

The death penalty shall not apply to a person who has reached the age of 75 at the time of the trial, except where he/she has caused the death of another person by using extremely brutal methods.

---

[5] This article was revised on 25 February 2011 by Amendment (VIII).

Article 50[6] Where a person sentenced to death with a suspension of execution does not intentionally commit a crime during the period of the suspension, his/her death sentence shall be commuted to life imprisonment upon the expiration of the two-year period; if he/she renders meritorious services, the death sentence shall be commuted to fixed-term imprisonment of 25 years upon the expiration of the two-year period; if investigation reveals evidence that he/she has intentionally committed a crime, the death penalty shall be executed upon the verification and approval of the Supreme People's Court.

Where a recidivist is to be sentenced to death with a suspension of execution, or a criminal is to be sentenced to death with a suspension of execution for his/her crime of intentional murder, rape, robbery, abduction, arson, explosion, spreading hazardous substances or organised crime of violence, the people's courts may in the meantime decide, in light of the circumstances of the crime and other factors, to restrict the application of reduction of his/her sentence.

Article 51 The term of suspension of execution of a death penalty is calculated from the date on which the judgment becomes final. The term of fixed-term imprisonment commuted from a death penalty with suspension of execution is to be calculated from the date on which the term of the suspended execution of the death penalty expires.

Section 6 Fines

Article 52 The amount of a fine imposed shall be determined according to the circumstances of the crime.

Article 53 A fine is to be paid in a lump sum or in instalments within the period specified in the judgment. In the case of failure to pay a fine upon the expiration of the period, the person fined shall be compelled to make the payment. If the person fined is unable to pay the fine in full, the people's court shall demand the payment whenever it finds that he/she holds executable property. If the person fined has true difficulties in paying due to an irresistible calamity he/she has suffered, the fine may be reduced or waived according to the circumstances.

---

[6] This article was revised on 25 February 2011 by Amendment (VIII).

Section 7 Deprivation of Political Rights

Article 54 Deprivation of political rights refers to the deprivation of the following rights:

(1) the right to vote and the right to stand for election;
(2) the rights of freedom of speech, of the press, of assembly, of association, of procession and of demonstration;
(3) the right to hold a position in a State organ; and
(4) the right to hold a leading position in a State-owned company, enterprise, or institution or people's organisation.

Article 55 The term of deprivation of political rights shall be more than one year and less than five (5) years, except as otherwise stipulated in Article 57 of this Law.

Where a sentence of deprivation of political rights is imposed as a supplementary punishment in addition to a sentence of control and surveillance, the term of deprivation of political rights shall be the same as the term of control and surveillance, and the punishments shall be executed concurrently.

Article 56 A criminal endangering State security shall be sentenced to deprivation of political rights as a supplementary punishment; a criminal who has committed a crime of murder, rape, arson, explosion, poisoning, robbery, or other crimes, which seriously undermine the social order, may be sentenced to deprivation of political rights as a supplementary punishment.

Where deprivation of political rights is imposed independently, provisions in the Special Provisions of this Law apply.

Article 57 A criminal sentenced to death or life imprisonment shall be deprived of political rights for life.

Where the death penalty with a suspension of execution is to be commuted to fixed-term imprisonment or where life imprisonment is to be commuted to fixed-term imprisonment, the term of the supplementary punishment of deprivation of political rights shall be changed to more than three (3) years and less than 10 years.

Article 58 The term of the supplementary punishment of deprivation of political rights is calculated from the date on which the execution of imprisonment or criminal detention comes to an end, or from the date on which a parole period begins; deprivation of political rights shall have effect during the period in which the principal punishment is being executed.

A criminal who is deprived of political rights must, during the period of execution, abide by laws, administrative regulations and relevant rules on supervision and administration made by the public security departments under the State Council, and submit him/herself to supervision. He/she is prohibited from exercising various rights stipulated in Article 54 of this Law.

Section 8 Confiscation of Property

Article 59 Confiscation of property refers to the confiscation of part or all of the property personally owned by the criminal. Where all of the property is confiscated, basic living expenses for the criminal personally and the family members depending on his/her support shall be set aside.

When a sentence of confiscation of property is imposed, property that belongs to the family members of the criminal or that the family members of the criminal are entitled to must not be confiscated.

Article 60 Where it is necessary to use the confiscated property to repay the lawful debts incurred by the criminal before the confiscation of the property, the debts shall be paid at the request of the creditors.

Chapter IV

Concrete Application of Punishments

Section 1 Sentencing

Article 61 When determining a sentence, the punishment shall be rendered on the basis of the facts of the crime, the nature and circumstances of the crime and the gravity of the harm done to the society, in accordance with the relevant provisions of this Law.

Article 62 Where the circumstances of a criminal accord with the provisions of this Law on bringing in a heavier or lighter punishment, he/she shall be sentenced to a punishment within the limits of the prescribed punishment.

Article 63[7] Where the circumstances of a criminal accord with the provisions of this Law on bringing in a mitigated punishment, he/she shall be sentenced to a punishment below the prescribed punishment; where this Law provides for several levels of scope for the measurement of punishment, the punishment shall be fixed within the next level below the statutorily prescribed level of punishment.

Even if the circumstances of a criminal do not accord with the provisions of this Law on bringing in a mitigated punishment, he/she may still, on the basis of the special situation of the case and with the approval of the Supreme People's Court, be sentenced to a punishment below the prescribed punishment.

Article 64 All money and property illegally obtained by the criminal must be recovered, or the criminal must be ordered to return it or pay compensation for it. The lawful property of victims must be returned without delay. Contraband and the criminal's personal property which has been used for the commission of a crime shall be confiscated. All confiscated property and fine money shall be turned over to the State Treasury and must not be misappropriated or disposed of without authority.

Section 2 Recidivists

Article 65[8] A recidivist is a criminal sentenced to fixed-term imprisonment or more who, within five years after the completion of his/her sentence or the receipt of a pardon, commits another crime punishable by fixed-term imprisonment or more. A recidivist must receive a heavier punishment, unless the crime is negligently committed or is committed by a person under the age of 18.

For a criminal released on parole, the period prescribed in the preceding Paragraph shall be calculated from the date of the expiration of the parole.

Article 66[9] A criminal guilty of endangering state security, of terrorism or organised crime of an underground gangland nature, who commits another such crime at any time after the completion of his/her sentence or the receipt of a pardon, shall be deemed a recidivist.

---

7 This article was revised on 25 February 2011 by Amendment (VIII).
8 This article was revised on 25 February 2011 by Amendment (VIII).
9 This article was revised on 25 February 2011 by Amendment (VIII).

Section 3 Voluntary Surrender and Rendering Meritorious Service

Article 67[10] Voluntary surrender means that a criminal, having committed a crime, voluntarily surrenders him/herself to the police and confesses truthfully his/her criminal acts. A voluntarily surrendered criminal may receive a lighter or mitigated punishment, and those whose crimes are relatively minor may be exempted from punishment.

A criminal suspect or accused person under coercive measures, or a criminal during the serving of his/her sentence confessing truthfully to another crime which is still unknown to the judicial organ, shall be deemed to have voluntarily surrendered.

A criminal suspect falling outside the circumstance of voluntary surrender as prescribed in the preceding Paragraphs who truthfully confesses his/her criminal acts, may be given a lighter punishment, or, where the truthful confession of his/her criminal acts leads to avoidance of the occurrence of a particularly serious consequence, may be given a mitigated punishment.

Article 68[11] A criminal who performs meritorious services such as exposing a crime committed by another person which is later verified, or providing important information leading to the discovery of another crime, may receive a lighter or mitigated punishment. A criminal who performs major meritorious services may be given a mitigated punishment or be exempted from punishment.

Section 4 Combined Punishment for Multiple Crimes

Article 69[12] Where a person commits more than one crime before a judgment has been rendered, except where a death sentence or life imprisonment is to be imposed, the term of sentence shall, depending on the circumstances, be less than the accumulated total of penal terms for all crimes committed, but more than the longest penal term for any of the crimes. However, the term of control and surveillance shall not exceed three (3) years, the term of criminal detention less than one year, and the term of fixed-term imprisonment shall not exceed 20 years where the cumulated term of punishment is less than 35 years, or not exceed 25 years where the cumulated term of punishment is more than 35 years.

---

10 This article was revised on 25 February 2011 by Amendment (VIII).

11 This article was revised on 25 February 2011 by Amendment (VIII).

12 This article was revised on 25 February 2011 by Amendment (VIII).

Where penalties imposed for crimes include supplementary punishments, the supplementary punishments shall also be executed. The supplementary punishments shall, if they are of the same type, be combined for execution, or if they are different types, be executed separately.

Article 70 Where, after a judgment has been rendered but before the sentence thereunder has been completely executed, it is discovered that the sentenced criminal had committed another crime before the said judgment, for which he/she has not been sentenced, a judgment for the newly-discovered crime must be rendered, and the combined punishment for this crime and for the earlier crime(s) shall be determined in accordance with the provisions of Article 69 of this Law. The term that has already been served shall be counted towards the term decided by the new judgment.

Article 71 Where, after a judgment has been rendered but before the sentence thereunder has been completely executed, the sentenced criminal commits another crime, a judgment for the newly committed crime shall be rendered, and the combined punishment for this crime and the remainder of punishment for the earlier crime(s) shall be determined in accordance with the provisions of Article 69 of this Law.

Section 5 Suspension of Execution of Sentence

Article 72[13] A suspension of execution of sentence may be granted for a criminal sentenced to criminal detention or fixed-term imprisonment of less than three (3) years if all the following conditions are met; a criminal under the age of 18, or who is a pregnant women or a criminal aged 75 or above shall be granted a suspension of execution of sentence:

(1) the criminal circumstances are relatively minor;
(2) the criminal has shown repentance;
(3) there will be no risk that the criminal will commit another crime; and
(4) the granting of a suspended sentence would not have a major adverse effect on the community in which the criminal lives.

A criminal granted a suspension of execution of sentence may also, in light of the circumstances of the crime, be ordered not to engage in

[13] This article was revised on 25 February 2011 by Amendment (VIII).

certain activities, to enter certain areas or places or to contact certain persons during the term of serving his/her sentence.

If a supplementary punishment is imposed on a criminal receiving a suspension of sentence, the supplementary punishment shall still be executed.

Article 73 The probation period for suspension of criminal detention shall be more than two (2) months but less than one year longer than the original term of the sentence.

The probation period for suspension of fixed-term imprisonment shall be more than one (1) year but less than five (5) years longer than the term originally decided.

The probation period for suspension shall be calculated from the date the judgment is made final.

Article 74[14] Suspension of sentence is not applicable to recidivists and ringleaders of criminal gangs.

Article 75 A criminal subject to a suspended sentence must observe the following provisions:

(1) abiding by laws and administrative regulations and submitting him/herself to supervision;
(2) reporting his/her activities in accordance with the provisions of the supervising organ;
(3) obeying the provisions regarding meeting visitors made by the supervising organ;
(4) reporting to and applying to the supervising organ for approval for a departure from the city or county where he/she lives, or a change of residence.

Article 76[15] A criminal subject to a suspended sentence is subject to community correction in accordance with the law during the probation period for suspension. If no circumstance prescribed in Article 77 of this Law occurs, the punishment originally decided on shall no longer be executed when the probation period for suspension of the sentence comes to an end, and a public pronouncement to this effect shall be made.

---

[14] This article was revised on 25 February 2011 by Amendment (VIII).
[15] This article was revised on 25 February 2011 by Amendment (VIII).

Article 77[16] If a criminal subject to a suspended sentence commits a new crime during the probation period for suspension of sentence, or is found to have committed another crime before the judgment was rendered, for which he/she has not been sentenced, the suspension must be revoked and the punishment to be executed shall be determined based on the punishments imposed for the earlier crime and the new crime in accordance with the provisions of Article 69 in this Law.

If, during the probation period for suspension of sentence a criminal subject to a suspended sentence violates laws, administrative regulations or provisions on the supervision and administration of suspension of sentence of the relevant departments under the State Council, or violates the prohibition order(s) in the judgment of the people's court, the suspension shall, where the circumstances are serious, be revoked and the punishments originally imposed shall be executed.

Section 6 Reduction of Criminal Sentence

Article 78[17] A criminal sentenced to control and surveillance, criminal detention, fixed-term imprisonment or life imprisonment may have his/her sentence reduced if, during the period of serving the sentence, he/she seriously observes prison rules, accepts education and reform, shows true repentance, or performs meritorious services. The sentence shall be reduced if any of the following meritorious services are performed:

(1) preventing someone from engaging in major criminal activities;
(2) reporting major criminal activities in or outside the prison, which are later verified;
(3) making inventions or major technological innovations;
(4) rescuing others during normal production and daily life by risking his/her own life;
(5) performing outstanding service in fighting against natural disasters or preventing major accidents; or
(6) making other major contributions to the state or society.

The term of the punishment actually executed after the counting of a reduction of the sentence may not be less than the following time periods:

---

16 This article was revised on 25 February 2011 by Amendment (VIII).
17 This article was revised on 25 February 2011 by Amendment (VIII).

(1) for those sentenced to control, criminal detention or fixed-term imprisonment, not less than half of the term originally decided;
(2) for those sentenced to life imprisonment, not less than 13 years;
(3) for those sentenced to death with suspended execution by the people's court in accordance with the provisions of Paragraph 2 of Article 50 of the Law, not less than 25 years where the sentence is reduced to life-imprisonment in accordance with the law after the expiration of the period of suspended execution, or not less than 20 years where the sentences is reduced to fixed-term imprisonment of 25 years after the expiration of the period of suspended execution.

Article 79 To have the punishment of a criminal reduced, the executing organ shall submit a recommendation on the reduction of the punishment to a people's court at intermediate level or above. The people's court shall form a collegial panel to adjudicate and, where the criminal demonstrates true repentance and performs meritorious service, render an order for reduction of punishment. No punishment may be reduced without legal procedures being followed.

Article 80 The term of fixed-term imprisonment reduced from life imprisonment shall be calculated from the date that the order for reducing the sentence is rendered.

Section 7 Parole

Article 81[18] A criminal sentenced to fixed-term imprisonment with more than half of the original sentence having been served, or a criminal sentenced to life imprisonment with more than 13 years of the original sentence having been actually served, may be granted parole if he/she seriously observes the prison rules, accepts education and reform, demonstrates true repentance, and will no longer pose a risk of committing another crime. Under special circumstances, upon the approval of the Supreme People's Court, the aforesaid restrictions with respect to the served term may not need to be followed.

Recidivists or criminals sentenced to fixed-term imprisonment of more than 10 years or life imprisonment for crimes of murder, rape, robbery, kidnap, arson, explosion, spreading hazardous substances or organised crimes of a violent nature must not be granted parole.

[18] This article was revised on 25 February 2011 by Amendment (VIII).

In granting parole, the impact on the community where the paroled criminal will live shall be taken into consideration.

Article 82 The granting of parole to a criminal shall be conducted in accordance with the procedures stipulated in Article 79 of this Law; no parole may be granted without legal procedures being followed.

Article 83 The parole probation period for fixed-term imprisonment is the remaining term that has not been served; the parole probation period for life imprisonment is 10 years.

The probation period for parole is calculated from the date the criminal is released on parole.

Article 84 A criminal granted parole must observe the following provisions:

(1) abiding by laws and administrative regulations and submitting him/herself to supervision;
(2) reporting his/her activities in accordance with the provisions of the supervising organ;
(3) observing rules on meeting visitors set by the supervising organ; and
(4) reporting and applying to the supervising organ for approval of a departure from the city or county where he/she lives or a change in residence.

Article 85[19] A criminal granted parole is subject to community correction during the probation period for parole pursuant to the law, and if no circumstance as stipulated in Article 86 of this Law exists, upon the expiration of the probation period for parole the punishment originally imposed shall be regarded as having been served, and a pronouncement to that effect shall be made in public.

Article 86[20] Where a criminal commits a new crime during the probation period for parole, the parole must be revoked and a combined punishment for his/her crimes shall be imposed in accordance with the provisions in Article 71 of this Law.

Where it is found that the criminal released on parole had committed another crime before the judgment was rendered, which has not been

[19] This article was revised on 25 February 2011 by Amendment (VIII).
[20] This article was revised on 25 February 2011 by Amendment (VIII).

sentenced, the parole must be revoked and a combined punishment for his/her crimes shall be imposed in accordance with the provisions in Article 70 of this Law.

Where a criminal violates laws, administrative regulations or provisions on the supervision and administration of parole of the relevant department under the State Council during the probation period for parole, which does not constitute a new crime, the parole must be revoked in accordance with the legal procedures and the parolee must be taken back to prison to serve the remaining term of the sentence.

Section 8 Statutory Limitations

Article 87 A crime shall not be prosecuted when the following periods have elapsed:

(1) the maximum prescribed punishment for the crime is fixed-term imprisonment of less than five (5) years, and five (5) years have elapsed;
(2) the maximum prescribed punishment for the crime is fixed-term imprisonment of more than five (5) years and less than 10 years, and 10 years have elapsed;
(3) the maximum fixed-term imprisonment for the crime is more than 10 years, and 15 years have elapsed;
(4) the maximum prescribed punishment for the crime is life-imprisonment or death, and 20 years have elapsed. If it is considered that a crime must be prosecuted after 20 years, the matter must be submitted to the Supreme People's Procuratorate for verification and approval.

Article 88 Where a criminal escapes from investigation or adjudication after his/her case has been filed by a people's procuratorate, a public security organ or a state security organ for investigation, or has been accepted by a people's court, the limitation period for prosecution shall have no effect.

Where the victim brings a complaint within the period for prosecution, and the people's court, the people's procuratorate, or the public security organ fail to file the case for investigation when they should do so, the limitation period for prosecution shall have no effect.

Article 89 The limitation period for prosecution shall be calculated from the date the crime is committed; where the criminal act is of a continuous or continuing nature, it shall be calculated from the date the criminal act is completed.

If any further crime is committed during the limitation period for prosecution, the limitation period for prosecution of the former crime shall be calculated from the date the new crime is committed.

Chapter V

Other Provisions

Article 90 Where an autonomous area inhabited with minority nationalities cannot completely apply the provisions in this Law, the people's congresses of the autonomous region or of the province may formulate alternative or supplementary provisions in line with the political, economic and cultural characteristics of the local nationalities and in accordance with the general principles of this Law. The provisions so formulated shall become effective after they have been submitted to and approved by the Standing Committee of the National People's Congress.

Article 91 For the purpose of this Law, the term "public property" refers to the following properties:

(1) state-owned property;
(2) property owned collectively by the working masses;
(3) public donations and special funds for purposes of poverty relief and other public welfare.

Private property that is managed, used or under transportation by a state organ, state-owned company, enterprise, collective enterprise or people's organisation, is deemed public property.

Article 92 For the purpose of this Law the term "private property owned by citizens" refers to the following properties:

(1) the lawful incomes, savings, houses and other means of livelihood, of a citizen;
(2) means of production which belong to individuals or families according to the law;
(3) property lawfully owned by individual commercial households or private enterprises;
(4) shares, stocks, bonds and other properties which belong to individuals according to the law.

Article 93 For the purpose of this Law the term "state functionaries" refers to persons who perform public service in state organs.

Persons performing public service in state-owned companies, enterprises, institutions, and people's organisations; persons assigned by state organs, state-owned companies, enterprises, and institutions to perform public service in non-state-owned companies, enterprises, institutions, and social organisations; and other persons performing public service according to the law, are regarded as state functionaries.

Article 94 For the purpose of this Law the term "judicial officials" refers to personnel who perform functions of investigation, prosecution, adjudication, supervision and control.

Article 95 For the purpose of this Law the term "grave injury" refers to any of the following injuries:

(1) injuries that result in the disability or disfigurement of a person;
(2) injuries that result in the loss of a person's hearing, sight, or the functions of other organs; or
(3) other injuries that cause grave harm to a person's physical health.

Article 96 For the purpose of this Law the term "violation of provisions of the State" refers to violation of laws and decisions enacted by the National People's Congress or the Standing Committee of the National People's Congress, and administrative regulations, administrative measures, decisions and orders formulated and issued by the State Council.

Article 97 For the purpose of this Law the term "ringleader" refers to a criminal who organises, plans or directs a criminal gang or gathers a crowd to commit a crime.

Article 98 For the purpose of this Law the term "to be handled only upon complaint" refers to a case which will only be handled after the victim lodges a complaint. If the victim is unable to lodge a complaint because of coercion or intimidation, a people's procuratorate or the victim's close relatives may also file the complaint.

Article 99 For the purpose of this Law the terms "more than", "less than" and "within" include the figures themselves.

Article 100[21] A person with a record of criminal punishment shall, when joining the army or seeking employment, report to the relevant units the punishment they received and not conceal it.

A person sentenced to fix-term imprisonment of less than five (5) years who has not reached the age of 18 at the time of committing the crime is exempted from the obligation of reporting as prescribed in the provisions of the preceding Paragraph.

Article 101 The General Provisions of this Law are applicable to other laws containing provisions on criminal penalty, unless special provisions are made in those laws.

[21] This article was revised on 25 February 2011 by Amendment (VIII).

Part II

Specific Provisions

Chapter I

Crimes of Endangering State Security

Article 102 Whoever colludes with a foreign state in plotting to endanger the sovereignty, territorial integrity and security of the People's Republic of China shall be sentenced to life imprisonment or fixed-term imprisonment of more than 10 years.

Whoever commits the crimes prescribed in the preceding Paragraph in collusion with an institution, organisation or individual outside the territory of China shall be punished in accordance with the provisions in the preceding Paragraph.

Article 103 In activities of organising, plotting or acting to split the country or undermine national unity, the ringleader and the person(s) committing a serious crime, shall be sentenced to life imprisonment or fixed-term imprisonment of more than 10 years; the active participants shall be sentenced to fixed-term imprisonment of more than three (3) and less than 10 years; other participants shall be sentenced to fixed-term imprisonment of less than three (3) years, criminal detention, control and surveillance, or deprivation of political rights.

Whoever incites others to split the country and undermine national unity shall be sentenced to fixed-term imprisonment of less than five (5) years, criminal detention, control and surveillance, or deprivation of political rights; the ringleader(s) and the person(s) committing a serious crime shall be sentenced to fixed-term imprisonment of more than five (5) years.

Article 104 In activities of organising, plotting, or carrying out armed rebellion or armed riots, the ringleaders and the person(s) participating in serious criminal activities shall be sentenced to life imprisonment or fixed-term imprisonment of more than 10 years; active participants shall be sentenced to fixed-term imprisonment of more than three (3) years and less than 10 years; other participants are to be sentenced to fixed-term imprisonment of less than three (3) years, criminal detention, control and surveillance, or deprivation of political rights.

Whoever incites, coerces, lures and bribes state functionaries, personnel of the armed forces, the people's police or people's militia to carry out armed rebellion or armed riot shall have a heavier punishment imposed in accordance with the provisions in the preceding Paragraph.

Article 105 In activities of organising, plotting or acting to subvert the political power of the State and to overthrow the socialist system, the ringleader(s) and the person(s) participating in serious criminal activities shall be sentenced to life imprisonment or fixed-term imprisonment of more than 10 years; active participants shall be sentenced to fixed-term imprisonment of more than three years and less than ten 10 years; other participants shall be sentenced to fixed-term imprisonment of less than three (3) years, criminal detention, control and surveillance, or deprivation of political rights.

Whoever incites others to subvert the power of the State and to overthrow the socialist system through such means as spreading rumours or slandering shall be sentenced to fixed-term imprisonment of less than five (5) years, criminal detention, control and surveillance, or deprivation of political rights; the ringleader(s) and the person(s) participating in serious criminal activities shall be sentenced to fixed-term imprisonment of more than five (5) years.

Article 106 Whoever colludes with an institution, organisation, or individual outside the territory of China and commits crimes as stipulated in Articles 103, 104 and 105 of this Chapter shall have a heavier punishment imposed in accordance with the provisions in these respective articles.

Article 107[22] Where an institution, organisation or individual either inside or outside the territory of China provides financial support for the commission of the crimes prescribed in Articles 102, 103, 104 and 105, the directly responsible person(s) shall be sentenced to fixed-term imprisonment of less than five (5) years, criminal detention, control and surveillance, or deprivation of political rights; where the circumstances are serious, the sentence shall be fixed-term imprisonment of more than five (5) years.

Article 108 Whoever defects to the enemy and turns traitor shall be sentenced to fixed-term imprisonment of more than three (3) years and less than 10 years; where the circumstances are serious or where armed

22 This article was revised on 25 February 2011 under the Revision Bill (VIII).

personnel, the people's police or people's militia are induced to defect to the enemy and turn traitor, such a person shall be sentenced to fixed-term imprisonment of more than 10 years or life imprisonment.

Article 109[23] Where a state functionary, in the course of discharging his/her official duties, leaves his/her post without permission and defects to another country or defects to another country when he/she is outside China, he/she shall be sentenced to fixed-term imprisonment of less than five (5) years, criminal detention, control and surveillance, or deprivation of political rights; where the circumstances are serious, the person shall be sentenced to fixed-term imprisonment of more than five (5) years but less than 10 years.

A state functionary in possession of state secrets who defects to another country or defects to another country when he/she is outside China, shall have a heavier punishment imposed in accordance with the provisions in the preceding Paragraph.

Article 110 Whoever commits one of the following acts of espionage and endangers state security shall be sentenced to fixed-term imprisonment of more than 10 years or life imprisonment; where the circumstances are relatively minor, the sentence is to be fixed-term imprisonment of more than three (3) years and less than 10 years:

(1) joining an espionage organisation or accepting a mission assigned by an espionage organisation or its agent; or
(2) directing the enemy towards shelling targets.

Article 111 Whoever steals, spies on or purchases, or illegally provides state secrets or intelligence information to an organisation, institution or individual outside China shall be sentenced to fixed-term imprisonment of more than five (5) years and less than 10 years; where the circumstances are particularly serious, the sentence is to be fixed-term imprisonment of more than 10 years or life imprisonment; or where the circumstances are relatively minor, he/she shall be sentenced to fixed-term imprisonment of less than five (5) years, criminal detention, control and surveillance, or deprivation of political rights.

Article 112 Whoever in times of war supplies the enemy with weapons and ammunition or other military materials shall be sentenced to fixed-term

23 This article was revised on 25 February 2011 by Amendment (VIII).

imprisonment of more than 10 years or life imprisonment; where the circumstances are relatively minor, he/she shall be sentenced to fixed-term imprisonment of more than three (3) years and less than 10 years.

Article 113 Whoever commits a crime of endangering state security as stipulated in this Chapter, and has thereby caused particularly grave harm to the State and the people, and where the circumstances are particularly serious, may be sentenced to death, except for the crimes prescribed in the second Paragraph of Article 103 and Articles 105, 107 and 109.

Whoever commits a crime prescribed in this Chapter may concurrently be sentenced to confiscation of property.

Chapter II

Crimes of Endangering Public Safety

Article 114[24] Whoever commits arson, causes a breach of a dyke, makes an explosion, spreads poisonous, radioactive materials or the pathogens of infectious diseases, or employs other dangerous means to harm public security, shall be sentenced to fixed-term imprisonment of more than three (3) years and less than 10 years where no serious consequence occurs.

Article 115[25] Whoever sets a fire, breaches dykes, makes an explosion, spreads poisonous, radioactive materials or the pathogens of infectious diseases, or employs other dangerous means to inflict grave bodily harm to, or causes the death of, other persons, or causes major losses of public or private property to be suffered, shall be sentenced to fixed-term imprisonment of more than 10 years, life imprisonment, or death.

Whoever negligently commits the crimes stipulated in the preceding Paragraph shall be sentenced to fixed-term imprisonment of more than three (3) years and less than seven (7) years; where the circumstances are relatively minor, he/she shall be sentenced to fixed-term imprisonment of less than three (3) years, or criminal detention.

Article 116 Whoever sabotages a train, motor vehicle, tram, vessel or aircraft where the damage is serious enough to overturn or destroy the train, motor vehicle, tram, vessel or aircraft, shall be sentenced to fixed-term

[24] This article was revised on 29 December 2001 by Amendment (III).
[25] This article was revised on 29 December 2001 by Amendment (III).

imprisonment of more than three (3) years and less than 10 years, where no serious consequences occur.

Article 117 Whoever sabotages a railway, bridge, tunnel, highway, airport, waterway, lighthouse or sign, or conducts other destructive activities where the damage is serious enough to overturn or destroy a train, motor vehicle, tram, vessel or aircraft, shall be sentenced to fixed-term imprisonment of more than three (3) years and less than 10 years, where no serious consequences occur.

Article 118 Whoever sabotages the electric power supply, gas or other inflammable and explosive equipment, thereby endangering public safety, shall be sentenced to fixed-term imprisonment of more than three (3) years and less than 10 years, where no serious consequences occur.

Article 119 Whoever sabotages means of transportation, transportation facilities, electric power facilities, gas facilities or other inflammable and explosive equipment, thereby endangering public safety and causing serious consequences, shall be sentenced to fixed-term imprisonment of more than 10 years, life imprisonment or death.

Whoever negligently commits the crimes in the preceding Paragraph shall be sentenced to fixed-term imprisonment of more than three (3) years and less than seven (7) years; where the circumstances are relatively minor, he/she shall be sentenced to fixed-term imprisonment of less than three (3) years or criminal detention.

Article 120[26] Whoever organises or leads a terrorist organisation shall be sentenced to fixed-term imprisonment of more than 10 years or life imprisonment; active participants shall be sentenced to fixed-term imprisonment of more than three (3) years and less than 10 years; other participants shall be sentenced to fixed-term imprisonment of less than three (3) years, criminal detention, control and surveillance, or deprivation of political rights.

Whoever commits the crimes in the preceding Paragraph and in addition commits a crime of murder, causing an explosion, or kidnapping shall have a punishment imposed for his/her multiple crimes according to the provisions on combined punishment.

---

[26] This article was revised on 29 December 2001 by Amendment (III).

Article 120(A).[27] Whoever provides financial support for terrorist activities or for persons engaged in terrorist activities shall be sentenced to fixed-term imprisonment of less than five (5) years, criminal detention, control and surveillance, or deprivation of political rights, with a fine; where circumstances are serious, he/she shall be sentenced to fixed-term imprisonment of five (5) years or longer, with a fine or confiscation of property.

A unit that commits the crimes prescribed in the preceding Paragraph shall have imposed a fine, and the directly responsible person(s)-in-charge and any other directly responsible person(s) shall be punished in accordance with the provisions in the preceding Paragraph.

Article 121 Whoever hijacks an aircraft by using violent or coercive means shall be sentenced to fixed-term imprisonment of more than 10 years or life imprisonment; where grave injury or death to a person or serious damage to the airliner is caused therefrom, he/she shall be sentenced to death.

Article 122 Whoever hijacks a vessel or motor vehicle by violent or coercive means shall be sentenced to fixed-termed imprisonment of more than five (5) years and less than 10 years or, where serious consequences are caused, be sentenced to fixed-term imprisonment of more than 10 years or life imprisonment.

Article 123 Whoever uses violence to attack a person on an in-flight aircraft, thereby endangering flying safety shall, where no serious consequences occur, be sentenced to fixed-termed imprisonment of less than five (5) years or criminal detention; where serious consequences occur, he/she shall be sentenced to fixed-term imprisonment of more than five (5) years.

Article 124 Whoever sabotages radio and television broadcasting facilities or public telecommunication facilities, thus endangering public safety, shall be sentenced to fixed-term imprisonment of more than three (3) years and less than seven (7) years; where serious consequences are caused, he/she shall be sentenced to fixed-term imprisonment of more than seven (7) years.

Whoever negligently commits the crimes prescribed in the preceding Paragraph shall be sentenced to fixed-term imprisonment of more than

[27] This article was added on 29 December 2001 by Amendment (III).

three (3) years and less than seven (7) years; where the circumstances are relatively minor, he/she shall be sentenced to fixed-term imprisonment of less than three (3) years or criminal detention.

Article 125[28] Whoever illegally manufactures, trades, transports, mails or stockpiles guns, ammunition or explosives shall be sentenced to fixed-termed imprisonment of more than three (3) years and less than 10 years; where circumstances are serious, he/she shall be sentenced to fixed-termed imprisonment of more than 10 years, life imprisonment, or death.

Whoever illegally manufactures, trades, transports, or stockpiles poisonous or radioactive materials, or pathogens of infectious diseases or other materials that harm public security shall be punished in accordance with the provisions in the preceding Paragraph.

A unit that commits the crimes prescribed in the preceding two Paragraphs shall be punished with a fine, and the directly responsible person(s)-in-charge and any other directly responsible person(s) shall be punished in accordance with the provisions in the first Paragraph.

Article 126 An enterprise which is designated or authorised pursuant to the law to manufacture or sell guns, and which commits, in violation of the provisions on gun control, one of the following acts, shall be punished with a fine and the directly responsible person(s)-in-charge and any other directly responsible person(s) shall be sentenced to fixed-term imprisonment of less than five (5) years; where circumstances are serious, he/she shall be sentenced to fixed-term imprisonment of more than five (5) years and less than 10 years; where the consequences are particularly serious, he/she shall be sentenced to fixed-term imprisonment of more than 10 years or life imprisonment:

(1) for the purpose of illegal sale, manufacturing or allocation of guns exceeding allocated quotas, or in contravention of the stipulated types;
(2) for the purpose of illegal sale, manufacturing unnumbered, repetitiously numbered or falsely numbered guns;
(3) illegally selling guns or selling guns which are manufactured in China for export.

[28] This article was revised on 29 December 2001 by Amendment (III).

Article 127[29] Whoever steals or seizes by force guns, ammunition or explosives, or steals or seizes by force poisonous, radioactive materials or pathogens of infectious diseases or other materials that endanger the public security, shall be sentenced to fixed-term imprisonment of more than three (3) years and less than 10 years; where the circumstances are serious, he/she shall be sentenced to fixed-term imprisonment of more than ten years, life imprisonment or death.

Whoever robs by force guns, ammunition or explosives, or robs by force poisonous, radioactive materials or pathogens of infectious diseases or other materials that endanger the public security, or steals or seizes by force guns, ammunition or explosives from a state organ, serviceperson or policeman or the people's militia, shall be sentenced to fixed-term imprisonment of more than 10 years, life imprisonment or death.

Article 128 Whoever violates the provisions on gun control by owning or unlawfully possessing guns and ammunition shall be sentenced to fixed-term imprisonment of less than three (3) years, criminal detention, or control and surveillance; where the circumstances are serious, he/she shall be sentenced to fixed-term imprisonment of more than three (3) years and less than seven (7) years.

A person lawfully equipped with a gun for his/her official duty who illegally leases or lends the gun out shall be punished in accordance with the provisions in the previous Paragraph.

A person lawfully equipped with a gun who illegally leases or lends the gun out thereby causing serious consequences shall be punished in accordance with the provisions in the first Paragraph.

A unit committing crimes stipulated in the second and third paragraphs shall have imposed a fine and the directly responsible person(s)-in-charge and any other directly responsible person(s) shall be punished in accordance with the provisions of the first Paragraph.

Article 129 A person lawfully equipped with guns for his/her official duty who loses the gun and fails to immediately make a report on the matter, thereby causing serious consequences, shall be sentenced to fixed-term imprisonment of less than three (3) years or criminal detention.

---

29 This article was revised on 29 December 2001 by Amendment (III).

Article 130 Whoever illegally carries guns, ammunition, controlled knives, tools or goods of an explosive, inflammable, radioactive, poisonous or corrosive nature into a public place or public transportation, thereby endangering public safety, shall be sentenced to fixed-term imprisonment of less than three (3) years, criminal detention, or control and surveillance, where the circumstances are serious.

Article 131 An aircrew member who violates rules and regulations thereby causing a major air accident shall, where serious consequences occur, be sentenced to fixed-term imprisonment of less than three (3) years or criminal detention; where the crash of the aircraft or the death of others is caused, he/she shall be sentenced to fixed-term imprisonment of more than three (3) years and less than seven (7) years.

Article 132 A railway worker who violates rules and regulations and causes a railway accident shall, where serious consequences are caused, be sentenced to fixed-term imprisonment of less than three (3) years or criminal detention; where the consequences are particularly serious, he/she shall be sentenced to fixed-term imprisonment of more than three (3) years and less than seven (7) years.

Article 133 Whoever violates regulations on traffic and causes a serious accident resulting in severe injuries to or the death of other persons or great losses of public and private property shall be sentenced to fixed-term imprisonment of less than three (3) years or criminal detention; where he/she flees from the scene after the accident or where there are other particularly odious circumstances, he/she shall be sentenced to fixed-term imprisonment of more than three (3) years and less than seven (7) years; where the fleeing causes the death of another person, he/she shall be sentenced to fixed-term imprisonment of more than seven (7) years.

Article 133(A)[30] Whoever drives a motor vehicle engaging in illegal racing with another vehicle in serious circumstances, or engages in drink-driving, shall be sentenced to criminal detention with a fine.

Where the act prescribed in the preceding Paragraph constitutes also another crime or crimes, conviction and sentencing shall be decided in accordance with provisions on the crime which attracts the heaviest punishment.

---

30 This article was added on 25 February 2011 by Amendment (VIII).

Article 134[31] Whoever in production or operation violates the relevant provisions on safety management, thereby causing a serious accident resulting in injuries or death to persons, or other serious consequences, shall be sentenced to fixed-term imprisonment of less than three (3) years or criminal detention; where the circumstances are particularly serious, he/she shall be sentenced to fixed-term imprisonment of more than three (3) years and less than seven (7) years.

Whoever forces another to work under hazardous conditions in violation of the rules, thereby causing a serious accident resulting in injuries or death to persons, or other serious consequences, shall be sentenced to fixed-term imprisonment of less than five (5) years or criminal detention; where the circumstances are particularly serious, he/she shall be sentenced to fixed-term imprisonment of more than five (5) years.

Article 135[32] Where production safety facilities or production safety conditions do not conform with the State regulations, thereby causing serious accidents resulting in injuries and death to persons or with other serious consequences, the directly responsible person(s) shall be sentenced to fixed-term imprisonment of less than three (3) years or criminal detention; where the circumstances are particularly serious, he/she shall be sentenced to fixed-term imprisonment of more than three (3) years and less than seven (7) years.

Article 135(A)[33] Where large-scale mass activities are conducted in violation of provisions on safety administration, thereby causing serious accidents resulting in injuries and death to persons, or other serious consequences, the directly responsible person(s) shall be sentenced to fixed-term imprisonment of less than three (3) years or criminal detention; where the circumstances are particularly serious, he/she shall be sentenced to fixed-term imprisonment of more than three (3) years and less than seven (7) years.

Article 136 Whoever violates regulations on the control of explosive, inflammable, radioactive, poisonous or corrosive goods, and causes a major accident during the course of production, storage, transportation or use of such goods, shall, where serious consequences are caused, be

---

[31] This article was added on 29 June 2006 by Amendment (VI).

[32] This article was revised on 29 June 2006 by Amendment (VI).

[33] This article was added on 29 June 2006 by Amendment (VI).

sentenced to fixed-term imprisonment of less than three (3) years or criminal detention; where the consequences are particularly serious, he/she shall be sentenced to fixed-term imprisonment of more than three (3) years and less than seven (7) years.

Article 137 Where a building, design, construction, or engineering supervisory unit, in violation of provisions of the State, lowers the standards for the quality of a project, and thereby causes a major accident, the directly responsible person(s) shall be sentenced to fixed-term imprisonment of less than five (5) years or criminal detention, with a fine; where the consequences are particularly serious, he/she shall be sentenced to fixed-term imprisonment of more than five (5) years and less than 10 years, with a fine.

Article 138 Where it is known that a school building or educational and teaching facility is dangerous but no measures are taken to remove the danger or to report the matter promptly, thereby causing a major accident resulting in injuries and death, the directly responsible person(s) shall be sentenced to fixed-term imprisonment of less than three (3) years or criminal detention; where the consequences are particularly serious, he/she shall be sentenced to fixed-term imprisonment of more than three (3) years and less than seven (7) years.

Article 139 Where there is a violation of rules on fire prevention and control and a refusal to adopt measures to correct the situation after notification to do so has been given by the supervisory organ for fire prevention and control, thereby causing severe consequences, the person(s) directly responsible shall be sentenced to fixed-term imprisonment of less than three (3) years or criminal detention; where the consequences are particularly serious, he/she shall be sentenced to fixed-term imprisonment of more than three (3) years and less than seven (7) years.

Article 139(A)[34] Where after the occurrence of an accident the person with the duty to report fails to report or makes a false report on the accident, thus delaying the rescue work, he/she shall, where the circumstances are serious, be sentenced to fixed-term imprisonment of less than three (3) years or criminal detention; where the consequences are particularly serious, he/she shall be sentenced to fixed-term imprisonment of more than three (3) years and less than seven (7) years.

---

[34] This article was added on 29 June 2006 by Amendment (VI).

Chapter III

Crimes of Undermining the Order of the Socialist Market Economy

Section 1 Crimes of Manufacturing and Selling Fake and Shoddy Commodities

Article 140 Where a producer or seller mixes products with inferior or adulterated materials, uses imitations in place of genuine items, offers low-quality products as high-quality products or substandard products as standard products, if the sales volume reaches an amount of more than 50,000 yuan and less than 200,000 yuan, he/she shall be sentenced to fixed-term imprisonment of less than two (2) years or criminal detention, with a fine equivalent to an amount of more than 50 per cent and less than 200 per cent of the products sold to be concurrently or independently imposed; where the sales volume reaches an amount of more than 200,000 yuan and less than 500,000 yuan, he/she shall be sentenced to fixed-term imprisonment of more than two (2) years and less than seven (7) years, with a fine equivalent to an amount of more than 50 per cent and less than 200 per cent of the products sold; where the sales volume reaches an amount of more than 500,000 yuan and less than 2 million yuan, he/she shall be sentenced to fixed-term imprisonment of more than seven (7) years, with a fine equivalent to an amount of more than 50 per cent and less than 200 per cent of the products sold; where the sales volume reaches an amount of more than two million yuan, he/she shall be sentenced to fixed-term imprisonment of 15 years or life imprisonment with a fine equivalent to an amount of more than 50 per cent and less than 200 per cent of the products sold, or confiscation of property.

Article 141[35] Whoever produces or sells fake medicines shall be sentenced to fixed-term imprisonment of less than three (3) years or criminal detention, with a fine; where serious harm to human health results or there are other serious circumstances, he/she shall be sentenced to fixed-term imprisonment of more than three (3) years and less than 10 years, with a fine; where death to a person results or there are other particularly serious circumstances, he/she shall be sentenced to fixed-term imprisonment of more than 10 years, life imprisonment, or death, with a fine or confiscation of property.

---

[35] This article was revised on 25 February 2011 by Amendment (VIII).

For the purpose of this Article, the term "fake medicines" refers to fake medicines and other medicines and non-medical substances that fall within the categories of fake medicines stipulated in, or deemed to be fake medicines by, the provisions of the "Law of the PRC on the Administration of Pharmaceutical Products".

Article 142 Whoever produces or sells medicines of inferior quality, and thereby causes grave harm to human health, shall be sentenced to fixed-term imprisonment of more than three (3) years and less than 10 years, with a fine of more than 50 per cent and less than 200 per cent of the amount of sales; where the consequences are particularly serious, he/she shall be sentenced to fixed-term imprisonment of more than 10 years or life imprisonment, with a fine of more than 50 per cent and less than 200 per cent of the sale amount or confiscation of property.

For the purpose of this Article the term "medicines of inferior quality" refers to those pharmaceutical products that are defined by the "Law of the PRC on the Management of Pharmaceutical Products" as medicines of inferior quality.

Article 143[36] Whoever produces or sells foods which do not accord with food safety standards and which are likely to cause a food poisoning accident or other serious food-related illnesses shall be sentenced to fixed-term imprisonment of less than three (3) years or criminal detention, with a fine; where grave harm to human health results or the circumstances are serious, he/she shall be sentenced to fixed-term imprisonment of more than three (3) years and less than seven (7) years, with a fine; where the consequences are particularly grave, he/she shall be sentenced to fixed-term imprisonment of more than seven (7) years or life imprisonment, with a fine or confiscation of property.

Article 144[37] Whoever mixes poisonous or harmful non-food materials into the foods he/she produces, or sells or knowingly sells foods that are mixed with poisonous or harmful non-food materials, shall be sentenced to fixed-term imprisonment of less than five (5) years or criminal detention, with a fine; where serious harm to human health is caused or the circumstances are serious, he/she shall be sentenced to fixed-term imprisonment of more than five (5) years and less than 10 years, with a fine;

---

36 This article was revised on 25 February 2011 by Amendment (VIII).

37 This article was revised on 25 February 2011 by Amendment (VIII).

where death to a person results or there are other particularly serious circumstances, he/she shall be punished in accordance with the provisions of Article 141 of the Law.

Article 145[38] Whoever produces medical apparatus and instruments or medical cleansing materials which do not accord with the state standards or the trade standards for protection of human health, or knowingly sells such products which are sufficient enough to cause serious harm to human health, shall be sentenced to fixed-term imprisonment of less than three (3) years or criminal detention, with a fine equivalent to an amount of more than 50 per cent and less than 200 per cent of the products sold; where serious harm to human health are caused, he/she shall be sentenced to fixed-term imprisonment of more than three (3) years and less than 10 years, with a fine equivalent to an amount of more than 50 per cent and less than 200 per cent of the products sold; where the consequences are particularly grave, he/she shall be sentenced to fixed-term imprisonment of more than 10 years or life imprisonment, with a fine equivalent to an amount of more than 50 per cent and less than 200 per cent of the products sold or confiscation of property.

Article 146 Whoever produces electrical appliances, pressurised containers, inflammable and explosive products or other products that do not accord with the state standards and the trade standards for protection of human safety and property, or whoever knowingly sells electrical appliances, pressurised containers, inflammable and explosive products or other products that do not accord with the state standards and the trade standards for protection of human safety and property, and thereby causes serious consequences, shall be sentenced to fixed-term imprisonment of less than five (5) years with a fine equivalent to an amount of more than 50 per cent and less than 200 per cent of the products sold; where the consequences are particularly serious, he/she shall be sentenced to fixed-term imprisonment of more than five (5) years, with a fine equivalent to an amount of more than 50 per cent and less than 200 per cent of the products sold.

Article 147 Whoever produces fake insecticides, fake veterinary medicines, fake chemical fertilisers or knowingly sells insecticides, veterinary medicines, chemical fertilisers or seeds, which are fake or are no longer

---

38 This article was revised on 28 December 2002 by Amendment (IV).

effective, or any producer or seller who passes off substandard insecticides, veterinary medicines, chemical fertilisers and seeds as standard ones, thereby causing relatively heavy losses in production, shall be sentenced to fixed-term imprisonment of less than three (3) years or criminal detention, with a fine equivalent to an amount of more than 50 per cent and less than 200 per cent of the products sold to be concurrently or independently imposed; where serious losses in production result, he/she shall be sentenced to fixed-term imprisonment of more than three (3) years and less than seven (7) years, with a fine equivalent to an amount of more than 50 per cent and less than 200 per cent of the products sold; where particularly serious losses in production result, he/she shall be sentenced to fixed-term imprisonment of more than seven (7) years or life imprisonment, with a fine equivalent to an amount of more than 50 per cent and less than 200 per cent of the products sold or confiscation of property.

Article 148 Whoever produces cosmetics that do not accord with hygienic standards or knowingly sells cosmetics that do not accord with hygienic standards, thereby causing serious consequences, shall be sentenced to imprisonment of less than three (3) years or criminal detention, with a fine equivalent to an amount of more than 50 per cent and less than 200 per cent of the products sold, to be concurrently or independently imposed.

Article 149 Whoever produces or sells products prescribed in Articles 141 to 148 of this Section shall, where the conduct does not constitute a crime as prescribed in the aforesaid Articles, but the sales volume exceeds 50,000 yuan, be convicted and punished in accordance with the provisions of Article 140 of this Section.

Whoever produces or sells products prescribed in Articles 141 to 148 of this Section and has committed a crime as prescribed in these Articles and also a crime as prescribed in Article 140, shall be convicted and punished in accordance with the provisions which impose a heavier penalty.

Article 150 A unit committing a crime as prescribed in Articles 140 to 148 of this Section shall be punished with a fine, and the directly responsible person(s)-in-charge and other directly responsible person(s) shall be punished in accordance with the relevant provisions in these respective articles.

Section 2 Crimes of Smuggling

Article 151[39] Whoever smuggles arms, ammunition, nuclear materials or counterfeit currency shall be sentenced to imprisonment of more than seven (7) years, with a fine or confiscation of property; where the circumstances are particularly serious, he/she shall be sentenced to life imprisonment or death, with confiscation of property; where the circumstances are relatively minor, he/she shall be sentenced to imprisonment of more than three (3) years and less than seven (7) years, with a fine.

Whoever smuggles cultural relics, gold, silver, other precious metals, or precious and rare species of animals and their products which are prohibited by the State for export, shall be sentenced to imprisonment of more than five (5) years and less than 10 years, with a fine; where the circumstances are particularly serious, he/she shall be sentenced to fixed-term imprisonment of more than 10 years or life imprisonment, with confiscation of property; where the circumstances are relatively minor, he/she shall be sentenced to imprisonment of less than five (5) years, with a fine.

Whoever smuggles precious and rare species of plants and their products, or other goods and articles which are prohibited by the State for import and export, shall be sentenced to imprisonment of less than five (5) years or criminal detention, with a fine to be concurrently or independently imposed; where the circumstances are serious, he/she shall be sentenced to imprisonment of more than five (5) years, with a fine.

A unit committing crimes prescribed in this Article shall be punished with a fine, and the directly responsible person(s)-in-charge and any other directly responsible person(s) shall be punished in accordance with the provisions of the various Paragraphs of this Article.

Article 152[40] Whoever smuggles obscene movies, video tapes, audio tapes, pictures, books, journals and other obscene materials for the purpose of making a profit or of dissemination, shall be sentenced to fixed-term imprisonment of more than three (3) years and less than 10 years, with a fine; where the circumstances are serious, he/she shall be sentenced to fixed-term imprisonment of more than 10 years or life imprisonment, with a fine or confiscation of property; where the circumstances are relatively

[39] This article was first revised on 28 February 2009 by Amendment (VII), and again on 25 February 2011 by Amendment (VIII).

[40] This article was revised on 28 December 2002 by Amendment (IV).

minor, he/she shall be sentenced to imprisonment of less than three (3) years, criminal detention, or control and surveillance, with a fine.

Whoever transports solid wastes, liquid wastes or gas wastes into China's territory in evasion of Customs supervision and administration shall, where circumstances are serious, be sentenced to imprisonment of less than five (5) years, with a fine to be independently or concurrently imposed; where circumstances are particularly serious, he/she shall be sentenced to imprisonment of more than five (5) years, with a fine.

A unit committing crimes prescribed in the preceding two Paragraphs shall be punished with a fine, and the directly responsible person(s)-in-charge and any other directly responsible person(s) shall be punished in accordance with the provisions of the preceding two Paragraphs.

Article 153[41] Whoever smuggles goods and objects which are not specified in Articles 151, 152 and 347, shall, depending on the circumstances of the case, be punished in accordance with the following respective provisions:

(1) the smuggling of goods and objects carrying a relatively large amount of tax, or the committing of smuggling even after having been subject to administrative punishment twice in the year for smuggling, shall incur a sentence of fixed-term imprisonment of less than tree (3) or criminal detention, with a fine of more than 100 per cent but less than 500 per cent of the amount of payable tax evaded.
(2) the smuggling of goods and objects carrying a very large amount of tax or with other serious circumstances, shall incur a sentence of fixed-term imprisonment of more than three (3) years and less than 10 years, with a fine of more than 100 per cent but less than 500 per cent of the amount of payable tax evaded.
(3) the smuggling of goods and objects carrying a particularly large amount of tax or with other particularly serious circumstances, shall incur a sentence of fixed-term imprisonment of more than 10 years or life imprisonment, with a fine of more than 100 per cent but less than 500 per cent of the amount of payable tax evaded or confiscation of property.

A unit committing the crimes prescribed in the preceding Paragraph shall be punished with a fine, and the directly responsible person(s)-in-charge

41 This article was revised on 25 February 2011 by Amendment (VIII).

and any other directly responsible person(s) shall be sentenced to fixed-term imprisonment of less than three (3) years or criminal detention; where the circumstances are serious, they shall be sentenced to fixed-term imprisonment of more than three (3) years and less than 10 years; where the circumstances are particularly serious, they shall be sentenced to fixed-term imprisonment of more than 10 years.

Where an offender has carried out smuggling on many occasions and remained uninvestigated, he/she shall be punished on the basis of the accumulated amount of tax payable on the smuggled goods and objects, which has been evaded.

Article 154 Whoever commits one of the following acts of smuggling which constitute crimes according to the provisions of this Section shall be convicted and sentenced in accordance with the provisions of Article 153 of this Law:

(1) selling for profit in China bonded goods such as raw materials, parts, finished products and equipment which are imported under authorisation for the purposes of assembling, processing and compensation trade, without the permission of the Customs and without paying the amount of tax payable; or
(2) selling for profit in China specific goods and objects which are imported under reduced or exempted duties, without the approval of the Customs and without paying the amount of tax payable.

Article 155[42] Whoever commits any of the following acts shall be deemed to be committing the crime of smuggling and shall be punished in accordance with the relevant provisions in this Section:

(1) directly and illegally buying from smugglers goods of which the import is prohibited by the State, or directly and illegally buying from smugglers other imported smuggled goods and objects in a relatively large quantity;
(2) transporting, buying or selling in inland seas, territorial waters, boundary rivers or boundary lakes goods of which the import and export is prohibited by the State; or transporting, buying or selling without legal documentation a relatively large quantity of goods of which the import and export are restricted by the State.

---

42 This article was revised on 28 December 2002 by Amendment (IV).

Article 156 Whoever colludes with smugglers and provides them with loans, funds, account numbers, invoices or proof documents, or other conveniences such as transportation, custody and mailing, shall be treated as a joint offender in the crime of smuggling and punished accordingly.

Article 157[43] Whoever provides smugglers with armed protection shall have a heavier punishment imposed in accordance with the provisions of the first Paragraphs of Article 151 of this Law.

Whoever resists by means of violence or threat any actions taken by the Customs to seize smuggled goods shall be deemed to be committing both the crime of smuggling and the crime of hindering state functionaries from performing their duties pursuant to the law as prescribed in Article 277 of this Law, and shall be punished in accordance with the provisions on combined punishment for multiple crimes.

Section 3 Crimes of Disrupting the Order of Company and Enterprise Administration

Article 158 Whoever uses false documents of proof or adopts other deceptive means to falsely declare registered capital when applying for company registration, and obtains company registration by deceiving the competent company registration organ shall, where the amount of falsely registered capital is large and the consequences are serious or there are other aggravating circumstances, be sentenced to fixed-term imprisonment of less than three (3) years or criminal detention, with a fine of more than one (1) per cent but less than five (5) per cent of the amount of the registered capital falsely declared, to be concurrently or independently imposed.

A unit committing the crime prescribed in the preceding paragraph shall be punished with a fine, and the directly responsible person(s)-in-charge and any other directly responsible person(s) shall be sentenced to fixed-term imprisonment of less than three (3) years or criminal detention.

Article 159 A company promoter or a shareholder who, in violation of the provisions of the Company Law, makes a false capital contribution by failing to pay in cash or in kind or to transfer the ownership rights of property, or who withdraws their capital contribution after the establishment of the company, if the amount involved is large and the consequences are serious or there are other aggravating circumstances, shall be sentenced to

43 This article was revised on 25 February 2011 by Amendment (VIII).

fixed-term imprisonment of less than five (5) years or criminal detention, and a fine of more than two (2) per cent but less than 10 percent of the amount of capital that was falsely declared as contribution capital, or that is withdrawn from contributed capital, to be imposed concurrently or independently.

A unit committing crimes prescribed in the preceding Paragraph shall be punished with a fine, and the directly responsible person(s)-in-charge and any other directly responsible person(s) shall be sentenced to fixed-term imprisonment of less than five (5) years or criminal detention.

Article 160 Whoever, in the course of issuance of shares or company bonds, conceals important facts or falsifies major contents in the prospectuses, subscription documents or measures for issuing company or enterprise bonds shall, if the amount involved is large, the consequences are serious or there are other aggravating circumstances, be sentenced to fixed-term imprisonment of less than five (5) years or criminal detention, with a fine of more than one (1) per cent and less than five (5) per cent of the amount of the funds illegally raised, to be concurrently or independently imposed.

A unit committing crimes prescribed in the preceding paragraph shall be punished with a fine, and the directly responsible person(s)-in-charge and any other directly responsible person(s) shall be sentenced to fixed-term imprisonment of less than five (5) years or criminal detention.

Article 161[44] Where a company with the legal obligation to disclose information provides its shareholders or the public at large with false financial and accounting reports or financial and accounting reports which conceal important facts, or fails to make disclosure as required by regulations of other major information that shall be disclosed in accordance with the law, and thus causes serious harm to the interests of shareholders or other people, or where there are other serious circumstances, the directly responsible person(s)-in-charge and any other directly responsible person(s) shall be sentenced to fixed-term imprisonment of less than three (3) years or criminal detention, with a fine of more than 20,000 yuan and less than 200,000 yuan to be concurrently or independently imposed.

Article 162 Where a company or an enterprise in the process of liquidation conceals property, makes false entries in its balance sheet or asset

---

[44] This article was revised on 29 June 2006 by Amendment (VI).

list, or distributes assets of the company or enterprise before making payment for its debts, thereby causing serious harm to the interests of creditors and other people, the directly responsible person(s)-in-charge and any other directly responsible person(s) shall be sentenced to fixed-term imprisonment of less than five (5) years or criminal detention, with a fine of more than 20,000 yuan and less than 200,000 yuan to be concurrently or independently imposed.

Article 162(A)[45] Whoever conceals or deliberately destroys accounting documents, accounting books or financial and accounting reports which must be kept according to law, shall, where the circumstances are serious, be sentenced to fixed-term imprisonment of less than five (5) years or criminal detention, with a fine of more than 20,000 yuan and less than 200,000 yuan to be concurrently or independently imposed.

A unit committing the crime prescribed in the preceding Paragraph shall be punished with a fine, and the directly responsible person(s)-in-charge and any other directly responsible person(s) shall be punished in accordance with the provisions in the preceding paragraph.

Article 162(B)[46] Where a company or enterprise transfers or disposes of assets, or claims false bankruptcy through such means as concealing assets and undertaking fabricated debts, thereby causing serious harm to the interests of shareholders or other people, the directly responsible person(s)-in-charge and any other directly responsible person(s) shall be sentenced to fixed-term imprisonment of less than five (5) years or criminal detention, with a fine of more than 20,000 yuan and less than 200,000 yuan to be concurrently or independently imposed.

Article 163[47] A staff member of a company, an enterprise or a unit of other types who, taking advantage of his/her position, demands money or property from other persons or illegally accepts money or property from other persons and in turn seeks benefits for these others, shall, where the amount involved is relatively large, be sentenced to fixed-term imprisonment of less than five (5) years or criminal detention; where the amount involved is large, he/she shall be sentenced to fixed-term imprisonment of more than five (5) years and may also be concurrently sentenced to confiscation of property.

---

45 This article was added on 5 December 1999 by Amendment (I).
46 This article was added on 29 June 2006 by Amendment (VI).
47 This article was revised on 29 June 2006 by Amendment (VI).

A staff member of a company, an enterprise or a unit of other types who, taking advantage of his/her position, accepts commissions and service fees in the guise of performing various functions in violation of provisions of the State, and takes them into his/her own possession shall be punished in accordance with the provisions in the preceding Paragraph.

A staff member who performs public duties in a state-owned company, state-owned enterprise or state-owned unit, or who is assigned by a state-owned company, enterprise or unit to a non-state-owned company, enterprise or unit to perform public duties, and who commits the acts prescribed in the preceding two Paragraphs, shall be convicted and punished in accordance with the provisions of Articles 385 and 386 of this Law.

Article 164[48] Whoever, in order to seek improper benefits, offers money or property to staff members of a company or an enterprise or a unit shall, if the amount involved is relatively large, be sentenced to fixed-term imprisonment of less than three (3) years or criminal detention; if the amount involved is very large, he/she shall be sentenced to fixed-term imprisonment of more than three (3) years and less than 10 years, with a fine.

Whoever, in order to seek improper commercial benefits, offers money or property to a foreign staff member performing public duties or to an official of an international organisation, shall be punished in accordance with the provisions in the preceding Paragraph.

A unit committing a crime as prescribed in the preceding two Paragraphs shall be punished with a fine, and the directly responsible person(s)-in-charge and any other directly responsible person(s) shall be punished in accordance with the provisions in the first Paragraph.

A briber who voluntarily confesses his/her bribery prior to being prosecuted may be given a mitigated punishment or be exempted from punishment.

Article 165 A director or manager of a state-owned company or enterprise who, taking advantage of his/her office, operates for him/herself or operates for another business which is of the same type as the business of the company or enterprise in which he/she holds the position, and illegally obtains benefits, shall, where the amount involved is very large,

[48] This article was first revised on 29 June 2006 by Amendment (VI), and again on 25 February 2011 by Amendment (VIII).

be sentenced to fixed-term imprisonment of less than three (3) years or criminal detention, with a fine to be imposed concurrently or independently; where the amount involved is particularly large, he/she shall be sentenced to fixed-term imprisonment of more than three (3) years and less than seven (7) years, with a fine.

Article 166 A staff member of a state-owned company, enterprise or institution who takes advantage of his/her position, is involved in any of the following conducts and seriously harms the interests of the State, shall be sentenced to fixed-term imprisonment of less than three (3) years or criminal detention, with a fine to be imposed concurrently or independently; where he/she causes the State to suffer particularly heavy losses, he/she shall be sentenced to fixed-term imprisonment of more than three (3) years and less than seven (7) years, with a fine:

(1) handing the unit's profitable business to relatives or friends for management;
(2) purchasing commodities from a unit operated and managed by relatives or friends at a price obviously higher than the market price, or selling commodities to the unit operated and managed by relatives or friends at a price obviously lower than the market price; or
(3) purchasing substandard commodities from a unit operated and managed by relatives or friends.

Article 167 A directly responsible person in charge of a state-owned company, enterprise or institution who is defrauded because of gross neglect of his/her duty in the process of signing or performing contracts and thus causes heavy losses to the State, shall be sentenced to fixed-term imprisonment of less than three (3) years or criminal detention; where he/she causes the State to suffer particularly heavy losses, he/she shall be sentenced to fixed-term imprisonment of more than three (3) years and less than seven (7) years.

Article 168[49] A directly responsible person in charge of a state-owned company or enterprise who causes the bankruptcy of or serious losses to his/her company or enterprise and causes major losses to the State due to his/her gross neglect of duty or the abuse of his/her position, shall be sentenced fixed-term imprisonment of less than three (3) years or criminal detention; where the losses suffered by the State are particularly serious,

[49] This article was revised on 25 December 1999 by Amendment (I).

he/she shall be sentenced to fixed-term imprisonment of more than three (3) years and less than seven (7) years.

Where a staff member of a state-owned institution commits the acts prescribed in the preceding Paragraph and causes major losses to the State, he/she shall be punished in accordance with the provisions in the preceding Paragraph.

Where a staff member of a state-owned company, enterprise or institution practises favouritism and irregularity and commits the crimes prescribed in the preceding two Paragraphs, he/she shall be given a heavier sentence in accordance with the provisions in the first Paragraph.

Article 169 A directly responsible person in charge of a state-owned company, enterprise or a competent department at the higher levels, who causes great losses to the State by practising favouritism and irregularity, and by converting state assets into shares at a low price or by selling them at a low price, shall be sentenced to fixed-term imprisonment of less than three (3) years or criminal detention; where the losses suffered by the State are particularly heavy, he/she shall be sentenced to fixed-term imprisonment of more than three (3) years and less than seven (7) years.

Article 169(A)[50] A director, supervisor or senior managerial member of a listed company, who, in betrayal of his/her obligation of loyalty to the company, by taking advantage of his/her position manipulates the listed company to engage in any of the following acts, thereby causing the listed company to suffer from heavy losses, shall be sentenced to fix-term imprisonment of less than three (3) years or criminal detention, with a fine to be imposed concurrently or independently; or where particularly serious losses are caused to the listed company, he/she shall be sentenced to fix-term imprisonment of more than three (3) years and less than seven (7) years, with a fine:

(1) gratuitously providing funds, commodities, services or other assets to another unit or individual;
(2) providing or receiving funds, commodities, services or other assets under obviously unfair conditions;

50 This article was added on 29 June 2006 by Amendment (VI).

(3) providing funds, commodities, services or other assets to another unit or individual that obviously does not have the capacity to make repayment;
(4) providing a guarantee to a unit or individual that obviously does not have the capacity to make repayment, or providing a guarantee to a unit or individual without proper reasons;
(5) waiving credits or undertaking debts without proper reasons; or
(6) damaging the listed company's interests in any other way.

The controlling shareholder or actual controller of the listed company who instructs directors, supervisors or senior managerial personnel to commit acts prescribed in the preceding Paragraph, is to be punished with reference to the provisions of the preceding Paragraph.

Where the controlling shareholder or actual controller of a listed company that commits a crime listed in the preceding Paragraph is a unit, the unit shall be punished with a fine, and the directly responsible person(s)-in-charge and any other directly responsible person(s) shall be punished in accordance with the provisions in the first Paragraph.

Section 4 Crimes of Undermining the Order of Financial Administration

Article 170 Whoever counterfeits currency shall be sentenced to fixed-term imprisonment of more than three (3) years and less than 10 years, with a fine of more than 50,000 yuan and less than 500,000 yuan; where this involves one of the following circumstances, he/she shall be sentenced to fixed-term imprisonment of more than 10 years, life imprisonment or death, with a fine of more than 50,000 yuan and less than 500,000 yuan or confiscation of property:

(1) being the ringleader of a gang involved in counterfeiting currency;
(2) having counterfeited a particularly large amount of currency;
(3) being involved in other particularly serious circumstances.

Article 171 Whoever sells or buys counterfeit currency or knowingly transports counterfeit currency shall be sentenced to fixed-term imprisonment of less than three (3) years or criminal detention, with a fine of more than 20,000 yuan and less than 200,000 yuan; where the amount involved is large, he/she shall be sentenced fixed-term imprisonment of more than three (3) years and less than 10 years with a fine of more than 50,000 yuan and less than 500,000 yuan; where the amount involved is particularly large, he/she shall be sentenced to fixed-term imprisonment of more than

10 years or life imprisonment with a fine of more than 50,000 yuan and less than 500,000 yuan or confiscation of property.

A staff member of a bank or other financial institution who buys counterfeit currency or takes advantage of his/her position to convert counterfeit currency into genuine currency shall be sentenced to fixed-term imprisonment of less than three (3) years or criminal detention with a fine of more than 20,000 yuan and less than 200,000 yuan; where the amount involved is large or there are other aggravating circumstances, he/she shall be sentenced to fixed-term imprisonment of more than 10 years or life imprisonment, with a fine of more than 20,000 yuan and less than 200,000 yuan or confiscation of property; where the circumstances are relatively minor, he/she shall be sentenced to fixed-term imprisonment of less than three (3) years or criminal detention, with a fine more than 10,000 yuan and less than 100,000 yuan to be concurrently or independently imposed.

Whoever counterfeits currency and also sells or transports counterfeit currency shall be convicted and given a heavier penalty in accordance with the provisions of Article 170 of this Law.

Article 172 Whoever knowingly possesses or uses counterfeit currency shall, where the amount involved is relatively large, be sentenced to fixed-term imprisonment of less than three (3) years or criminal detention, with a fine of more than 10,000 yuan and less than 100,000 yuan to be concurrently or independently imposed; where the amount involved is large, he/she shall be sentenced to fixed-term imprisonment of more than three (3) years and less than 10 years with a fine of more than 20,000 yuan and less than 200,000 yuan; where the amount is particularly large, he/she shall be sentenced to fixed-term imprisonment of more than 10 years with a fine of more than 50,000 yuan and less than 500,000 yuan or confiscation of property.

Article 173 Whoever produces fake currency involving a relatively large amount shall be sentenced to fixed-term imprisonment of less than three (3) years or criminal detention, with a fine of more than 10,000 yuan and less than 100,000 yuan to be concurrently or independently imposed; where the amount involved is large, he/she shall be sentenced to fixed-term imprisonment of more than three (3) years and less than 10 years with a fine of more than 20,000 yuan and less than 200,000 yuan.

Article 174[51] Whoever sets up a commercial bank, stock exchange, futures exchange, securities company, futures brokerage company, insurance company or any other financial institution without the permission of the relevant competent department of the State, shall be sentenced to fixed-term imprisonment of less than three (3) years or criminal detention, with a fine of more than 20,000 yuan and less than 200,000 yuan to be concurrently or independently imposed; where the circumstances are serious, he/she shall be sentenced to fixed-term imprisonment of more than three (3) years and less than 10 years with a fine of more than 50,000 yuan and less than 500,000 yuan.

Whoever forges, alters or transfers the business license or approval document of a commercial bank, stock exchange, futures exchange, securities company, futures brokerage company, insurance company or any other financial institution, shall be punished in accordance with the provisions in the preceding Paragraph.

A unit committing the crimes prescribed in the preceding two Paragraphs shall be punished with a fine, and the directly responsible person(s)-in-charge and any other directly responsible person(s) shall be punished in accordance with the first Paragraph.

Article 175 Whoever, for the purpose of making a profit, illegally acquires credit funds from a financial institution and re-lends them at a high interest rate to other people shall, where the amount of profit illegally obtained is relatively large, be sentenced to fixed-term imprisonment of less than three (3) years or criminal detention, with a fine of more than 100 per cent and less than 500 per cent of the amount of the profit illegally obtained; where the amount involved is large, he/she shall be sentenced to fixed-term imprisonment of more than three (3) years and less than seven (7) years, with a fine of more than 100 per cent and less than 500 per cent of the amount of the profit illegally obtained.

A unit committing the crimes prescribed in the preceding Paragraph, shall be punished with a fine, and the directly responsible person(s)-in-charge and any other directly responsible person(s) shall be sentenced to fixed-term imprisonment of less than three (3) years or criminal detention.

51 This article was revised on 25 December 1999 by Amendment (I).

Article 175(A)[52] Whoever obtains through fraudulent means loans, convertible instruments, letter of credit, letter of guarantee, etc. from a bank or any other financial institution shall, where it causes the bank or the financial institution to suffer from major losses or where there are other serious circumstances, be sentenced to fixed-term imprisonment of less than three (3) years or criminal detention, with a fine to be imposed concurrently or independently; where it causes the bank or financial institution to suffer from particularly heavy losses or where there are other particularly serious circumstances, be sentenced to fix-term imprisonment of more than three (3) years and less than seven (7) years, with a fine.

A unit committing the crimes prescribed in the preceding Paragraph, shall be punished with a fine, and the directly responsible person(s)-in-charge and any other directly responsible person(s) shall be punished in accordance with provisions of the preceding Paragraph.

Article 176 Whoever illegally absorbs deposits from the public or does so in a disguised form, thereby disrupting the financial order, shall be sentenced to fixed-term imprisonment of less than three (3) years or criminal detention, with a fine of more than 20,000 yuan and less than 200,000 yuan to be concurrently or independently imposed; where the amount involved is large or there are other aggravating circumstances, he/she shall be sentenced to fixed-term imprisonment of more than three (3) years and less than 10 years, with a fine of more than 50,000 yuan and less than 500,000 yuan.

A unit committing the crimes prescribed in the preceding paragraph shall be punished with a fine, and the directly responsible person(s)-in-charge and any other directly responsible person(s) shall be punished in accordance with the provisions in the preceding Paragraph.

Article 177 Whoever forges or alters financial bills in any of the following ways shall be sentenced to fixed-term imprisonment of less than five (5) years or criminal detention, with a fine of more than 20,000 yuan and less than 200,000 yuan to be concurrently or independently imposed; where the circumstances are serious, he/she shall be sentenced to fixed-term imprisonment of more than five (5) years and less than 10 years with a fine of more than 50,000 yuan and less than 500,000 yuan; where the circumstances are particularly serious, he/she shall be sentenced to fixed-term

[52] This article was revised on 29 June 2006 by Amendment (VI).

imprisonment of more than 10 years or life imprisonment with a fine of more than 50,000 yuan and less than 500,000 yuan or confiscation of property:

(1) forging or imitating money orders, promissory notes or cheques;
(2) forging or imitating power of attorney for payments, remittance documents, deposit receipts or other account-settlement documents;
(3) forging or imitating letters of credit or the bills or documents attached;
(4) forging credit cards.

A unit committing the crimes prescribed in the preceding Paragraph shall be punished with a fine, and the directly responsible person(s)-in-charge or any other directly responsible person(s) shall be punished in accordance with the provisions in the preceding Paragraph.

Article 177(A)[53] Whoever hinders the administration of credit cards in any of the following ways shall be sentenced to fixed-term imprisonment of less than three (3) years or criminal detention, with a fine of more than 10,000 yuan and less than 100,000 yuan to be concurrently or independently imposed; where the amount involved is large or there are other serious circumstances, he/she shall be sentenced to fixed-term imprisonment of more than three (3) years and less than 10 years, with a fine of more than 20,000 yuan and less than 200,000 yuan:

(1) knowingly holding or transporting forged credit cards, or knowingly holding or transporting a relatively large quantity of forged blank credit cards;
(2) illegally holding a relatively large quantity of credit card of other persons;
(3) using false identity certificates to fraudulently obtain credit cards; or
(4) selling, purchasing or providing other persons with forged credit cards or credit cards which he/she has obtained with false identity certificates.

Whoever steals, purchases or illegally provides information about the credit card of another person, shall be punished in accordance with the provisions of the preceding Paragraph.

A staff member of a bank or another financial institution, taking advantage of his/her position, who commits the crime prescribed in the

---

53 This article was added on 28 February 2005 by Amendment (V).

preceding second paragraph of this Article, shall have a heavier penalty imposed.

Article 178 Whoever forges or alters treasury bonds or other negotiable instruments issued by the State shall, where the amount involved is relatively large, be sentenced to fixed-term imprisonment of less than three (3) years or criminal detention, with a fine of more than 20,000 yuan and less than 200,000 yuan to be concurrently or independently imposed; where the amount involved is large, he/she shall be sentenced to fixed-term imprisonment of more than three (3) years and less than 10 years, with a fine of more than 50,000 yuan and less than 500,000 yuan; where the amount is particularly large, he/she shall be sentenced to fixed-term imprisonment of more than 10 years or life imprisonment, with a fine of more than 50,000 yuan and less than 500,000 yuan or confiscation of property.

Whoever forges or alters shares or company or enterprise bonds shall, where the amount involved is relatively large, be sentenced to fixed-term imprisonment of less than three (3) years or criminal detention, with a fine of more than 10,000 yuan and less than 100,000 yuan to concurrently or independently imposed; where the amount involved is large, he/she shall be sentenced to fixed-term imprisonment of more than three (3) years and less than 10 years, with a fine of more than 20,000 yuan and less than 200,000 yuan.

A unit committing the crimes prescribed in the preceding two Paragraphs shall be punished with a fine, and the directly responsible person(s)-in-charge or any other directly responsible person(s) shall be punished in accordance with the provisions in the preceding two paragraphs.

Article 179 Whoever issues shares or company and enterprise bonds without the permission of the relevant competent departments of the State shall, where the amount involved is large and the circumstances are serious or there are other aggravating circumstances, be sentenced to fixed-term imprisonment of less than five (5) years or criminal detention, with a fine of more than one (1) per cent and less than five (5) per cent of the funds illegally raised, to be concurrently or independently imposed.

A unit committing the crimes prescribed in the preceding paragraph shall be punished with a fine, and the directly responsible person(s)-in-charge or any other directly responsible person(s) shall be sentenced to fixed-term imprisonment of less than five (5) years or criminal detention.

Article 180[54] Where an insider who holds inside information on securities and futures trading or a person who illegally obtains inside information on securities and futures trading, and before the information on the issuance of the securities or the trade of the securities and futures or other information which will have a major impact on the trading price of the securities and futures is published, purchases or sells such securities or engages in the trading of futures which is related to the inside information, or leaks the information, or explicitly or implicitly instructs any other person(s) to engage in the aforesaid trading activities, shall, where the circumstances are serious, be sentenced to fixed-term imprisonment of less than five (5) years or criminal detention, with a fine of more than 100 per cent and less than 500 per cent of the amount of gains illegally obtained to be concurrently or independently imposed; where the circumstances are particularly serious, he/she shall be sentenced to fixed-term imprisonment of more than five (5) years and less than 10 years, with a fine of more than 100 per cent and less than 500 per cent of the amount of gains illegally obtained.

A unit committing the crimes prescribed in the preceding Paragraph shall be punished with a fine, and the directly responsible person(s)-in-charge or any other directly responsible person(s) shall be sentenced to fixed-term imprisonment of less than five (5) years or criminal detention.

The extent of inside information and the meaning of insiders shall be determined in accordance with the provisions of laws and administrative regulations.

A staff member of a stock exchange, futures exchange, securities company, futures brokerage company, fund management company, commercial bank, insurance company or any other financial institution, or a staff member of a relevant supervision and administration department or trade association, who, taking advantage of his/her position, obtains unpublished information other than inside information and engages in securities or futures trading activities related to such information, or explicitly or implicitly instructs any other person(s) to engage in the relevant trading activities, shall, where the circumstances are serious, be punished in accordance with provisions of the first Paragraph.

---

[54] This article was first revised on 25 December 1999 by Amendment (I), and again on 28 February 2009 by Amendment (VII).

Article 181[55] Whoever fabricates or disseminates false information on the securities and futures markets, thereby disrupting the securities and futures markets, shall, where this causes serious consequences, be sentenced to fixed-term imprisonment of less than five (5) years or criminal detention, with a fine of more than 10,000 yuan and less than 100,000 yuan to be concurrently or independently imposed.

A staff member of a stock exchange, futures exchange, securities company, futures brokerage company, or a staff member of a securities industry association, futures industry association, or a securities supervision and administration department, who intentionally provides false information, or forges, alters or destroys trading records and induces investors to buy or sell securities or futures contracts shall, where serious consequences result, be sentenced to fixed-term imprisonment of less than five (5) years or criminal detention, with a fine of more than 10,000 yuan and less than 100,000 yuan to be concurrently or independently imposed; where the circumstances are particularly odious, he/she shall be sentenced to fixed-term imprisonment of more than five (5) years and less than the 10 years, with a fine of more than 20,000 yuan and less than 200,000 yuan to be concurrently imposed.

A unit committing the crimes prescribed in the preceding two Paragraphs shall be punished with a fine, and the directly responsible person(s)-in-charge or any other directly responsible person(s) shall be sentenced to fixed-term imprisonment of less than five (5) years or criminal detention.

Article 182[56] Whoever rigs the securities or futures markets in any of the following ways shall, where the circumstances are serious, be sentenced to fixed-term imprisonment of less than five (5) years or criminal detention with a fine; where circumstances are particularly serious, be sentenced to fixed-term imprisonment of more than five (5) years and less than 10 years, with a fine:

(1) either on his/her own or by conspiring with others, taking advantage of his/her financial strength or combined financial strength, or shareholding or stock holding strength or information strength to jointly or

---

[55] This article was revised on 25 December 1999 by Amendment (I).

[56] This article was first revised on 25 December 1999 by Amendment (I), and again on 29 June 2006 by Amendment (VI).

continuously sell or buy securities or futures, thereby rigging the trading prices or volumes of securities or futures;

(2) colluding with others to trade with them securities or futures at pre-agreed times, prices and forms, thereby influencing the trading prices or volumes of securities or futures;

(3) trading securities between accounts that are actually controlled by him/herself, or buying from or selling to him/herself, or buying from and selling to him/herself futures contracts, thereby influencing the trading prices or volumes of securities or futures; or

(4) rigging securities or futures trading prices by other means.

A unit committing the crimes prescribed in the preceding Paragraph shall be punished with a fine, and the directly responsible person(s)-in-charge or any other directly responsible person(s) shall be punished in accordance with provisions of the preceding Paragraph.

Article 183 A staff member of an insurance company who, taking advantage of his/her position, intentionally fabricates a non-existing insured accident and settles a false claim thereupon, thereby deceitfully taking the insurance money into his/her own possession, shall be convicted and punished in accordance with the provisions of Article 271 of this Law.

A staff member of a state-owned insurance company or a staff member assigned by a state-owned insurance company to perform official duties in a non-state-owned insurance company, who commits the acts prescribed in the preceding Paragraph shall be convicted and punished in accordance with the provisions of Articles 382 and 383 of this Law.

Article 184 A staff member of a bank or any other financial institution who, in conducting financial business activities, demands money or goods from others or illegally accepts money or goods from others as the price of seeking benefits for those others or, in violation of provisions of the State, accepts commissions or service charges in the guise of performing various functions and takes them into his/her own possession, shall be convicted and punished in accordance with the provisions of Article 163 of this Law.

A staff member of a state-owned financial institution or a staff member assigned by a state-owned financial institution to perform official duties in a non-state-owned financial institution, who commits the acts prescribed in the preceding Paragraph shall be convicted and punished in accordance with the provisions of Article 385 and Article 386 in this Law.

Article 185[57] A staff member of a commercial bank, stock exchange, futures exchange, securities company, futures brokerage company, insurance company or any other financial institution, who, taking advantage of his/her position, misappropriates funds from his/her unit or customers shall be convicted and punished in accordance with the provisions of Article 272 of this Law.

A staff member of a state-owned commercial bank, stock exchange, futures exchange, securities company, futures brokerage company, insurance company or any other state-owned financial institution, or a person who is assigned by a state-owned commercial bank, stock exchange, futures exchange, securities company, futures brokerage company, insurance company or a state-owned financial institution of another kind to perform official duties in a non-state-owned institution as prescribed in the preceding Paragraph, who commits the acts prescribed in the preceding Paragraph shall be convicted and punished in accordance with the provisions of Article 384 of this Law.

Article 185(A)[58] A commercial bank, stock exchange, future exchange, securities company, future brokerage company, insurance company or any other financial institution that, in violation of trust obligations, uses under its own volition customers' funds or other commissioned property or entrusted property, shall, where the circumstances are serious, be punished with a fine, and the directly responsible person(s)-in-charge or any other directly responsible person(s) shall be sentenced to fixed-term imprisonment of less than three (3) years or criminal detention, with a fine of more than 30,000 yuan and less than 300,000 yuan; where the circumstance are particularly serious, be sentenced to fixed-term imprisonment of more than three (3) years and less than 10 years, with a fine of more than 50,000 yuan and less than 500,000 yuan.

Where a social security funds management institution, housing public reserve funds management institution or a public funds management institution of another kind, or an insurance company, insurance assets management company, or a securities investment funds management company, utilises funds in violation of State provisions, the directly responsible person(s)-in-charge or any other directly responsible

[57] This article was revised on 25 December 1999 by Amendment (I).
[58] This article was added on 29 June 2006 by Amendment (VI).

person(s) shall be punished by reference to the provisions of the preceding Paragraph.

Article 186[59] A staff member of a bank or a financial institution of another kind who grants loans in violation of the provisions of the State, shall, where the amount involved is large or heavy losses are caused, be sentenced to fixed-term imprisonment of less than five (5) years or criminal detention with a fine of more than 10,000 yuan and less than 100,000 yuan; where the amount involved is particularly large or the losses are particularly heavy, he/she shall be sentenced to fixed-term imprisonment of more than five (5) years with a fine of more than 20,000 yuan and less than 200,000 yuan.

A staff member of a bank or a financial institution of another kind who, in violation of the provisions of the State, grants loans to related persons, shall have imposed a heavier penalty in accordance with the provisions of the preceding Paragraph.

A unit committing the crimes prescribed in the preceding two Paragraphs shall be punished with a fine, and the directly responsible person(s)-in-charge and any other directly responsible person(s) shall be punished in accordance with the provisions in the preceding two Paragraphs.

The meaning of "related persons" shall be determined in accordance with the "Law of the People's Republic of China Governing Commercial Banks" and other relevant financial laws and regulations.

Article 187[60] A staff member of a bank or a financial institution of another kind who absorbs customers' funds without entering them into their accounts, shall, where the amount involved is large or large losses are caused, be sentenced to fixed-term imprisonment of less than five (5) years or criminal detention with a fine of more than 20,000 yuan and less than 200,000 yuan; where the amount involved is particularly large or the losses are particularly heavy, he/she shall be sentenced to fixed-term imprisonment of more than five (5) years with a fine of more than 50,000 yuan and less than 500,000 yuan.

A unit committing the crimes prescribed in the preceding Paragraph shall be punished with a fine, and the directly responsible person(s)-in-charge

---

[59] This article was revised on 29 June 2006 by Amendment (VI).
[60] This article was revised on 29 June 2006 by Amendment (VI).

and any other directly responsible person(s) shall be punished in accordance with the provisions in the preceding Paragraph.

Article 188[61] A staff member of a bank or a financial institution of another kind who, in violation of provisions, issues to others letters of credit, letters of guarantee, negotiable instruments, deposit receipts, or other credit certificates, shall, where the circumstances are serious, be sentenced to fixed-term imprisonment of less than five (5) years or criminal detention; where the circumstances are particularly serious, he/she shall be sentenced to fixed-term imprisonment of more than five (5) years.

A unit committing the crimes prescribed in the preceding Paragraph shall be punished with a fine, and the directly responsible person(s)-in-charge and any other directly responsible person(s) shall be punished in accordance with the provisions in the preceding Paragraph.

Article 189[62] A staff member of a bank or a financial institution of another kind who, in the course of handling negotiable instruments, accepts, pays or provides guarantees for negotiable instruments which do not accord with laws on negotiable instruments, shall, where serious losses are caused, be sentenced to fixed-term imprisonment of less than five (5) years or criminal detention; where the losses are particularly heavy, he/she shall be sentenced to fixed-term imprisonment of more than five (5) years.

A unit committing the crimes prescribed in the preceding Paragraph shall be punished with a fine, and the directly responsible person(s)-in-charge and any other directly responsible person(s) shall be punished in accordance with the provisions in the preceding Paragraph.

Article 190[63] A company, an enterprise or a unit of another kind which, in violation of provisions of the State, deposits foreign exchange abroad without authorisation or illegally transfers foreign exchange from China to overseas, shall, where the amount involved is relatively large, be sentenced to a fine of more than five (5) per cent and less than 30 per cent of

---

[61] This article was revised on 29 June 2006 by Amendment (VI).

[62] This Article needs to be read in conjunction with "Decision of on the Punishment of Crimes Involving Fraudulent Purchasing, Evasion and Illegal Trading of Foreign Exchange" (29 December 1998).

[63] This article was revised on 29 December 1998 by the "Decision of on the Punishment of Crimes Involving Fraudulent Purchasing, Evasion and Illegal Trading of Foreign Exchange".

the amount of foreign exchange evaded, and the directly responsible person(s)-in-charge and any other directly responsible person(s) shall be sentenced to fixed-term imprisonment of less than five (5) years or criminal detention; where the amount involved is large or there are other serious circumstances, the unit concerned shall be punished with a fine of more than five (5) per cent and less than 30 per cent of the amount of foreign exchange evaded, and the direct responsible person(s)-in-charge and other direct responsible person(s) shall be sentenced to fixed-term imprisonment of more than five (5) years.

Article 191[64] Whoever knows clearly that the income and the gains derived therefrom are obtained from committing drug-related crimes, crimes committed by underground organisations of a gangland nature, crimes of terrorism, crimes of smuggling, crimes of corruption and bribery, crimes of undermining the order of financial administration, or crimes of financial fraud, but covers up or conceals the source or nature of the income and the gains by committing any of the following acts, shall be sentenced to fixed-term imprisonment of less than five (5) years or criminal detention, confiscation of gains and income derived from the above crimes, and a fine of more than five (5) per cent and less than 20 per cent of the amount of money laundered to be concurrently or independently imposed; where the circumstances are serious, he/she shall be sentenced to fixed-term imprisonment of more than five (5) years and less than 10 years, with a fine of more than five (5) per cent and less than 20 per cent of the amount of money laundered:

(1) providing funds accounts;
(2) assisting to convert property into cash, financial instruments, or valuable securities;
(3) assisting to transfer capital by transferring accounts or by other account settlement means;
(4) assisting to remit funds overseas; or
(5) using other means to cover up and conceal the nature and sources of the illegally obtained income and the gains therefrom.

A unit committing the crimes prescribed in the preceding Paragraph shall be punished with a fine, and the directly responsible person(s)-in-charge and any other directly responsible person(s) shall be sentenced to

[64] This article was first revised on 29 December 2001 by Amendment (III), and again on 29 June 2006 by Amendment (VI).

fixed-term imprisonment of less than five (5) years or criminal detention; where the circumstances are serious, he/she shall be sentenced to fixed-term imprisonment of more than five (5) years and less than 10 years.

Section 5 Crimes of Financial Fraud

Article 192 Whoever illegally raises funds by fraudulent means for the purpose of unlawful possession shall, if the amount involved is relatively large, be sentenced to fixed-term imprisonment of less than five (5) years or criminal detention with a fine of more than 20,000 yuan and less than 200,000 yuan; where the amount involved is large or there are other aggravating circumstances, he/she shall be sentenced to fixed-term imprisonment of more than five (5) years and less than 10 years with a fine of more than 50,000 yuan and less than 500,000 yuan; where the amount is particularly large or there are other particularly aggravating circumstances, he/she shall be sentenced to fixed-term imprisonment of more than 10 years or life imprisonment with a fine more than 50,000 yuan and less than 500,000 yuan or confiscation of property.

Article 193 Whoever, for the purpose of illegal possession, commits any of the following acts to deceive a bank or any other financial institution for loans shall, if the amount involved is relatively large, be sentenced to fixed-term imprisonment of less than five (5) years or criminal detention with a fine of more than 20,000 yuan and less than 200,000 yuan; where the amount involved is large or there are other aggravating circumstances, he/she shall be sentenced to fixed-term imprisonment of more than five (5) years and less than 10 years with a fine of more than 50,000 yuan and less than 500,000 yuan; where the amount involved is particularly large or there are other particularly aggravating circumstances, he/she shall be sentenced to fixed-term imprisonment of more than 10 years or life imprisonment with a fine of more than 50,000 yuan and less than 500,000 yuan or confiscation of property:

(1) fabricating reasons for attracting funds or projects;
(2) using false economic contracts;
(3) using false proof certificates;
(4) using false certificates of property rights as guarantee or providing a duplicate guarantee exceeding the value of the mortgaged property; and
(5) obtaining loans by other fraudulent means.

Article 194 Whoever engages in activities of fraud with financial bills which fall within one of the following categories, shall, if the amount involved is relatively large, be sentenced to fixed-term imprisonment of less than five (5) years or criminal detention with a fine of more than 20,000 yuan and less than 200,000 yuan; where the amount is large or there are other aggravating circumstances, he/she shall be sentenced to fixed-term imprisonment of more than five (5) years and less than 10 years with a fine of more than 50,000 yuan and less than 500,000 yuan; where the amount is particularly large or there are other particularly aggravating circumstances, he/she shall be sentenced to fixed-term imprisonment of more than 10 years or life imprisonment with a fine of more than 50,000 yuan and less than 500,000 yuan or confiscation of property:

(1) knowingly using forged or altered drafts, promissory notes or cheques;
(2) knowingly using invalid drafts, promissory notes or cheques;
(3) using another's drafts, promissory notes or cheques;
(4) signing a bad cheque or a cheque with a seal different from the preserved specimen seal in order to defraud someone of money or property; or
(5) issuing drafts or promissory notes which have no guaranteed funds, or making false records while issuing drafts or promissory notes in order to defraud someone of money and property.

Whoever uses forged and altered documents of authorisation to collect money, documents of remittance, bank deposit receipts or other bank documents of settlement, shall be punished in accordance with the provisions of the preceding Paragraph.

Article 195 Whoever engages in activities of fraud with credit certificates which fall within one of the following categories, shall, if the amount involved is relatively large, be sentenced to fixed-term imprisonment of less than five (5) years or criminal detention, with a fine of more than 20,000 yuan and less than 200,000 yuan; where the amount is large or there are other aggravating circumstances, he/she shall be sentenced to fixed-term imprisonment of more than five (5) years and less than 10 years with a fine of more than 50,000 yuan and less than 500,000 yuan; where the amount is particularly large or there are other particularly aggravating circumstances, he/she shall be sentenced to fixed-term imprisonment of more than 10 years or life imprisonment with a fine of more than 50,000 yuan and less than 500,000 yuan or confiscation of property:

(1) using forged or altered letters of credit or bills and attached documents;
(2) using invalid letters of credit;

(3) fraudulently obtaining letters of credit; or
(4) engaging in fraudulent activities with letters of credit in other ways.

Article 196[65] Whoever engages in activities of fraud with credit cards which fall within one of the following categories shall, if the amount involved is relatively large, be sentenced to fixed-term imprisonment of less than five (5) years or criminal detention with a fine of more than 20,000 yuan and less than 200,000 yuan; where the amount involved is large or there are other aggravating circumstances, he/she shall be sentenced to fixed-term imprisonment of more than five (5) years and less than 10 years with a fine of more than 50,000 yuan and less than 500,000 yuan; where the amount involved is particularly large or there are other particularly aggravating circumstances, he/she shall be sentenced to fixed-term imprisonment of more than 10 years or life imprisonment with a fine more than 50,000 yuan and less than 500,000 yuan or confiscation of property:

(1) using a forged credit card or a credit card obtained with a false identification document;
(2) using an invalid credit card;
(3) using another person's credit card; or
(4) overdrawing with malicious intent.

The term "overdrawing with malicious intent" used in the preceding Paragraph means that the card holder, for the purpose of unlawful possession, overdraws money in excess of the limit of the amount or the time, and refuses to return the money after being ordered to do so by the bank which issued the card.

Whoever steals a credit card and uses it shall be convicted and punished in accordance with the provisions of Article 264 in this law.

Article 197 Whoever uses forged or altered Treasury bonds or other negotiable instruments issued by the State to engage in fraudulent activities shall, if the amount involved is relatively large, be sentenced to fixed-term imprisonment of less than five (5) years or criminal detention with a fine of more than 20,000 yuan and less than 200,000 yuan; where the amount is large or there are other aggravating circumstances, he/she shall be sentenced to fixed-term imprisonment of more than five (5) years and less

---

65 This article was revised on 28 February 2005 by Amendment (V).

than 10 years with a fine of more than 50,000 yuan and less than 500,000 yuan; where the amount is particularly large or there are other particularly aggravating circumstances, he/she shall be sentenced to fixed-term imprisonment of more than 10 years or life imprisonment with a fine of more than 50,000 yuan and less than 500,000 yuan or confiscation of property.

Article 198 Whoever engages in fraudulent insurance activities which fall within one of the following categories shall, if the amount involved is relatively large, be sentenced to fixed-term imprisonment of less than five (5) years or criminal detention with a fine of more than 10,000 yuan and less than 100,000 yuan; where the amount involved is large or there are other aggravating circumstances, he/she shall be sentenced to fixed-term imprisonment of more than five (5) years and less than 10 years with a fine of more than 20,000 yuan and less than 200,000 yuan; where the amount involved is particularly large or there are other particularly aggravating circumstances, he/she shall be sentenced to fixed-term imprisonment of more than 10 years with a fine of more than 20,000 yuan and less than 200,000 yuan or confiscation of property:

(1) a policy holder intentionally fabricating insurance objects to deceitfully claim insurance money;
(2) a policy holder, the insured or the beneficiary fabricating false causes of an insurance incident or inflating the extent of loss to deceitfully claim insurance money;
(3) a policy holder, the insured, or the beneficiary fabricating a non-existing insurance incident to deceitfully claim insurance money;
(4) a policy holder, the insured, or the beneficiary intentionally creating an insurance incident with property loss in order to deceitfully claim insurance money; or
(5) a policy holder or the beneficiary intentionally causing the death, injury, or sickness of the insured in order to deceitfully claim insurance money.

A person whose actions fall into the categories prescribed in (4) and (5) of the preceding Paragraph and whose act also constitutes another crime, shall have a combined punishment imposed for all the crimes committed.

A unit committing a crime prescribed in the first Paragraph shall be punished with a fine, and the directly responsible person(s)-in-charge and any other directly responsible person(s) shall be sentenced to fixed-term imprisonment of less than five (5) years or criminal detention; where the amount involved is large or there are other aggravating circumstances, he/she shall be sentenced to fixed-term imprisonment of more than five (5) years and less than 10 years; where the amount involved is particularly large or there are other particularly aggravating circumstances, they shall be sentenced to fixed-term imprisonment of more than 10 years.

An appraiser, assessor or property valuator, who intentionally provides false certificates and provides conditions for another person to commit fraud, shall be punished as an accomplice in the crime of insurance fraud.

Article 199[66] Whoever commits crimes prescribed in Article 192 of this Section, involving a particularly large amount of money and causing particularly serious losses to the State and the people, shall be sentenced to life imprisonment or death with confiscation of property.

Article 200[67] A unit committing crimes prescribed in Articles 192, 194, and 195 of this Section shall be punished with a fine, and the directly responsible person(s)-in-charge and any other directly responsible person(s) shall be sentenced to fixed-term imprisonment of less than five years or criminal detention, and may also be imposed a fine concurrently; where the amount involved is large or there are other aggravating circumstances, they shall be sentenced to fixed-term imprisonment of more than five (5) years and less than 10 years with a fine; where the amount involved is particularly large or there are other particularly aggravating circumstances, they shall be sentenced to fixed-term imprisonment of more than 10 years or life imprisonment with a fine.

Section 6 Crimes of Disrupting the Administration of Tax Collection

Article 201[68] A taxpayer who submits false tax returns by using such means as cheating and concealing or does not submit tax returns, shall, where the amount of tax evaded is relatively large and in excess of 10 per cent of the tax payable, be sentenced to fixed-term imprisonment of less than three (3) years or criminal detention with a fine; where the amount of tax evaded is large and in excess 30 per cent of the tax payable, he/she shall be sentenced to fixed-term imprisonment of more than three (3) years and less than seven (7) years with a fine.

---

66 This article was revised on 25 February 2011 by Amendment (VIII).
67 This article was revised on 25 February 2011 by Amendment (VIII).
68 This article was revised on 28 February 2009 by Amendment (V).

A tax withholding agent who fails to pay or who underpays the tax which he/she has withheld or collected by means prescribed in the preceding Paragraph shall, if the amount involved is relatively large, be punished in accordance with the provisions in the preceding Paragraph.

Whoever has repeatedly committed the acts prescribed in the preceding two Paragraphs without being punished shall be punished on the basis of the accumulated amount of tax evaded.

A taxpayer who commits the acts prescribed in the first Paragraph and has, after being notified by the taxation authority in accordance with the law, paid the tax in arrears and the surcharge for late payment and has received administrative punishment, will not be investigated for criminal responsibility, except where he/she has, in the past five (5) years, had imposed a criminal penalty for tax evasion or twice been subject to administrative sanctions imposed by tax authorities for tax evasion.

Article 202 Whoever refuses to pay tax by means of violence or threat shall be sentenced to fixed-term imprisonment of less than three (3) years or criminal detention, with a fine of more than 100 per cent but less than 500 per cent of the amount of unpaid tax; where the circumstances are serious, he/she shall be sentenced to fixed-term imprisonment of more than three (3) years and less than seven (7) years with a fine of more than 100 per cent and less than 500 per cent of the amount of unpaid tax.

Article 203 A taxpayer who fails to pay payable tax in time and uses means of transferring or concealing his/her assets to make the tax authority unable to recover the tax in arrears shall, where the amount involved is more than 10,000 yuan but less than 100,000 yuan, be sentenced to fixed-term imprisonment of less than three (3) years or criminal detention, with a fine of more than 100 per cent but less than 500 per cent of the amount in arrears to be concurrently or independently imposed; where the amount involved exceeds 100,000 yuan, he/she shall be sentenced to fixed-term imprisonment of more than three (3) years and less than seven (7) years, with a fine of more than 100 per cent but less than 500 per cent of the amount in arrears.

Article 204 Whoever makes a false export declaration to fraudulently claim export tax refunds from the State shall, where the amount involved is relatively large, be sentenced to fixed-term imprisonment of less than five (5) years or criminal detention with a fine of more than 100 per cent but less than 500 per cent of the amount of the defrauded tax refunds;

where the amount involved is large or there are other aggravating circumstances, he/she shall be sentenced to fixed-term imprisonment of more than five (5) years and less than 10 years with a fine of more than 100 per cent but less than 500 per cent of the amount of the defrauded tax refunds; where the amount involved is particularly large or there are other particularly aggravating circumstances, he/she shall be sentenced to fixed-term imprisonment of more than 10 years or life imprisonment with a fine of more than 100 per cent but less than 500 per cent of the amount of the defrauded tax refunds, or confiscation of property.

A taxpayer who, after having paid the tax, deceptively obtains a tax refund by using the fraudulent means prescribed in preceding Paragraph shall be convicted and punished in accordance with the provisions of Article 201; where the amount of the tax refund deceptively obtained is more than the amount he/she paid, he/she shall be punished according to provisions of the preceding Paragraph.

Article 205[69] Whoever falsely produces special invoices for value-added tax or other invoices for fraudulently claiming export tax refunds or offsetting taxes shall be sentenced to fixed-term imprisonment of less than three (3) years or criminal detention with a fine of more than 20,000 yuan and less than 200,000 yuan; where the amount of the falsely produced claims is relatively large or there are other aggravating circumstances, he/she shall be sentenced to fixed-term imprisonment of more than three (3) years and less than 10 years with a fine of more than 50,000 yuan but less than 500,000 yuan; where the amount of the falsely produced claims is particularly large or there are other particularly aggravating circumstances, he/she shall be sentenced to fixed-term imprisonment of more than 10 years or life imprisonment with a fine of more than 50,000 yuan but less than 500,000 yuan or confiscation of property.

A unit committing crimes prescribed in this Article shall be punished with a fine, and the directly responsible person(s)-in-charge and any other directly responsible person(s) shall be sentenced to fixed-term imprisonment of less than three (3) years or criminal detention; where the amount of the falsely produced claims is relatively large or there are other aggravating circumstances, he/she shall be sentenced to fixed-term imprisonment of more than three (3) years and less than 10 years; where the amount of the falsely produced claims is large or there are other

69 This article was revised on 25 February 2011 by Amendment (VIII).

particularly aggravating circumstances, they shall be sentenced to fixed-term imprisonment of more than 10 years or life imprisonment.

The phrase "falsely producing special invoices for value-added tax invoices or other invoices for defrauding export tax refunds or offsetting taxes" refers to the acts of falsely producing for others or for oneself, or having another to falsely produce for oneself, or introducing another person to falsely produce, the aforesaid invoices.

Article 205(A)[70] Whoever falsely produces invoices other than those prescribed in Article 205 of this Law, shall, where the circumstances are serious, be sentenced to fixed-term imprisonment of less than two (2) years, criminal detention, or control and surveillance, with a fine; where the circumstances are particularly serious, he/she shall be sentenced to fixed-term imprisonment of more than two (2) years and less than seven (7) years, with a fine.

A unit committing crimes prescribed in the preceding Paragraph shall be punished with a fine, and the directly responsible person(s)-in-charge and any other directly responsible person(s) shall be punished in accordance with the provisions of the preceding Paragraph.

Article 206[71] Whoever forges or sells forged special invoices for value-added tax shall be sentenced to fixed-term imprisonment of less than three (3) years, criminal detention, or control and surveillance, with a fine of more than 20,000 yuan but less than 200,000 yuan; where the amount involved is relatively large or there are other aggravating circumstances, he/she shall be sentenced to fixed-term imprisonment of more than three (3) years and less than 10 years, with a fine of more than 50,000 yuan but less than 500,000 yuan; where the amount involved is large or there are other particularly aggravating circumstances, he/she shall be sentenced to fixed-term imprisonment of more than 10 years or life imprisonment, with a fine of more than 50,000 yuan but less than 500,000 yuan, or confiscation of property.

A unit committing crimes prescribed in this Article shall be punished with a fine, and the directly responsible person(s)-in-charge and any other directly responsible person(s) shall be sentenced to fixed-term imprisonment of less than three (3) years, criminal detention, or control

---

70 This article was added on 25 February 2011by Amendment (VIII).

71 This article was revised on 25 February 2011 by Amendment (VIII).

and surveillance; where the amount involved is relatively large or there are other aggravating circumstances, they shall be sentenced to fixed-term imprisonment of more than three (3) years and less than 10 years; where the amount involved is large or there are other particularly aggravating circumstances, they shall be sentenced to fixed-term imprisonment of more than 10 years or life imprisonment.

Article 207 Whoever illegally sells special invoices for value-added tax shall be sentenced to fixed-term imprisonment of less than three (3) years, criminal detention, or control and surveillance, with a fine of more than 20,000 yuan but less than 200,000 yuan; where the amount involved is relatively large, he/she shall be sentenced to fixed-term imprisonment of more than three (3) years and less than 10 years with a fine of more than 50,000 yuan but less than 500,000 yuan; where the amount involved is large, he/she shall be sentenced to fixed-term imprisonment of more than 10 years or life imprisonment with a fine of more than 50,000 yuan but less than 500,000 yuan, or confiscation of property.

Article 208 Whoever illegally purchases special invoices for value-added tax or purchases forged special invoices for value-added tax shall be sentenced to fixed-term imprisonment of less than five (5) years or criminal detention, with a fine of more than 20,000 yuan but less than 200,000 yuan to be concurrently or independently imposed.

Whoever, after illegally purchasing special invoices for value-added tax or purchasing forged special invoices for value-added tax, also produces or sells such invoices, shall be convicted and punished in accordance with the provisions of Articles 205, 206, and 207 of this Law.

Article 209 Whoever forges, produces without authority or sells forged or illegally produced invoices of other kinds which may be used to deceitfully claim export tax refunds or offset taxes, shall be sentenced to fixed-term imprisonment of less than three (3) years, criminal detention, or control and surveillance, with a fine of more than 20,000 yuan but less than 200,000 yuan; where the amount involved is large, he/she shall be sentenced to fixed-term imprisonment of more than three (3) years and less than seven (7) years, with a fine of more than 50,000 yuan but less than 500,000 yuan; where the amount involved is particularly large, he/she shall be sentenced to fixed-term imprisonment of more than seven (7) years, with a fine of more than 50,000 yuan but less than 500,000 yuan or confiscation of property.

Whoever forges or produces invoices without authority, or sells forged or illegally produced invoices other than those prescribed in the preceding Paragraph, shall be sentenced to fixed-term imprisonment of less than two (2) years, criminal detention, or control and surveillance, with a fine of more than 10,000 yuan but less than 50,000 yuan; where the circumstances are serious, he/she shall be sentenced to fixed-term imprisonment of more than two (2) years and less than seven (7) years, with a fine of more than 50,000 yuan but less than 500,000 yuan.

Whoever illegally sells other types of invoices which may be used to deceitfully claim export tax refunds or offset taxes shall be punished in accordance with the provisions of the first Paragraph.

Whoever illegally sells invoices other than those prescribed in the third Paragraphs shall be punished in accordance with the provisions of the second Paragraph.

Article 210 Whoever steals special invoices for value-added tax or other types of invoices that may be used for deceitfully claiming export tax refunds or offsetting taxes, shall be convicted and punished in accordance with the provisions of Article 264 of this Law.

Whoever uses other methods to deceitfully obtain special invoices for value-added tax or other types of invoices that may be used for deceitfully claiming export tax refunds or offsetting taxes, shall be convicted and punished in accordance with the provisions of Article 266 of this Law.

Article 210(A)[72] Whoever knowingly possesses forged invoices shall, where the amount involved is relatively large, be sentenced to fixed-term imprisonment of less than two (2) years, criminal detention, or control and surveillance, with a fine; where the amount involved is large, he/she shall be sentenced to fixed-term imprisonment of more than two (2) years and less than seven (7) years, with a fine.

A unit committing crimes prescribed in the preceding Paragraph shall be punished with a fine, and the directly responsible person(s)-in-charge and any other directly responsible person(s) shall be punished in accordance with the provisions of the preceding Paragraph.

[72] This article was added on 25 February 2011 by Amendment (VIII).

Article 211 A unit committing crimes prescribed in Articles 201, 203, 204, 207, 208, and 209 of this Section shall be punished with a fine, and the directly responsible person(s)-in-charge and any other directly responsible person(s) shall be punished in accordance with the respective provisions of these articles.

Article 212 Where an offender is fined or sentenced to confiscation of property for a crime prescribed in Articles 201 to 205, the sentence may only be enforced after the taxation authority has recovered the payable tax and the fraudulently obtained export tax refunds.

Section 7 Crime of Infringing Upon Intellectual Property Rights

Article 213 Whoever, without permission of the owner of a registered trade mark, uses a trademark identical to the registered trade mark for the same type of commodity shall, where the circumstances are serious, be sentenced to fixed-term imprisonment of less than three (3) years or criminal detention, with a fine to be concurrently or independently imposed; where the circumstances are particularly serious, he/she shall be sentenced to fixed-term imprisonment of more than (3) years and less than seven (7) years with a fine.

Article 214 Whoever knowingly sells commodities with a faked trademark shall, where the sales volume involved is relatively large, be sentenced to fixed-term imprisonment of less than three (3) years or criminal detention, with a fine to be imposed concurrently or independently; where the sales volume involved is large, he/she shall be sentenced to fixed-term imprisonment of more than (3) years and less than seven (7) years with a fine.

Article 215 Whoever forges or produces the symbols of a registered trademark of another person without authorisation or sells forged or illegally produced symbols of another person's registered trademark shall, where the circumstances are serious, be sentenced to fixed-term imprisonment of less than three (3) years, criminal detention, or control and surveillance, with a fine to be concurrently or independently imposed; where the circumstances are particularly serious, he/she shall be sentenced to fixed-term imprisonment of more than three (3) years and less than seven (7) years with a fine.

Article 216 Whoever counterfeits another person's patent shall, where the circumstances are serious, be sentenced to fixed-term imprisonment of less than three (3) years or criminal detention, with a fine to be imposed concurrently or independently.

Article 217 Whoever, for the purpose of making a profit, commits one of the following acts of infringement of copyright shall, where the amount of profit illegally obtained is relatively large or there are other serious circumstances, be sentenced to fixed-term imprisonment of less than three (3) years or criminal detention, with a fine to be concurrently or independently imposed; where the amount of profit illegally obtained is large or there are other particularly serious circumstances, he/she shall be sentenced to fixed-term imprisonment of more than three (3) years and less than seven (7) years, with a fine:

(1) copying and distributing without the permission of the owner of the copyright the written works, musical works, film, television or video works, computer software or other works of the owner;
(2) publishing a book of which the copyright is exclusively owned by another;
(3) duplicating and distributing audio-visual works without the permission of the author of the audio or video works;
(4) producing and selling a work of fine art which is marked with the forged signature of another.

Article 218 Whoever, for the purpose of making a profit, knowingly sells duplicated works which infringe upon the owner's copyright as described in Article 217 of this Law shall, where the amount illegally obtained is large, be sentenced to fixed-term imprisonment of less than three (3) years or criminal detention, with a fine to be concurrently or independently imposed.

Article 219 Whoever commits one of the following acts which infringes upon commercial secrets and results in major losses to the rightful owner of the commercial secrets, shall be sentenced to fixed-term imprisonment of less than three (3) years or criminal detention, with a fine to be concurrently or independently imposed; where particularly serious consequences result, he/she shall be sentenced to fixed-term imprisonment of more than three (3) years and less than seven (7) years, with a fine:

(1) obtaining commercial secrets from the rightful owner by stealing, inducing, threatening or other improper means;
(2) disclosing, using, or allowing another person to use the commercial secrets of a rightful owner which are obtained through the means mentioned in Item (1) above; or

(3) disclosing, using, or allowing another person to use the commercial secrets he/she holds, in violation of the agreement or of the requests of the rightful owner to keep the commercial secrets confidential.

Whoever obtains, uses or discloses another's commercial secrets shall, if he/she knows or should have known that these commercial secrets have been acquired through the aforementioned means, be regarded as an offender infringing upon commercial secrets.

The commercial secrets mentioned in this Article refer to technical and business information which is unknown to the public, which is able to bring economic profit to the rightful owner, is of practical use and for which the rightful owner has adopted measures to keep their confidentiality.

A rightful owner mentioned in this Article refers to the owner of a commercial secret or a user who obtains the permission of the owner to use the commercial secret.

Article 220 A unit committing the crimes prescribed in Articles 213 to 219 shall be sentenced to a fine, and the directly responsible person(s)-in-charge and other direct responsible person(s) shall be punished in accordance with the provisions of the respective articles in this Section.

Section 8 Crimes of Disrupting the Market Order

Article 221 Whoever fabricates and spreads false stories to damage another person's commercial reputation and commodity reputation shall, where the circumstances are serious or serious losses result, be sentenced to fixed-term imprisonment of less than two (2) years or criminal detention, with a fine to be concurrently or independently imposed.

Article 222 An advertiser, advertising agent or advertising issuer who, in violation of provisions of the State, makes false claims for commodities or services by means of advertisements shall, where the circumstances are serious, be sentenced to fixed-term imprisonment of less than two (2) years or criminal detention, with a fine to be concurrently or independently imposed.

Article 223 A bidder who colludes with other bidders in the submission of tenders and the offer of bidding prices, thereby harming the interests of the tender inviters or other bidders, shall, where the circumstances are serious, be sentenced to fixed-term imprisonment of less than three (3) years or criminal detention, with a fine to be concurrently or independently imposed.

Where a bidder and inviter of tenders collude with each other in the tendering and thus harm the legitimate interests of the State, collectives and citizens, they shall be punished in accordance with the provisions of the preceding Paragraph.

Article 224 Whoever, in the course of concluding and performing a contract, defrauds the other party of money or property for the purpose of unlawful possession by using one of the following means shall, where the amount involved is relatively large, be sentenced to fixed-term imprisonment of less than three (3) years or criminal detention, with a fine to be concurrently or independently imposed; where the amount involved is large or the circumstances are serious, he/she shall be sentenced to fixed-term imprisonment of more than three (3) and less than 10 years, with a fine; where the amount involved is particularly large or the circumstances are particularly serious, he/she shall be sentenced to fixed-term imprisonment of more than 10 years or life imprisonment, with a fine to be concurrently imposed, or confiscation of property:

(1) signing a contract in the name of a fictitious unit or in the name of another person;
(2) using forged, altered or invalid negotiable instruments or other false certificates of property title as guarantees;
(3) having no ability to actually perform a contract but inducing the other party to continue to enter into and perform the contract by first performing small contracts or performing part of the contract;
(4) fleeing into hiding after receiving from the other party goods, payment for goods, advanced payment, or property for guarantee;
(5) defrauding the other party of property by other means.

Article 224(A)[73] Whoever, for purposes of deceitfully obtaining funds and property and thereby disrupting economic and social order, organises or leads pyramid sale activities in the name of the marketing and provision of services, which require the payment of a fee or purchasing of commodities or services, etc. in order to be qualified as a participant, and in which participants are organised under pyramid levels according to certain orders and their rewards or share of profits are based on the number of new members they have directly or indirectly attracted, thereby to induce or coerce participants to attract other members, shall be sentenced to fixed-term imprisonment of less than five (5) years or criminal detention,

[73] This article was added on 28 February 2009 by Amendment (VII).

with a fine; where the circumstances are serious, he/she shall be sentenced to fixed-term imprisonment of more than five (5) years, with a fine.

Article 225[74] Whoever, in violation of the provisions of the State, engages in one of the following acts of illegal operation thereby disrupting the market order shall, where the circumstances are serious, be sentenced to fixed-term imprisonment of less than five (5) years or criminal detention, with a fine of more than 100 per cent and less than 500 per cent of the income illegally obtained, to be concurrently or independently imposed; where the circumstances are particularly serious, he/she shall be sentenced to fixed-term imprisonment of more than five (5) years, with a fine of more than 100 per cent and less than 500 per cent of the income illegally obtained, or confiscation of property:

(1) operating without permission a business engaging in trade of goods which, as stipulated by laws and administrative regulations, are under monopolised operation or for monopolised selling, or engaging in trade of other goods of which the buying and selling is restricted;
(2) purchasing or selling import-export licenses, certificates of origin, or other business operation permits and approval documents required by laws and administrative regulations;
(3) illegally operating securities, futures or insurance businesses without the approval of the competent departments of the State, or illegally engaging in business of fund-payment settlement;
(4) engaging in other illegal business activities that seriously disrupt the market order.

Article 226[75] Whoever commits one of the following acts by means of violence or coercion, shall, where the circumstances are serious, be sentenced to fixed-term imprisonment of less than three (3) years or criminal detention, with a fine to be concurrently or independently imposed, where the circumstances are particularly serious, he/she shall be sentenced to fixed-term imprisonment of more than three (3) years and less than seven (7) years, with a fine:

(1) buying or selling commodities by means of violence or coercion;
(2) forcing another person to provide or to accept services;

[74] This article was first revised on 25 December 1999 by Amendment (I), and again on 28 February 2009 by Amendment (VII).

[75] This article was a revised on 25 February 2011 by Amendment (VIII).

(3) forcing another person to participate in or withdraw from a bidding or auction;
(4) forcing another person to transfer or to buy shares, bonds or other assets of a company or enterprise; or
(5) forcing another person to participate in or withdraw from certain specific operational activities.

Article 227 Whoever forges or re-sells for profit counterfeit land and water transport tickets, stamps or other valuable coupons shall, where the amount involved is relatively large, be sentenced to fixed-term imprisonment of less than two (2) years, criminal detention, or control and surveillance, with a fine of more than 100 per cent and less than 500 per cent of the price of the tickets or coupons to be concurrently or independently imposed; where the amount involved is large, he/she shall be sentenced to fixed-term imprisonment of more than two (2) years and less than seven (7) years, with a fine of more than 100 per cent and less than 500 per cent of the price of the tickets or coupons.

Whoever sells for profit land and water transport tickets shall, where the circumstances are serious, be sentenced to fixed-term imprisonment of less than three (3) years, criminal detention, or control and surveillance, with a fine of more than 100 per cent and less than 500 per cent of the price of the tickets and coupons to be concurrently or independently imposed.

Article 228 Whoever, in violation of laws and regulations on land management, illegally transfers or resells for profit land use rights shall, where the circumstances are serious, be sentenced to fixed-term imprisonment of less than three (3) years or criminal detention, with a fine of more than five per cent and less than 20 per cent of the money illegally obtained from the transferring or reselling of the land use rights to be concurrently or independently imposed; where the circumstances are particularly serious, he/she shall be sentenced to fixed-term imprisonment of more than three (3) years and less than seven (7) years, with a fine of more than five per cent and less than 20 per cent of the money illegally obtained from the transferring or reselling of the land use rights.

Article 229 A staff member of an intermediary organisation, who is responsible for asset assessment, capital verification, certificate verification, accounting, auditing, legal services or other tasks, and who intentionally provides false certificates shall, where the circumstances are serious, be sentenced to fixed-term imprisonment of less than five (5) years or criminal detention, with a fine.

Where a person described in the preceding Paragraph demands money and goods from others or illegally accepts money and goods from others, which constitutes a crime prescribed in the preceding Paragraph, he/she shall be sentenced to fixed-term imprisonment of more than five (5) years and less than 10 years, with a fine.

Where a person described in the first Paragraph produces certificates which are seriously inconsistent with the facts due to gross neglect of his/her duty, he/she shall, where serious consequences result, be sentenced to fixed-term imprisonment of less than three (3) years or criminal detention, with a fine to be concurrently or independently imposed.

Article 230 Whoever, in violation of the provisions of laws on import-export commodity inspection, evades commodity inspection and sells or uses without authorisation imported goods which are subject to inspection by the commodity inspection organ, but which have not been declared to such organ for inspection, or exports without authorisation goods which are subject to inspection by the commodity inspection organ but which have not passed the inspection, shall, where the circumstances are serious, be sentenced to fixed-term imprisonment of less than three (3) years or criminal detention, with a fine to be concurrently or independently imposed.

Article 231 A unit committing the crimes prescribed in Articles 221 to 230 of this Section shall be punished with a fine and the directly responsible person(s)-in-charge and any other directly responsible person(s) shall be punished in accordance with the respective provisions in these articles.

Chapter IV

Crimes of Infringing Upon the Personal Rights and the Democratic Rights of Citizens

Article 232 Whoever intentionally kills another person shall be sentenced to death, life imprisonment or fixed-term imprisonment of more than 10 years; where the circumstances are relatively minor, he/she shall be sentenced to fixed-term imprisonment of more than three (3) years and less than 10 years.

Article 233 Whoever negligently causes the death of another person shall be sentenced to fixed-term imprisonment of more than three (3) years and less than seven (7) years; where the circumstances are relatively minor, he/she shall be sentenced to fixed-term imprisonment of less than three (3) years. Where provisions in this Law provide otherwise, those provisions shall apply.

Article 234 Whoever intentionally inflicts bodily harm on another person shall be sentenced to fixed-term imprisonment of less than three (3) years, criminal detention, or control and surveillance.

Whoever commits the crime prescribed in the preceding Paragraph and causes serious injury to the other person shall be sentenced to fixed-term imprisonment of more than three (3) years and less than 10 years; if he/she causes the death of the person, or resorts to extremely brutal means to inflict grave bodily harm to the person, thus resulting in the person's disability, he/she shall be sentenced to fixed-term imprisonment of more than 10 years, life imprisonment or death. Where provisions in this Law provide otherwise, those provisions shall apply.

Article 234(A)[76] Whoever organises another person to sell human organs shall be sentenced to fixed-term imprisonment of less than five (5) years, with a fine; where the circumstances are serious, he/she shall be sentenced to fixed-term imprisonment of more than five (5) years, with a fine or confiscation of property.

Whoever harvests a person's organ without his/her consent or harvests the organ of a person under the age of 18, or forces or cheats a person to donate his/her organ, shall be punished in accordance with provisions of Articles 234 and 232 of this Law.

Whoever harvests an organ from a deceased person against that person's will expressed when he/she was alive, or harvests an organ from a deceased person in violation of the provisions of the State and against the will of the close relatives of that deceased person, shall be punished in accordance with the provisions of Article 302 of this Law.

Article 235 Whoever negligently injures another person and causes serious injury to that person shall be sentenced to fixed-term imprisonment

[76] This article was added on 25 February 2011 by Amendment (VIII).

of less than three (3) years or criminal detention. Where provisions of this Law provide otherwise, those provisions shall apply.

Article 236 Whoever rapes a woman by violence, coercion or other means shall be sentenced to fixed-term imprisonment of more than three (3) years and less than 10 years.

Whoever has sexual intercourse with an under-aged girl shall be deemed to have committed a rape and have a heavier punishment imposed.

Whoever rapes a woman or has sexual intercourse with a girl under the age of 14 in one of the following circumstances, shall be sentenced to fixed-term imprisonment of more than 10 years, life imprisonment, or death:

(1) raping a woman or having sexual intercourse with an under-aged girl, where the circumstances are odious;
(2) raping several women or having sexual intercourse with several under-aged girls;
(3) raping a woman in a public place and in front of the public;
(4) the raping of a woman by two or more persons in turn;
(5) causing serious injury or death to the victim or causing other serious consequences.

Article 237 Whoever indecently insults or humiliates a woman by violence, coercion or other means shall be sentenced to fixed-term imprisonment of less than five (5) years or criminal detention.

Whoever gathers a crowd to commit the crime prescribed in the preceding Paragraph or who commits the crime in a public place and in front of the public shall be sentenced to fixed-term imprisonment of more than five (5) years.

Whoever indecently assaults a child shall have a heavier punishment imposed in accordance with the provisions of the two preceding Paragraphs.

Article 238 Whoever unlawfully detains a person or deprives the person of his/her personal freedom by other means shall be sentenced to fixed-term imprisonment of less than three (3) years, criminal detention, control and surveillance, or deprivation of political rights. Where battery or humiliation is involved, a heavier punishment shall be imposed.

Whoever commits a crime prescribed in the preceding Paragraph and causes serious injury to another person shall be sentenced to fixed-term imprisonment of more than three (3) years and less than 10 years; where he/she causes the death of another person, he/she shall be sentenced to fixed-term imprisonment of more than 10 years; where violence is used to cause another person's disability or death, he/she shall be convicted and punished in accordance with the provisions in Articles 234 and 232 of this Law.

Whoever unlawfully imprisons or detains a person in order to demand the payment of a debt shall be sentenced in accordance with the provisions of the two preceding Paragraphs.

A state functionary, taking advantage of his/her office, who commits the crimes prescribed in the preceding three Paragraphs, shall have a heavier punishment imposed in accordance with the provisions of the three preceding Paragraphs.

Article 239[77] Whoever kidnaps a person for the purpose of extorting money or kidnaps a person as a hostage shall be sentenced to fixed-term imprisonment of more than 10 years or life imprisonment, with a fine or confiscation of property; where the circumstances are relatively minor, he/she shall be sentenced to fixed-term imprisonment of more than five (5) and less than 10 years, with a fine.

Whoever commits a crime prescribed in the preceding Paragraph and causes the death of the person kidnapped or kills the person kidnapped, shall be sentenced to death with confiscation of property.

Whoever steals an infant or a baby for the purpose of extorting money shall be punished in accordance with the provisions of the preceding two Paragraphs.

Article 240 Whoever abducts and traffics in a woman or child shall be sentenced to fixed-term imprisonment of more than five (5) years and less than 10 years, with a fine; where the act falls within one of the following categories, he/she shall be sentenced to fixed-term imprisonment of more than 10 years or life imprisonment with a fine or confiscation of property; where the circumstances are particularly serious, he/she shall be sentenced to death with confiscation of property:

---

[77] This article revised on 28 February 2009 by Amendment (VII).

(1) being a ringleader of a gang engaging in abducting and trafficking in women and children;
(2) abducting and trafficking in more than three women and/or children;
(3) raping an abducted woman;
(4) seducing or forcing an abducted woman to engage in prostitution, or selling an abducted woman to another person so as to force her to engage in prostitution;
(5) kidnapping a woman or child by means of violence, coercion or anaesthesia for the purpose of selling them;
(6) stealing an infant or a baby for the purpose of selling it;
(7) causing death or serious injury to an abducted woman or child or his/her family members, or causing other grave consequences;
(8) selling women or children overseas.

The term "abducting and trafficking in a woman or child" refers to any one of the acts of abducting, kidnapping, buying, selling, picking up and sending away, or transferring a woman or child, for the purpose of selling them.

Article 241 Whoever buys an abducted woman or child shall be sentenced to fixed-term imprisonment of less than three (3) years, criminal detention, or control and surveillance.

Whoever buys an abducted woman and has sexual intercourse with her by force shall be convicted and punished in accordance with the provisions of Article 236.

Whoever buys an abducted woman or child and illegally deprives her/it of personal freedom or restricts her/its personal freedom, or inflicts bodily harm on her/it or insults her/it, shall be convicted and punished in accordance with the relevant provisions of this Law.

Whoever buys an abducted woman or child and commits the crimes prescribed in Paragraphs (2) and (3) of this Article shall be punished in accordance with the provisions on combined punishment for multiple crimes.

Whoever buys and then sells an abducted woman or child shall be convicted and punished in accordance with the provisions of Article 240 of this law.

A person who buys an abducted woman or child but does not obstruct the woman bought from returning to her original residence as she wishes, or does not abuse the child bought and does not obstruct a rescuer's actions, may be exempted from criminal liability.

Article 242 Whoever uses means of violence and coercion to obstruct state functionaries from rescuing a sold women or child shall be convicted and punished in accordance with the provisions of Article 277 of this law.

A ringleader who gathers a crowd to obstruct state functionaries from rescuing a sold women or child shall be sentenced to fixed-term imprisonment of less than five (5) years or criminal detention. Other participants who use means of violence or coercion in the perpetrating of the offence shall be punished in accordance with the provisions in the preceding Paragraph.

Article 243 Whoever fabricates stories to frame another person in order to have him/her become subject to criminal investigation shall, where the circumstances are serious, be sentenced to fixed-term imprisonment of less than three (3) years, criminal detention, or control and surveillance; where serious consequences result, he/she shall be sentenced to fixed-term imprisonment of more than three (3) years and less than 10 years.

A state functionary committing the crimes prescribed in the preceding Paragraph shall have a heavier punishment imposed.

Provisions in the preceding two Paragraphs do not apply to cases where one does not intentionally frame another but accuses another by mistake or makes reports which contain factual mistakes.

Article 244[78] Whoever compels another person to work by means of violence, coercion or restriction of personal freedom, shall be sentenced to fixed-term imprisonment of less than three (3) years or criminal detention, with a fine; where the circumstances are serious, he/she shall be sentenced to fixed-term imprisonment of more than three (3) years and less than 10 years with a fine.

Whoever knowingly recruits or transports labourers for a person who commits the crime prescribed in the preceding Paragraph, or provides other assistances to a person in compelling other persons to work, shall be punished in accordance with the provisions of preceding Paragraph.

---

[78] This article was revised on 25 February 2011 by Amendment (VIII).

A unit committing a crime prescribed in the preceding two Paragraphs, shall be punished with a fine, and the directly responsible person(s)-in-charge and any other directly responsible person(s) shall be punished in accordance with the provisions of the first Paragraph.

Article 244(A)[79] When employing, in violation of labour management regulations, a minor under the age of 16 to conduct extreme physically demanding work or to engage in high-altitude or underground mining work, or to work with explosive, flammable, radioactive or poisonous materials or under other dangerous conditions, the directly responsible person(s) shall, where the circumstances are serious, be sentenced to fixed-term imprisonment of less than three (3) years or criminal detention, with a fine; where the circumstances are particularly serious, he/she shall be sentenced to fixed-term imprisonment of more than three (3) years and less than seven (7) years with a fine.

Whoever commits the above crime and thereby causes accidents, which constitute another crime, shall be punished in accordance with the provisions on combined punishment for multiple crimes.

Article 245 Whoever illegally searches another person's body or residence, or illegally intrudes into another person's residence, shall be sentenced to fixed-term imprisonment of less than three (3) years or criminal detention.

A judicial official committing the crimes prescribed in the preceding Paragraph by abusing his/her office shall have a heavier punishment imposed.

Article 246 Whoever humiliates another person in public by such means as violence, or fabricates stories to defame another person shall, where the circumstances are serious, be sentenced to fixed-term imprisonment of less than three (3) years, criminal detention, control and surveillance, or deprivation of political rights.

A crime prescribed in the preceding Paragraph may only be handled upon a complaint, except where it seriously undermines the social order or the interests of the State.

Article 247 A judicial official who extorts a confession from a criminal suspect or defendant by torture, or extorts testimony from a witness by force,

---

[79] This article was added on 28 December 2002 by Amendment (IV).

shall be sentenced to fixed-term imprisonment of less than three (3) years or criminal detention; where another person's injury, disability or death are caused, he/she shall be convicted and have a heavier penalty imposed in accordance with the provisions of Articles 234 and 232 of this Law.

Article 248 A staff member of a prison, criminal detention centre, custody centre or other supervisory and administration organ who beats or abuses by violence a prisoner or detainee shall, where the circumstances are serious, be sentenced to fixed-term imprisonment of less than three (3) years or criminal detention; where the circumstances are particularly serious, he/she shall be sentenced to fixed-term imprisonment of more than three (3) years and less than 10 years; where another person's injury, disability or death are caused, he/she shall be convicted and have a heavier penalty imposed in accordance with the provisions of Articles 234 and 232 of this Law.

A staff member of supervisory and administration personnel who orders one prisoner or detainee to beat or abuse by violence another prisoner or detainee shall be punished in accordance with the provisions of the preceding Paragraph.

Article 249 Whoever incites ethnic hatred or discrimination shall, where the circumstances are serious, be sentenced to fixed-term imprisonment of less than three (3) years, criminal detention, control and surveillance, or deprivation of political rights; where the circumstances are particularly serious, he/she shall be sentenced to fixed-term imprisonment of more than three (3) years and less than ten (10) years.

Article 250 Where a publication contains materials that discriminate or insult minority nationalities, if the circumstances are odious and the consequences are serious, the directly responsible person(s) shall be sentenced to fixed-term imprisonment of less than three (3) years, criminal detention, or control and surveillance.

Article 251 A state functionary who illegally deprives a citizen of freedom of religion or infringes upon the customs and ways of life of minority nationalities shall, where the circumstances are serious, be sentenced to fixed-term imprisonment of less than two (2) years or criminal detention.

Article 252 Whoever hides, destroys or unlawfully opens another person's letters thereby infringing upon a citizen's right to freedom of communication shall, where the circumstances are serious, be sentenced to fixed-term imprisonment of less than one year or criminal detention.

Article 253 An employee of a postal office who opens, hides or destroys mail or telegrams without authorisation shall be sentenced to fixed-term imprisonment of less than two (2) years or criminal detention.

Where an employee of a postal office steals money or articles while committing the crime prescribed in the preceding Paragraph, he/she shall be convicted and have a heavier punishment imposed in accordance with the provisions of Article 264 of this law.

Article 253(A)[80] A staff member of a State organ or a unit in such sectors as finance, telecommunication, transportation, education, and medical care, who, in violation of the provisions of the State, sells to or unlawfully provides for another person a citizen's personal information which he/she obtains in the course of performing his/her functions or providing services for his/her work unit, shall, where the circumstances are serious, be sentenced to fixed-term imprisonment of less than three (3) years or criminal detention, with a fine to be concurrently or independently imposed.

Whoever steals or unlawfully obtains the above information by other means shall, where the circumstances are serious, be convicted and sentenced in accordance with the provisions of the preceding Paragraph.

A unit committing crimes prescribed in the preceding two Paragraphs shall be punished with a fine, and the directly responsible person(s)-in-charge and any other directly responsible person(s) shall be punished in accordance with the provisions of the preceding two Paragraphs.

Article 254 A state functionary who abuses his/her position, uses official power to serve his/her own aims, or retaliates against or frames complainants, petitioners, critics or informers, shall be sentenced to fixed-term imprisonment of less than two (2) years or criminal detention; where the circumstances are serious, he/she shall be sentenced to fixed-term imprisonment of more than two (2) years and less than seven (7) years.

Article 255 A leader of a company, enterprise, institution, state agency or organisation who retaliates against accountants or statisticians who perform their duty according to law and resist acts that violate the accounting laws and statistics laws, shall, where the circumstances are odious, be sentenced to fixed-term imprisonment of less than three (3) years or criminal detention.

---

80 This article was added on 28 February 2009 by Amendment (VII).

Article 256 Whoever, in the electing of deputies to the People's Congresses or leaders of State organs at various levels, disrupts the elections or obstructs voters and deputies from freely exercising their right to vote or right to stand for election by such means as violence, threats, deception, bribes, falsifying election documents, falsely reporting ballots, shall, where the circumstances are serious, be sentenced to fixed-term imprisonment of less than three (3) years, criminal detention, or deprivation of political rights.

Article 257 Whoever uses force to interfere with another person's freedom of marriage shall be sentenced to fixed-term imprisonment of less than two (2) years or criminal detention.

Whoever commits the crimes prescribed in the preceding Paragraph and causes the death of the victim shall be sentenced to fixed-term imprisonment of more than two (2) years and less than seven (7) years.

A crime prescribed in the first Paragraph may only be handled upon complaint.

Article 258 Whoever has a spouse and marries again or knowingly marries a person who has a spouse shall be sentenced to fixed-term imprisonment of less than two (2) years or criminal detention.

Article 259 Whoever knowingly cohabits with the spouse of an active serviceperson or knowingly marries the spouse of an active serviceperson, shall be sentenced to fixed-term imprisonment of less than three (3) years or criminal detention.

Whoever, taking advantage of his office or the subordinate relationship, compels the wife of an active serviceperson to have sexual intercourse by means of coercion, shall be convicted and punished in accordance with the provisions of Article 236 of this Law.

Article 260 Whoever abuses his/her family member(s) shall, where the circumstances are serious, be sentenced to fixed-term imprisonment of less than two (2) years, criminal detention, or control and surveillance.

Whoever commits the crimes prescribed in the preceding Paragraph and causes serious injuries or death to the victims shall be sentenced to fixed-term imprisonment of more than two (2) years and less than seven (7) years.

A crime prescribed in the first Paragraph may only be handled upon complaint.

Article 261 Whoever refuses to support a person who is aged, young, ill or with no ability to live independently while he/she is under the obligation to do so, shall, where the circumstances are odious, be sentenced to fixed-term imprisonment of less than five (5) years, criminal detention, or control and surveillance.

Article 262 Whoever abducts a minor under the age of 14 to leave his/her family or guardians shall be sentenced to fixed-term imprisonment of less than five (5) years or criminal detention.

Article 262 (A)[81] Whoever organizes by means of violence or coercion, handicapped or minors under the age of 14 to act as beggars, shall be sentenced to fixed-term imprisonment of less than three (3) years or criminal detention, with a fine; where the circumstances are serious, he/she shall be sentenced to fixed-term imprisonment of more than three (3) years and less than seven (7) years, with a fine.

Article 262 (B)[82] Whoever organises minors to commit theft, deception, robbery, extortion by blackmail or other activities in violation of social order administration, shall be sentenced to fixed-term imprisonment of less than three (3) years or criminal detention, with a fine; where the circumstances are serious, he/she shall be sentenced to fixed-term imprisonment of more than three (3) years and less than seven (7) years, with a fine.

Chapter V

Crimes of Encroaching upon Property

Article 263 Whoever robs public or private property by force, coercion and other means shall be sentenced to fixed-term imprisonment of more than three (3) and less than 10 years, with a fine; where the act falls into one of the following categories he/she shall be sentenced to fixed-term imprisonment of more than 10 years, life imprisonment or death, with a fine or confiscation of property:

---

81 This article was added on 29 June 2006 by Amendment (VI).
82 This article was added on 28 February 2009 by Amendment (VII).

(1) intruding into a house for robbery;
(2) robbing in public conveyances;
(3) robbing a bank or a financial institution of another kind;
(4) committing robbery repeatedly or robbing a large amount of money or property;
(5) committing robbery causing serious injuries to or the death of another person;
(6) committing robbery under the guise of being a serviceperson or police officer;
(7) committing armed robbery;
(8) robbing military supplies, materials for emergency rescue, disaster relief or social welfare.

Article 264[83] Whoever steals a relatively large amount of public or private property or money, or commits theft repeatedly, or commits breaking-in theft or armed theft or pocket-picking, shall be sentenced to fixed-term imprisonment of less than three (3) years, criminal detention, or control and surveillance, with a fine to be concurrently or independently imposed; where the amount involved is large or the circumstances are serious, he/she shall be sentenced to fixed-term imprisonment of more than three (3) years and less than 10 years, with a fine; where the amount involved is particularly large or the circumstances are particularly serious, he/she shall be sentenced to fixed-term imprisonment of more than 10 years or life imprisonment, with a fine or confiscation of property.

Article 265 Whoever, for the purpose of making a profit, penetrates another person's communication lines without that person's knowledge, or duplicates another person's telecommunication codes, or knowingly uses stolen or duplicated telecommunication equipment or facilities, shall be convicted and punished in accordance with the provisions of Article 264 in this Law.

Article 266 Whoever fraudulently obtains public or private property of a relatively large amount shall be sentenced to fixed-term imprisonment of less than three (3) years, criminal detention, or control and surveillance, with a fine to be concurrently or independently imposed; where the amount involved is large or the circumstances are serious, he/she shall be sentenced to fixed-term imprisonment of more than three (3) years

83 This article was revised on 25 February 2011 by Amendment (VIII).

and less than 10 years, with a fine; where the amount involved is particularly large or the circumstances are particularly serious, he/she shall be sentenced to fixed-term imprisonment of more than 10 years or life imprisonment, with a fine or confiscation of property. Where provisions in this Law provide otherwise, those provisions apply.

Article 267 Whoever seizes by force public or private property of a relatively large amount shall be sentenced to fixed-term imprisonment of less than three (3) years, criminal detention, or control and surveillance, with a fine to be concurrently or independently imposed; where the amount involved is large or the circumstances are serious, he/she shall be sentenced to fixed-term imprisonment of more than three (3) years and less than 10 years, with a fine; where the amount involved is particularly large or the circumstances are particularly grave, he/she shall be sentenced to fixed-term imprisonment of more than 10 years or life imprisonment, with a fine or confiscation of property.

Whoever commits armed seizure shall be convicted and punished in accordance with the provisions of Article 263 in this Law.

Article 268 In cases where a crowd is gathered to seize by force public or private property, the ringleader and the active participants shall, where the amount involved is relatively large or the circumstances are serious, be sentenced to fixed-term imprisonment of less than three (3) years, criminal detention, or control and surveillance, with a fine; where the amount involved is large or the circumstances are particularly grave, they shall be sentenced to fixed-term imprisonment of more than three (3) years and less than 10 years, with a fine.

Article 269 Whoever commits crimes of theft, fraud or seizure by force and, in order to conceal booty, resists arrest or destroys criminal evidence, uses outright violence or threats to use violence, shall be convicted and punished in accordance with the provisions of Article 263 in this Law.

Article 270 Whoever illegally takes possession of another person's property under his/her custody and refuses to return it shall, where the amount involved is relatively large, be sentenced to fixed-term imprisonment of less than two (2) years, criminal detention, or a fine; where the amount involved is large and the circumstances are serious, he/she shall be sentenced to fixed-term imprisonment of more than two (2) years and less than five (5) years, with a fine.

Whoever illegally takes possession of the property of another person which has been left behind or buried and refuses to return it shall, where the amount involved is relatively large, be punished according to the provisions of the preceding Paragraph.

The crimes prescribed in this Article may only be handled upon complaint.

Article 271 A staff member of a company, enterprise or unit, who, taking advantage of his/her position, illegally takes the property of his/her unit into his/her own possession shall, where the amount involved in relatively large, be sentenced to fixed-term imprisonment of less than five (5) years or criminal detention; where the amount involved is large, he/she shall be sentenced to fixed-term imprisonment of more than five (5) years, and may also in addition be sentenced to confiscation of property.

A staff member responsible for public duty in a state-owned company, enterprise or unit, or a person assigned by a state-owned company, enterprise or unit to a non-state-owned company, enterprise or unit to perform public duty, who commits the crime prescribed in the preceding Paragraph shall be convicted and punished in accordance with the provisions of Articles 382 and 383 of this Law.

Article 272 A staff member of a company, enterprise or unit, who, taking advantage of his/her position, misappropriates the unit's funds for his/her own use or lends them to another person shall, if the amount involved is relatively large and the money is not repaid to the unit within three (3) months, or if the money is repaid to the unit within three (3) months but the amount involved is relatively large and used for profit-making or unlawful activities, be sentenced to fixed-term imprisonment of less than three (3) years or criminal detention; if the amount of money misappropriated from the unit is large or is relatively large but the staff member fails to repay it, he/she shall be sentenced to fixed-term imprisonment of more than three (3) years but less than 10 years.

A staff member responsible for public duty in a state-owned company, enterprise or unit, or a person assigned by a state-owned company, enterprise or unit to a non-state-owned company, enterprise or unit to perform public duty, who commits the crime prescribed in the preceding Paragraph shall be convicted and punished in accordance with the provisions of Article 384 of this Law.

Article 273 Where funds and goods for disaster relief, emergency rescue, flood prevention and control, assisting disabled servicepersons and the families of revolutionary martyrs and servicepersons, poverty relief, migrant resettlement and social welfare, are misappropriated, the directly responsible person(s) shall, where the circumstances are serious and the interests of the State and the people have been seriously harmed, be sentenced to fixed-termed imprisonment of less than three (3) years or criminal detention; where the circumstances are particularly serious, he/she/they shall be sentenced to fixed-termed imprisonment of more than three (3) years but less than seven (7) years.

Article 274[84] Whoever extorts public or private property by blackmail shall, where the amount involved is relative large or he/she has committed such a crime repeatedly, be sentenced to fixed-termed imprisonment of less than three (3) years, criminal detention, or control and surveillance, with a fine to be concurrently or independently imposed; where the amount involved is large or there are other aggravating circumstances, he/she shall be sentenced fixed-termed imprisonment of more than three (3) years and less than 10 years, with a fine; where the amount involved is particularly large or there are other particularly aggravating circumstances, he/she shall be sentenced fixed-termed imprisonment of more than 10 years with a fine.

Article 275 Whoever intentionally damages public or private property shall, where the amount involved is relatively large or the circumstances are serious, be sentenced to fixed-termed imprisonment of less than three (3) years, criminal detention, or a fine; where the amount involved is large or the circumstances are particularly serious, he/she shall be sentenced to fixed-termed imprisonment of more than three (3) years and less than seven (7) years.

Article 276 Whoever, in order to exact revenge or to fulfil other personal aims, damages machinery equipment, brutally injures or slaughters farm animals or uses other means to sabotage production and management, shall be sentenced to fixed-termed imprisonment of less than three (3) years, criminal detention, or control and surveillance; where the circumstances are serious, he/she shall be sentenced to fixed-termed imprisonment of more than three (3) years and less than seven (7) years.

84 This article was revised on 25 February 2011 by Amendment (VIII).

Article 276(A)[85] Whoever uses such methods as transferring assets and fleeing and hiding so as to avoid payment to workers of their labour remuneration, or refuses to pay labour remuneration to workers when he/she has the capacity to pay and it involves a relatively large amount of money, shall, if he/she still refuses to make the payment after having been ordered by the relevant government department to do so, be sentenced to fixed-termed imprisonment of less than three (3) years, criminal detention, or control and surveillance, with a fine to be concurrently or independently imposed; where a serious consequence results, he/she shall be sentenced to fixed-termed imprisonment of more than three (3) years and less than seven (7) years, with a fine.

A unit committing a crime prescribed in the preceding Paragraph shall be punished with a fine, and the directly responsible person(s)-in-charge and any other directly responsible person(s) shall be punished in accordance with provisions of the preceding Paragraph.

Whoever commits an act prescribed in the preceding two Paragraphs but has paid labour remuneration to the workers before a public prosecution is initiated, and has undertaken the corresponding liability for compensation in accordance with the law, he/she may, where no serious consequence has resulted, receive a lighter penalty or be exempted from punishment.

CHAPTER VI

CRIMES OF DISRUPTING THE SOCIAL ADMINISTRATION ORDER

Section 1 Crimes of Disrupting the Public Order

Article 277 Whoever uses means of violence or threat to obstruct state functionaries from discharging their duties shall be sentenced to fixed-termed imprisonment of less than three (3) years, criminal detention, or a fine.

Whoever uses means of violence or threats to obstruct the deputies of the National People's Congress or deputies of the local people's congresses from discharging their duties as deputies pursuant to the law shall be punished in accordance with the provisions in the preceding Paragraph.

[85] This article was added on 25 February 2011 by Amendment (VIII).

Whoever, in the event of a natural disaster or an emergency, uses means of violence or threats to obstruct personnel of the Red Cross from discharging their duties pursuant to the law shall be punished in accordance with the provisions in the first Paragraph.

Whoever intentionally obstructs a state security organ or public security organ from performing state security tasks in accordance with the law and, though without resorting to violence or threat, has caused serious consequences, shall be punished in accordance with the provisions in the first Paragraph.

Article 278 Whoever incites the masses to use violence to resist the implementation of laws and administrative regulations of the State shall be sentenced to fixed-term imprisonment of less than three (3) years, criminal detention, control and surveillance, or deprivation of political rights; where serious consequences are caused, he/she shall be sentenced to fixed-term imprisonment of more than three (3) years and less than seven (7) years.

Article 279 Whoever pretends to be a state functionary to swindle and deceive others shall be sentenced to fixed-term imprisonment of less than three (3) years, criminal detention, control and surveillance, or deprivation of political rights; where the circumstances are serious, he/she shall be sentenced to fixed-term imprisonment of more than three (3) years and less than 10 years.

Whoever pretends to be a people's police officer to swindle and deceive others shall have a heavier sentence imposed in accordance with the preceding Paragraph.

Article 280 Whoever forges, alters, buys or sells, steals, seizes by force or destroys official documents, certificates or seals of State organs shall be sentenced to fixed-term imprisonment of less than three (3) years, criminal detention, control and surveillance, or deprivation of political rights; where the circumstances are serious, he/she shall be sentenced to fixed-term imprisonment of more than three (3) years and less than 10 years.

Whoever forges the seals of a company, enterprise, institution or people's organisation shall be sentenced to fixed-term imprisonment of less than three (3) years, criminal detention, control and surveillance, or deprivation of political rights.

Whoever forges or alters a resident identification card shall be sentenced to fixed-term imprisonment of less than three (3) years, criminal detention, control and surveillance, or deprivation of political rights; where the circumstances are serious he/she shall be sentenced to fixed-term imprisonment of more than three (3) years and less than seven (7) years.

Article 281 Whoever illegally manufactures, buys or sells police uniforms, plates of motor vehicles or other specific symbols or other police instruments shall, where the circumstances are serious, be sentenced to fixed-term imprisonment of less than three (3) years, criminal detention, or control and surveillance, with a fine to be concurrently or independently imposed.

A unit committing the crimes prescribed in the preceding Paragraph shall be punished with a fine, and the directly responsible person(s)-in-charge and any other directly responsible person(s) shall be punished in accordance with the provisions in the preceding Paragraph.

Article 282 Whoever illegally acquires State secrets by means of stealing, spying or buying, shall be sentenced to fixed-term imprisonment of less than three (3) years, criminal detention, control and surveillance, or deprivation of political rights; where the circumstances are serious, he/she shall be sentenced to fixed-term imprisonment of more than three (3) years and less than seven (7) years.

Whoever illegally holds documents, information or other articles of the State that are classified as absolutely confidential or confidential, and refuses to explain their source or usage, shall be sentenced to fixed-term imprisonment of less than three (3) years, criminal detention, or control and surveillance.

Article 283 Whoever illegally manufactures or sells such special espionage equipment as tapping devices and photographic devices shall be sentenced to fixed-term imprisonment of less than three (3) years, criminal detention, or control and surveillance.

Article 284 Whoever illegally uses espionage equipment specially for tapping or photographing and causes serious consequences shall be sentenced to fixed-term imprisonment of less than two (2) years, criminal detention, or control and surveillance.

Article 285[86] Whoever, in violation of the provisions of the State, intrudes into computer information systems which contain information on State affairs, defence facilities or the most advanced science and technology, shall be sentenced to fixed-term imprisonment of less than three (3) years or criminal detention.

Whoever, in violation of the provisions of the State, by intruding into a computer information system other than the one prescribed in the preceding Paragraph, or by using other technical means so as to obtain the data stored in or processed or transmitted by that computer information system, or to implement unlawful control over that computer information system, shall, where the circumstances are serious, be sentenced to fixed-term imprisonment of less than three (3) years or criminal detention, with a fine to be concurrently or independently imposed; where the circumstances are particularly serious, he/she shall be sentenced to fixed-term imprisonment of more than three (3) years and less than seven (7) years, with a fine.

Whoever provides programs or tools specially for intruding into or unlawfully controlling a computer information system, or knowingly provides programs or tools to a person who is committing a criminal act of intruding into or unlawful control of a computer information system, shall, where the circumstances are serious, be punished in accordance with the provisions in the preceding Paragraph.

Article 286 Whoever, in violation of the provisions of the State, deletes, alters or adds data, or interrupts the functioning of the computer information system and causes the malfunction of the computer information system, shall, where the consequences are serious, be sentenced to fixed-term imprisonment of less than five (5) years or criminal detention; where the consequences are particularly serious, he/she shall be sentenced to fixed-term imprisonment of more than five (5) years.

Whoever, in violation of the provisions of the State, deletes, alters or adds to data installed in or processed and transmitted by the computer systems or application programs shall, where the consequences are serious, be sentenced in accordance with the provisions in the preceding Paragraph.

---

[86] Paragraphs 2 and 3 of this article were added on 28 February 2009by Amendment (VII).

Whoever deliberately creates and propagates computer viruses or other programs of a destructive nature so as to disrupt the normal functioning of the computer system, shall, where the consequences are serious, be punished in accordance with the provisions in the first Paragraph.

Article 287 Whoever uses a computer to commit such crimes as financial fraud, theft, embezzlement, misappropriation of public funds or the stealing of State secrets shall be convicted and punished in accordance with the relevant provisions in this Law.

Article 288 Whoever, in violation of the provisions of the State, installs and uses radio stations (transmitters) or occupies frequencies without authorisation, and refuses to cease the usage of such after being ordered to do so, thereby disrupting the normal operation of the radio communication, shall, where serious consequences are caused, be sentenced to fixed-term imprisonment of less than three (3) years, criminal detention, or control and surveillance, with a fine to be concurrently or independently imposed.

A unit committing the crimes prescribed in the preceding Paragraph shall be punished with a fine, and the directly responsible person(s)-in-charge and any other directly responsible person(s) shall be punished in accordance with the provisions in the preceding Paragraph.

Article 289 Whoever gathers a crowd to commit "beating, smashing and robbing" and causes injury, disability or the death of a person, shall be convicted and punished in accordance with the provisions of Articles 234 and 232 of this Law. Where public or private property is damaged or stolen, the ringleader(s) shall, in addition to being ordered to make restitution and compensation, be convicted and punished in accordance with the provisions in Articles 263 of this Law.

Article 290 In cases where a crowd is gathered to disturb the public order and the circumstances are so serious that the normal processes of work, production, business, teaching, and scientific research are disrupted thereby, if major losses are caused, the ringleader(s) shall be sentenced to fixed-term imprisonment of more than three (3) years and less than seven (7) years; other active participants shall be sentenced to fixed-term imprisonment of less than three (3) years, criminal detention, control and surveillance, or deprivation of political rights.

Where a crowd is gathered to attack a State organ and causes the State organ to be unable to perform its normal functions, if major losses are caused, the ringleader(s) shall be sentenced to fixed-term imprisonment of more than five (5) years and less than 10 years, and other active participants shall be sentenced to fixed-term imprisonment of less than five (5) years, criminal detention, control and surveillance, or deprivation of political rights.

Article 291 Where a crowd is gathered to disturb the order at stations, wharves, civil airports, market places, parks, theatres, exhibition centres, sports grounds or other public places, blocking traffic or undermining traffic order, and resisting or obstructing personnel of public order administration in the performance of their functions pursuant to the law, where the circumstances are serious, the ringleader(s) shall be sentenced to fixed-term imprisonment of less than five (5) years, criminal detention, or control and surveillance.

Article 291(A)[87] Whoever casts false explosives, poisonous or radioactive substances, pathogens of infectious diseases or other such substances, or fabricates news about a risk of explosion, a biochemical threat or radioactive threat or other terrifying information, or intentionally disseminates fabricated terrifying information, thereby seriously disrupting the social order, shall be sentenced to fixed-term imprisonment of less than five (5) years, criminal detention, or control and surveillance; where serious consequences are caused, he/she shall be sentenced to fixed-term imprisonment of more than five (5) years.

Article 292 Where a crowd is gathered to fight, the ringleader(s) and other active participants shall be sentenced to fixed-term imprisonment of less than three (3) years, criminal detention, or control and surveillance; where one of the following situations is involved, the ringleader(s) and other active participants shall be sentenced to fixed-term imprisonment of more than three (3) years and less than 10 years:

(1) gathering a crowd to cause affray on many occasions;
(2) gathering a large number of people to cause a large scale affray and causing a very bad impact on society;
(3) gathering a crowd to cause an affray in a public place or a vital transport system and causing serious social chaos; or
(4) gathering an armed crowd to cause an affray.

[87] This article was added on 29 December 2001 by Amendment (III).

Whoever gathers a crowd to cause an affray and causes serious injuries or death to a person shall be convicted and punished in accordance with the provisions in Articles 234 and 232 of this Law.

Article 293[88] Whoever acts to undermine the public order through one of the following provocative conducts shall be sentenced to fixed-term imprisonment of less than five (5) years, criminal detention, or control and surveillance:

(1) battering another person at will under odious circumstances;
(2) chasing, intercepting, insulting or intimidating another person under odious circumstances;
(3) forcibly seizing and taking away or indiscriminately damaging or occupying public or private property, under serious circumstances;
(4) jeering and making trouble in a public place and causing major chaos.

Whoever gathers other persons to repeatedly commit the act(s) prescribed in the preceding Paragraph whereby seriously disrupting the social order, shall be sentenced to fixed-term imprisonment of more than five (5) years and less than 10 years, and a fine may also be imposed.

Article 294[89] Whoever organises or leads an underground organisation of a gangland nature shall be sentenced to fixed-term imprisonment of more than seven (7) years with a fine; active participants shall be sentenced to fixed-term imprisonment of more than three (3) years and less than seven (7) years, and may also have a fine or confiscation of property imposed; other participants shall be sentenced to fixed-term imprisonment of less than three (3) years, criminal detention, control and surveillance, or deprivation of political rights, and may also have a fine imposed.

A member of an overseas underground gangland organisation who enters into the territory of the People's Republic of China to recruit members to the organisation shall be sentenced to fixed-term imprisonment of more than three (3) years and less than 10 years.

A state functionary who harbours an underground organisation of a gangland nature or connives at an underground organisation of a gangland nature committing lawless and criminal activities, shall be sentenced to fixed-term imprisonment of less than five (5) years; where the

88 This article was revised on 25 February 2011 by Amendment (VIII).
89 This article was revised on 25 February 2011 by Amendment (VIII).

circumstances are serious, he/she shall be sentenced to fixed-term imprisonment of more than five (5) years.

Whoever commits other crimes, in addition to the crimes prescribed in the preceding three Paragraphs, shall be punished in accordance with the provisions on combined punishment for multiple crimes.

An underground organisation of a gangland nature is defined as one involving all the following characteristics:

(1) A relatively stable criminal organisation is formed, which has a relatively large number of members, and has definite organisers or leaders and generally stable key members.
(2) It obtains economic benefits through organised illegal and criminal activities or other means, and possesses considerable financial strength to support its activities.
(3) It uses such means as violence and coercion to repeatedly carry out illegal and criminal activities, commits lawless activities and crimes, and bullies and harms ordinary people.
(4) It plays the role of a tyrant in a locality through committing illegal and criminal activities or by taking advantage of being harboured or connived at by state functionaries, and thereby gaining unlawful control or major influence in a certain area or a trade, which seriously undermines the economic and social order.

Article 295[90] Whoever teaches methods of committing crimes shall be sentenced to fixed-term imprisonment of less than five (5) years, criminal detention, or control and surveillance; where the circumstances are serious, he/she shall be sentenced to fixed-term imprisonment of more than five (5) years and less than 10 years; where the circumstances are particularly serious, he/she shall be sentenced to fixed-term imprisonment of more than 10 years or life imprisonment.

Article 296 Where an assembly, procession or demonstration takes place without, as required by law, approval having been applied for or obtained, or takes place and departs from the starting and ending time, the place, or the route as permitted by the competent authorities, and the order to dismiss is refused to be obeyed, thereby having the social order seriously disrupted, the person(s)-in-charge of and the person(s) directly responsible for the assembly, procession or demonstration shall be sentenced to

90 This article was revised on 25 February 2011 by Amendment (VIII).

fixed-term imprisonment of less than five (5) years, criminal detention, control and surveillance, or deprivation of political rights.

Article 297 Whoever, in violation of the provisions of laws, brings with him/her weapons, controlled knives or explosive objects to participate in an assembly, procession or demonstration shall be sentenced to fixed-term imprisonment of less than three (3) years, criminal detention, control and surveillance, or deprivation of political rights.

Article 298 Whoever disturbs, acts violently or carries out other acts to sabotage a legally held assembly, procession or demonstration, thereby causing public chaos, shall be sentenced to fixed-term imprisonment of less than five (5) years, criminal detention, control and surveillance, or deprivation of political rights.

Article 299 Whoever deliberately desecrates the National Flag or National Emblem of the People's Republic of China in a public place by such means as burning, damaging, scribbling on, soiling and disfiguring shall be sentenced to fixed-term imprisonment of less than three (3) years, criminal detention, control and surveillance, or deprivation of political rights.

Article 300 Whoever hinders the implementation of laws and administrative regulations of the State by organising or utilising superstitious sects or religious cults, or utilising superstition, shall be sentenced to fixed-term imprisonment of more than three (3) years and less than seven (7) years; where the circumstances are particularly serious, he/she shall be sentenced to fixed-term imprisonment of more than seven (7) years.

Whoever organises and utilises superstitious sects or religious cults, or utilises superstition to deceive others and cause the death of a person shall be punished in accordance with the provisions in the preceding Paragraph.

Whoever organises and utilises superstitious sects or religious cults, or utilises superstition to have sexual intercourse with a woman or to defraud someone of money and property, shall be convicted and punished in accordance with the provisions of Articles 236 and 266 of this Law respectively.

Article 301 Where a group of people is gathered to engage in obscene activities, the ringleader(s) and those who participate in such activities on many occasions shall be sentenced to fixed-term imprisonment of less than five (5) years, criminal detention, or control and surveillance.

Whoever induces a minor to participate in such a group's obscene activities shall have a heavier penalty imposed in accordance with the preceding Paragraph.

Article 302 Whoever steals or insults a corpse shall be sentenced to fixed-term imprisonment of less than three (3) years, criminal detention, or control and surveillance.

Article 303[91] Whoever, for the purpose of making a profit, gathers a group of people to engage in gambling or makes gambling his/her occupation, shall be sentenced to fixed-term imprisonment of less than three (3) years, criminal detention, or control and surveillance, with a fine.

Whoever runs a gambling house shall be sentenced to fixed-term imprisonment of less than three (3) years, criminal detention, or control and surveillance, with a fine; where the circumstances are serious, he/she shall be sentenced to fixed-term imprisonment of more than three (3) years and less than 10 years, with a fine.

Article 304 An employee of a postal service who in gross neglect of his/her duty deliberately delays delivery of mail and causes serious losses to public property and the interests of the State and the people, shall be sentenced to fixed-term imprisonment of less than two (2) years or criminal detention.

Section 2 Crimes of Disrupting the Administration of Justice

Article 305 A witness, expert witness, recorder or translator in a criminal proceeding who, in order to frame others or conceal criminal evidence, intentionally gives false testimony or gives a false expert evaluation, or makes a false record or a false translation regarding circumstances which have a major effect on the case, shall be sentenced to fixed-term imprisonment of less than three (3) years or criminal detention; where the circumstances are serious, he/she shall be sentenced to fixed-term imprisonment of more than three (3) years and less than seven (7) years.

Article 306 A defence counsel or litigation agent in a criminal proceeding who destroys or forges evidence, assists the parties concerned to destroy or falsify evidence, or threatens or induces a witness to change his/her testimony to depart from the facts or to make false testimony, shall be sentenced to fixed-term imprisonment of less than three (3) years or criminal

[91] This article was revised on 29 June 2006 by Amendment (VI).

detention; where the circumstances are serious, he/she shall be sentenced to fixed-term imprisonment of more than three (3) years and less than seven (7) years.

A defence counsel or litigation agent who provides, presents or quotes a witness's testimony or other evidence which does not conform with the facts but is not intentionally forged, is not regarded as falsifying the evidence.

Article 307 Whoever uses violence, threats, bribery or other means to obstruct a witness from testifying or to instigate another person to give false testimony, shall be sentenced to fixed-term imprisonment of less than three (3) years or criminal detention; where the circumstances are serious, he/she shall be sentenced to fixed-term imprisonment of more than three (3) years and less than seven (7) years.

Whoever assists a party to the case to destroy or falsify evidence shall, where the circumstances are serious, be sentenced fixed-term imprisonment of less than three (3) years or criminal detention.

A judicial official committing the crimes prescribed in the previous two Paragraphs shall have a heavier punishment imposed.

Article 308 Whoever retaliates against or takes revenge on a witness shall be sentenced to fixed-term imprisonment of less than three (3) years or criminal detention; where the circumstances are serious, he/she shall be sentenced to fixed-term imprisonment of more than three (3) years and less than seven (7) years.

Article 309 Whoever gathers a crowd to create a disturbance in the courtroom, to disrupt the courtroom order, or to attack judicial personnel, thereby severely disrupting the order of the court shall be sentenced to fixed-term imprisonment of less than three (3) years, criminal detention, control and surveillance, or a fine.

Article 310 Whoever knowingly provides a criminal offender with a hiding place, money or goods, or helps him/her to escape or gives false testimony to protect him/her, shall be sentenced to fixed-term imprisonment of less than three (3) years, criminal detention, or control and surveillance; where the circumstances are serious, he/she shall be sentenced to fixed-term imprisonment of more than three (3) years and less than 10 years.

Whoever commits a crime prescribed in the preceding Paragraph involving conspiracy shall be treated as a joint offender.

Article 311 Whoever clearly knows the criminal espionage activities of another person but refuses to provide information on such when being interviewed and required by the State security organ to provide relevant evidence shall, where the circumstances are serious, be sentenced to fixed-term imprisonment of less than three (3) years, criminal detention, or control and surveillance.

Article 312[92] Whoever knowingly conceals, transfers, purchases or sells, or uses other methods to disguise or conceal for another person booty and gains acquired from the commission of a crime, shall be sentenced to fixed-term imprisonment of less than three (3) years, criminal detention, or control and surveillance, with a fine to be concurrently or independently imposed; where the circumstances are serious, be sentenced to fixed-term imprisonment of more than three (3) years and less than seven (7) years, with a fine.

A unit committing the crimes prescribed in the preceding Paragraph shall be punished with a fine, and the directly responsible person(s)-in-charge and any other directly responsible person(s) shall be punished in accordance with the provisions of the preceding Paragraph.

Article 313 Whoever possesses the ability to fulfil a judgment or ruling rendered by a people's court but refuses to carry it out shall, where the circumstances are serious, be sentenced to fixed-term imprisonment of less than three (3) years or criminal detention.

Article 314 Whoever hides, transfers, sells or intentionally damages property which has already been sealed, seized or frozen by the judicial organ shall, where the circumstances are serious, be sentenced to fixed-term imprisonment of less than three (3) years, criminal detention, or a fine.

Article 315 A criminal held in custody pursuant to the law who commits one of the following acts to subrogate the order of supervision and control shall, where the circumstances are serious, be sentenced to fixed-term imprisonment of less than three (3) years:

(1) attacking the supervising personnel;
(2) organising other persons held in custody to subrogate the order of supervision and control;

---

92 This article was revised on 29 June 2006 by Amendment (VI).

(3) gathering a crowd of persons in custody to create a disturbance and subrogate the normal order of supervision and control;
(4) beating or torturing persons in custody or instigating a person in custody to beat or torture another person in custody.

Article 316 A criminal, or criminal accused, or criminal suspect who is held in custody pursuant to law and who escapes from custody, shall be sentenced to fixed-term imprisonment of less than five (5) years or criminal detention.

Whoever takes over by force a criminal, criminal accused, or criminal suspect under escort shall be sentenced to fixed-term imprisonment of more than three (3) years and less than seven (7) years; where the circumstances are serious, he/she shall be sentenced to fixed-term imprisonment of more than seven (7) years.

Article 317 Whoever plays the role of organiser in an attempt to escape from a prison, and those who participate actively in the attempt, shall be sentenced to fixed-term imprisonment of more than five (5) years; other participants in the attempt shall be sentenced to fixed-term imprisonment of less than five (5) years or criminal detention.

Whoever plays the role of organiser in a riotous breach of prison order, or who gathers a crowd of people with weapons to break out of a prison, and those who participate actively in the action shall be sentenced to fixed-term imprisonment of more than 10 years or life imprisonment; where the circumstances are particularly serious, he/she shall be sentenced to death; other participants in the attempt shall be sentenced to fixed-term imprisonment of more than three (3) years and less than 10 years.

Section 3 Crimes of Undermining National Border (Frontier) Control

Article 318 Whoever organises people to illegally cross the national border (frontier) shall be sentenced to fixed-term imprisonment of more than two (2) years and less than seven (7) years, with a fine; where the act falls within one of the following categories, he/she shall be sentenced to fixed-term imprisonment of more than seven (7) years or life imprisonment, with a fine or confiscation of property:

(1) taking the role of a ringleader in organising other people to illegally cross the national border (frontier);
(2) repeatedly organising people to illegally cross the national border (frontier) or organising a large number of people to illegally cross the national border (frontier);

(3) causing serious injury or death to a person whom he/she has organised;
(4) depriving of or restricting the personal freedom of the person whom he/she has organised;
(5) resisting inspection by means of violence or threats;
(6) illegally deriving a large amount of income;
(7) other particularly serious circumstances.

Whoever, in addition to the commission of a crime prescribed in the preceding Paragraph, kills, injures, rapes or abducts and sells a person whom he/she has organised, or kills or injures an investigating official shall be punished in accordance with the provisions on combined punishment for multiple crimes.

Article 319 Whoever, for the purpose of organising for another person to illegally cross the national border (frontier), obtains by deceit a passport, visa or other border exit document in the name of such activities as labour export, economic cooperation and trade, shall be sentenced to fixed-term imprisonment of less than three (3) years with a fine; where the circumstances are serious, he/she shall be sentenced to fixed-term imprisonment of more than three (3) years and less than 10 years, with a fine.

A unit committing the crimes prescribed in the preceding Paragraph shall be sentenced to a fine, and the directly responsible person(s)-in-charge and any other directly responsible person(s) shall be punished in accordance with the provisions of the preceding Paragraph.

Article 320 Whoever provides another person with a forged or altered passport, visa or other kind of border exit and entry document, or who sells a passport, visa or other kind of border exit and entry document, shall be sentenced to fixed-term imprisonment of less than five (5) years with a fine; where the circumstances are serious, he/she shall be sentenced to fixed-term imprisonment of more than five (5) years with a fine.

Article 321 Whoever transports another person illegally across the national border (frontier) shall be sentenced to fixed-term imprisonment of less than five (5) years, criminal detention, or control and surveillance, with a fine; where the act falls within one of the following categories, he/she shall be sentenced to fixed-term imprisonment of more than five (5) years and less than 10 years, with a fine:

(1) repeatedly committing such transportation activities or transporting a large number of people;
(2) using vessels, vehicles or other means of transportation which do not fulfil necessary safety conditions and are dangerous enough to cause serious consequences;
(3) having obtained a large amount of illegal gains;
(4) other particularly serious circumstances.

Whoever, when transporting another person to illegally across the national border (frontier), causes serious injury and death to the person being transported or uses means of violence or threats to resists inspection, shall be sentenced to fixed-term imprisonment of more than seven (7) years with a fine.

Whoever, in addition to the commission of a crime prescribed in the two preceding Paragraphs kills, injures, rapes or abducts and sells a person being transported, or kills or injures an inspection official shall be punished in accordance with the provisions on combined penalty for multiple crimes.

Article 322 Whoever, in violation of laws and regulations on border control, illegally crosses the national border (frontier) shall, where the circumstances are serious, be sentenced to fixed-term imprisonment of less than one year, criminal detention, or control and surveillance, with a fine.

Article 323 Whoever intentionally sabotages boundary tablets, boundary markers or permanent survey indicators erected along the borders of the country shall be sentenced to fixed-term imprisonment of less than three (3) year or criminal detention.

Section 4 Crimes of Disrupting the Administration of Cultural Relics

Article 324 Whoever intentionally damages precious cultural relics under the protection of the State or cultural relics which are listed as key units to be protected at national level or provincial level, shall be sentenced to fixed-term imprisonment of less than three (3) years or criminal detention, with a fine to be concurrently or independently imposed; where the circumstances are serious, he/she shall be sentenced to fixed-term imprisonment of more than three (3) years and less than 10 years, with a fine.

Whoever intentionally damages sites of historic interest or scenic beauty which are protected by the State shall be sentenced to fixed-term imprisonment of less than five (5) years or criminal detention, with a fine to be concurrently or independently imposed.

Whoever negligently damages precious cultural relics which are under State protection or listed as key units to be protected at national level or provincial level shall be sentenced to fixed-term imprisonment of less than three (3) years or criminal detention.

Article 325 Whoever, in violation of laws and regulations on the protection of cultural relics, sells without permission precious cultural relics in his/her collection, of which the export is prohibited by the State, or gifts them to a foreigner without authorisation, shall be sentenced to fixed-term imprisonment of less than five (5) years or criminal detention, and may also have a fine imposed.

A unit committing the crime prescribed in the preceding Paragraph shall be sentenced to a fine, and the directly responsible person(s)-in-charge and any other directly responsible person(s) shall be punished in accordance with the provisions in the preceding Paragraph.

Article 326 Whoever, for the purpose of making a profit, re-sells cultural relics of which the trade is prohibited by the State shall, where the circumstances are serious, be sentenced to fixed-term imprisonment of less than five (5) years or criminal detention, with a fine; where the circumstances are particularly serious, he/she shall be sentenced to fixed-term imprisonment of more than five (5) years and less than 10 years, with a fine.

A unit committing the crime prescribed in the preceding Paragraph shall be sentenced to a fine, and the directly responsible person(s)-in-charge and any other directly responsible person(s) shall be punished in accordance with the provisions in the preceding Paragraph.

Article 327 A state-owned museum, library or unit, which, in violation of laws and regulations on protection of cultural relics, sells without authorisation works of a cultural relic collection protected by the State or sends them to a non-state-owned unit or individuals without authorisation, shall be punished with a fine, and the directly responsible person(s)-in-charge and any other directly responsible person(s) shall be sentenced to fixed-term imprisonment of less than three (3) years or criminal detention.

Article 328[93] Whoever digs up and robs ancient cultural ruins or an ancient tomb with historical, artistic or scientific value, shall be sentenced to fixed-term imprisonment of more than three (3) years and less than 10 years with a fine; where the circumstances are relatively minor, he/she shall be sentenced to fixed-term imprisonment of less than three (3) years, criminal detention, or control and surveillance, with a fine; where the act falls within one of the following categories, he/she shall be sentenced to fixed-term imprisonment of more than 10 years or life imprisonment with a fine or confiscation of property:

(1) digging up and robbing ruins of ancient culture or ancient tombs which are listed as key units of national cultural relics protected at national and provincial levels;
(2) being the ringleader of a gang engaged in robbing ancient cultural ruins and tombs;
(3) digging up and robbing ruins of ancient culture or ancient tombs on many occasions;
(4) digging up and robbing ruins of ancient culture or ancient tombs, and at the same time also stealing precious cultural relics or causing great damage to precious cultural relics.

Whoever digs up and robs ancient human fossils and ancient vertebrate fossils with scientific value and under State protection shall be punished in accordance with the provisions of the preceding Paragraph.

Article 329 Whoever seizes by force or steals archives in the possession of the State shall be sentenced to fixed-term imprisonment of less than five (5) years or criminal detention.

Whoever, in violation of the provisions of archive laws, sells or assigns archive records in the possession of the State without authorisation shall, where the circumstances are serious, be sentenced to fixed-term imprisonment of less than three (3) years or criminal detention.

Where the commission of an act prescribed in the preceding two Paragraphs has also constituted another crime prescribed in this Law, the person shall be convicted and punished in accordance with the provisions which carry the heavier sentence.

---

[93] This article was revised on 25 February 2011 by Amendment (VIII).

Section 5 Crimes of Endangering Public Health

Article 330 Whoever, in violation of the provisions of laws on prevention and treatment of infectious diseases, causes the spread or the high danger of the spread of Class A infectious diseases shall, where the act falls within one of the following categories, be sentenced to fixed-term imprisonment of less than three (3) years or criminal detention; where the consequences are particularly serious, he/she shall be sentenced to fixed-term imprisonment of more than three (3) years and less than seven (7) years:

(1) a water supply unit supplying drinking water which does not meet the hygienic standards set by the State;
(2) refusing to undertake sterilisation treatment for sewage, pollutants, excrement and urine that contain pathogens of infectious diseases in accordance with the sanitary requirements set by the sanitation and anti-epidemic organs;
(3) allowing or conniving at infectious disease patients, infectious disease pathogen carriers, or those suspected of having an infectious disease to undertake work which they are prohibited by the health administrative department of the State Council from engaging in because of the high possibility of spreading the infection; or
(4) refusing to implement other prevention and control measures put forward by the sanitation and anti-epidemic organs in accordance with the laws of the People's Republic of China on the prevention and treatment of infectious diseases.

A unit committing the crime prescribed in the preceding Paragraph shall be punished with a fine, and the directly responsible person(s)-in-charge and any other directly responsible person(s) shall be punished in accordance with the provisions in the preceding Paragraph.

The extent of Class A infectious diseases shall be determined in accordance with the Law of the People's Republic of China on Prevention and Treatment of Infectious Diseases and the relevant provisions of the State Council.

Article 331 Whoever is engaged in experimentation, safekeeping, carriage or transportation of bacterial strains and viruses of infectious diseases, and violates the relevant provisions of the health administrative departments under the State Council and causes the spread of the bacterial and viral infectious diseases, shall, where the consequences are serious, be sentenced to fixed-term imprisonment of less than three (3) years or criminal detention; where the consequences are particularly serious, he/she shall be sentenced to fixed-term imprisonment of more than three (3) years and less than seven (7) years.

Article 332 Whoever violates the provisions on national border health and quarantine and causes the spread or the great danger of the spread of infectious diseases under quarantine, shall be sentenced to fixed-term imprisonment of less than three (3) years or criminal detention, with a fine to be concurrently or independently imposed.

A unit committing the crime prescribed in the preceding Paragraph shall be punished with a fine, and the directly responsible person(s)-in-charge and any other directly responsible person(s) shall be punished in accordance with the provisions in the preceding Paragraph.

Article 333 Whoever illegally organises for people to sell their blood shall be sentenced to fixed-term imprisonment of less than five (5) years with a fine; where violent means and threats are used to compel others to sell blood, he/she shall be sentenced to fixed-term imprisonment of more than five (5) years and less than 10 years, with a fine.

Whoever causes injury to another person when committing the act prescribed in the preceding Paragraph shall be convicted and punished in accordance with the provisions of Article 234 of this Law.

Article 334 Whoever illegally collects and supplies blood or produces and supplies blood products that do not meet the standards stipulated by the State and are dangerous enough to threaten human health, shall be sentenced to fixed-term imprisonment of less than five (5) years or criminal detention, with a fine; where serious harm to human health results, he/she shall be sentenced to fixed-term imprisonment of more than five (5) years and less than 10 years with a fine; where particularly serious harm to human health results, he/she shall be sentenced to fixed-term imprisonment of more than 10 years or life imprisonment with a fine or confiscation of property.

A unit which is authorised by a relevant competent department of the State to engage in collecting and supplying blood or producing and supplying blood products, and which fails to carry out tests as required, or violates provisions on operation procedures and thus causes harm to a person's health, shall be punished with a fine, and the directly responsible person(s)-in-charge and any other directly responsible person(s) shall be sentenced to fixed-term imprisonment of less than five (5) years or criminal detention.

Article 335 A member of medical staff who in gross neglect of his/her duty causes death to a patient or serious harm to a patient's health shall be sentenced to fixed-term imprisonment of less than three years or criminal detention.

Article 336 Whoever illegally engages in medical practice without obtaining the qualification for medical practice, shall, where the circumstances are serious, be sentenced to fixed-term imprisonment of less than three (3) years, criminal detention, or control and surveillance, with a fine to be concurrently or independently imposed; where serious harm to the health of a patient results, he/she shall be sentenced to fixed-term imprisonment of more than three (3) years and less than 10 years with a fine; where the death of a patient results, he/she shall be sentenced to fixed-term imprisonment of more than 10 years with a fine.

Whoever, without obtaining the qualification for medical practice, engages in practices of reversing birth control surgery, undertaking false birth control surgery, terminating pregnancy or removing intra-uterine devices from the womb shall, where the circumstances are serious, be sentenced to fixed-term imprisonment of less than three (3) years, criminal detention, or control and surveillance, with a fine to be concurrently or independently imposed; where serious harm to the health of a patient results, he/she shall be sentenced to fixed-term imprisonment of more than three (3) years and less than 10 years, with a fine; where the death of a patient results, he/she shall be sentenced to fixed-term imprisonment of more than 10 years and a fine.

Article 337[94] Whoever violates the provisions of the State on animal and plant quarantine and therefore causes an outbreak of serious animal and plant epidemic disease or brings a risk of the outbreak of serious animal and plant epidemic disease, shall be sentenced to fixed-term imprisonment of less than three (3) years or criminal detention, with a fine to be concurrently or independently imposed.

A unit committing the crime prescribed in the preceding Paragraph shall be punished with a fine, and the directly responsible person(s)-in-charge

---

94 This article was revised on 28 February 2009 by Amendment (VII).

and any other directly responsible person(s) shall be punished in accordance with the provisions in the preceding Paragraph.

Section 6 Crimes of Undermining the Protection of Environmental Resources

Article 338[95] Whoever discharges, dumps or disposes of radioactive waste, waste containing pathogens of infectious diseases, toxic materials or other dangerous waste in violation of the provisions of the State, and thereby causes serious environmental pollution, shall be sentenced to fixed-term imprisonment of less than three (3) years or criminal detention with a fine to be concurrently or independently imposed; where the consequences are particularly serious, he/she shall be sentenced to fixed-term imprisonment of more than three (3) years and less than seven (7) years, with a fine.

Article 339[96] Whoever, in violation of the provisions of the State, transports from abroad solid waste into China for the purpose of dumping, storage or treatment shall be sentenced to fixed-term imprisonment of less than five (5) years or criminal detention, with a fine; where this causes a serious environmental pollution accident resulting in great harm to public or private property or serious danger to the health of others, he/she shall be sentenced to fixed-term imprisonment of more than five (5) years and less than 10 years, with a fine; where the consequences are particularly serious, he/she shall be sentenced to fixed-term imprisonment of more than 10 years, with a fine.

Whoever, without the permission of the relevant competent department of the State Council, imports solid waste to use as raw material, thereby causing a major environmental pollution accident and great harm to public or private property or serious danger to human health, shall be sentenced to fixed-term imprisonment of less than five (5) years or criminal detention, with a fine; if the consequences are particularly serious, he/she shall be sentenced to fixed-term imprisonment of more than five (5) years and less than 10 years, with a fine.

Whoever imports solid waste, liquid waste or gas waste which cannot be used as raw material, in the guise of utilising it as raw material, shall be punished in accordance with the provisions of Paragraphs (2) and (3) of Article 152 in this Law.

---

95 This article was revised on 25 February 2011 by Amendment (VIII).
96 This article was revised on 28 December 2002 by Amendment (IV).

Article 340 Whoever, in violation of laws and regulations on the protection of aquatic resources, harvests aquatic products in an area in which, or in a season during which fishing is forbidden, or uses implements and methods which are forbidden from being used in fishing shall, where the circumstances are serious, be sentenced to fixed-term imprisonment of less than three (3) years, criminal detention, control and surveillance, or a fine.

Article 341 Whoever illegally hunts and kills precious and endangered species of wildlife which are under the special protection of the State, or illegally purchases, transports or sells precious and endangered species of wildlife or their products which are under the special protection of the State, shall be sentenced to fixed-term imprisonment of less than five (5) years or criminal detention, with a fine; where the circumstances are serious, he/she shall be sentenced to fixed-term imprisonment of more than five (5) years and less than 10 years, with a fine; where the circumstances are particularly serious, he/she shall be sentenced to fixed-term imprisonment of more than 10 years, with a fine or confiscation of property.

Whoever, in violation of laws and regulations governing hunting, hunts wildlife in an area in which, or in a season during which hunting is forbidden, or uses implements and methods which are forbidden from being used in hunting, thus endangering the source of wildlife, shall, where the circumstances are serious, be sentenced to fixed-term imprisonment of less than three (3) years, criminal detention, control and surveillance, or a fine.

Article 342[97] Whoever, in violation of land management laws and regulations, illegally converts arable land, forest land or other agricultural land into land for other uses shall, if the area involved is relatively large and a large area of arable land, forest land or other agricultural land is damaged, be sentenced to fixed-term imprisonment of less than five (5) years or criminal detention, with a fine to be concurrently or independently imposed.

Article 343[98] Whoever, in violation of the provisions of the laws on mineral resources, exploits mines without obtaining a mining licence, enters without authorisation into a mining area, which is subject to the State

97 This article was revised on 31 August 2001 by Amendment (II).

98 This article was revised on 25 February 2011 by Amendment (VIII).

plan or is valuable for the national economy, or which belongs to other people, in order to exploit mines, or who exploits without authorisation specific types of minerals, the exploitation of which is subject to the protective provisions of the State shall, where the circumstances are serious, be sentenced to fixed-term imprisonment of less than three (3) years, criminal detention, or control and surveillance, with a fine to be concurrently or independently imposed; where circumstances are particularly serious, he/she shall be sentenced to fixed-term imprisonment of more than three (3) years and less than seven (7) years, with a fine.

Whoever, in violation of the provisions of laws on mineral resources, uses methods of a destructive nature to exploit mineral resources and causes serious damage to the mineral resources shall be sentenced to fixed-term imprisonment of less than five (5) years or criminal detention, with a fine.

Article 344[99] Whoever, in violation of the provisions of the State, illegally logs or destroys precious species of trees or other plants under the key protection of the State, or illegally purchases, transports, processes or sells precious species of trees or other plants and their products under the key protection of the State, shall be sentenced to fixed-term imprisonment of less than three (3) years, criminal detention, or control and surveillance, with a fine; where the circumstances are serious, he/she shall be sentenced to fixed-term imprisonment of more than three (3) years and less than seven (7) years, with a fine.

Article 345[100] Whoever illegally fells forests or trees and woods shall, if the amount involved is relatively large, be sentenced to fixed-term imprisonment of less than three (3) years, criminal detention, or control and surveillance, with a fine to be concurrently or independently imposed; where the amount involved is large, he/she shall be sentenced to fixed-term imprisonment of more than three (3) years and less than seven (7) years, with a fine.

Whoever, in violation of the provisions of laws on forests, fells in an arbitrary manner forests or trees and woods shall, where the amount involved is relatively large, be sentenced to fixed-term imprisonment of less than three (3) years, criminal detention, or control and surveillance, with a fine to be concurrently or independently imposed; where the amount involved

99 This article was revised on 28 December 2002 by Amendment (IV).
100 This article was revised on 28 December 2002 by Amendment (IV).

is large, he/she shall be sentenced to fixed-term imprisonment of more than seven (7) years, with a fine.

Whoever illegally purchases or transports logs and timber which he/she knows clearly have been illegally felled or felled in an arbitrary manner, shall, where the circumstances are serious, be sentenced to fixed-term imprisonment of less than three (3) years, criminal detention, or control and surveillance, with a fine to be concurrently or independently imposed; where the circumstances are particularly serious, he/she shall be sentenced to fixed-term imprisonment of more than three (3) years and less than seven (7) years, with a fine.

Whoever illegally fells or fells in an arbitrary manner forests or trees and woods in a national natural reserve shall have a heavier punishment imposed.

Article 346 A unit committing the crimes prescribed in Articles 338 to 345, shall be punished with a fine, and the directly responsible person(s)-in-charge and any other directly responsible person(s) shall be punished in accordance with the provisions of the relevant articles in this Section.

Section 7 Crimes of Smuggling, Trafficking, Transporting and Manufacturing Narcotic Drugs

Article 347 Whoever smuggles, traffics in, transports and manufactures narcotic drugs, regardless of the amount of narcotic drugs, shall be pursued with criminal liability and sanctioned by criminal penalty.

Whoever smuggles, traffics, transports or manufactures narcotic drugs, where the act falls within one of the following categories, shall be sentenced to fixed-term imprisonment of 15 years, life imprisonment, or death, with confiscation of property:

(1) smuggling, trafficking, transporting or manufacturing opium of more than 1,000 grams, heroin or methylaniline of more than 50 grams, or other narcotic drugs of a large amount;
(2) being the ringleader of a criminal gang engaged in smuggling, trafficking, transporting and manufacturing narcotic drugs;
(3) using arms to protect the smuggling, trafficking, transporting and manufacturing of narcotic drugs;
(4) using violent force to resist inspection, detention, or arrest where the circumstances are serious; and
(5) participating in organised international narcotic drug trafficking.

Whoever smuggles, traffics, transports or manufactures opium of an amount of more than 200 grams and less than 1,000 grams, heroin or methylaniline of an amount of more than 10 grams and less than 50 grams, or other narcotic drugs of a relatively large amount, shall be sentenced to fixed-term imprisonment of more than seven (7) years, with a fine.

Whoever smuggles, traffics, transports or manufactures opium of an amount of less than 200 grams, heroin or methylaniline of an amount of less than 10 grams, or other narcotic drugs of a small amount, shall be sentenced to fixed-term imprisonment of less than three (3) years, criminal detention, or control and surveillance, with a fine; where the circumstances are serious, he/she shall be sentenced to fixed-term imprisonment of more than three (3) years and less than seven (7) years, with a fine.

A unit committing the crimes prescribed in the preceding Paragraphs (2), (3) and (4) shall be punished with a fine, and the directly responsible person(s)-in-charge and any other directly responsible person(s) shall be punished in accordance with the provisions in the relevant paragraphs of this Article.

Whoever makes use of or instigates minors to engage in smuggling, trafficking in, transporting or manufacturing narcotic drugs or sells narcotic drugs to minors shall have a heavier punishment imposed.

Where a person has repeatedly been involved in smuggling, trafficking in, transporting and manufacturing narcotic drugs and has not be dealt with, the amount of narcotic drugs involved shall be calculated by accumulation.

Article 348 Whoever illegally possesses more than 1,000 grams of opium or more than 50 grams of heroin or methylaniline or a large amount of other narcotic drugs shall be sentenced to fixed-term imprisonment of more than seven (7) years or life imprisonment, with a fine. Whoever illegally possesses more than 200 grams of opium but less than 1,000 grams or more than 10 grams but less than 50 grams of heroin or methylaniline, or a large amount of other narcotic drugs shall be sentenced to fixed-term imprisonment of less than three (3) years, criminal detention, or control and surveillance, with a fine; where the circumstances are serious, he/she shall be sentenced to fixed-term imprisonment of more than three years (3) and less than seven (7) years, with a fine.

Article 349 Whoever harbours a criminal engaged in smuggling, trafficking, transporting or manufacturing narcotic drugs, and hides, transfers or covers up for the criminal narcotic drugs or money and properties obtained from the commission of the crime, shall be sentenced to fixed-term imprisonment of less than three (3) years, criminal detention, or control and surveillance; where the circumstances are serious, he/she shall be sentenced to fixed-term imprisonment of more than three (3) years and less than 10 years.

Where an anti-drug official or a state functionary shields or harbours a criminal who engages in smuggling, trafficking in, transporting or manufacturing narcotic drugs, he/she shall have a heavier punishment imposed in accordance with the provisions of the preceding Paragraph.

Whoever conspires in advance with other to commit the crimes prescribed in the preceding two Paragraphs shall be regarded as a joint offender in the crimes of smuggling, trafficking, transporting or manufacturing narcotic drugs.

Article 350 Whoever, in violation of the provisions of the State, illegally transports or carries into or out of China acetic anhydride, ether, chloroform or other raw materials or elixirs which are used for the manufacture of narcotic drugs or, in violation of the provisions of the State, illegally sells or buys the aforesaid materials inside the country, shall be sentenced to fixed-term imprisonment of less than three (3) years, criminal detention, or control and surveillance, with a fine; where the amount involved is large, he/she shall be sentenced to fixed-term imprisonment of more than three (3) years and less than 10 years, with a fine.

Whoever provides the aforementioned materials to a person whom he/she knows clearly to be manufacturing narcotic drugs, shall be regarded as a joint offender in the crime of manufacturing narcotic drugs.

A unit committing the crimes prescribed in the preceding two Paragraphs shall be punished with a fine, and the directly responsible person(s)-in-charge and any other directly responsible person(s) shall be punished in accordance with the provisions in the preceding two Paragraphs.

Article 351 All illegal plantings of opium poppies, marijuana, etc shall be completely destroyed. Whoever illegally grows them, where the act falls within one of the following categories, shall be sentenced to fixed-term imprisonment of less than five (5) years, criminal detention, or control and surveillance, with a fine:

(1) growing more than 500 plants but less than 3,000 plants of opium poppies, or other original drug plants in relatively large numbers;
(2) growing again the aforesaid plants after being handled by the public security organ; or
(3) refusing to root out the plants.

Whoever illegally grows more than 3,000 plants of opium poppies, or other narcotic drug plants in large numbers, shall be sentenced to fixed-term imprisonment of more than five (5) years, with a fine or confiscation of property.

Whoever illegally grows opium poppy plants or other narcotic drug plants but voluntarily roots them out before harvesting them may be exempted from punishment.

Article 352 Whoever illegally purchases, sells, transports, carries or possesses seeds or seedlings of opium poppies or other original drug plants whose plant life has not been terminated, shall, if the amount involved is relatively large, be sentenced to fixed-term imprisonment of less than three (3) years, criminal detention, or control and surveillance, with a fine to be concurrently or independently imposed.

Article 353 Whoever lures, teaches or tricks another person into drug taking or injection shall be sentenced to fixed-term imprisonment of less than three (3) years, criminal detention, or control and surveillance, with a fine; where the circumstances are serious, he/she shall be sentenced to fixed-term imprisonment of more than three (3) years and less than seven (7) years, with a fine.

Whoever compels another person to take or inject narcotic drugs shall be sentenced to fixed-term imprisonment of more than three (3) years and less than 10 years, with a fine.

Whoever lures, teaches, tricks or compels a minor into narcotic drug taking or injection shall have a heavier punishment imposed.

Article 354 Whoever shelters a person for his/her narcotic drug taking or injection shall be sentenced to fixed-term imprisonment of less than three (3) years, criminal detention, or control and surveillance, with a fine.

Article 355 Whoever, engaging in the production, transport, administration and utilisation of State controlled drugs for anaesthesia or psychiatric treatment pursuant to the law, in violation of provisions of the State, provides drug addicts or persons using drug injections with State controlled drugs for anaesthesia or psychiatric treatment which are addictive, shall be sentenced to fixed-term imprisonment of less than three (3) years or criminal detention, with a fine; where the circumstances are serious, he/she shall be sentenced to fixed-term imprisonment of more than three (3) years and less than seven (7) years, with a fine.

Those who provide criminals engaged in smuggling or drug trafficking or, for the purpose of making a profit, provide drug addicts or persons using drug injections with State controlled drugs for anaesthesia or psychiatric treatment which are addictive, shall be convicted and punished in accordance with the provisions in Article 347 of this Law.

A unit committing the crimes prescribed in the preceding Paragraph shall be punished with a fine, and the directly responsible person(s)-in-charge and any other directly responsible person(s) shall be punished in accordance with the provisions in the preceding Paragraph.

Article 356 Whoever, having been sentenced for the commission of a crime of smuggling, trafficking, transporting, making or illegally possessing narcotic drugs, again commits the crime prescribed in this Section, shall have a heavier punishment imposed.

Article 357 For the purpose of the Law, "narcotic drug" refers to opium, heroin, methylaniline (ice), morphine, marijuana, cocaine, and state controlled drugs for anaesthesia or psychiatric treatment which are addictive.

The amount of narcotic drugs smuggled, sold, transported, manufactured or illegally possessed shall be calculated on the basis of the amount that has been proved and verified and shall not be calculated according to the purity of the narcotic drugs.

Section 8 Crimes of Organising, Forcing, Luring, Harbouring or Introducing Prostitution

Article 358[101] Whoever organises for a person to engage in prostitution or forces a person into prostitution shall be sentenced to fixed-term imprisonment of more than five (5) years and less than 10 years with a fine; where the act falls within one of the following categories, he/she shall be sentenced to fixed-term imprisonment of more than 10 years or life imprisonment, with a fine or confiscation of property:

---

[101] This article was revised on 25 February 2011 by Amendment (VIII).

(1) organising others to engage in prostitution, where the circumstances are serious;
(2) forcing a girl under the age of 14 into prostitution;
(3) forcing many persons into prostitution, or forcing persons into prostitution on many occasions;
(4) raping a person and then forcing that person into prostitution;
(5) causing serious injuries, death or other serious consequences to the person who is forced into prostitution.

Whoever commits an act within one of the categories listed in the preceding Paragraph, where the circumstances are particularly grave, shall be sentenced to life imprisonment or death, with confiscation of property.

Whoever recruits or transports persons for a prostitution organiser, or commits other acts in assisting the organising of persons to engage in prostitution shall be sentenced to fixed-term imprisonment of less than five (5) years with a fine; where the circumstances are serious, he/she shall be sentenced to fixed-term imprisonment of more than five (5) years and less than 10 years, with a fine.

Article 359 Whoever lures, harbours or introduces others to engage in prostitution shall be sentenced to a fixed term of imprisonment of less than five (5) years, criminal detention, or control and surveillance, with a fine; where the circumstances are serious, he/she shall be sentenced to fixed-term imprisonment of more than five (5) years, with a fine.

Whoever lures a girl under the age of 14 to engage in prostitution shall be sentenced to fixed-term imprisonment of more than five (5) years, with a fine.

Article 360 Whoever knows clearly that he/she suffers from syphilis, gonorrhoea/baptothecorrhea or other serious venereal diseases but engages in prostitution or visits prostitutes, shall be sentenced to fixed-term imprisonment of less than five (5) years, criminal detention, or control and surveillance, with a fine.

Whoever visits a young girl prostitute under the age of 14 shall be sentenced to fixed-term imprisonment of more than five (5) years with a fine.

Article 361 Any employee in such industries as hotels, food service and restaurants, culture and recreation, and the taxi industry who, taking advantage of his/her work unit, arranges, forces, lures, harbours or introduces another person to engage in prostitution shall be convicted and punished in accordance with the provisions of Articles 358 and 359 in this Law.

Any person taking the main responsibility for a unit listed above committing the crime prescribed in the preceding Paragraph shall have a heavier punishment imposed.

Article 362 Any employee in the hotel, food service and restaurant, culture and recreation or taxi industry, or in any other unit, who divulges secret information to criminals when the public security organ is taking action in investigating and dealing with activities involved in prostitution and visits to prostitutes, shall be convicted and punished in accordance with the provision of Article 310 in this Law, if the circumstances are serious.

Section 9 Crimes of Manufacturing, Selling, or Disseminating Obscene Materials

Article 363 Whoever, for the purpose of making a profit, manufactures, copies, publishes, sells, or disseminates obscene materials shall be sentenced to fixed-term imprisonment of less than three (3) years, criminal detention, or control and surveillance, with a fine; where the circumstances are serious, he/she shall be sentenced to fixed-term imprisonment of more than three (3) years and less than 10 years with a fine; where the circumstances are particularly serious, he/she shall be sentenced to fixed-term imprisonment of more than 10 years or life imprisonment, with a fine or confiscation of property.

Whoever provides [International] Standard Book Numbers to a person who uses them for the publishing of obscene books or magazines shall be sentenced to fixed-term imprisonment of less than three (3) years, criminal detention, or control and surveillance, with a fine to be concurrently or independently imposed. Whoever knowingly provides a person with [International] Standard Book Numbers for his/her use for the publishing of obscene books or magazines shall be punished in accordance with the provisions in the preceding Paragraph.

Article 364 Whoever disseminates obscene books, magazines, films, audio or video products, pictures or other kinds of obscene materials shall, where the circumstances are serious, be sentenced to fixed-term imprisonment of less than two (2) years, criminal detention, or control and surveillance.

Whoever organises to show obscene movies, video-tapes or other audio-visual products shall be sentenced to fixed-term imprisonment of less than three (3) years, criminal detention, or control and surveillance, with a fine; where the circumstances are serious, he/she shall be sentenced to fixed-term imprisonment of more than three (3) years and less than 10 years, with a fine.

Whoever produces or re-produces obscene movies, video-tapes or other audio-visual products and organises to show them shall be given a heavier punishment in accordance with the provisions in the second Paragraph.

Whoever disseminates obscene materials to minors under the age of 18 years shall have a heavier punishment imposed.

Article 365 Whoever organises obscene performances shall be sentenced to fixed-term imprisonment of less than three (3) years, criminal detention, or control and surveillance, with a fine; where the circumstances are serious, he/she shall be sentenced to fixed-term imprisonment of more than three (3) years and less than 10 years, with a fine.

Article 366 A unit committing crimes prescribed in Articles 363, 364 or 365 of this Section shall be punished with a fine, and the directly responsible person(s)-in-charge and any other directly responsible person(s) shall be punished in accordance with the relevant provisions in these articles.

Article 367 For the purpose of this Law, the term "obscene materials" refers to obscene books, magazines, movies, video-tapes, audio-tapes, pictures and other obscene materials that describe in detail sexual behaviour or explicitly propagates pornography.

Scientific works on human physiology or medical knowledge are not obscene materials.

Literary and artistic works of artistic value which contain pornographic contents are not regarded as obscene materials.

Chapter VII

Crimes of Endangering the Interests of National Defence

Article 368 Whoever uses means of violence or threats to obstruct a serviceperson from performing his/her duties pursuant to the law, shall be sentenced to fixed-term imprisonment of less than three (3) years, criminal detention, or control and surveillance, or a fine.

Whoever intentionally obstructs any military actions of the armed forces and causes serious consequences shall be sentenced to fixed-term imprisonment of less than five (5) years or criminal detention.

Article 369[102] Whoever sabotages weaponry, military facilities or military communications shall be sentenced to fixed-term imprisonment of less than three (3) years, criminal detention, or control and surveillance; where important weaponry, military facilities or military communications are sabotaged, he/she shall be sentenced to fixed-term imprisonment of more than three (3) years and less than 10 years; where the circumstances are particularly serious, he/she shall be sentenced to fixed-term imprisonment of more than 10 years, life imprisonment or death.

Whoever negligently commits the crimes prescribed in the preceding Paragraph and causes serious consequences shall be sentenced to fixed-term imprisonment of less than three (3) years or criminal detention; where particularly serious consequences result, he/she shall be sentenced to fixed-term imprisonment of more than three (3) years and less than seven (7) years.

In times of war, a heavier punishment shall be imposed.

Article 370 Whoever knowingly supplies substandard weapons, equipment or other military facilities to the armed forces shall be sentenced to fixed-term imprisonment of less than five (5) years or criminal detention; where the circumstances are serious, he/she shall be sentenced to fixed-term imprisonment of more than five (5) years and less than 10 years; where the circumstances are particularly serious, he/she shall be sentenced to fixed-term imprisonment of more than 10 years, life imprisonment or death.

Whoever negligently commits the crimes prescribed in the preceding Paragraph and causes serious consequences shall be sentenced to fixed-term imprisonment of less than three (3) years or criminal detention; where particularly serious consequences result, he/she shall be sentenced to fixed-term imprisonment of more than three (3) years and less than seven (7) years.

---

102 This Article was revised on 28 February 2005 by Amendment (V).

A unit committing the crimes prescribed in the first Paragraph shall be punished with a fine, and the directly responsible person(s)-in-charge and any other directly responsible person(s) shall be punished in accordance with the provisions in the first Paragraph.

Article 371 Where a gathered crowd forces its way into a military prohibited zone to create a disturbance, and thereby seriously disturbs the order of the military prohibited zone, the ringleader(s) shall be sentenced to fixed-term imprisonment of more than five (5) years and less than 10 years; other active participants shall be sentenced to fixed-term imprisonment of less than five (5) years, criminal detention, control and surveillance, or deprivation of political rights.

Where the circumstances of the disturbance of the order of a military prohibited zone by the crowd are serious, and as a result the administration work in the zone cannot be carried out and heavy losses are caused, the ringleader(s) shall be sentenced to fixed-term imprisonment of more than three (3) years and less than seven (7) years, and other active participants shall be sentenced to fixed-term imprisonment of less than three (3) years, criminal detention, control and surveillance, or deprivation of political rights.

Article 372 Whoever pretends to be a serviceperson in order to swindle and deceive others shall be sentenced to fixed-term imprisonment of less than three (3) years, criminal detention, control and surveillance, or deprivation of political rights; where the circumstances are serious, he/she shall be sentenced to fixed-term imprisonment of more than three (3) years and less than 10 years.

Article 373 Whoever incites a serviceperson to desert from the armed forces or knowingly employs a deserted serviceperson shall, where the circumstances are serious, be sentenced to fixed-term imprisonment of less than three (3) years, criminal detention, or control and surveillance.

Article 374 Whoever practises favouritism for his/her own benefit during the work of recruitment and supplies unqualified army recruits shall, where the circumstances are serious, be sentenced to fixed-term imprisonment of less than three (3) years or criminal detention; if particularly grave consequences are caused, he/she shall be sentenced to fixed-term imprisonment of more than three (3) years and less than seven (7) years.

Article 375[103] Whoever forges, alters, buys, sells, steals or seizes by force official documents, certificates or seals of the armed forces shall be sentenced to fixed-term imprisonment of less than three (3) years, criminal detention, control and surveillance, or deprivation of political rights; where the circumstances are serious, he/she shall be sentenced to fixed-term imprisonment of more than three (3) years and less than 10 years.

Whoever illegally manufactures or trades uniforms of the armed forces shall, where the circumstances are serious, be sentenced to fixed-term imprisonment of less than three (3) years, criminal detention, or control and surveillance, with a fine to be concurrently or independently imposed.

Whoever forges, steals, trades or illegally supplies or uses vehicle number plates or other symbols of the armed forces, shall, where the circumstances are serious, be sentenced to fixed-term imprisonment of less than three (3) years, criminal detention, or control and surveillance, with a fine to be concurrently or independently imposed; where the circumstances are particularly serious, he/she shall be sentenced to fixed-term imprisonment of more than three (3) years and less than seven (7) years, with a fine.

A unit committing the crimes prescribed in the second and third Paragraphs shall be punished with a fine, and the directly responsible person(s)-in-charge and any other directly responsible person(s) shall be punished in accordance with the provisions in the respective Paragraph.

Article 376 A person on reserve duty who, during the time of war, refuses or escapes from conscription to the army or to military training shall, where the circumstances are serious, be sentenced to fixed-term imprisonment of less than three (3) years or criminal detention.

A citizen who, during times of war, refuses to serve or deserts from serving military duty shall, where the circumstances are serious, be sentenced to fixed-term imprisonment of less than two (2) years.

Article 377 Whoever during times of war intentionally provides false information on the enemy's situation to the armed forces and causes serious consequences shall be sentenced to fixed-term imprisonment of more than three (3) years and less than 10 years; where particularly serious consequences are caused, he/she shall be sentenced to fixed-term imprisonment of more than 10 years or life imprisonment.

---

103 This article was revised on 28 February 2009 by Amendment (VII).

Article 378 Whoever in times of war makes up and spreads rumours to confuse and undermine the morale of the army shall be sentenced to fixed-term imprisonment of less than three (3) years, criminal detention, or control and surveillance, where the circumstances are serious, he/she shall be sentenced to fixed-term imprisonment of more than three (3) years and less than 10 years.

Article 379 Whoever in times of war knowingly provides a serviceperson who has deserted the army with shelter, money or goods shall, where the circumstances are serious, be sentenced to fixed-term imprisonment of less than three (3) years or criminal detention.

Article 380 A unit which in times of war refuses or intentionally delays orders for military supplies shall be punished with a fine; the directly responsible person(s)-in-charge and any other directly responsible person(s) shall be sentenced to fixed-term imprisonment of less than five (5) years or criminal detention; where the circumstances are serious, he/she shall be sentenced to fixed-term imprisonment of more than five (5) years.

Article 381[104] Whoever in times of war refuses military acquisition and requisition shall, where the circumstances are serious, be sentenced to fixed-term imprisonment of less than three (3) years or criminal detention.

Chapter VIII

Crimes of Embezzlement and Bribery

Article 382 A crime of embezzlement refers to an act committed by a state functionary who, in taking advantage of his/her office, appropriates, steals, swindles or uses other illegal means to acquire public property.

A person entrusted by a State organ, State-owned company and enterprise or institution, or a people's organisation to manage and operate State property, who takes advantage of his/her office to appropriate, steal, deceive or use other illegal means to acquire public property shall be treated as having committed the crime of embezzlement.

104 This article was revised by the The "Decision of the Standing Committee of the NPC on Revision of Certain Laws" (27 August 2009).

Whoever acts in conspiracy with a person described in the preceding two Paragraphs to engage in embezzlement is treated as a joint offender in the crime of embezzlement.

Article 383 Whoever commits the crime of embezzlement shall be punished in accordance with to the following provisions, depending on the gravity of the circumstances:

(1) An individual who embezzles an amount of more than 100,000 yuan shall be sentenced to fixed-term imprisonment of more than 10 years or life imprisonment and may also have confiscation of property additionally imposed; where the circumstances are particularly serious, he/she shall be sentenced to death with confiscation of property;
(2) An individual who embezzles an amount of more than 50,000 yuan but less than 100,000 yuan shall be sentenced to fixed-term imprisonment of more than five (5) years and may also have confiscation of property additionally imposed; where the circumstances are particularly serious, he/she shall be sentenced to life imprisonment with confiscation of property;
(3) An individual who embezzles an amount of more than 5,000 yuan but less than 50,000 yuan shall be sentenced to fixed-term imprisonment of more than one (1) year and less than seven (7) years; where the circumstances are serious, he/she shall be sentenced to more than seven (7) years and less than 10 years. An individual who embezzles an amount of more than 1,000 yuan but less than 10,000 yuan, and shows repentance after the commission of the crime and promptly returns the illegally acquired money, may be given a mitigated criminal punishment or be exempted from criminal punishment, but shall be subject to administrative sanction by the unit where he/she works or by a competent organ at a higher level;
(4) An individual who embezzles an amount of less than 5,000 yuan, shall, where the circumstances are relatively serious, be sentenced to fixed-term imprisonment of less than two (2) years or criminal detention; where the circumstances are relatively minor; he/she shall be subject to administrative sanction by the unit where he/she works or by a competent organ at a higher level.

Those who repeatedly commit the crime of embezzlement and have not been pursued shall be punished on the basis of the accumulated amount of money embezzled.

Article 384 A state functionary who, in taking advantage of his/her office, misappropriates public funds for his/her own use and engages in illegal activities, or misappropriates a relatively large amount of public funds and engages in profit-making activities, or misappropriates a relatively large amount of public funds and fails to return it within three (3) months, is guilty of the crime of misappropriation of public funds and shall be sentenced to fixed-term imprisonment of less than five (5) years or criminal detention; where the circumstances are serious, he/she shall be sentenced to fixed-term imprisonment of more than five (5) years; where misappropriating a huge amount of public funds without returning it, he/she shall be sentenced to fixed-term imprisonment of more than 10 years or life imprisonment.

Whoever misappropriates funds intended for disaster relief, emergency rescue, flood prevention and control, support of revolutionary martyrs and servicepersons and family members, poverty aid, migrant settlement or social welfare and converts them to his/her own use, shall have a heavier punishment imposed.

Article 385 The crime of acceptance of bribes refers to an act by a state functionary who, taking advantage of his/her office, demands money and property from another person or illegally accepts money and property from another person as the price of providing benefits for that person.

A state functionary who, in violation of the provisions of the State accepts commissions and service fees in economic activities under various guises, and takes them into his/her own possession, shall be treated as having committed the crime of acceptance of bribes.

Article 386 Whoever is guilty of the crime of acceptance of bribes shall be punished in accordance with the provisions of Article 383 of this Law and on the basis of the amount of properties obtained from the bribes and of the gravity of the circumstances. Whoever extorts a bribe shall have a heavier punishment imposed.

Article 387 A State organ, State-owned company and enterprise or institution, or a people's organisation which extorts or illegally accepts money or property from another person and in turn seeks benefits for that person, shall, where the circumstances are serious, be punished with a fine, the directly responsible person(s)-in-charge and any other directly responsible person(s) shall be sentenced to fixed-term imprisonment of less than five (5) years or criminal detention.

Where a unit listed in the preceding Paragraph secretly accepts unrecorded commissions and service fees of various kinds in its economic activities, it shall be treated as having committed the crime of acceptance of bribes and be punished in accordance with the provisions in the preceding Paragraph.

Article 388 A state functionary who, taking advantage of his/her power or position, seeks, through the official act of another state functionary, illegitimate benefits for a person who requests him/her and in turn extorts or accepts money or property from that person, shall be deemed as having committed the crime of acceptance of bribes.

Article 388(A)[105] A close relative of a state functionary or any other person with a close relationship with the state functionary, who, through the official act of the said state functionary or, taking advantage of the power or position of that state functionary, through the official act of another state functionary, seeks illegitimate benefits for a person who requests them and in turn extorts or accepts money or property from that person, shall, where the amount involved is relatively large or there are other relatively serious circumstances, be sentenced to fixed-term imprisonment of less than three (3) years or criminal detention, with a fine; where the amount involved is large or there are other serious circumstances, be sentenced to fixed-term imprisonment of more than three (3) years and less than seven (7) years, with a fine; where the amount involved is extremely large or there are other particularly serious circumstances, be sentenced to fixed-term imprisonment of more than seven (7) years, with a fine or confiscation of property.

A state functionary retired from his/her official position or his/her close relative or any other person with a close relationship with him/her, who, taking advantage of the pre-retirement power or position of the said state functionary, commits acts prescribed in the preceding Paragraph, shall be convicted and punished in accordance with the provisions of the preceding Paragraph.

Article 389 Whoever for the purpose of obtaining illegitimate benefits gives state functionaries money or property is guilty of the crime of offering bribes.

---

105 This article was added on 28 February 2009 by Amendment (VII).

Whoever, in economic activities, offers a relatively large amount of money or property to state functionaries in violation of the provisions of the State, or offers commissions or service fees of various kinds to state functionaries in violation of the provisions of the State, shall be deemed as having committed the crime of offering bribes.

Whoever gives money or property to a state functionary under extortion and receives no illegitimate benefits therefrom shall not be deemed as having committed the crime of offering bribes.

Article 390 Whoever commits the crime of offering bribes shall be sentenced to fixed-term imprisonment of less than five (5) years or criminal detention; where bribes are offered for the purpose of obtaining illegitimate benefits and the circumstances are serious or the interests of the State thereby are seriously harmed, he/she shall be sentenced to fixed-term imprisonment of more than five (5) years and less than 10 years; where the circumstances are particularly serious, he/she shall be sentenced to fixed-term imprisonment of more than 10 years or life imprisonment, and may in addition be sentenced to confiscation of property.

A briber who takes the initiative to confess his/her act of offering bribes before being prosecuted may be given a mitigated punishment or be exempted from punishment.

Article 391 Whoever for the purpose of seeking illegitimate benefits offers a State organ, State-owned company and enterprise, institution or a people's organisation money or property, or in economic activities gives various kinds of commissions and service fees to such aforesaid units in violation of the provisions of the State, shall be sentenced to fixed-term imprisonment of less than three (3) years or criminal detention.

A unit committing the crime prescribed in the preceding Paragraph shall be punished with a fine, and the directly responsible person(s)-in-charge and any other directly responsible person(s) shall be punished in accordance with the provisions in the preceding Paragraph.

Article 392 Whoever introduces another to bribe a state functionary shall, where the circumstances are serious, be sentenced to fixed-term imprisonment of less than three (3) years or criminal detention.

If the person introducing the briber takes the initiative to confess his/her act of offering bribes before being prosecuted, he/she may be given a mitigated punishment or be exempted from punishment.

Article 393 A unit which offers bribes for the purpose of seeking illegitimate benefits, or gives commissions or service fees to state functionaries in violation of the provisions of the State shall, if the circumstances are serious, be sentenced to a fine, and the directly responsible person(s)-in-charge and any other directly responsible person(s) shall be sentenced to fixed-term imprisonment of less than five (5) years or criminal detention. Where a briber takes the illegal gains obtained from the offering of bribes into his/her own possession, he/she shall be convicted and punished in accordance with the provisions in Articles 389 and 390 of this Law.

Article 394 A state functionary who accepts gifts during the course of performing his/her official duties at home or during foreign cooperation and fails to turn over the gifts as required by the provisions of the State shall, if the amount involved is relatively large, be convicted and punished in accordance with the provisions in Articles 382 and 383 of this Law.

Article 395[106] Where a state functionary has property or expenses which obviously exceed his/her legitimate income, if the difference is large, he/she may be ordered to explain the sources of his/her property. If he/she fails to prove the legitimacy of the property, the amount of income that is discrepant shall be deemed illegal income, and he/she shall be sentenced to fixed-term imprisonment of less than five (5) years or criminal detention; where the amount of discrepant is particularly large, he/she shall be sentenced to fixed-term imprisonment of more than five (5) years and less than 10 years. The amount of income that is discrepant shall be recovered.

A state functionary who holds deposits overseas must declare them in accordance with the provisions of the State. Whoever holds a relatively large amount of such deposits and conceals the matter, shall be sentenced to fixed-term imprisonment of less than two (2) years or criminal detention; where the circumstances are minor, an administrative sanction shall be imposed by the unit with which he/she works or by a competent organ at the higher level depending on the circumstances.

Article 396 Where a State organ a State-owned company and enterprise or institution, or a people's organisation which, in violation of the provisions of the State, distributes, in the name of the unit, state-owned assets to

106 This article was revised on 28 February 2009 by Amendment (VII).

individuals in the unit, where the amount involved is relatively large, the directly responsible person(s)-in-charge and any other directly responsible person(s) shall be sentenced to fixed-term imprisonment of less than three (3) years or criminal detention, with a fine to be imposed concurrently or independently; where the amount involved is large, he/she shall be sentenced to fixed-term imprisonment of more than three (3) years and less than seven (7) years, with a fine.

A judicial organ or an administrative law enforcement organ which, in violation of the provisions of the State, privately distributes, in the name of the unit, to individuals in the unit any fines collected or any money and property confiscated which should have been turned over to the State, shall be punished in accordance with the provisions in the preceding Paragraph.

Chapter IX

Crimes of Dereliction of Duty

Article 397 A state functionary who abuses his/her power or neglects his/her duty and thereby causes major losses to public property and the interests of the State and the people, shall be sentenced to fixed-term imprisonment of less than three (3) years or criminal detention; where the circumstances are particularly serious, he/she shall be sentenced to fixed-term imprisonment of more than three (3) years and less than seven (7) years. Where this Law provides otherwise elsewhere, those provisions apply.

A state functionary who practises favouritism and irregularities and commits the crime prescribed in the preceding Paragraph shall be sentenced to fixed-term imprisonment of less than five (5) years or criminal detention; where the circumstances are particularly serious, he/she shall be sentenced to fixed-term imprisonment of more than five (5) years and less than 10 years. Where this Law provides otherwise elsewhere, those provisions apply.

Article 398 A state functionary who, in violation of the provisions of the law on the protection of State secrets, intentionally or negligently leaks State secrets shall, where the circumstances are serious, be sentenced to fixed-term imprisonment of less than three (3) years or criminal detention; where the circumstances are particularly serious, he/she shall be sentenced to fixed-term imprisonment of more than three (3) years and less than seven (7) years.

A person other than a state functionary who commits the crime prescribed in the preceding Paragraph shall be punished in accordance with the provisions of the preceding Paragraph and relative to the gravity of the circumstances.

Article 399[107] A judicial official who, in bending the law for his/her own benefit or bending the law for a favour, knowingly subjects an innocent person to prosecution or intentionally harbours a person, whom he/she knows clearly to be guilty, from being pursued with criminal liability, or in the course of adjudication intentionally departs from the facts and the law, and renders judgment or rulings that pervert the law, shall be sentenced to fixed-term imprisonment of less than five (5) years or criminal detention; where the circumstances are serious, he/she shall be sentenced to fixed-term imprisonment of more than five (5) years and less than 10 years; where the circumstances are particularly serious, he/she shall be sentenced to fixed-term imprisonment of more than 10 years.

A judicial official who, in the course of civil or administrative adjudication, intentionally departs from the facts and the law and renders judgment or orders that pervert the law, shall, where the circumstances are serious, be sentenced to fixed-term imprisonment of less than five (5) years or criminal detention; where the circumstances are particularly serious, he/she shall be sentenced to fixed-term imprisonment of more than five (5) years and less than 10 years.

A judicial official who, in the activities of execution of a judgment or ruling, grossly neglects his/her duty or abuses his/her position and fails to adopt litigation preservation measures according to the law, or to perform the statutory function of execution, or adopts litigation preservation measures or coercive execution measures in violation of the law, shall, where the party concerned or another person thus suffers from major losses, be sentenced to fixed-term imprisonment of less than five (5) years or criminal detention; where losses suffered by the party concerned or another person are particularly serious, he/she shall be sentenced to fixed-term imprisonment of more than five (5) years and less than 10 years.

---

[107] This article was revised on 28 December 2002 by Amendment (IV).

A judicial official who takes bribes and commits the acts prescribed in the preceding three Paragraphs, which at the same time also constitute the crime prescribed in Article 385 of this Law, shall be convicted and punished in accordance with the provisions that impose a heavier penalty.

Article 399(A)[108] A person performing the functions of arbitration according to law, who in the course of arbitration intentionally departs from the facts and the law, and renders judgments or rulings that pervert the law, shall, where the circumstances are serious, be sentenced to fixed-term imprisonment of less than three (3) years or criminal detention; where the circumstances particularly serious, he/she shall be sentenced to fixed-term imprisonment of more than three (3) years and less than seven (7) years.

Article 400 A judicial official who releases without authority a crime suspect, criminal accused or criminal from custody shall be sentenced to fixed-term imprisonment of less than five (5) years or criminal detention; where the circumstances are serious, he/she shall be sentenced to fixed-term imprisonment of more than five (5) years and less than 10 years; where the circumstances are particularly serious, he/she shall be sentenced to fixed-term imprisonment of more than 10 years.

A judicial official whose gross neglect of duty causes the escape of a crime suspect, criminal accused or criminal under custody shall, where serious consequences result, be sentenced to fixed-term imprisonment of less than three (3) years or criminal detention; where particularly serious consequences are caused, he/she shall be sentenced to fixed-term imprisonment of more than three (3) years and less than 10 years.

Article 401 A judicial official who, practising favouritism and irregularity, grants a reduction of sentence, parole, or temporary service of sentence outside prison for criminals who do not meet the conditions for the reduction of sentence, parole, or temporary service of sentence outside prison, shall be sentenced to fixed-term imprisonment of less than three (3) years or criminal detention; where the circumstances are serious, he/she shall be sentenced to fixed-term imprisonment of more than three (3) years and less than seven (7) years.

---

108 This article was added on 29 June 2006 by Amendment (VI).

Article 402 An official of an administrative law enforcement organ who, practising favouritism and irregularity, does not transfer cases to judicial organs for investigation of criminal liabilities in accordance with the law where he/she should have done so, shall, where the circumstances are serious, be sentenced to fixed-term imprisonment of less than three (3) years or criminal detention; where serious consequences result, he/she shall be sentenced to fixed-term imprisonment of more than three (3) years and less than seven (7) years.

Article 403 A state functionary in a department with the relevant competence who, practising favouritism and irregularity and abusing his/her powers, approves or registers the establishment of companies which do not meet the conditions for being companies, or approves applications of companies for the issue and listing of shares or bonds, shall, where this results in serious losses to public property and the State and the people, be sentenced to fixed-term imprisonment of less than five (5) years or criminal detention.

Where a competent department at a higher level arbitrarily orders a registration organ or its personnel to commit acts prescribed in the preceding Paragraph, the directly responsible person(s)-in-charge shall be punished in accordance with the provisions in the preceding Paragraph.

Article 404 An official of a taxation authority who, practising favouritism and irregularity, fails to collect or under-collects payable taxes, resulting in heavy losses of State revenues, shall be sentenced to fixed-term imprisonment of less than five (5) years or criminal detention; where particularly heavy losses are caused, he/she shall be sentenced to fixed-term imprisonment of more than five (5) years.

Article 405 An official of a taxation authority who, in violation of the provisions of laws and administrative regulations, practises favouritism and irregularity in the work of handling the distribution and sale of invoices, offsetting taxes and export tax refunds and causes great losses to the State, shall be sentenced to fixed-term imprisonment of less than five (5) years or criminal detention; where the State suffers particularly heavy losses, he/she shall be sentenced to fixed-term imprisonment of more than five (5) years.

A state functionary who, in violation of the provisions of the State, practises favouritism and irregularity in the work of providing declaration forms for export goods and verification and cancellation forms for collecting foreign exchanges from export or other documents for export tax refunds, shall, where heavy losses to the State are caused, be punished in accordance with the provisions of the preceding Paragraph.

Article 406 A state functionary who, in the course of concluding and performing a contract, is defrauded due to his/her gross neglect of duty shall, where heavy losses to the State are caused, be sentenced to fixed-term imprisonment of less than three (3) years or criminal detention; where particularly heavy losses to the State are caused, he/she shall be sentenced to fixed-term imprisonment of more than three (3) years and less than seven (7) years.

Article 407 A state functionary in a department with competence for forestry who, in violation of the provisions of the forestry laws, issues logging permits in excess of the approved annual quota, or in violation of provisions issues logging permits improperly shall, where the circumstances are serious and the forests suffer serious damage, be sentenced to fixed-term imprisonment of less than three (3) years or criminal detention.

Article 408 A state functionary in a competent department responsible for supervision and administration of environmental protection, whose gross neglect of duty causes a major environmental pollution accident which results in serious damage to public and private property or injuries or death to persons, shall be sentenced to fixed-term imprisonment of less than three (3) years or criminal detention.

Article 408(A)[109] A state functionary with the responsibility for food safety supervision and administration, who abuses his/her position or neglects his/her duties shall, where a serious food safety accident or other serious consequence results, be sentenced to fixed-term imprisonment of less than five (5) years or criminal detention; where a particularly serious consequence results, he/she shall be sentenced to fixed-term imprisonment of more than five (5) years and less than 10 years.

Where a crime prescribed in the preceding Paragraph is committed by practising favouritism and irregularity, a heavier penalty shall be imposed.

Article 409 A functionary of a government health administrative department who is responsible for the prevention and treatment of infectious diseases, and who causes the spread of infectious diseases due to his/her

109 This article was added on 25 February 2011 by Amendment (VIII).

gross neglect of duty, shall be sentenced to fixed-term imprisonment of less than three (3) years or criminal detention, where the circumstances are serious.

Article 410[110] A state functionary, who practises favouritism and irregularity in violation of laws and regulations on land management and by abusing his/her powers illegally approves acquisition, requisition, and occupation of land, or illegally grants land use rights at a price lower than the market value, shall, where the circumstances are serious, be sentenced to fixed-term imprisonment of less than three (3) years or criminal detention; where particularly heavy losses to the State or collectives result, he/she shall be sentenced to fixed-term imprisonment of more than three (3) years and less than seven (7) years.

Article 411 A customs official who practises favouritism and irregularity and connives at smuggling, shall, where the circumstances are serious, be sentenced to fixed-term imprisonment of less than five (5) years or criminal detention; where the circumstances are particularly serious, he/she shall be sentenced to fixed-term imprisonment of more than five (5) years.

Article 412 An official in a state commodity inspection department or a commodity inspection organ who practises favouritism and irregularity and falsifies inspection results, shall be sentenced to fixed-term imprisonment of less than five (5) years or criminal detention; where particularly serious consequences result, he/she shall be sentenced to fixed-term imprisonment of more than five (5) years and less than 10 years.

An official described in the preceding Paragraph who, due to his/her gross neglect of duty, fails to inspect goods which are subject to inspection, or delays in issuing inspection certificates or wrongly issues certificates, resulting in serious losses to the State, shall be sentenced to fixed-term imprisonment of less than three (3) years or criminal detention.

Article 413 A quarantine official in an animal and plant quarantine organ who, practising favouritism and irregularity, falsifies quarantine results, shall be sentenced to fixed-term imprisonment of less than five (5) years or criminal detention; where this causes grave consequences, he/she shall be sentenced to fixed-term imprisonment of more than five (5) years and less than 10 years.

---

110 This article was revised by the The "Decision of the Standing Committee of the NPC on Revision of Certain Laws" (27 August 2009).

An official described in the preceding Paragraph who, due to his/her gross neglect of duty, fails to quarantine goods which are subject to quarantine, or delays in issuing quarantine certificates or wrongly issues certificates, and as a result the State suffers serious losses, shall be sentenced to fixed-term imprisonment of less than three (3) years or criminal detention.

Article 414 A state functionary responsible for investigating criminal acts involved in the manufacturing and selling of fake and shoddy commodities who practises favouritism and irregularity and fails to perform his/her investigating function pursuant to law shall, where the circumstances are serious, be sentenced to fixed-term imprisonment of less than five (5) years or criminal detention.

Article 415 A state functionary responsible for handling passports, visas and other border exit/entry documents, who knowingly issues a border exit/entry document to a person attempting to illegally cross the national border (frontier), or a frontier official or a customs official who knowingly lets a person illegally cross the national border (frontier), shall be sentenced to fixed-term imprisonment of less than three (3) years or criminal detention; where the circumstances are serious, he/she shall be sentenced to fixed-term imprisonment of more than three (3) years and less than seven (7) years.

Article 416 A state functionary responsible for rescuing abducted or kidnapped women and children who fails to act to rescue abducted or kidnapped women and children after receiving requests from the abducted or kidnapped women or children or their family members or receiving information from other persons, and causes serious consequences, shall be sentenced to fixed-term imprisonment of less than five (5) years or criminal detention.

A state functionary responsible for rescuing abducted or kidnapped women and children who obstructs rescue efforts by using his/her power, shall be sentenced to fixed-term imprisonment of more than two (2) years and less than seven (7) years; where the circumstances are relatively minor, he/she shall be sentenced to fixed-term imprisonment of less than two (2) years or criminal detention.

Article 417 A state functionary responsible for investigating and stopping criminal activities who divulges secret information or provides assistance to criminals so as to help them escape from punishment, shall be sentenced to fixed-term imprisonment of less than three (3) years or criminal detention; where the circumstances are serious, he/she shall be sentenced to fixed-term imprisonment of more than three (3) years and less than 10 years.

Article 418 A state functionary who practises favouritism and irregularity in work relating to the recruitment of public servants or students, shall, where the circumstances are serious, be sentenced to fixed-term imprisonment of less than three (3) years or criminal detention.

Article 419 A state functionary who is in gross neglect of duty and thus causes precious cultural relics to be damaged or lost, shall be sentenced to fixed-term imprisonment of less than three (3) years or criminal detention, where the circumstances are serious.

Chapter X

Crimes of Violation of Duty by Servicepersons

Article 420 The crime of violation of duty by a serviceperson refers to an act committed by a serviceperson in violation of his/her duty, which jeopardises national and military interests and which is punishable by criminal sentence in accordance with the law.

Article 421 A serviceperson in times of war who disobeys an order, thereby endangering the battle, shall be sentenced to fixed-term imprisonment of more than three (3) years and less than 10 years; where heavy losses are caused to the combat or campaign, he/she shall be sentenced to fixed-term imprisonment of more than 10 years, life imprisonment or death.

Article 422 A serviceperson who deliberately conceals or falsely reports information on military actions or refuses to transmit or transmits false military orders, thereby jeopardising battles, shall be sentenced to fixed-term imprisonment of more than three (3) years and less than 10 years; where heavy losses are caused to the combat or campaign, he/she shall be sentenced to fixed-term imprisonment of more than 10 years, life imprisonment or death.

Article 423 A serviceperson who is mortally afraid of death and voluntarily lays down his/her arms and surrenders to the enemy, shall be sentenced to fixed-term imprisonment of more than three (3) years and less than 10 years; where the circumstances are serious, he/she shall be sentenced to fixed-term imprisonment of more than 10 years or life imprisonment.

Those who work for the enemy after surrender shall be sentenced to fixed-term imprisonment of more than 10 years, life imprisonment or death.

Article 424 A serviceperson who flees from the battlefield shall be sentenced to fixed-term imprisonment of less than three (3) years; where the circumstances are serious, he/she shall be sentenced to fixed-term imprisonment of more than three (3) years and less than 10 years; where heavy losses are caused to the combat or campaign, he/she shall be sentenced to fixed-term imprisonment of more than 10 years, life imprisonment or death.

Article 425 A commander or a person on duty who leaves his/her post on his/her own accord or neglects his/her duty shall, where this causes serious consequences, shall be sentenced to fixed-term imprisonment of less than three (3) years or criminal detention; where this causes particularly serious consequences, he/she shall be sentenced to fixed-term imprisonment of more than three (3) years and less than seven (7) years.

Those who commit the crimes prescribed in the preceding Paragraph in times of war shall be sentenced to fixed-term imprisonment of more than five (5) years.

Article 426 A person who obstructs a commander or a person on duty from performing his/her duty by means of violence or threat, shall be sentenced to fixed-term imprisonment of less than five (5) years or criminal detention; where the circumstances are serious, he/she shall be sentenced to fixed-term imprisonment of more than five (5) years; where serious injury or death to another person is caused or there are other serious consequences, he/she shall be sentenced to life imprisonment, or death. Committing such crimes in times of war shall have a heavier punishment imposed.

Article 427 Whoever instructs his/her subordinates to commit activities in violation of their duties in abusing his/her powers shall, where this causes serious consequences, be sentenced to fixed-term imprisonment of less than five (5) years or criminal detention; where the circumstances are particularly serious, he/she shall be sentenced to fixed-term imprisonment of more than five (5) years and less than 10 years.

Article 428 A commander who disobeys an order and shrinks back at a battle or acts passively in a battle shall, where serious consequences are caused, be sentenced to fixed-term imprisonment of less than five (5) years; where heavy losses are caused in the combat or campaign or there are other particularly serious consequences, he/she shall be sentenced to fixed-term imprisonment of more than five (5) years.

Article 429 A commander on the battlefield who does not rescue his/her friendly troops which are in a dangerous situation and ask for help, when he/she has the ability to do so, therefore causing the friendly troops to suffer heavy losses, shall be sentenced to fixed-term imprisonment of less than five (5) years.

Article 430 Whoever, in the course of performing his/her official duties, leaves his/her post without permission and defects to another country or commits desertion while being outside China, thereby endangering the State's military interests, shall be sentenced to fixed-term imprisonment of less than five (5) years or criminal detention; where the circumstances are serious, he/she shall be sentenced to fixed-term imprisonment of more than five (5) years.

Whoever commits desertion by piloting an aircraft or a ship, or in other particularly serious circumstances, shall be sentenced to fixed-term imprisonment of more than 10 years, life imprisonment or death.

Article 431 Whoever illegally obtains military secrets by means of stealing, spying or buying shall be sentenced to fixed-term imprisonment of less than five (5) years; where the circumstances are serious, he/she shall be sentenced to fixed-term imprisonment of more than five (5) years and less than 10 years.

Whoever steals, spies, buys or illegally provides military secrets for an overseas institution, organisation or individual, shall be sentenced to fixed-term imprisonment of more than 10 years, life imprisonment or death.

Article 432 Whoever, in violation of the regulations on the maintenance of State secrets, intentionally or negligently leaks military secrets shall, where the circumstances are serious, be sentenced to fixed-term imprisonment of less than five (5) years or criminal detention; where the circumstances are particularly serious, he/she shall be sentenced to fixed-term imprisonment of more than five (5) years and less than 10 years.

Whoever, in times of war, commits the crimes prescribed in the preceding Paragraph shall be sentenced to fixed-term imprisonment of more than five (5) years and less than 10 years; where the circumstances are particularly serious, he/she shall be sentenced to fixed-term imprisonment of more than 10 years or life imprisonment.

Article 433 Whoever in times of war fabricates rumours to confuse people and undermines the morale of the troops shall be sentenced to fixed-term imprisonment of less than three (3) years; where the circumstances are serious, he/she shall be sentenced to fixed-term imprisonment of more than three (3) years and less than 10 years.

Whoever colludes with the enemy to fabricate rumours to confuse people and undermines the morale of the troops shall be sentenced to fixed-term imprisonment of more than 10 years or life imprisonment; where the circumstances are particularly serious, he/she may be sentenced to death.

Article 434 Whoever in times of war inflicts injuries on him/herself so as to escape from military duties shall be sentenced to fixed-term imprisonment of less than three (3) years; where the circumstances are serious, he/she shall be sentenced to fixed-term imprisonment of more than three (3) years and less than seven (7) years.

Article 435 Whoever in violation of the regulations on conscription deserts his/her troops shall be sentenced to fixed-term imprisonment of less than three (3) years or criminal detention, if the circumstances are serious.

Committing the crime prescribed in the preceding Paragraph in times of war shall have a sentence of fixed-term imprisonment of more than three (3) years and less than seven (7) years imposed.

Article 436 Whoever seriously violates regulations on the use of weaponry and thereby causes an accident resulting in serious injuries or deaths to persons or other serious consequences, shall be sentenced to fixed-term imprisonment of less than three (3) years or criminal detention; where the consequences are particularly serious, he/she shall be sentenced to fixed-term imprisonment of more than three (3) years and less than seven (7) years.

Article 437 Whoever, in violation of regulations on the use of weaponry, changes the prescribed use of weaponry on his/her own accord, thereby causing serious consequences, shall be sentenced to fixed-term imprisonment of less than three (3) years or criminal detention; where particularly grave consequences are caused, he/she shall be sentenced to fixed-term imprisonment of more than three (3) years and less than seven (7) years.

Article 438 Whoever steals or seizes by force weaponry or military supplies shall be sentenced to fixed-term imprisonment of less than five (5) years or criminal detention; where the circumstances are serious, he/she shall be sentenced to fixed-term imprisonment of more than five (5) years and less than 10 years; where the circumstances are particularly serious, he/she shall be sentenced to fixed-term imprisonment of more than 10 years, life imprisonment or death.

Those who steal or seize guns, ammunition or explosives shall be punished in accordance with the provisions in Article 127 of this law.

Article 439 Whoever illegally sells or transfers military weaponry shall be sentenced to fixed-term imprisonment of more than three (3) years and less than 10 years; where the sale or transfer involves a large amount of weaponry or there are other particularly serious circumstances, he/she shall be sentenced to fixed-term imprisonment of more than 10 years, life imprisonment or death.

Article 440 Whoever abandons weaponry in defiance of orders shall be sentenced to fixed-term imprisonment of less than five (5) years or criminal detention; where important weaponry or a large number of weapons are abandoned or there are other serious circumstances, he/she shall be sentenced to fixed-term imprisonment of more than five (5) years.

Article 441 Whoever loses weaponry but fails to report this promptly, or where there are other serious circumstances, shall be sentenced to fixed-term imprisonment of less than three (3) years or criminal detention.

Article 442 Wherever, in violation of the provisions, the sale or transfer of real estate of the armed forces occurs without authorisation, if the circumstances are serious, the directly responsible person(s) shall be sentenced to fixed-term imprisonment of less than three (3) years or criminal detention; where the circumstances are particularly serious, he/she shall be sentenced to fixed-term imprisonment of more than three (3) years and less than 10 years.

Article 443 Whoever abuses his/her powers and mistreats his/her subordinates shall, where the circumstances are odious, or grave injuries or other serious consequences result, be sentenced to fixed-term imprisonment of less than five (5) years or criminal detention; where death to a person is caused, he/she shall be sentenced to fixed-term imprisonment of more than five (5) years.

Article 444 In cases of intentionally abandoning injured or sick servicepersons on the battlefield, the person(s) directly responsible shall, where the circumstances are serious, be sentenced to fixed-term imprisonment of less than five (5) years.

Article 445 A person responsible for providing rescue and medical treatment in times of war, who refuses to rescue and give treatment to seriously injured or sick servicepersons when he/she is able to do so, shall be sentenced to fixed-term imprisonment of less than five (5) years or criminal detention; where serious disability, death to the serviceperson or other grave consequences are caused, he/she shall be sentenced to fixed-term imprisonment of more than five (5) years and less than 10 years.

Article 446 Whoever, in times of war and in military operation areas, cruelly injures or kills innocent residents or seizes by force money or properties from innocent residents, shall be sentenced to fixed-term imprisonment of less than five (5) years; where the circumstances are serious, he/she shall be sentenced to fixed-term imprisonment of more than five (5) years and less than 10 years; where the circumstances are particularly serious, he/she shall be sentenced to fixed-term imprisonment of more than 10 years, life imprisonment or death.

Article 447 Whoever releases prisoners of war without authorisation shall be sentenced to fixed-term imprisonment of less than five (5) years; where without authorisation important prisoners of war or a large number of prisoners of war are released, or there are other serious circumstances, he/she shall be sentenced to fixed-term imprisonment of more than five (5) years.

Article 448 Whoever mistreats prisoners of war shall to be sentenced to fixed-term imprisonment of less than three (3) years, if the circumstances are odious.

Article 449 In times of war, a serviceperson who is sentenced to fixed-term imprisonment of less than three (3) years with a suspension of execution of sentence on the grounds of there being no immediate danger, shall be allowed to atone for his/her crime by performing good service; where he/she actually performs meritorious service, the original sentence may be withdrawn and he/she shall not be deemed to have committed a crime.

Article 450 This Chapter applies to active service officers, civilian cadres, soldiers, and students with military status in the Chinese People's Liberation Army, active service police officers, civilian cadres, soldiers, and students with military status in the Chinese People's Armed Police, and persons on reserve duty and other persons who are in the position to execute military tasks.

Article 451 For the purpose of this Chapter, the term "in times of war" refers to the time from which the country, upon the declaration of the State, enters into a state of war and the troops have been assigned to combat missions, or the time at which the troop suffers a surprise attack by the enemy.

The time during which servicepersons enforce a curfew or deal with a sudden incident of violence is considered to be a time of war.

Supplementary Provisions

Article 452 This Law takes effect on 1 October 1997.

Regulations, supplementary provisions and decisions enacted by the Standing Committee of the National People's Congress listed in Appendix I of this Law, which have either been included in this Law or are no longer applicable, shall be nullified from the date on which this Law becomes effective.

Supplementary provisions and decisions enacted by the Standing Committee of the National People's Congress listed in Appendix II of this Law shall be retained. Among them, provisions governing administrative sanctions and administrative measures remain effective; provisions governing criminal liability which have been included in this Law shall be superseded by this Law from the date on which this Law becomes effective.

Appendix I

The following regulations, supplementary provisions and decisions enacted by the Standing Committee of the National People's Congress listed in Appendix 1 of this Law, which have either been included in this Law or are no longer applicable, shall be nullified from the date on which this Law becomes effective.

1. Provisional Regulations of the People's Republic of China on Punishing Servicepersons for Crimes of Violation of Duty;
2. Decisions on Severely Punishing Criminals for Engaging in Seriously Undermining the Economy;
3. Decisions on Severely Punishing Criminals for Engaging in Seriously Jeopardising Social Order;
4. Supplementary Provisions on Punishment for Crimes of Smuggling;

5. Supplementary Provisions on Punishment for Crimes of Embezzlement and Bribery;
6. Supplementary Provisions on Punishment for Crimes of Leaking State Secrets;
7. Supplementary Provisions on Punishment for Crimes of Hunting and Slaughtering Rare and Endangered Species of Wildlife under the State's Special Protection;
8. Decisions on Punishment for Crimes of Insulting the National Flag or Emblem of the People's Republic of China;
9. Supplementary Provisions on Punishment for Crimes of Robbing Ancient Cultural Ruins or Ancient Tombs;
10. Decision on Punishing Criminals for Hijacking Aircraft;
11. Supplementary Provisions on Punishment for Crimes of Falsifying Registered Trademarks;
12. Decisions on Punishment for Crimes of Manufacturing or Selling Fake and Shoddy Commodities;
13. Decisions on Punishment for Crimes of Infringing upon Copyright;
14. Decisions on Punishment for Crimes of Violation of the Company Law;
15. Decisions on Handling Criminals under Reform through Labor or Offenders under Re-education through Labor for Escaping or Committing Crimes Again.

Appendix II

The following supplementary provisions and decisions enacted by the Standing Committee of the National People's Congress listed in Appendix II of this Law shall be retained. Among them, provisions governing administrative sanctions and administrative measures remain effective; provisions governing criminal liability which have been included in this Law shall be superseded by this Law from the date on which this Law becomes effective.

1. Decisions on Prohibition of Narcotic Drugs;
2. Decisions on Punishing Criminals for Engaging in Smuggling, Producing, Selling, or Disseminating Obscene Materials;
3. Decisions on Punishing Criminals for Engaging in Abducting and Selling or Kidnapping Women or Children;
4. Decisions on Strict Prohibition of Prostitution and Visiting Prostitutes;
5. Supplementary Provisions on Punishment for Crimes of Tax Evasion and Refusal to Pay Tax;

6. Supplementary Provisions on Severe Punishment for Crimes of Organising or Transporting People to Illegally Cross National Borders (Frontiers);
7. Decisions on Punishment for Crimes of Undermining the Financial Order;
8. Decisions on Punishment for Crimes of Fraudulently Issuing, Forging or Illegally Selling Special Invoices for Value-Added Taxes.

II DECISION OF THE STANDING COMMITTEE OF THE NATIONAL PEOPLE'S CONGRESS ON THE PUNISHMENT OF CRIMES INVOLVING FRAUDULENT PURCHASING, EVADING AND ILLEGAL TRADING OF FOREIGN EXCHANGE

Adopted 29 December 1998 at the 6th Meeting of the Standing Committee of the 9th National People's Congress

Promulgated 29 December 1998 by Presidential Order No 14 (9th NPC) Effective on Promulgation

In order to punish criminal behaviour involving the fraudulent purchase, evasion and illegal trade of foreign exchange and to safeguard the order of the state foreign exchange control, the following supplementary provisions and revisions to the Criminal Law are hereby enacted:

1. Whoever fraudulently purchase foreign exchange in one of the following circumstances shall be sentenced to fixed-term imprisonment of less than five (5) year or criminal detention, with a fine of more than five (5) per cent and less than 30 per cent of the amount of foreign exchange fraudulently purchased to be concurrently imposed; where the amount involved is large or there are other serious circumstances, he or she shall be sentenced to fixed-term imprisonment of more than five (5) years and less than 10 years, with a fine of more than five (5) per cent and less than 30 per cent of the amount of foreign exchange fraudulently purchased to be concurrently imposed; where the amount involved is particularly large or there are other particularly serious circumstances, he or she shall be sentenced to fixed-term imprisonment of more than 10 years or life imprisonment, with a fine of more than five (5) per cent and less than 30 per cent of the amount of foreign exchange fraudulently purchased or confiscation of property to be concurrently imposed:

(1) using forged or altered customs declaration forms or import certificates issued by customs, or approval documents or certificates issued by foreign exchange control authorities;
(2) repeatedly using customs declaration forms or import certificates issued by customs, or approval documents or certificates issued by foreign exchange control authorities; or
(3) fraudulently purchasing foreign exchange by other means.

Whoever forges or alters customs declaration forms or import certificates issued by customs, or approval documents or certificates issued by foreign exchange control authorities, and uses them to fraudulently purchase foreign exchange, shall be punished severely in accordance with provisions in the preceding paragraph.

Whoever supplies Renminbi funds knowing that they are to be used to fraudulently purchase foreign exchange shall be deemed joint offenders.

Where a unit has committed the crimes stipulated in the preceding three paragraphs, it shall be fined in accordance with the provisions in the first paragraph. The direct responsible person(s)-in-charge and other direct responsible person(s) shall be sentenced to fixed-term imprisonment of less than five (5) years or criminal detention; where the amount involved is large or there are other serious circumstances, they shall be sentenced to fixed-term imprisonment of more than five (5) years and less than 10 years; where the amount involved is particularly large or there are particularly serious circumstances, they shall be sentenced to fixed-term imprisonment of more than 10 years or life imprisonment.

2. Whoever purchases forged or altered customs declaration forms or import certificates issued by customs, approval documents or certificates issued by foreign exchange control authorities, or other official documents, certificates or seals of state organs, shall be convicted and punished in accordance with the provisions of Article 280 of the Criminal Law.

3. Article 190 of the Criminal Law shall be revised as follows: A company, an enterprise, or a unit of another kind which, in violation of provisions of the State, deposits foreign exchange abroad without authorisation or illegally transfers foreign exchange from China to overseas, shall, where the amount involved is relatively large, be sentenced to a fine of more than five (5) per cent and less than 30 per cent of the amount of foreign exchange evaded, and the directly responsible person(s)-in-charge and any other directly responsible person(s) shall be sentenced to fixed-term imprisonment of less than five (5) years or criminal detention; where the amount involved is large or there are other serious circumstances, the unit concerned shall be sentenced to a fine of more than five (5) per cent and less than 30 per cent of the amount of foreign exchange evaded, and the direct responsible person(s)-in-charge and other direct responsible person(s) shall be sentenced to fixed-term imprisonment of more than five (5) years.

4. Whoever illegally trades foreign exchange in places other than the trading places designated by the State and disturbs the market order shall, where the circumstances are serious, be convicted and punished in accordance with the provisions of Article 225 of the Criminal Law.

A unit that commits a crime stipulated in the preceding paragraph shall be punished in accordance with the provisions of Article 231 of the Criminal Law.

5. Staff members of customs, foreign exchange control authorities, financial institutions, companies, enterprises or other units engaged in foreign trade operation activities, who collude with those engaged in fraudulent purchase or evasion of foreign exchange, and provide to the latter relevant documents for purchasing foreign exchange or other conveniences, or who sell or pay foreign exchange knowing that the relevant documents or certificates are falsified or altered, shall be deemed joint offenders and be punished severely in accordance with this Decision.

6. Staff members of customs or foreign exchange control authorities who, as a result of serious negligence, cause the fraudulent purchase or evasion of a large amount of foreign exchange and major losses to the interests of the State, shall be convicted and punished in accordance with the provisions of Article 397 of the Criminal Law.

7. Staff members of companies or enterprises engaged in foreign trade operation activities, who, as a result of serious negligence, cause the fraudulent purchase or evasion of a large amount of foreign exchange and major losses to the interests of the State, shall be convicted and punished in accordance with the provisions of Article 167 of the Criminal Law.

8. Property recovered or confiscated and fines collected in accordance with the law, in pursuing punishment for commission of crimes stipulated in this Decision, shall be turned over to the State Treasury without exception.

9. This Decision shall take effect from the date of promulgation.

III CRIMINAL PROCEDURE LAW OF THE PEOPLE'S REPUBLIC OF CHINA

Adopted 1 July 1979 at the 2nd Session of the Fifth National People's Congress

Revised 17 March 1996 at the Fourth Session of the Eighth National People's Congress in accordance with the "Decision concerning the Revision of the Criminal Procedure Law of the People's Republic of China"
Re-promulgated by Presidential Order No 64 (8th NPC)

Revised 14 March 2012 at the Fifth Session of the Eleventh National People's Congress in accordance with the "Decision concerning the Revision of the Criminal Procedure Law of the People's Republic of China"
Re-promulgated by Presidential Order No 55 (11th NPC), 14 March 2012
Effective from 1 January 2013

TABLE OF CONTENTS

Part I

General Provisions

Chapter I

Tasks and Basic Principles

Article 1 This Law is formulated in accordance with the Constitution, in order to ensure the proper enforcement of the Criminal Law, to punish crimes, to protect people, to safeguard state security and public safety, and to maintain a socialist social order.

Article 2 The tasks of the Criminal Procedure Law of the People's Republic of China are to ensure that the facts of crimes are determined correctly and promptly, laws are applied properly, criminals are punished, and innocent people are protected from being pursued for criminal liability; to educate citizens to abide by the law and to fight actively against criminal activities, so as to uphold the socialist legal system, to respect and protect human rights, to protect citizens' personal rights, property rights, democratic rights and other rights, and to safeguard the smooth progress of the course of socialist construction.

Article 3 The public security organs are responsible for the investigation, detention and execution of arrests and the preliminary interrogation [of criminal suspects] in criminal cases. The people's procuratorates are responsible for procuratorial work, approval of arrest, investigation of cases accepted directly by the procuratorial organs, and initiation of public prosecution. The people's courts are responsible for adjudication. No other institution, organisation or individual, other than those specifically authorised by law, has the authority to exercise such powers.

In conducting criminal proceedings, the people's courts, the people's procuratorates and the public security organs shall strictly observe this Law and relevant provisions in other laws.

Article 4 The state security organs shall handle criminal cases involved in endangering state security in accordance with the law, and perform functions and exercise powers in the same way as the public security organs.

Article 5 The people's courts exercise adjudication power independently in accordance with the law; the people's procuratorates exercise procuratorial power independently in accordance with the law, and they are not to be interfered with by any administrative organ, social organisation or individual.

Article 6 In the course of criminal proceedings, the people's courts, the people's procuratorates and the public security organs shall rely on the masses and take facts as the basis and law as the criterion. The law shall be applied equally to all citizens and no privilege is permitted before the law.

Article 7 In the course of criminal proceedings, the people's courts, the people's procuratorates or the public security organs shall each take responsibility for their own work and coordinate and check with each other, so as to ensure the correct and effective enforcement of the law.

Article 8 The people's procuratorates conduct legal supervision over criminal proceedings in accordance with the law.

Article 9 Citizens of all nationalities are entitled to use their own spoken and written languages in court proceedings. The people's courts, the people's procuratorates and the public security organs shall provide interpretation and translation for any participant in the proceedings who does not properly understand the language which is commonly spoken or written in the locality.

In regions where a minority nationality is concentrated, or where a number of different nationalities live together, court hearings shall be conducted in the language commonly spoken in the locality, and judgments, public notices and other documents shall be issued in the language commonly written in the locality.

Article 10 The people's courts shall implement an adjudication system in which the second instance adjudication is final.

Article 11 All cases, except those otherwise provided by this Law, shall be heard in public by the people's courts. An accused person has the right to defence and the people's courts have the duty to guarantee that the accused person obtains defence.

Article 12 Without a verdict by a people's court in accordance with the law, no one shall be found guilty.

Article 13 In court proceedings the people's courts shall implement the system of people's assessors playing role in trials in accordance with this Law.

Article 14 The people's courts, the people's procuratorates and the public security organs shall safeguard the right to defence and other procedural rights of criminal suspects, accused persons and other participants in court proceedings, to which they are entitled under the law.

A participant in the proceedings has the right to make complaints against any act of an adjudicating official or a procuratorial official or an investigatory officer which has infringed upon his/her procedural rights as a citizen or has constituted a personal insult.

Article 15 In any of the following situations no criminal liability shall be pursued; where the pursuit of criminal liability is already under way the case shall be withdrawn, or prosecution must not take place, or court proceedings shall be terminated or the accused person shall be declared innocent:

(1) the circumstance is obviously minor, causing no serious harm and therefore not to be deemed as a crime;
(2) the time limit for initiating prosecution has expired;
(3) the act has been exempted from punishment by a special amnesty decree;
(4) in accordance with the Criminal Law, the crime will only be handled upon a complaint, and no complaint has been filed or the complaint has been withdrawn;
(5) the criminal suspect or the accused person is deceased; or
(6) the offence has been exempted from criminal liability by other laws.

Article 16 Provisions of this Law apply to foreigners who commit crimes for which criminal liability shall be pursued.

Where foreigners with diplomatic privilege and immunity commit crimes for which criminal liability shall be pursued, such cases shall be handled through diplomatic channels.

Article 17 In accordance with the international treaties concluded or acceded to by the People's Republic of China, or in line with the principles of reciprocity, the judicial organs of China and the judicial organs of other countries may request judicial assistance in criminal matters from each other.

Chapter II

Jurisdiction

Article 18 Investigations of criminal cases are to be conducted by the public security organs, unless the law provides otherwise.

Filing and investigation of cases involving crimes of embezzlement and bribery, crimes of dereliction of duty committed by state functionaries or crimes committed by functionaries of state organs taking advantage of their positions, which infringe the personal rights of citizens, including illegal detention, extortion of confessions by torture, retaliation and illegal search, or infringement of the democratic rights of citizens, are to be conducted by the people's procuratorates. For other major cases committed by functionaries of state organs taking advantage of their positions, the people's procuratorates may, where their direct handling of the case is necessary and upon the decision of the people's procuratorates at provincial level and above, file such cases for investigation.

Cases of private prosecution are to be handled directly by the people's courts.

Article 19 The basic people's courts have jurisdiction over ordinary criminal cases as courts of first instance, except those cases which fall within the jurisdiction of the courts at the higher levels in accordance with this Law.

Article 20 The intermediate people's courts exercise jurisdiction over the following criminal cases as courts of first instance:

(1) cases involving the endangering of state security or involving terrorist activities; and
(2) cases for which life imprisonment or the death penalty are likely to be imposed.

Article 21 The High People's Courts exercise jurisdiction as courts of first instance over major criminal cases that affect an entire province (autonomous region or directly administered municipality).

Article 22 The Supreme People's Court exercises jurisdiction as the court of first instance over major criminal cases that affect the whole country.

Article 23 The people's courts at the higher levels may, where it is necessary, try criminal cases which are within the jurisdiction of the people's courts of first instance at the lower levels; people's courts at the lower level may, where it is considered that a case is major and complex and should be tried by a people's court at the higher level in the first instance, request that the case to be transferred to the people's court at the next higher level for trial.

Article 24 Jurisdiction over a criminal case is assumed by the people's court of the place where the crime was committed. If it is more appropriate for the case to be tried by the people's court in the place where the accused person resides, the case may be handled by the people's court in the place where the accused person resides.

Article 25 Where a case over which several people's courts at the same level have the same jurisdiction, the case shall be handled by the people's court which first accepts the case. Where it is necessary, the case may be transferred for trial to the people's court in the place where the principal crime was committed.

Article 26 A people's court at the higher levels may instruct a people's court at a lower level to try a case over which jurisdiction is unclear. It may also instruct a people's court at a lower level to transfer the case to another people's court for trial.

Article 27 Jurisdictions of specialised people's courts are to be stipulated separately.

Chapter III

Withdrawal

Article 28 In any of the following situations, the adjudicating, procuratorial or investigatory personnel shall withdraw on their own accord from a case; parties to the case and their statutory representatives also have the right to demand this withdrawal, where:

(1) the person is a party to, or a close relative of a party to, the case;
(2) the person or one of his/her close relatives has an interest in the case;
(3) the person has been a witness, expert witness, defence counsel or litigation representative in the case; or
(4) the person is related in some other way to a party to the case and may influence the fair handling of the case.

Article 29 An adjudicating, procuratorial or investigatory official must not accept any dinner invitation or gift from a party to the case or from a person entrusted by such a party, and must not, in violation of provisions, meet with a party to the case or a person entrusted by that party.

An adjudicating, procuratorial or investigatory official violating the provisions in the preceding Paragraph, shall be pursued with legal liability in accordance with the law. Parties to the case and their statutory representatives have the right to demand his/her withdrawal.

Article 30 Withdrawal of an adjudicating, procuratorial or investigatory official is to be determined separately by the president of a court, the president of a procuratorate, or the head of the public security organ. Withdrawal of the president of a court is to be determined by the adjudication committee of the court. Withdrawal of the president of a procuratorate and the head of a public security organ is to be determined by the procuratorial committee of the people's procuratorate at the same level.

Before a decision is made on the withdrawal of an investigatory officer, the investigatory officer may not cease the investigation of the case.

Where a decision is made in rejection of an application for withdrawal, the party to the case and his/her statutory representative may apply for a re-consideration once.

Article 31 The provisions of this Chapter on withdrawal apply also to clerks, interpreters and expert witnesses.

A defence council or a litigation representative may request withdrawal and apply for reconsideration in accordance with the provisions of this Chapter.

Chapter IV

Defence and Representation

Article 32 A criminal suspect or an accused person may, in addition to exercising the right of defence by him/her self, appoint one or two persons as defence counsels. The following persons may be appointed as defence counsels:

(1) lawyers;
(2) persons recommended by a community organisation or by the unit which the criminal suspect or the accused person works with; or

(3) guardians, relatives or friends of the criminal suspect or the accused person.

A person who is serving a criminal sentence, or who has been deprived of personal freedom or those whose personal freemen is restricted in accordance with the law, must not be appointed as defence counsel.

Article 33 A criminal suspect has the right to appoint his/her defence counsel(s) from the date on which he/she is first interrogated by the investigation organ or is subject to coercive measure(s); during the investigation period only a lawyer may be appointed as a defence counsel. An accused person has the right to appoint a person/persons as his/her defence counsel(s) at any time.

The investigation organ shall inform the criminal suspect of his/her right to appoint defence counsel(s) when it first interrogates the criminal suspect or subjects a criminal suspect to coercive measure(s). The people's procuratorate shall, within three (3) days from the date of receipt of a transferred case dossier for examination for prosecution, inform the criminal suspect that he/she has the right to appoint defence counsel/s. A people's court shall, within three (3) days from the date of the acceptance of a prosecution case, inform the accused person that he/she has the right to appoint defence counsel/s. Where, during the period of detention, the criminal suspect or the accused person requests the appointment of a defence counsel, the people's court, the people's prosecutorate or the public security organ shall promptly convey the request.

Where the criminal suspect or the accused person is in detention, a defence counsel may be appointed by his/her custodian or close relative on his/her behalf.

The defence counsel shall, upon acceptance of the appointment by the criminal suspect or the accused person, promptly notify the organs handling the case.

Article 34 Where a criminal suspect or an accused person has not appointed a person as his/her defence counsel because of financial difficulty or other reasons, he/she or his/her close relatives may apply to a legal aid organisation for assistance. The legal aid organisation shall assign a lawyer to provide defence for the criminal suspect or the accused person where conditions for legal aid are met.

Where a criminal suspect or an accused person is blind, deaf or mute, or is a mentally ill person who has not completely lost his/her capacity to comprehend or to control his/her behaviour, and who has not appointed for him/her self a defence counsel, the people's court, the people's procuratorate or the public security organ shall notify a legal aid organisation to assign a lawyer to provide defence for the criminal suspect or the accused person.

Where a criminal suspect or an accused person is likely to be sentenced to life imprisonment or death and he/she has not appointed a person as his/her defence counsel, the people's court, the people's procuratorate or the public security organ shall notify a legal aid organisation to assign a lawyer to provide defence for the criminal suspect or the accused person.

Article 35 A defence counsel's duties are, in accordance with the law and in light of the facts, to provide materials and opinions proving the innocence of the criminal suspect or the accused person, the limited seriousness of the crime, showing the mitigating circumstances of the case or grounds for exempting the criminal suspect or the accused person from criminal liability, and to protect the procedural rights and other legitimate rights and interests of the criminal suspect and the accused person.

Article 36 During the investigation period, a defence lawyer may provide legal assistance to the criminal suspect; make a petition and accusation on his/her behalf; apply for alteration of coercive measures; seek from the investigation organ information on the crime of the criminal suspect and situations relevant to the case; and provide opinions.

Article 37 A defence lawyer may meet the detained criminal suspect or the accused person and communicate with him/her by mail. Other defence counsels, with the permission of the people's court or people's procuratorate, may meet the detained criminal suspect or the accused person and communicate with him/herby mail.

Where a defence lawyer holds a practice certificate, a law firm certificate and a letter of attorney or an official letter of legal aid to request to meet a criminal suspect or an accused person in custody, the detention centre shall arrange the meeting in a timely manner but not later than within 48 hours.

In a case involving a crime of endangering state security or engaging in terrorism, or a particularly serious crime of bribery, if the defence lawyer intends to meet the criminal suspect during the investigation period, he/she must have permission from the investigation organ. The investigation organ shall notify the detention centre in advance of the above cases.

During any meeting with a criminal suspect or an accused person in custody the defence lawyer may inquire about situations relevant to the case, provide legal advice, etc; and from the date on which the case is referred for examination for prosecution he/she may verify the relevant evidence with the criminal suspect or the accused person. The meeting between the defence lawyer and the criminal suspect or the accused person shall not be monitored.

Provisions of Paragraphs 1, 3 and 4 apply to where a defence lawyer meets or communicates by mail with a criminal suspect or an accused person under house surveillance.

Article 38 A defence lawyer may, from the date on which the procuratorate begins to examine the case for prosecution, inspect, extract and copy the materials in the case dossier. Other defence counsels with permission from the people's court or the procuratorate may also inspect, extract and copy such materials.

Article 39 Where a defence counsel is of the opinion that during the period of investigation or examination for prosecution, evidentiary material collected by the public security organ or the people's procuratorate have not been submitted which may prove the innocence of the criminal suspect or the accused person or the lesser seriousness of a crime, he/she has the right to apply to the people's procuratorate or the people's court to obtain such evidence.

Article 40 Where a defence counsel has collected evidence which may prove that the criminal suspect was not present at the crime scene, or has not reached the age of criminal liability, or is mentally ill and exempted from criminal liability pursuant to the law, he/she shall notify the public security organ or the people's procuratorate promptly.

Article 41 With the consent of witnesses or other relevant units or individuals, a defence lawyer may collect from them materials relevant to the case. He/she may also apply to the people's procuratorate or the people's court for the collection and acquisition of evidence, or apply to the people's court to subpoena witnesses to appear in the court to testify.

A defence lawyer may, with the permission of the people's procuratorate or the people's court and the consent of the victim, the close relatives of the victim, or the witnesses recommended by the victim, collect from them materials relevant to the case.

Article 42 A defence counsel or any other person must not assist a criminal suspect or an accused person to conceal, destroy or falsify evidence or to make a collusive confession, must not threaten or induce a witness to alter his/her testimony, or commit perjury or adopt other acts to interfere with the activities of a judicial organ.

Violations of the provisions in the preceding paragraph shall be pursued with legal liability in accordance with the law. Where a defence counsel is suspected of having committed a crime, the matter shall be handled by an investigatory organ other than the one that handles the case represented by the defence counsel. Where a defence counsel is a lawyer, the law firm with which he/she works or the lawyers' association to which he/she belongs shall be informed promptly.

Article 43 During a court trial an accused person may refuse to have his/her defence counsel(s) to continue the defence for him/her; he/she may also appoint another person as his/her defence counsel.

Article 44 A victim in a public prosecution case and his/her statutory representative(s) or close relative(s), and a party to an incidental civil action and his/her statutory representative, has the right to appoint a person as his/her litigation representative from the date on which the case is transferred for examination for prosecution. A private prosecutor in a private prosecution case and his/her statutory representative, or a party to an incidental civil action and his/her statutory representative, has the right to appoint a person as his/her litigation representative at any time.

A people's procuratorate shall, within three (3) days from the date of the receipt of the referred case dossier for examination for prosecution, inform the victim and his/her statutory representative or close relatives and the parties to an incidental civil action and their statutory representatives, of the right to appoint litigation representatives. A people's court shall, within three (3) days from the date of the acceptance of a private prosecution case, inform the private prosecutor and his/her statutory representative, and the parties to an incidental civil action and their statutory representatives, of their right to appoint persons as their litigation representatives.

Article 45 Provisions of Article 32 in this Law apply in reference to matters regarding the appointment of litigation representatives.

Article 46 A defence lawyer has the right to keep confidential any relevant information of his/her client obtained in the course of performing professional activities. But if a defence lawyer, during the course of performing professional activities, becomes aware that his/her client or any other person is preparing for or is committing a crime that endangers state security or public security, or seriously harms other persons' personal safety, he/she shall promptly notify the judicial organs.

Article 47 Where a defence counsel or a litigation representative considers that a public security organ, a people's procuratorate, a people's court or their personnel hinder his/her exercise of procedural rights, he/she has the right to make a complaint or an accusation with the people's procuratorate at the same level or at the next higher level. The people's procuratorate shall promptly examine the complaint or accusation and, if verified as true, notify the relevant organ(s) to make correction.

Chapter V

Evidence

Article 48 Any material that is able to prove the facts of a case is evidence:

Evidence includes:

(1) physical evidence;
(2) documentary evidence;
(3) testimony of witnesses;
(4) statements of victims;
(5) statements and defence of criminal suspects and accused persons;
(6) opinions of expert witnesses;
(7) records of inspection, examination, identification, investigative experiments, etc.; and
(8) audio and visual materials, and electronic data.

Any of the evidence listed above may only be relied on for the deciding of a case after it has been verified as reliable.

Article 49 The people's procuratorate bears the onus of proof of guilt of the accused person in a pubic prosecution case; the private prosecutor bears the onus of proof of guilt of the accused person in a private prosecution case.

Article 50 Adjudicating, procuratorial and investigatory personnel must, in accordance with procedures stipulated by law, collect all the evidence required to prove the guilt or innocence of the criminal suspect or the accused person, and to determine the gravity of the circumstances of the crime. Extortion of confessions by torture and collection of evidence through threats, inducement, deceit or other unlawful means are strictly prohibited, and no person shall be forced to prove his/her own guilt. A citizen involved in a case, or with knowledge about a case, must be provided with conditions under which he/she may objectively and fully provide evidence, and, except in special circumstances, he/she may also be invited to assist the investigation.

Article 51 All documents of a public security organ authorising arrest, all bills of prosecution of a people's procuratorate and all judgments of a people's court, must truly rest on facts. Whoever intentionally conceals facts must be pursued for liability.

Article 52 The people's courts, the people's procuratorates and the public security organs have the power to collect and gather evidence from relevant units and individuals. The units and individuals concerned must provide evidence based on the truth.

Physical evidence, documentary evidence, audio and visual evidence, electronic data and other evidence collected by administrative organs in the course of administrative law enforcement or of handling a case may be used as evidence in criminal procedures.

Evidence involving state secrets, commercial secretes or personal privacy must be kept confidential.

Whoever forges, conceals or destroys evidence, no matter which side they are on in the case, must be pursued by law.

Article 53 In deciding a case, emphasis must be placed on evidence, investigation and analysis, and shall not readily rely on confessions. An accused person shall not be found guilty and have imposed a criminal penalty where there is only his/her confession but no other evidence; however, an accused person may be found to be guilty and have imposed a criminal penalty where no confession of the accused person exists but the evidence is reliable and sufficient.

"Reliable and sufficient evidence" shall meet the following requirements:

(1) all facts used for determining guilt and sentencing are proven with evidence;
(2) all evidence relied on to decide the case has been verified and proven to be true through procedures prescribed by law; and
(3) based on overall evaluation of the evidence, all facts are proven beyond reasonable doubt.

Article 54 Confessions by a criminal suspect or an accused person obtained through torture, extortion or other illegal methods, and witness testimony and victim statements obtained through the use of violence, threats and other illegal methods shall be excluded. Where the collection of physical evidence and documentary evidence violates the legal procedures in a way which may seriously affect judicial justice, correction and supplementation shall be made or a reasonable explanation shall be given; if correction and supplementation are not made or a reasonable explanation provided, the evidence shall be excluded.

Where evidence that should be excluded is identified during the course of investigation, examination for prosecution or adjudication, such evidence shall be excluded pursuant to the law and shall not be used as a basis for prosecution opinions, prosecution decisions or judgements.

Article 55 Where a people's procuratorate receives a report, an accusation, or information on an offence, or discovers that the investigatory personnel collected evidence through unlawful means, it shall investigate and verify the matter. Where the people's procuratorate determines that the evidence has been collected through unlawful means, it shall issue an opinion on correction of the situation, and, if a crime is constituted, pursue criminal liability in accordance with the law.

Article 56 Where, during the course of adjudication, the adjudicating personnel is of the opinion that there may be an aspect of evidence being collected through the unlawful means prescribed in Article 54 of this Law, a court enquiry shall be conducted into the legality of the collection of the evidence.

A party to a case and his/her defence counsel and litigation representative has the right to apply to the people's court for exclusion of evidence collected through unlawful means. An application for exclusion of illegally collected evidence shall include relevant information or materials.

Article 57 During a court enquiry into the legality of the collection of evidence, the people's procuratorate shall prove the legality of the collection of evidence.

Where the existing evidentiary material is unable to prove the legality of evidence collection, the people's procuratorate may request the people's court to notify the relevant investigatory personnel or other persons to explain the situation before the court; the people's court may notify the relevant investigatory personnel or other persons to explain the situation before the court. Investigatory personnel and other persons may also request to give explanations before the court. Upon notification by a people's court, the relevant persons shall attend the court.

Article 58 Where, after a court hearing, evidence is confirmed to have been obtained illegally or where the possibility of collecting evidence through unlawful means as prescribed in Article 54 of this Law cannot be excluded, the evidence shall be excluded.

Article 59 The testimony of a witness may only be used as the basis for deciding a case after the witness has been questioned and cross-examined in a courtroom by the public procurator, the victim, the accused person, and defence counsels of both sides, and after the testimony of witnesses of both sides has been heard and verified. Where a court confirms that a witness has deliberately given false testimony or concealed evidence of a crime, it shall handle the matter in accordance with the law.

Article 60 Anyone with knowledge of a case has a duty to testify.

A person who is physically or mentally handicapped or is a juvenile or is unable to distinguish right from wrong or unable to accurately express him/herself, cannot be a witness.

Article 61 The people's courts, the people's procuratorates and the public security organs must ensure the safety of witnesses and their close relatives.

Where an act of threatening, insulting, beating or retaliating against a witness or his/her close relative constitutes a crime, criminal liability shall be pursued in accordance with the law; where the act is not punishable under the criminal law, penalties relating to the administration of public order shall be imposed in accordance with the law.

Article 62 In cases involving a crime of endangering state security, a terrorism crime, the organised crime of underworld characters, drug related crimes, etc, where the personal safety of a witness, expert witness or victim or their close relatives is at risk because of his/her testimony in a court proceeding, the people's court, the people's procuratorate and the public security organ shall take one or several of the following protective measures:

(1) withholding their true names, addresses, work units and other personal details;
(2) taking such measures so as not to expose their appearance and reveal their real voice in court testimony;
(3) prohibiting particular person(s) from contacting the witnesses, expert witnesses or victims and their close relatives;
(4) adopting special measures to protect their personal and residential safety;
(5) any other necessary protective measures.

Where a witness, an expert witness or a victim considers that his/her personal safety or the personal safety of his/her close relatives is at risk because of his/her testimony in a legal proceeding, he/she may apply to the people's court, the people's procuratorate or the public security organ for protection.

The people's court, people's procuratorate or the public security organ shall take protective measures in accordance with the law; relevant units and individuals shall provide cooperation.

Article 63 The expenses of a witness, such as transportation, accommodation and meals incurred when performing a testimonial duty shall be compensated. Compensation for the testimonial expenses of witnesses is to be included in the work expenses of judicial organs and be guaranteed in the financial budget of the government at the same level.

Where a witness providing testimony is employed, the unit with which he/she works shall not reduce, or reduce in a disguised way, the witness's remuneration, bonuses and other social benefits.

Chapter VI

Coercive Measures

Article 64 A people's court, a people's procuratorate and a public security organ may, in light of the circumstances of a case, detain a criminal suspect or an accused person, or place the criminal suspect or the accused person on bail or under residential surveillance.

Article 65 A people's court, a people's procuratorate and a public security organ may place a criminal suspect or an accused person on bail in one of the following situations:

(1) the criminal suspect or the accused person is likely to be sentenced to pubic surveillance, detention, or an independently applicable supplementary penalty;
(2) the criminal suspect or the accused person is likely to have imposed a penalty of fixed-term imprisonment or a heavier penalty, and the placement of this person on bail would not endanger the society;
(3) where the criminal suspect or the accused person has a serious illness and cannot take care of him/her self, or is a pregnant woman or is breastfeeding her own baby, and the releasing of him/her on bail does not pose a risk to the public;
(4) the case has not been closed at the end of the time limitation for detention, and the placement of this person on bail is necessary.

A bail order is to be executed by a public security organ.

Article 66 Where a people's court, a people's procuratorate or a public security organ decides to place a criminal suspect or an accused person on bail, it shall order the criminal suspect or the accused person to provide a guarantor or to pay a guarantee bond.

Article 67 A guarantor must meet the following conditions:

(1) he/she is not involved in the case concerned;
(2) he/she possesses the capacity to perform his/her obligations;
(3) he/she enjoys political rights and is not subject to any restriction of personal freedom; and
(4) he/she has a stable domicile and a steady income.

Article 68 A guarantor shall fulfil the following obligations:

(1) to supervise the person on bail in observing the provisions of Article 69 of this Law; and
(2) to report immediately to the execution organ once it has been found that a violation of the provisions of Article 69 by the person on bail is likely to happen or has already happened.

Where a person on bail has violated the provisions of Article 69 and the guarantor fails to perform his/her obligation as a guarantor, the guarantor shall be fined, and, where the failure has constituted a crime, be pursued for criminal liability.

Article 69 A criminal suspect or an accused person on bail shall observe the following provisions:

(1) not to leave the city or county where he/she lives without the permission of the execution organ;
(2) to report to the execution organ within 24 hours in the event of a change of address, place of work or contact details;
(3) to appear on time when summoned;
(4) not to interfere in any way with a witness in testifying; and
(5) not to destroy or falsify evidence or make a collusive confession with others.

The people's court, the people's procuratorate and the public security organ may, depending on the circumstances of the case, order a criminal suspect or an accused person on bail to comply with one or several of the following provisions:

(1) not to enter particular venues;
(2) not to meet or correspond with particular persons;
(3) not to engage in particular activities; and
(4) to surrender his/her passport or other border-crossing documents, and driver's licence to the execution organ for safekeeping.

Where a criminal suspect or an accused person on bail violates the provisions in the preceding two Paragraphs, the guarantee bond paid shall be partially or wholly confiscated, and, depending on the seriousness of circumstances, the criminal suspect or the accused person shall be ordered to submit a statement of repentance for his/her wrong doing, pay a new guarantee bond, provide another guarantor, or be placed under residential surveillance, or be arrested.

Where the criminal suspect or the accused person has violated the provisions on bail and needs to be arrested, he/she may be detained first.

Article 70 When determining the amount of a guarantee bond, the organ making the decision on granting bail shall consider the overall situation, such as the need to ensure the normal operation of the legal proceedings, the risk the person to be placed on bail may pose to the society, the nature and circumstances of the case, the gravity of the possible punishment and the financial situation of the person to be placed on bail.

The person who provides a guarantee bond shall deposit the guarantee bond in a special account of a bank designated by the execution organ.

Article 71 Where a criminal suspect or an accused person has not violated the provision in Article 69 of this Law during the period of bail, he/she may, by presenting the notice of release of bail or other relevant legal documents, collect the guarantee bond from the bank at the end of the bail period.

Article 72 Where any of the following circumstances apply to a criminal suspect or an accused person who meets the conditions for arrest , the people's court, the people's procuratorate or the public security organ may place the criminal suspect or the accused person under residential surveillance:

(1) being seriously ill and unable to take care of him/her self;
(2) being a pregnant woman or breastfeeding her own baby;
(3) being the only supporter of a person who cannot take care of him/herself;
(4) it is more appropriate to adopt the measure of residential surveillance due to the special situation of the case or the need for the handling of the case; or
(5) although the time limitation period for detention has expired, the case has not been closed yet, and the adoption of residential surveillance measures is necessary.

A criminal suspect or an accused person who meets the conditions for bail but cannot provide a guarantor and pay a guarantee bond may be placed under residential surveillance.

Residential surveillance is to be conducted by the public security organs.

Article 73 Residential surveillance shall be conducted in the domicile of the criminal suspect or the accused person; where there is no fixed domicile, residential surveillance may be conducted at a designated residence. Where there is suspicion of a crime of endangering state security, a terrorism crime or a particularly serious crime of bribery, and the conduct of residential surveillance at a domicile may impede the investigation, upon approval of the people's procuratorate or the public security organ at the next higher level, residential surveillance may also be conducted at a designated residence. However, residential surveillance may not be conducted at a detention centre or a venue which is used especially for handling cases.

Where residential surveillance is to be conducted at a designated residence, the family members of the person under residential surveillance shall be notified within 24 hours of the implementation of residence surveillance, unless it is impossible do so.

The provisions of Article 33 of this Law apply to matters concerning the appointment of defence counsels by a criminal suspect or an accused person under residential surveillance.

The people's procuratorate exercises supervision over the legality of the decisions of residential surveillance at a designated residence and its execution.

Article 74 The period of surveillance at a designated place of residence shall be deducted from the term of the sentence. For those sentenced to public surveillance, the term of the sentence shall be reduced by one day for each day under residential surveillance; for those sentenced to criminal detention or fixed-term imprisonment, the term of the sentence shall be reduced by one day for each two days under residential surveillance.

Article 75 A criminal suspect or an accused person under residential surveillance shall abide by the following provisions:

(1) not to leave his/her domicile without the permission of the execution organ;
(2) not to meet or correspond with any person without the permission of the execution organ;
(3) to appear on time when so summoned;
(4) not to interfere in any way with a witness in testifying;
(5) not to destroy or falsify evidence or make a collusive confession with others; and
(5) to surrender his/her passport or other border-crossing documents, identity card and driver's licence to the execution organ for safekeeping.

Where a criminal suspect or an accused person under residential surveillance violates the provisions of the preceding Paragraph, he/she may, where the circumstances are serious, be arrested; where arrest is necessary, the criminal suspect or the accused person may be detained first.

Article 76 In order to supervise the compliance of a criminal suspect or an accused person with the provisions on residential surveillance, the execution organ may take various surveillance measures, such as electronic monitoring and random inspection of the criminal suspect or the accused person; during the period of investigation, the execution organ may monitor the correspondence of the criminal suspect or the accused person under residential surveillance.

Article 77 A people's court, a people's procuratorate or a public security organ shall not place a criminal suspect or an accused person on bail for a period in excess of twelve (12) months, or under residential surveillance for a period in excess of six (6) months.

During the period of bail or residential surveillance, the investigation, prosecution and court handling of the case must not be suspended. Where it is found that criminal liability should not have been pursued, or the period of bail or residential surveillance has expired, the bail or residential surveillance must be terminated without delay. The person on bail or under residential surveillance and the relevant units shall be notified of the termination of the bail or residential surveillance immediately.

Article 78 The arrest of a criminal suspect or an accused person must be approved by a people's procuratorate or upon a decision of a people's court, and executed by a public security organ.

Article 79 Where there is evidence of a crime, and the criminal suspect or the accused person is likely to be sentenced to a criminal penalty of imprisonment or a more severe penalty, if the placement of the criminal suspect or the accused person on bail will not be enough to prevent the following social risks, the criminal suspect or the accused person shall be arrested in accordance with the law:

(1) the criminal suspect or the accused person may commit a new crime;
(2) the criminal suspect or the accused person poses a real risk to state security, public security or the social order;
(3) it is possible that the criminal suspect or the accused person will destroy or falsify evidence, interfere with the testimony of witnesses, or collude with witnesses in making statements;
(4) it is likely that the criminal suspect or the accused person will retaliate against the victim, informant or complainant; or
(5) the criminal suspect or the accused person may attempt to commit suicide or escape.

Where there is evidence proving the facts of a crime which is likely to be punished by fixed-term imprisonment of ten (10) years or longer, or by a more severe criminal penalty, or where there is evidence proving the facts of a crime which is likely to be punished by fixed-term imprisonment and the person in question has previously intentionally committed a crime, or his/her identity is unknown, that person shall be arrested.

A criminal suspect or an accused person on bail or under residential surveillance who violates the provisions on bail and residential surveillance, may, where the circumstances are serious, be arrested.

Article 80 A public security organ may detain an active offender or a major suspect in one of the following situations:

(1) the person is preparing for a crime, is committing a crime or is found right after a crime has been committed;
(2) the person is identified by the victim or other eye-witnesses as an offender who has committed a crime;
(3) evidence of a crime is found in the surroundings of the person or in his/her residence;
(4) the person attempts to commit suicide or escape or is on the run after committing a crime;
(5) evidence is likely to be destroyed or falsified, or the person is likely to make a collusive confession;
(6) the person refuses to provide his/her true name and address, and his/her identity is unknown; or
(7) there is strong suspicion that the person has committed crimes in different places, or has repeatedly committed crimes or committed gang crimes.

Article 81 When a public security organ executes a detention or an arrest order in another place, it shall notify the public security organ in the place where the person who is to be detained or arrested lives, and the public security organ in the place where the person who is to be detained or arrested lives shall co-operate.

Article 82 A citizen may catch and send a person directly to a public security organ, a people's procuratorate, or a people's court for handling in one of the following situations:

(1) the person is committing a crime or is found right after the committing of a crime;
(2) the person is under a circular order for arrest;
(3) the person has escaped from a prison; or
(4) the person is being pursued for arrest.

Article 83 When detaining a person, the public security organ must produce a detention warrant.

After a person has been detained, he/she shall be sent immediately, and no later than within 24 hours, to a detention centre for custody. The family members of the detainee must be notified within 24 hours, unless such notification is impossible to be delivered or where it involves a crime of endangering State security or a terrorism crime, and the notification would impede the investigation. The family members of the detainee must be notified immediately once the circumstances that impede investigation no longer exist.

Article 84 A public security organ must interrogate a detainee within 24 hours after his/her detention. If it is found that the person should not have been detained, he/she must be released immediately and be issued with a certificate of release.

Article 85 When making a request for arresting a criminal suspect, the public security organ shall prepare a written application for approval of the arrest and submit it along with the case materials and evidence to the people's procuratorate at the same level for examination and approval. Where it is necessary, the people's procuratorate may send its official to attend the discussion of a major case in the public security organ.

Article 86 When a people's procuratorate conducts examination and approval of the arrest of a criminal suspect, it may interrogate the criminal suspect, and, where any of the following circumstances exists, shall interrogate the criminal suspect:

(1) there is a doubt as to whether or not the conditions for arrest are met;
(2) the criminal suspect requests to give a statement to the procuratorial official face-to-face; or
(3) the investigation conduct may involve a serious violation of the law.

When a people's procuratorate conducts examination and approval of the arrest of a criminal suspect, it may question witnesses and other participants in the proceedings and hear opinions from the defence lawyer; and shall, where the defence lawyer requests to express his/her opinion, hear the opinion of the defence lawyer.

Article 87 When a people's procuratorate conducts examination and approval of the arrest of a criminal suspect, the decision shall be made by the president of the procuratorate. Major cases shall be submitted to the procuratorial committee for discussion and a decision.

Article 88 After having examined a case submitted by the public security organ, the people's procuratorate shall, in light of the circumstances of the case, make a decision on whether or not the request for arrest is approved. Where a decision is made for the arrest, the public security organ shall execute it immediately and inform the people's procuratorate of the execution without delay. Where the request for arrest is not approved, the people's procuratorate shall give reasons for the rejection and, if further investigation is required, notify the public security organ of the matter in the meantime.

Article 89 Where a public security organ is of the opinion that the arrest of a detainee is essential, it shall apply to the people's procuratorate for examination and approval of the arrest within three (3) days of the detention. The time limit for the submission of an application for examination and approval may, in exceptional cases, be extended by one to four (1–4) days.

For the arrest of a major criminal suspect who is involved in widespread crimes, or repeated crimes or gang crimes, the time limit for the submission of an application for examination and approval may be extended to 30 days.

The people's procuratorate shall, within seven (7) days from the date of the receipt of the application for approval of arrest submitted by a public security organ, make a decision as to whether or not the application for arrest is approved. Where the people's procuratorate does not approve the arrest, the public security organ shall, upon the receipt of the notification, release the detainee immediately, and inform the people's procuratorate of the result without delay. Where further investigation is required and conditions for placing the person on bail or under residential surveillance are met, bail or residential surveillance may be implemented in accordance with the law.

Article 90 If a public security organ is of the opinion that the decision of a people's procuratorate in not approving an arrest is incorrect, it may request reconsideration; but the detainee must be released immediately. If the opinion of the public security organ is not accepted, it may apply to the people's procuratorate at the next higher level for review. The people's procuratorate at the next higher level shall review the case immediately and make a decision as to whether the original decision should be altered, and notify the people's procuratorate at the lower level and the public security organ to execute its decision.

Article 91 When executing an arrest, the public security organ must produce an arrest warrant.

A person, after his/her arrest, shall be sent immediately to a detention centre for custody. The family members of the arrested person shall be notified within 24 hours of the arrest, unless the notification is impossible to be delivered.

Article 92 An arrested person whose arrest is decided by either a people's court or a people's procuratorate or whose arrest is approved by a people's procuratorate at the request of a public security organ, must be interrogated within 24 hours after the arrest. Where it is found that the arrest is incorrect, the person arrested must be released immediately and issued with a certificate of release.

Article 93 After a criminal suspect or an accused person is arrested, the people's procuratorate shall still examine the necessity for detention. Where further detention is no longer necessary, the people's procuratorate shall recommend the release of the arrested or the alteration of the coercive measures. The relevant organ shall notify the people's procuratorate within 10 days on how it has handled the case.

Article 94 If a people's court, a people's procuratorate or a public security organ finds that the coercive measure imposed on a criminal suspect or an accused person is inappropriate, such measure must be terminated or altered immediately. Where an arrested person is to be released or another measure of arrest is adopted, the public security organ shall notify the people's procuratorate which originally approved the arrest.

Article 95 A criminal suspect or an accused person, and his/her statutory representative, close relatives or defence counsel has the right to apply for alteration of coercive measures. Upon receiving such an application, the people's court, the people's procuratorate and the public security organ shall make its decision within three (3) days. Where application for the alteration of coercive measures is rejected, the applicant shall be notified and reasons for the rejection shall be provided.

Article 96 Where a case in which the criminal suspect or the accused person is detained cannot be closed within the time limit stipulated in this Law for investigation, examination and prosecution, and for first and second instance adjudication, the criminal suspect or the accused person shall be released; where further investigation and verification and court handling are required, the criminal suspect or the accused person may be placed on bail or under residential surveillance.

Article 97 The people's court, people's procuratorate and the public security organ shall, upon expiration of the legally prescribed period for coercive measures, release the criminal suspect or the accused person, terminate the bail or residential surveillance, or adopt another coercive measure. A criminal suspect or an accused person and his/her statutory representative, close relatives or defence counsel have the right to request the termination of coercive measures imposed by the people's court, the people's procuratorate or the public security organ when the statutory period for the coercive measures expires.

Article 98 In the process of examination and approval, if a people's procuratorate finds any violation of the law in the investigation conducted by a public security organ, it must notify the public security organ to correct the situation, and the public security organ shall inform the people's procuratorate of the correction.

Chapter VII

Incidental Civil Actions

Article 99 A victim who suffers economic loss as a result of the criminal acts of the accused person has the right to bring to the court an incidental civil action during the course of the criminal proceedings. If the victim is dead or loses capacity for action, his/her statutory representative and close relatives have the right to initiate incidental civil action.

Where state property or collectively owned property suffers losses, the people's procuratorate may bring an incidental civil action while initiating a public prosecution.

Article 100 A people's court may, where necessary, take reservation measures to seal, seize or freeze the property of the accused person. The plaintiff of an incidental civil action or the people's procuratorate may apply to the people's court for the adoption of reservation measures. The relevant provisions of the Civil Procedure Law apply to matters concerning the adoption of reservation measures by the people's court.

Article 101 When adjudicating an incidental civil case, the people's court may conduct mediation, or make a judgment or order according to the situation of property losses.

Article 102 An incidental civil action shall be heard at the same time as the criminal case. An incidental civil action may only be handled by the same adjudicating organ after completion of the criminal trial for the purpose of preventing excessive delay in the trial of the criminal case.

Chapter VIII

Time Periods and Service

Article 103 Time periods are calculated by the hour, day and month.

The hour and day on which the time period begins are not counted as within the time period.

A legally prescribed time period does not include the time for travelling. Appeal statements or other documents which have been sent by mail before the expiry of the time period are not regarded as overdue.

Where the last day of a time period is a public holiday, the expiration date shall be the first day after the holiday. However, where a criminal suspect, an accused person or a criminal is held in detention, the expiration date shall be the last day of the time period and may not be postponed due to a public holiday.

Article 104 Where a party to a case fails to meet the deadline, due to *force majeure* or other proper reasons, he/she may, within five (5) days from the date of the removal of the obstacle, apply for the continuation of the litigation activities which should have been completed before the expiry of the time period.

The approval or rejection of an application described in the preceding Paragraph is to be decided by a people's court.

Article 105 All summonses, notices and other litigation documents shall be served in person to the addressee; if the addressee is away, the documents may be delivered instead to an adult relative or the person in charge of the unit where the addressee works.

If the addressee or the receiver on the addressee's behalf refuses to accept the documents or sign or affix his/her seal, the sender may invite the addressee's neighbour or other witnesses to the scene, explain the situation, leave the documents at the addressee's residence, record the particulars of the refusal and the date and time of the service in the service certificate, and sign his/her name to it. The documents will then be deemed to have been served.

Chapter IX

Other Provisions

Article 106 For the purpose of this Law, the terms below are defined as follows:

(1) "Investigation" refers to the specialised investigatory work conducted by the public security organs and the people's procuratorates and the related coercive measures;
(2) "Parties to a case" refers to victims, private prosecutors, criminal suspects, accused parties, and plaintiffs and accused parties in incidental civil actions;
(3) "Statutory representatives" refers to the parents, foster parents or guardians of the person being represented, and representatives of organisations and bodies responsible for the protection of the person being represented;
(4) "Litigation participants" refers to parties to the case, statutory representatives, litigation representatives, defence counsels, witnesses, expert witnesses and interpreters;
(5) "Litigation representatives" refers to persons who have been appointed to participate in legal proceedings in public prosecution cases, by victims or their statutory representatives or close relatives acting on their behalf, or in private prosecution cases by private prosecutors or their statutory representatives, and persons appointed by parties in incidental civil actions and their statutory representatives acting on their behalf.
(6) "Close relatives" refers to husband, wife, father, mother, son(s), daughter(s), and brother(s) and sister(s) from the same parents.

Part II

Filing, Investigation and Initiation of Public Prosecution

Chapter I

Filing a Case

Article 107 When a public security organ or a people's procuratorate discovers the facts of a crime or a criminal suspect, it shall, within the scope of its jurisdiction, file a case for investigation.

Article 108 Upon discovering the facts of a crime or a criminal suspect, a unit or individual has the right as well as the duty to report it or provide information to a public security organ, a people's procuratorate or a people's court.

When the personal or property rights of a victim have been infringed upon, the victim has the right to make a report or bring a complaint to a public security organ, a people's procuratorate or a people's court.

A public security organ, a people's procuratorate or a people's court shall accept all such reports, complaints and information provided. Where a case falls outside the jurisdiction of the organ which accepts it, the case shall be transferred to the competent organ and the reporter, complainant or the informant of the matter shall be notified. Where a case falls outside the jurisdiction of the organ which accepts the case, but the adoption of emergency measures is required, the said organ shall first take emergency measures and then refer the case to the competent organ.

Provisions in Paragraph 3 shall apply to cases in which an offender has voluntarily surrendered him/her self to a public security organ, a people's procuratorate or a people's court.

Article 109 Reports, complaints or information on offences may be submitted in writing or verbally. Where a report of a crime, a complaint or information about an offence is in verbal form, the officer who receives it shall make a written record which shall be signed or sealed by the reporter, complainant or informant after it has been read out to him/her and confirmed by him/her as accurate.

The officer who receives a complaint or information about an offence shall explain to the complainant or the informant the legal liability incurred for making a false accusation. However, a complaint or information about an offence which does not accord with the facts or even turns out to be mistaken shall be strictly distinguished from a false accusation, so long as it does not involve any fabrication of facts or falsification of evidence.

A public security organ, a people's procuratorate and a people's court shall ensure the safety of reporters, complainants, informants and their close relatives. Where a reporter, complainant or informant is unwilling to reveal to the pubic his/her name and the action of making a report or a complaint, or to provide information about an offence, such matters must be kept confidential.

Article 110 A public security organ, a people's procuratorate or a people's court shall examine without delay the materials provided by a reporter, complainant, informant or a voluntarily surrendered offender. Where it is considered that the facts of a crime exist and criminal liability shall be pursued, the case shall be filed immediately. Where no fact of a crime is found, or the facts of a crime are obviously minor and therefore there is no need to pursue any criminal liability, no case shall be filed and the complainant shall be notified of the reasons for not filing the case. If the complainant is not satisfied with the decision, he/she may apply for reconsideration.

Article 111 Where a people's procuratorate is of the opinion that the public security organ has failed to file a case where it should have done so, or where a victim brings to the people's procuratorate a case because he/she is of the opinion that the public security organ has failed to file the case where it should have done so, the people's procuratorate shall request the public security organ concerned to explain the reasons for not filing the case. Where the people's procuratorate is of the opinion that the reasons for not filing the case provided by the public security organ are not acceptable, it shall instruct the public security organ to file the case, and the public security organ shall file the case after receipt of the instruction.

Article 112 A victim in a private prosecution case has the right to directly lodge a law suit in a people's court. Where the victim has died or has lost his/her capacity for action, the statutory representative and the close relatives of the victim have the right to lodge a law suit in a people's court. The people's court shall accept the case in accordance with the law.

CHAPTER II

INVESTIGATION

Section 1 General Provisions

Article 113 After filing a criminal case, the public security organ shall conduct an investigation, and collect and gather evidence which is able to prove the guilt or innocence of the criminal suspect or the gravity of the crime. An active offender or a major criminal suspect may be detained in accordance with the law; where conditions for arrest are met, a criminal suspect may be arrested in accordance with the law.

Article 114 After investigation, where there is evidence of the existence of facts of a crime, the public security organ shall conduct preliminary interrogation and verify the evidentiary materials collected and gathered.

Article 115 Where a judicial organ or its personnel have committed any of the following acts, a party to the case, defence counsel, litigation representative and interested party has the right to present a petition or complaint to the judicial organ concerned:

(1) failing to release, terminate or alter a coercive measure when the statutory time period has expired;
(2) failing to return a guarantee bond paid for bail when it should have been returned;
(3) sealing, seizure or freezing of assets that are irrelevant to the case;
(4) failing to terminate the sealing, seizure or freezing when it should have been done; or
(5) embezzling, appropriating, distributing without authorisation, exchanging , or using in violation of provisions, assets that have been sealed, seized or frozen.

The organ that accepts the petition or complaint shall process the case without delay. If there is dissatisfaction with the disposition, a complaint may be lodged with the people's procuratorate at the same level, or, where the case is accepted directly by the people's procuratorate, to the people's procuratorate at the next higher level. The people's procuratorate shall examine the complaint without delay, and, where the complaint is verified, instruct the relevant organ(s) to make a correction.

Section 2 Interrogation of Criminal Suspects

Article 116 Interrogation of a criminal suspect must be conducted by investigatory personnel of a people's procuratorate or a public security organ. During the interrogation there must be at least two (2) investigatory personnel present.

Where investigatory personnel interrogate a criminal suspect after he/she has been sent to a detention centre, the interrogation shall be conducted within the detention centre.

Article 117 A criminal suspect who does not need to be arrested or detained may be summoned to a designated place in the city or county where the criminal suspect lives for interrogation, or the interrogation may be conducted in his/her residence, but when this is done a certificate issued by a people's procuratorate or a public security organ must be produced. A criminal suspect who is identified on the spot may be summoned orally upon presentation of a work unit identification card, but the matter should be noted in the record of the interrogation.

The time for interrogation through summons or through a detention warrant shall not exceed 12 hours; for particularly serious or complex cases which require taking measures of detention or arrest, the time for interrogation through summons or through a detention warrant shall not exceed 24 hours.

No criminal suspect may be detained under the guise of repeated summonses or repeated detention warrants. A criminal suspect who is under summons or detention warrant shall be guaranteed food, drink and necessary time for rest.

Article 118 When interrogating a criminal suspect, the investigatory personnel shall first ask whether or not he/she has committed a crime, let him/her to state details of the crime or explain his/her innocence, and then ask him/her other questions. A criminal suspect must answer the questions of the investigatory personnel truthfully. However, he/she is entitled to refuse to answer a question that is irrelevant to the case.

When interrogating a criminal suspect, the investigatory personnel shall inform the criminal suspect of the legal provisions that he/she may receive lenient treatment if he/she honestly confesses his/her crime.

Article 119 When interrogating a criminal suspect who is deaf or mute, there must be a person who is proficient in sign language to participate in the interrogation, and such circumstance shall be recorded in writing.

Article 120 The written record of an interrogation shall be presented to the criminal suspect for confirmation. Where the criminal suspect is unable to read, the written record shall be read out to him/her. The criminal suspect may, where any omission or error is found, request to make additions or corrections. After the criminal suspect confirms the written record as accurate, he/she shall sign it or affix his/her seal to it. The investigatory personnel shall also sign the written record. Where the criminal suspect petitions to write a statement by him/her self, it shall be permitted. Where it is necessary, investigatory personnel may also request the criminal suspect to provide a statement written by the criminal suspect personally.

Article 121 When interrogating a criminal suspect, the investigatory personnel may make an audio or visual record of the interrogation process; for crimes that are likely to be punished by life imprisonment or death, or for other serious crimes, the interrogation process shall be audio or video recorded.

The audio or video record shall cover the entire process and be complete.

Section 3 Questioning of Witnesses

Article 122 Investigatory personnel may question a witness on the spot, at the unit which the witness works with, or at the witness's residence, or at a place suggested by the witness, and may, where it is necessary, subpoena the witness to provide testimony at the people's procuratorate or the public security organ. To question a witness on the spot, the investigatory personnel must produce a work unit identification card; to question a witness at the unit he/she works with, or at his/her domicile or the place of his/her suggestion, a certificate issued by the people's procuratorate or the public security organ shall be produced.

Witnesses must be questioned individually.

Article 123 When questioning a witness, the witness shall be informed that evidence or testimony given by him/her shall be based on the truth, and that intentional provision of false testimony or the concealing of evidence of a crime will be pursued with legal liability.

Article 124 Provisions in Article 120 also apply to the questioning of witnesses.

Article 125 Provisions of all articles in this section apply to the questioning of victims.

Section 4 Inspection and Examination

Article 126 Investigatory personnel must inspect or examine all sites, objects, persons and corpses related to a crime. Where it is necessary, experts with special knowledge may be assigned or invited to conduct inspection and examination under the instruction of the investigatory personnel.

Article 127 All units and individuals have a duty to protect the scene of a crime and to notify immediately the public security organ to send officials to undertake an inspection.

Article 128 Investigatory personnel conducting inspection and examination must hold a certificate issued by a people's procuratorate or a public security organ.

Article 129 Where the cause of a death is not clear, a public security organ has the authority to conduct an autopsy and notify the family members of the deceased to be present at the autopsy.

Article 130 In order to ascertain certain characteristics, the gravity of an injury or the psychological status of a victim or criminal suspect, personal examination may be conducted on the victim or the criminal suspect, the fingerprints of the victim or the criminal suspect may be taken, and their blood, urine or other biological samples may be collected.

If a criminal suspect refuses to be examined, the investigatory personnel may compel him/her to be examined where they consider it to be necessary.

The examination of women must be conducted by female personnel or physicians.

Article 131 The circumstances of an inspection or examination must be recorded in written form, and shall be signed by or affixed with the seals of the inspecting personnel and witnesses.

Article 132 In the course of examination of a case, if a people's procuratorate is of the opinion that re-inspection or re-examination of an inspection or examination conducted by a public security organ is necessary, it may request the public security organ to re-inspect or re-examine the matter, and may also send its personnel to participate.

Article 133 In order to clarify the circumstances of a case an investigative experiment may be conducted where it is necessary, upon the approval of the person in charge of the public security bureau.

The investigative experiment shall be recorded in written form, and the record shall be signed by or affixed with the seals of the participants of the experiment.

No action which is dangerous, humiliating or offensive to public decency is permitted in an investigative experiment.

Section 5 Search

Article 134 In order to collect evidence of a crime and catch an offender, investigatory personnel may search the person, belongings, residence and other relevant places of a criminal suspect, or of a person who might conceal criminals or criminal evidence.

Article 135 All units and individuals have the duty to hand over physical evidence, documentary evidence, audio-visual materials or other evidence which may prove the guilt or innocence of a criminal suspect, on the demand of a people's procuratorate or a public security organ.

Article 136 A search warrant must be shown to the person to be searched when a search is to be conducted.

When an arrest or detention is being carried out and an emergency situation occurs, a search may be conducted without a search warrant.

Article 137 During the search, the person being searched or his/her relatives, and neighbours or other eye-witnesses shall be present at the scene.

The searching of women shall be conducted by female personnel.

Article 138 The circumstances of a search shall be recorded in written form and be signed by or affixed with the seals of the investigatory personnel, the person searched or his/her relatives, and neighbours or other eye-witnesses. If the person searched or his/her relative is on the run or refuses to sign or affix his/her seal, the situation shall be noted in the record.

Section 6 Sealing and Seizure of Physical Evidence and Documentary Evidence

Article 139 All assets, articles and documents discovered during investigatory activities which may be used as evidence of the guilt or innocence of a criminal suspect shall be sealed and seized; irrelevant assets, articles and documents must not be sealed or seized.

All assets, articles and documents sealed or seized shall be kept properly, or be sealed up for safekeeping and must not be used, exchanged or damaged.

Article 140 All sealed or seized assets, articles and documents shall be checked clearly by the investigatory personnel together with eye-witnesses and the holder of the sealed or seized assets, articles and documents, and a list of the objects seized and a duplicate of the list shall be produced and be signed by or affixed with the seals of the investigatory personnel, eye-witnesses and the holder of the seized objects. One copy of the list is to be given to the holder of the seized objects and the other copy is to be kept on file for reference.

Article 141 Where the investigatory personnel are of the opinion that it is essential to have the mail and telegrams of a criminal suspect seized, they may, with the approval of the public security organ or the people's procuratorate, notify the post office to check and hand over the relevant mail and telegrams.

When the continuation of the seizure of mail and telegrams becomes unnecessary, the post office shall be so notified immediately.

Article 142 A people's procuratorate or a public security organ may, where it is necessary for the investigation of a crime, inquire into or freeze the bank deposits and remittances, bonds, shares, unit-holdings of funds and other assets of the criminal suspect in accordance with the provisions. The relevant units and individuals shall provide cooperation.

Bank deposits and remittances, bonds, shares, unit-holdings of funds and other assets of a criminal suspect which have been frozen must not be frozen repeatedly.

Article 143 Where sealed or seized assets, articles, documents, mail or telegrams, frozen bank deposits or remittances, bonds, shares, unit-holdings of funds and other assets have been identified as irrelevant to a case, the sealing, seizure and freezing shall be terminated and the objects must be returned within three (3) days.

Section 7 Examination and Evaluation

Article 144 Where certain specific problems relating to a case need to be resolved so that the circumstances of the case may be clarified, persons with specialised knowledge may be assigned or invited to conduct examination and evaluation.

Article 145 After completion of examination and evaluation, the expert shall produce an evaluation opinion and sign it.

An expert who deliberately presents a false examination and evaluation shall bear legal liability.

Article 146 An investigating organ shall inform the criminal suspect and the victim of the opinion of the expert evaluation which is to be used as evidence. If the criminal suspect or the victim applies for it, a supplementary examination and evaluation or a re-evaluation may be carried out.

Article 147 The period during which a criminal suspect is under evaluation for mental illness is not to be included in the time period for the handling of a case.

Section 8 Technical Investigation Measures

Article 148 After a public security organ has filed a case, if the case involves the crime of endangering State security, terrorism crime, organised crime of an underworld nature, major drug-related crime or other crimes with great harm to the society, it may take technical investigation measures in light of the requirement of the crime investigation and following strict approval procedures.

After a people's procuratorate has filed a case, if the case involves a crime of serious corruption or bribery, or a major crime of serious infringement upon a citizen's personal rights by using one's position, it may adopt technical investigation measures in light of the requirement of the crime investigation and following strict approval procedures, and entrust the relevant organ to carry out the implementation in accordance with the provisions.

In the pursuing of an on-the-run criminal suspect or an accused person who is under a circular order for arrest, or whose arrest has been approved or decided, technical measures necessary for the pursuit may be taken upon approval.

Article 149 The approval or decision shall determine, in light of the need of the crime investigation, the types of technical investigation measures to be taken and the intended target. An approval or decision is effective within three (3) months from the date on which it is issued. Where the continuation of the adoption of technical investigation measures becomes unnecessary, the measures shall be terminated without delay. For a complex or difficult case, if the taking of technical investigation measures is still necessary upon the expiry of an effective period of approval, the effective period may be extended upon approval. Each extension shall not be in excess of three (3) months.

Article 150 Technical investigation measures must be executed strictly in accordance with the approved type, target and duration of the measures.

Investigatory personnel shall maintain the confidentiality of any State secrets, commercial secrets or personal privacy that they become aware of during the execution of a technical investigation measure; materials irrelevant to the case obtained during the execution of a technical investigation measure must be destroyed without delay.

Materials obtained during the execution of a technical investigation measure may only be used for criminal investigation, prosecution and adjudication, and may not be used for any other purpose.

A relevant unit or individual shall provide cooperation when a public security organ implements technical investigation measures pursuant to the law, and shall maintain the confidentiality of the relevant situation.

Article 151 In order to ascertain the situation of a case, and where it is necessary, the relevant personnel may, upon approval of the person-in-charge of the public security organ, conceal their identity when conducting an investigation. However, they must not induce a person to commit a crime or use any other means that are likely to endanger public security or pose serious personal risks to other persons.

For criminal activities involving the delivery of and payment for drugs or other banned substances and assets, the public security organ may, in light of the need for criminal investigation, operate controlled delivery of and payment for such articles in accordance with the provisions.

Article 152 Materials collected during the implementation of investigation measures in accordance with the provisions of this Section may be used as evidence in criminal proceedings. Where the use of such evidence may pose risks to the relevant personnel, or may bring other serious consequences, protective measures such as concealing the identity of the relevant personnel and technical methods shall be adopted; where it is necessary, the verification of the evidence may be conducted by adjudicating personnel outside the court.

Section 9 Circular Orders for Arrest

Article 153 Where a criminal suspect who should be arrested is on the run, a public security organ may issue a Circular Order for Arrest and take effective measures to pursue and arrest the criminal suspect.

Public security organs at various levels may, within their respective jurisdictions, directly issue Circular Orders for Arrest; for areas beyond their jurisdictions, they shall request an organ at the higher level which has proper authority to issue such circular orders.

Section 10 Conclusion of Investigation

Article 154 The time limit for holding a criminal suspect in custody for investigation after his/her arrest must not be in excess of two (2) months. If a case is complex and cannot be concluded within the time limit, an extension of one (1) month may be permitted upon the approval of the people's procuratorate at the next higher level.

Article 155 Where a case is particularly grave and complex, and where for specific reasons it will be not appropriate to hand over the case for trial for a relatively long period of time, the Supreme People's Procuratorate shall report the matter to the Standing Committee of the National People's Congress and apply for a postponement of the hearing of the case.

Article 156 For the following cases, if investigation cannot be concluded within the time limit prescribed by the provisions of Article 154, an extension of two (2) months may be permitted with the approval or decision of the people's procuratorate at the level of province, autonomous region, or directly administered municipality:

(1) major and complex cases committed in remote areas where transport is particularly inconvenient;
(2) major cases committed by criminal gangs;
(3) major and complex cases committed by persons who go from place to place to commit crimes; and
(4) major and complex cases which involve large areas and for which gathering evidence is difficult.

Article 157 Where a criminal suspect is likely to be sentenced to 10 years of fixed-term imprisonment or more, and the investigation still cannot be concluded upon the expiry of the extended time period as provided in Article 156 of this Law, a further extension of two (2) months may be permitted with the approval or decision of the people's procuratorate at the level of province, autonomous region, or directly administered municipality.

Article 158 During the course of investigation, if a criminal suspect is found to have committed other major crime(s), the time period shall, in accordance with the provisions of Article 154 of this Law, be re-calculated from the date on which such a crime is discovered.

Where a criminal suspect refuses to provide his/her true name and address and his/her identity is unknown, his/her identity shall be investigated; the time limit for holding him/her in custody during investigation shall be calculated from the date on which his/her identity is established, but the investigation of his/her criminal acts and the gathering of evidence must not be suspended. Where the facts of a crime are clear and evidence is reliable and sufficient, and it is impossible to have the identity of the criminal suspect confirmed, the case may be transferred for prosecution and adjudication, using the name given by the criminal suspect him/herself as the name for the accused person.

Article 159 Before the investigation in a case is concluded, where a defence lawyer expresses his/her opinion, the investigation organ shall listen to the opinion and document it in the records. Where a defence lawyer submits a written opinion, the document shall be filed in the case dossier.

Article 160 Where an investigation in a case has been concluded, the public security organ shall ensure that the facts of the crime in the case are clear and evidence is reliable and sufficient, and shall draw up a prosecution recommendation and submit it together with the case dossier and evidence to the people's procuratorate for examination and determination, and in the meantime notify the criminal suspect and his/her defence lawyer of the transfer of the case.

Article 161 During the course of investigation, if it is found that a criminal suspect should not be pursued with criminal liability, the case shall be withdrawn; where the criminal suspect has been arrested, he/she shall be released immediately and be issued with a release certificate. The people's procuratorate which originally approved the arrest shall also be informed of the matter.

Section 11 Investigation of Cases Directly Accepted by the People's Procuratorates

Article 162 The provisions in this Chapter apply to investigation of cases conducted directly by the people's procuratorates.

Article 163 Where a case accepted directly by a people's procuratorate accords with the provisions of Article 79 and Article 80(4) and (5) in this Law and arrest or detention of the criminal suspect is necessary, the arrest or detention shall be decided by the people's procuratorate and executed by a public security organ.

Article 164 A detainee in a case accepted directly by a people's procuratorate shall be interrogated within 24 hours after the detention. Where it is found that the detainee should not have been detained, he/she must be released immediately and be issued with a release certificate.

Article 165 Where a people's procuratorate considers that arrest of a detainee in a case accepted directly by it is necessary, a decision on this shall be made within 14 days after the detention. In exceptional circumstances, the time limit for such decision-making may be extended for one to four (1–4) days. If arrest is unnecessary, the detainee shall be released immediately; if a further investigation is required and the case meets the conditions for setting bail or residential surveillance, the detainee may be placed on bail or under residential surveillance in accordance with the law.

Article 166 After the conclusion of the investigation of a directly accepted case, the people's procuratorate shall make a decision on whether or not to initiate a public prosecution or to dismiss the case.

CHAPTER III

INITIATION OF PUBLIC PROSECUTIONS

Article 167 All cases in which public prosecution is required shall be examined and determined by the people's procuratorates.

Article 168 When examining a case, the people's procuratorate must ascertain:

(1) whether the facts and details of a crime are clear, the evidence is reliable and sufficient, and the nature of the crime and the charge are correctly determined;
(2) whether any other crime or person liable for criminal responsibility has been omitted;
(3) whether the accused person should not be pursued with criminal liability;
(4) whether there is any incidental civil action; and
(5) whether the investigative activities are lawfully conducted.

Article 169 For a case transferred by a public security organ for the initiation of a public prosecution, the people's procuratorate shall make its decision within one (1) month; for major and complex cases, an extension of half a month may be permitted.

Where the jurisdiction over a case being examined by a people's procuratorate is changed, the time period for examination and prosecution shall be calculated from the date on which the people's procuratorate which has obtained the jurisdiction after the change receives the case.

Article 170 In examining a case, the people's procuratorate shall interrogate the criminal suspect and listen to the opinions of the defence counsel, the victim and his/her litigation representative, and document the opinions in the records. Where the defence counsel or the victim or his/her litigation representative submits a written opinion, the document shall be filed in the case dossier.

Article 171 When examining a case, the people's procuratorate may request a public security organ to provide evidential materials necessary for a court trial, and may request an explanation on the legality of the collection of the evidence where it is of the opinion that there may be a circumstance of collecting evidence through unlawful means as prescribed by Article 54 of this Law.

During the course of examination, where supplementary investigation is required, a people's procuratorate may return the case to the public security organ for supplementary investigation or may conduct the investigation itself.

A supplementary investigation must be completed within one (1) month. A supplementary investigation may only be conducted twice at the most. After the supplementary investigation has been completed and transferred to the people's procuratorate, the people's procuratorate shall recalculate the time limit for examination for prosecution.

Where a people's procuratorate is of the opinion that there is still a lack of sufficient evidence in the case, even after the second supplementary investigation, and thus the conditions for prosecution are not satisfied, it shall make a decision not to initiate a prosecution.

Article 172 Where a people's procuratorate is of the opinion that the facts of a crime committed by the criminal suspect are clear, the evidence is reliable and sufficient, and criminal liability must be pursued according to the law, it shall make a decision on the initiation of a prosecution and, in accordance with provisions on adjudication jurisdiction, initiate in the people's court a public prosecution and transfer the case materials and evidence to the people's court.

Article 173 Where a criminal suspect is found to have committed no criminal act, or falls within one of the situations prescribed by Article 15 of this Law, the people's procuratorate shall make a decision not to initiate a prosecution.

Where the circumstance of a crime is minor and criminal punishment is not necessary or may be exempted according to the provisions of the Criminal Law, the people's procuratorate may make a decision not to initiate a prosecution.

Where a people's procuratorate decides not to initiate a case, it shall in the meantime release all assets and articles sealed, seized or frozen during the investigation. Where it is necessary to impose an administrative penalty or administrative sanction on a person against whom no prosecution is initiated, or to have his/her illegally obtained profits confiscated, the people's procuratorate shall submit a recommendation to this effect and transfer the case to the relevant competent organ for handling, and the relevant competent organ shall promptly inform the people's procuratorate of the result of the case.

Article 174 A decision not to initiate a prosecution shall be announced in public, and the bill not to initiate a prosecution shall be served on the person concerned and the unit he/she works with. Where the said person is in custody, he/she shall be released immediately.

Article 175 Where a people's procuratorate decides not to initiate a case transferred by a public security organ, it shall deliver the bill not to initiate a prosecution to the public security organ. If the public security organ is of the opinion that the decision not to initiate prosecution is not correct, it may request reconsideration; if its opinion is not accepted, it may apply to the people's procuratorate at the next higher level for review.

Article 176 Where a people's procuratorate decides not to initiate a public prosecution in a case in which a victim is involved, it shall serve the bill not to initiate prosecution on the victim. If the victim is not satisfied with the decision, he/she may, within seven (7) days of the receipt of the bill, file a petition with the people's procuratorate at the next higher level for initiating a public prosecution. The people's procuratorate shall inform the victim of its review decision. Where the people's procuratorate upholds the decision not to initiate prosecution, the victim may lodge a suit in a people's court. A victim may also lodge a direct suit in a people's court without going through a petition. Where the people's court accepts the case, the people's procuratorate shall transfer all materials relevant to the case to the people's court.

Article 177 Where a person against whom a decision of non-prosecution is made is not satisfied with the decision made by a people's procuratorate under provisions of Paragraph 2 of Article 173 in this Law, he/she may file a petition with the people's procuratorate within seven (7) days of the receipt of the decision. The people's procuratorate shall make its review decision, notify the person not to be prosecuted, and deliver a copy of the decision to the public security organ.

Part III

Adjudication

Chapter I

Organisation of Adjudication

Article 178 Cases of first instance in a basic people's court or an Intermediate people's court shall be adjudicated by a collegial panel composed of three (3) judges, or composed of judges and people's assessors numbering three (3) in total. However, cases in a basic people's court for which summary procedures apply may be tried by a single sitting judge alone.

Cases of first instance in a High People's Court or the Supreme People's Court shall be adjudicated by a collegial panel composed of three to seven (3–7) judges, or composed of judges and people's assessors numbering three to seven (3–7) in total.

A people's assessor performing functions in a people's court has power equivalent to that of a judge.

Adjudication of an appeal case or a protested case in a people's court shall be conducted by a collegial panel composed of three to five (3–5) judges.

The number of members of a collegial panel shall be odd.

The president of a people's court or the chief judge of a division of the court shall appoint one judge to be the presiding judge of a collegial panel. Where the president of the court or the chief judge of a division of the court sits over the trial, he/she serves as the presiding judge.

Article 179 Where there is a divergence of opinion during the deliberation of a collegial panel, the decision shall be made on the basis of the view of the majority, and the opinions of the minority shall be recorded in the transcript. The transcript is to be signed by members of the collegial panel.

Article 180 A collegial panel shall make its judgment after the court hearing and deliberation. Where a collegial panel is unable to make a decision on a difficult, major and complex case, it may refer the case to the president of the court for his/her decision on whether to submit the case to the adjudication committee for discussion and decision. The decision of the adjudication committee shall be carried out by the collegial panel.

Chapter II

First Instance Procedure

Section 1 Cases of Public Prosecution

Article 181 After having examined a public prosecution case, the people's court shall make a decision on opening a court hearing where the facts of a charged crime are clearly presented in the bill of prosecution.

Article 182 After a people's court has decided to conduct a court hearing, it shall decide on the membership of the collegial panel, and serve a copy of the bill of prosecution of the people's procuratorate on the accused person and his/her defence counsel at least 10 days before the court hearing.

Before the court hearing the adjudicating personnel may convene the public prosecutor and the parties to the case and their defence counsels and litigation representatives to discuss issues of withdrawal, the list of witnesses, the exclusion of unlawfully obtained evidence and other issues relating to the trial, and listen to their opinions.

After the date of the court hearing is determined, the people's court shall notify the people's procuratorate of the time and place of the court hearing, summon the parties to the case, and notify the defence counsels, the litigation representative, witnesses, expert witnesses and interpreters; the summonses and notices shall be served at least three (3) days before the opening of the court hearing. For a case to be tried in public the main facts of the case, the name of the accused person, and the time and place of the hearing shall be announced three (3) days before the opening of the court hearing.

The above mentioned activities must be recorded in writing and signed by the adjudicating official and the court clerk.

Article 183 A case of first instance in a people's court shall be heard in public. But a case involving state secrets or personal privacy shall not be heard in public. Where a case involves commercial secrets and the parties to the case apply to not have the hearing conducted in public, a closed hearing may be conducted.

Reasons for a case not to be heard in public shall be announced openly in the court hearing session.

Article 184 When a public prosecution case is heard by a people's court, the people's procuratorate shall send its procurators to be present in the court to support the public prosecution.

Article 185 When a court proceeding begins, the presiding judge shall check whether the parties to the case appear in the court, announce the main facts of the case, the membership of the collegial panel, the names of the court clerk, public procurators, defence counsel(s), litigation representatives(s), expert witness(es) and interpreter(s), inform the parties to the case of their right to request the members of the collegial panel, the court clerk, the public procurator(s), expert witness(es) or interpreter(s) to withdraw from the proceeding, and inform the accused person of his/her entitlement to defence.

Article 186 After the public procurator has read out the bill of prosecution in the court, the accused person and the victim may make a statement on the crime alleged in the bill of prosecution, and the procurator may interrogate the accused person.

The victim, the plaintiff in an incidental civil action, the defence counsel and the litigation representatives may, with the permission of the presiding judge, question the accused person.

The adjudicating personnel may interrogate the accused person.

Article 187 Where the public procurator, a party to the case or his/her defence counsel or litigation representative has objections to a witness's testimony which has material influence on the criminality or sentencing, and the people's court believes that it is necessary to have the witness appear in the court to testify, the witness shall attend the court for testimony.

The provisions in the preceding Paragraph apply to where a member of the people's police force attends the court as a witness to give testimony about the situation of a crime he/she witnessed when on duty.

Where the public procurator, a party to the case or his/her defence counsel or litigation representative has objections to the opinion of an expert witness, and the people's court believes that it is necessary to have the expert appear in the court to testify, the expert witness shall attend the court for testimony. Where the expert witness, upon notification by the people's court, refuses to attend the court for testimony, the examination opinion may not be used as a basis for the determination of the case.

Article 188 Where a witness fails to attend the court for testimony after having been notified by the people's court, the people's court may compel the witness to attend the court, except where the spouse, parents and children of the accused person are the witnesses.

A witness who refuses to attend the court without proper reason, or refuses to give testimony after attending the court, shall receive admonition and, where circumstances are serious, be subject to detention of ten days or less upon approval by the president of the court. Where the person subject to the punishment is not satisfied with the detention decision, he/she may apply to the people's court at the next higher level for a review. During the period of review, the implementation of the decision is not to be suspended.

Article 189 Before a witness gives testimony the adjudicating personnel shall inform him/her that testimony must be given on the basis of the truth and that intentionally giving false testimony or concealing evidence of a crime will incur legal liability. The public procurator, the parties to the case, the defence counsel(s) and the litigation representative(s) may, with the permission of the presiding judge, question the witness(es) and the expert witness(es). Where the presiding judge considers that a question is irrelevant to the case, he/she shall stop the questioning of the issue.

The adjudicating personnel may question witnesses and expert witnesses.

Article 190 The public procurator and defence counsel(s) shall present physical evidence to the court for the parties to identify; transcripts of witnesses' testimonies, evaluation opinions of expert witnesses, written records of inspection and other evidential documents of which the authors are not present in the court must be read out in the court. The adjudicating personnel shall listen to the opinions of the public procurator, the parties to the case and their defence counsel(s) and litigation representatives.

Article 191 During the court hearing, the collegial panel may, where it has doubts regarding the evidence, announce an adjournment so as to conduct investigation and verification of the evidence.

When conducting investigation and verification of evidence, the people's court may adopt such measures as inspection, examination, seizure, evaluation, inquiry and the freezing of assets.

Article 192 During the court hearing, parties to the case and their defence counsels and litigation representatives are entitled to request the summoning of new witnesses to the court, to gather new physical evidence and to conduct re-evaluation or re-inspection.

The public prosecutor, parties to the case and their defence counsels and litigation representatives may apply to the court to summon persons with specific expertise to attend the court to provide opinions on the evaluation opinion of an expert witness.

The court shall make a decision on whether or not the above mentioned requests are to be approved.

The provisions on expert witnesses apply to cases where persons with specific expertise attend the court as provided under Paragraph 2.

Article 193 During the court hearing all facts and evidence relevant to criminality and sentencing shall be investigated and debated.

With the permission of the presiding judge, the public procurator, the parties to the case and their defence counsels and litigation representatives may deliver their opinion on the evidence and the circumstances of the case. They may also debate with each other.

After the presiding judge announces the conclusion of the court debate, the accused person has the right to make a final statement.

Article 194 During the court hearing, if any participant to the proceeding or an attendant violates a court order, the presiding judge shall give him/her a warning. If the warning is ignored, the person may be taken out of the court by force; where the circumstance is serious he/she shall have imposed a fine of not more than 1,000 *yuan* or a detention of not more than 15 days. A fine or detention shall be approved by the president of the court. If the person to be fined or detained is not satisfied with the decision, he/she may apply to the people's court at the next higher level for a review. During the period of review, the execution of the penalty shall not be suspended.

Anyone who gathers a crowd to create chaos in the court or to interrupt the court, or insults, slanders, threatens or beats up adjudicating personnel or parties to the case and thereby seriously disturbs the court order and commits a crime, shall be pursued with criminal liability.

Article 195 After the accused person has given his/her final statement, the presiding judge will announce an adjournment and the collegial panel will retire to deliberate. The court, in line with the facts and evidence that have been ascertained and relevant provisions of the law, will render its judgment in accordance with the following rules:

(1) if the facts of the case are clear, the evidence is reliable and sufficient and the accused person is found guilty in accordance with the law, a judgment of guilty shall be rendered;
(2) if the accused person is found not guilty in accordance with law, a judgment of not guilty shall be rendered; or
(3) where there is lack of sufficient evidence and the accused person therefore cannot be found guilty, a judgment of not guilty, stating that the crime charged cannot be established because there is insufficient evidence, shall be rendered.

Article 196 All judgments must be announced in public.

Where a judgment is announced in the courtroom immediately after the hearing, the judgment shall, within five (days) days, be served on the parties to the case and the people's procuratorate which initiated the public prosecution. Where a judgment is to be announced at a prescribed later time the judgment shall be served on the parties to the case and the people's procuratorate initiating the public prosecution right after the announcement. The judgment shall be served upon the defence counsels and litigation representatives at the same time.

Article 197 A judgment must be signed by the adjudicating official and the court clerk, and must state clearly the time period for appeal and the appellate court.

Article 198 A court hearing may be postponed in any one of the following situations which may affect the court hearing:

(1) it is necessary to summon a new witness to appear in court, or it is necessary to gather new physical evidence or to conduct re-verification or re-inspection;
(2) the procuratorial personnel consider that a supplementary investigation for the public prosecution case is needed and so suggest; or
(3) the hearing cannot proceed because of an application for withdrawal.

Article 199 Where the hearing of a case is postponed in accordance with the provisions of Article 198(2) of this Law, the people's procuratorate shall complete the supplementary investigation within one month.

Article 200 In the course of adjudication, if any of the following situations occurs and as a result the trial cannot be continued for a relatively long period of time, the trial may be suspended:

(1) the accused person is seriously ill and unable to attend the court;
(2) the accused person escapes;
(3) the private prosecutor falls seriously ill and is unable to attend the court, and has not yet appointed a litigation representative; or
(4) an event of *force majeure* occurs.

The trial shall be resumed after the reason for the suspension of the trial no longer exists. The time period during the suspension is not to be counted as adjudication time.

Article 201 A transcript recording the entire court proceeding shall be made by the court clerk, and shall, after examination by the presiding judge, be signed by the presiding judge and the court clerk.

Testimony of witnesses recorded in the court transcript shall be read out in the court or given to the witnesses to read. Where a witness confirms that the transcript is accurate, he/she shall sign it or affix his/her seal to it.

The court transcript must be given to the parties to the case to read or have read out to them. Where a party considers that there are omissions or errors in the transcript, he/she may request to make additions or corrections. After the party confirms that the transcript is accurate, he/she shall sign it or affix his/her seal to it.

Article 202 The judgment on a public prosecution case shall be announced by the people's court within two (2) months, or at the most within three (3) months, after the acceptance of the case by the court. For cases where the death sentence is likely to be imposed, cases accompanied by a civil action and cases falling within one of the circumstances as prescribed by Article 156 of the Law, an extension of three (3) months may be permitted with the approval of the next higher people's court; where a further extension is needed due to exceptional circumstances, it shall be reported to the People's Supreme Court for approval.

Where the jurisdiction of a people's court over a case has been changed, the time limit for the adjudication of the case is to be calculated from the date on which the people's court that obtained the jurisdiction after the change receives the case.

Once a case subject to supplementary investigation by a people's procuratorate is transferred to the people's court after the completion of the supplementary investigation, the people's court will re-calculate the time period for the adjudication of the case.

Article 203 Where a people's procuratorate discovers that a people's court has violated litigation procedures prescribed by law, it has the power to request the people's court to make corrections.

Section 2 Cases of Private Prosecution

Article 204 Cases of private prosecution include the following:

(1) cases to be handled upon complaint only;
(2) minor criminal cases in which the victim holds evidence; and
(3) cases in which the victim holds evidence proving that the accused person has infringed his/her personal or property rights, committed a crime and should be pursued with criminal liability in accordance with the law, but the public security organ or the people's procuratorate decides not to pursue the criminal liability of the accused person.

Article 205 After having examined a private prosecution case, the people's court is to handle the case in accordance with the following rules:

(1) opening a court hearing where the facts of a crime are clear and evidence is sufficient; or
(2) convincing the complainant to withdraw the case or ordering the dismissal of the case, where the private prosecution case lacks evidence and the complainant is unable to provide supplementary evidence.

Where a private prosecutor refuses to attend the court after being summoned for the second time without proper reason, or withdraws from the court hearing without the permission of the court, the case shall be treated as having been withdrawn.

During a court hearing, if the adjudicating personnel have doubts regarding a piece of evidence and investigation and verification are required, the provisions of Article 191 of this Law apply.

Article 206 A people's court may conduct mediation in a private prosecution case. The private prosecutor may arrange a settlement with the accused person or withdraw the complaint before the announcement of the judgment. Mediation does not apply to cases which fall within the provisions of Article 204(3).

With regard to the time period for a private prosecution case adjudicated by a people's court, where the accused person is in custody, the provisions of Paragraph 1 and 2 under Article 202 of the Law apply; where the accused person is not in custody the judgment shall be announced within six (6) months of the acceptance of the case by the people's court.

Article 207 An accused person in a private prosecution case may bring a counter-action against the private prosecutor during litigation. Provisions governing private prosecution apply to any counter-action.

Section 3 Summary Procedures

Article 208 Cases within the jurisdiction of the basic people's courts may be adjudicated under summary procedures if the case satisfies the following conditions:

(1) the facts of the case are clear and the evidence is sufficient;
(2) the accused person has admitted his/her crime and has no objection to the criminal facts charged; and
(3) the accused person has no objection to the application of summary procedures.

When initiating a public prosecution, the people's procuratorate may suggest that the people's court apply summary procedures.

Article 209 Summary procedures do not apply to any of the following situations:

(1) the accused person is blind, mute or deaf, or is mentally ill but has not completely lost his/her capacity to comprehend or control his/her behaviour;
(2) there is a major social impact;
(3) some accused persons in a joint crime do not admit their guilt, or object to the application of summary procedures; or
(4) other situations where the application of summary procedures is not appropriate.

Article 210 In cases where summary procedures apply, if a punishment of fixed term imprisonment of three years or less is likely to be imposed the trial may be conducted by a collegial panel or by a single judge, or, if a punishment of fixed term imprisonment of three years or more is likely to be imposed, by a collegial penal.

For a public prosecution case which is tried under summary procedures, the people's procuratorate shall send its procurator to be present in the court.

Article 211 In a case which is to be tried under summary procedures, the adjudicating personnel shall question the accused person about his/her opinion on the criminal facts charged, inform the accused person of the provisions of the law concerning the application of summary procedures, and ascertain whether or not the accused person agrees to have summary procedures applied for the trial.

Article 212 In a case which is tried under summary procedures, the accused person and his/her defence counsel may, with the permission of the adjudicating personnel, debate with the public procurator or the private prosecutor or his/her litigation representative.

Article 213 Cases to be tried under summary procedures are not subject to the provisions of Section 1 of this Chapter on limitation periods for the service of legal documents, interrogation of the accused person, questioning of witnesses and expert witnesses, presentation of evidence and procedures for court debate. However, the final statement of the accused person must be heard before the announcement of the judgment.

Article 214 A people's court shall conclude a case which is tried under summary procedures within 20 days after the acceptance of the case; where fixed-term imprisonment of more than three (3) years is likely to be imposed the period may be extended up to one and a half months.

Article 215 Where a people's court discovers during the course of adjudication that it is inappropriate to apply summary procedures for the case, it shall re-try the case in accordance with the provisions of Section 1 or 2 in this Chapter.

Chapter III

Second Instance Procedure

Article 216 If an accused person, a private prosecutor, or his/her statutory representative is not satisfied with the judgment or order of first instance made by a people's court at various levels, he/she has the right to make a written or verbal appeal to the people's court at the next higher level. Defence counsels and close relatives of the accused person may, with the consent of the accused person, file an appeal.

Parties to an incidental civil action and their statutory representatives may file an appeal against the relevant party regarding the incidental civil action in a judgment or order of first instance made by a local people's court at various levels.

The right of an accused person to appeal must not be withheld under any circumstances.

Article 217 Where a people's procuratorate at various levels is of the opinion that the judgment or order of first instance made by a people's court is not correct, it shall lodge a protest to the people's court at the next higher level.

Article 218 If a victim or his/her statutory representative is not satisfied with the judgment of first instance made by a people's court at various levels, he/she has the right, within five (5) days of the receipt of the judgment, to request the people's procuratorate to lodge a protest. The people's procuratorate shall, within five (5) days of the receipt of the request made by the victim or his/her statutory representative, decide whether or not to lodge a protest and reply to the person who made the request.

Article 219 The time limit for appeal or protest against a judgment is 10 days. The time limit for appeal or protest against an order is five (5) days. The time period shall be calculated from the day after the date of the receipt of the judgment or order.

Article 220 Where an accused person or a private prosecutor, or a plaintiff or an accused person in an incidental civil action makes an appeal through the people's court which originally tried the case, the people's court which originally tried the case shall within three (3) days transfer the appeal statement together with the case dossier and evidence to the people's court at the next higher level, and in the meantime send duplicates of the appeal statement to the people's procuratorate at the same level and the parties on the opposing side.

Where an accused person or a private prosecutor, or a plaintiff or an accused person in an incidental civil action makes an appeal directly to the people's court of second instance, the people's court of second instance shall within three (3) days deliver the appeal statement to the people's court that originally tried the case, the people's procuratorate at the same level, and the parties on the opposing side.

Article 221 A people's procuratorate at various levels lodging a protest against a judgment or order of first instance made by a people's court at the same level, shall submit the bill of protest through the people's court which originally tried the case, and send a copy of the bill of protest to the people's procuratorate at the next higher level. The people's court which originally tried the case shall transfer the bill of protest together with the case dossier and evidence to the people's court at the next higher level, and serve duplicates of the bill of protest on the parties to the case.

Where the people's procuratorate at the next higher level is of the opinion that the protest is inappropriate, it may withdraw the protest from the people's court at the same level and notify the people's procuratorate at the lower level.

Article 222 A people's court of second instance shall examine comprehensively the facts found and the application of law in the judgment of the first instance, and is not limited to the scope of the appeal or protest.

Where only some of the accused persons in a jointly committed crime case lodge an appeal, the case shall still be examined and handled as a whole.

Article 223 A people's court of second instance shall form a collegial panel and conduct a court hearing for any of the following cases:

(1) cases of appeal in which the accused person, the private prosecutor, or their statutory representative raises objections to a fact confirmed or evidence admitted in the first instance, which may influence the finding of criminality and sentencing;
(2) cases of appeal in which the accused person is sentenced to death;
(3) cases where the people's procuratorate has lodged a protest; and
(4) other cases for which a court hearing shall be conducted.

Where the people's court of second instance decides not to open a court hearing, it shall interrogate the accused person and listen to the opinions of other parties to the case, of the defence counsels and of litigation representatives.

A people's court of second instance may hear an appeal case or a protest case in the place where the case occurred, or in the place where the people's court which originally tried the case is located.

Article 224 For cases protested by a people's procuratorate, and cases of public prosecution tried by a people's court of second instance under a court hearing, the people's procuratorate at the same level shall send its procurator(s) to be present in the court. The people's court of second instance shall promptly notify the people's procuratorate to examine the case files after it has decided to open a court hearing. The people's procuratorate shall complete such examination within one month. The time used by the people's procuratorate in examining the case files is not to be included in the time limit for trial.

Article 225 After a case of appeal or protest against a judgment of first instance has been heard, the people's court of second instance shall handle the case in accordance with the following rules:

(1) if the original judgment is correct in the determination of the facts and the application of law, and appropriate in imposing the penalty, the appeal or protest shall be dismissed and the original judgment shall be upheld;
(2) if the original judgment is correct in the determination of facts but is incorrect in the application of law or the imposing of the penalty, the judgment shall be altered; or
(3) if the facts in the original judgment are unclear or evidence is insufficient, the judgment may be altered after the facts have been clarified; or the original judgment may also be quashed and the case remitted to the people's court which originally tried the case for retrial.

Where the original people's court has rendered its judgment for a case remitted to it for retrial pursuant to the provisions of Item (3) in the preceding Paragraph, and the accused person has filed an appeal or the people's procuratorate has lodged a protest, the people's court of second instance shall make a judgment or an order in accordance with the law, and shall not remit the case to the original people's court for another trial.

Article 226 When a people's court of second instance adjudicates an appeal case made by the accused person or his/her statutory representative, or by the defence counsel(s) or close relatives of the accused person, it must not impose a heavier criminal punishment on the accused person. When the original people's court re-tries a case remitted by a people's court of second instance, unless new criminal facts are found and the people's procuratorate has made a supplementary prosecution, it also must not impose a heavier criminal punishment on the accused person.

For cases protested by the people's procuratorates or appealed by private prosecutors, the restrictions stipulated in the preceding Paragraph do not apply.

Article 227 Where a people's court of second instance discovers that the people's court of first instance has in its adjudication violated the litigation procedures prescribed by law in one of the following ways, it shall quash the original judgment and remit the case to the people's court which originally tried the case for retrial:

(1) violating the relevant provisions of this Law on public trials;
(2) violating the system of withdrawal;
(3) withholding or restricting the procedural rights of the parties to the case to which they are entitled under the law, whereby a fair trial is likely to be impaired;
(4) the composition of the adjudication organisation is unlawful; or
(5) other conduct in violation of litigation procedures prescribed by law, whereby a fair trial is likely to be impaired.

Article 228 For a case to be remitted for retrial, the people's court which originally tried the case shall form a new collegial panel and conduct adjudication in accordance with procedures for the first instance. The judgment rendered after the re-trial may, in accordance with the provisions of Articles 216, 217 and 218 in this Law, be appealed or protested against.

Article 229 After a case of appeal or protest against an order of first instance has been examined, the people's court of second instance shall, in reference to the provisions of Articles 225, 227 and 228 in this Law and in light of the circumstances of the case, make an order to dismiss the appeal or protest, quash the original order or alter the original order.

Article 230 The time period for adjudicating a case remitted by a people's court of second instance for retrial by the people's court which originally tried the case shall be re-calculated from the date of the receipt of the remitted case.

Article 231 The adjudication of cases of appeal or protest by a people's court of second instance is to be conducted in reference to the procedures for first instance cases, except for those matters that are governed by the provisions in this Chapter.

Article 232 A people's court of second instance shall conclude an appeal or protest case within two (2) months. For cases where the death sentence is likely to be imposed, cases accompanied by a civil action, and cases falling within one of the situations prescribed in Article 156 of this Law, an extension of two (2) months may be permitted with the approval or decision of the High People's Court at the level of province, autonomous region or directly administered municipality; where there are exceptional circumstances and the period needs to be further extended, this needs to be reported to the Supreme People's Court for approval.

The time period for adjudicating an appeal or protest case accepted by the Supreme People's Court is to be decided by the Supreme People's Court.

Article 233 Judgments or orders of second instance and judgments and orders of the Supreme People's Court are final.

Article 234 The public security organs, the people's procuratorates and the people's courts shall have all sealed, seized and frozen assets and articles of criminal suspects and accused persons and assets propagated therefrom properly kept for verification, and shall produce a list of the assets and articles and have this transferred together with the case files. No unit or individual may be allowed to misappropriate or dispose of such items without authorisation. The legally obtained property of victims must be returned to them in good time. Prohibited goods or perishable articles shall be disposed of in accordance with the relevant provisions of the State.

Tangible goods to be used as evidence shall be transferred together with the case, and for those that are not transferable, a list, photos and other certified documents shall be transferred together with the case.

Judgments rendered by the people's courts shall include a decision on the disposal of the sealed, seized and frozen assets and articles, and assets propagated therefrom.

After a judgment rendered by a people's court becomes effective, the relevant organs shall dispose of the sealed, seized and frozen assets and articles and assets propagated therefrom in accordance with the judgment. All sealed, seized or frozen illicit money and goods and assets propagated therefrom shall be confiscated and turned over to the State Treasury, except for those to be returned to the victims in accordance with the law.

Where a judicial officer embezzles or misappropriates sealed, seized or frozen illicit money and goods, or disposes without authorisation of the assets propagated therefrom, he/she must be pursued with criminal liability in accordance with the law; where a crime is not constituted, a disciplinary sanction shall be imposed.

Chapter IV

Procedures for Review of Death Sentences

Article 235 Death sentences are to be verified and approved by the Supreme People's Court.

Article 236 A case of first instance in which a death sentence is imposed by an intermediate people's court where the accused person does not file an appeal, shall, after review by a High People's Court, be submitted to the Supreme People's Court for verification and approval. Where the High People's Court does not agree with the death sentence, it may have the case tried by itself or remit the case for retrial.

All cases of first instance in which a death sentence is imposed by a High People's Court and where the accused person does not file an appeal, and all cases of second instance in which a death sentence is imposed, shall be submitted to the Supreme People's Court for verification and approval.

Article 237 Cases in which a death sentence with a two-year suspension of execution is imposed by an intermediate people's court are to be verified and approved by a High People's Court.

Article 238 Review of the case of a death sentence by the Supreme People's Court and review of the case of a death sentence with a two-year suspension of execution by a High People's Court shall be conducted by a collegial panel composed of three (3) judges.

Article 239 When reviewing the case of a death sentence, the Supreme People's Court shall make an order on whether or not it approves the death sentence. Where it does not approve the death sentence, the Supreme People's Court may remit the case for a retrial or alter the sentence.

Article 240 When reviewing the case of a death sentence, the Supreme People's Court shall interrogate the accused person, and, where the defence lawyer makes a request, shall hear the opinion of the defence lawyer.

During the course of reviewing the case of a death sentence, the Supreme People's Procuratorate may advise the Supreme People's Court of its opinion. The Supreme People's Court shall inform the Supreme People's Procuratorate of the result of the review of the death sentence.

CHAPTER V

PROCEDURES FOR ADJUDICATION SUPERVISION

Article 241 A party to a case and his/her statutory representative(s) and close relative(s) may file with a people's court or a people's procuratorate a petition against a legally effective judgment or order, but the enforcement of the judgment or order shall not be suspended.

Article 242 Where a petition made by a party to a case or his/her statutory representative(s) or close relative(s) satisfies one of the following conditions, the people's court shall undertake a new trial for the case:

(1) there is new evidence proving that the determination of facts in the original judgment or order was clearly incorrect, which may affect the finding of criminality and sentencing;
(2) evidence used as the basis for criminal charges and penalty is unreliable or insufficient, or should have been excluded pursuant to the law, or the major pieces of evidence in proving the facts of the case contradict each other;
(3) the application of law in the original judgment or order was clearly incorrect;
(4) the litigation procedure violated the provisions of the law and thus a fair trial was likely to be impaired; or
(5) when trying the case, the adjudicating personnel was involved in embezzlement, accepting bribes, practising favouritism, or bending the law in passing judgment.

Article 243 Where the president of a people's court at various levels discovers that the determination of facts or the application of law in a legally effective judgment or an order is clearly incorrect, he/she shall submit the case to the adjudication committee for handling.

Where the Supreme People's Court discovers that a legally effective judgment or an order of a people's court is clearly incorrect, or where a people's court at a higher level discovers that a legally effective judgment or an order of a people's court at a lower level is clearly incorrect, it has the power to have the case tried by itself or to instruct the people's court at a lower level to re-try the case.

Where the Supreme People's Procuratorate discovers that a legally effective judgment or an order of a people's court is clearly incorrect, or where a people's procuratorate at a higher level discovers that a legally effective judgment or an order of a people's court at a lower level is clearly incorrect, it has the power to lodge a protest to a people's court at the same level in accordance with the procedures of adjudication supervision.

For cases protested by a people's procuratorate, the people's court which accepts the protest shall form a collegial panel and conduct a new trial; where the facts in the original judgment are unclear or the evidence is insufficient, it may instruct the people's court at the lower level to re-try the case.

Article 244 Where a people's court at a higher level instructs a people's court at a lower level to re-try a case it shall instruct a people's court at a lower level other than the people's court that originally tried the case to conduct the trial; where it is more appropriate for the people's court of the original trial to try the case, the people's court at the higher level may also order the people's court of the original trial to try the case.

Article 245 When a new trial is to be conducted in accordance with the procedures of adjudication supervision, and the trial is to be conducted by the original trial court, a new collegial panel for the trial shall be established. If the case is originally a case of first instance, it shall be tried under the procedures for first instance, and the new judgment or order may be appealed or protested; if the case is originally a case of second instance, or is a case taken up by a people's court at a higher level for trial, it shall be tried under the procedures for second instance, and the new judgment or order will be final.

Where the people's court holds a court hearing for a retrial case, the people's procuratorate shall send its procurator(s) to be present in the court.

Article 246 Where the decision for the retrial of a case is made by a people's court, and where it is necessary to impose coercive measures upon the accused person, the people's court is to make the decision on such a matter; where the retrial of a case is the result of the protest of the people's procuratorate, and where it is necessary to impose coercive measures upon the accused person, the people's procuratorate is to make the decision on the matter.

When a new trial is to be conducted in accordance with the procedures of adjudication supervision, the people's court may make decisions on the suspension of the execution of the original judgment or order.

Article 247 A case to be re-tried in accordance with the procedures of adjudication supervision shall be concluded by the people's court within three (3) months from the date on which it made the decision to have the case brought up for trial or to have it re-tried; where an extension of the time limit is needed, the extended period shall not exceed six (6) months.

The provisions in the preceding Paragraph apply to protested cases tried in accordance with the procedures of adjudication supervision by the people's court which accepts the protest. Where it is necessary to order a people's court at a lower level to re-try the case, such a decision shall be made within one month from the date on which the protest is accepted. The provisions in the preceding Paragraph apply to the time limit for adjudicating a case by a people's court at the lower level.

Part IV

Execution

Article 248 A judgment or an order shall be executed after it becomes legally effective.

The following judgments and orders are judgments and orders that are legally effective:

(1) judgments or orders against which no appeal or protest is made within the legally prescribed time period;
(2) final judgments or orders; and
(3) judgments of death sentence which have been verified and approved by the Supreme People's Court and judgments of death sentence with a two-year suspension of execution which have been verified and approved by a High People's Court.

Article 249 Where an accused person is found not guilty or is exempted from criminal penalty by a people's court of first instance, he/she shall be released immediately after the announcement of the judgment if he/she is in custody.

Article 250 For a judgment of death sentence with immediate execution made or approved by the Supreme People's Court, the order of execution shall be signed and issued by the president of the Supreme People's Court.

Where a criminal who is sentenced to death with a two-year suspension of execution does not intentionally commit any new crime during the period of the suspension of execution, the penalty imposed on him/her shall be reduced at the end of the period of the suspension of execution; the execution organ shall produce a written recommendation on the matter and submit it to the High People's Court for an order. Where the criminal intentionally commits a new crime and the crime has been proven, the death sentence shall be executed; the High People's Court shall submit the matter to the Supreme People's Court for verification and approval.

Article 251 When a people's court at a lower level receives an order from the Supreme People's Court to execute a death sentence, it shall carry out the sentence of execution within seven (7) days. However, if one of the following situations arises, the sentence shall be suspended, and the matter shall be reported to the Supreme People's Court immediately, and the Supreme People's Court shall make an order:

(1) before the execution it is discovered that the judgment is likely to be mistaken;
(2) before the execution the criminal reveals the facts of a major crime or performs other significant meritorious acts, and therefore the judgment may possibly be altered; or
(3) the criminal is pregnant.

After a condition for the suspension of the execution prescribed in (1) and (2) of the preceding Paragraph no longer exists, the death sentence may only be executed after it has been reported to the president of the Supreme People's Court and the president has re-signed and re-issued an order of execution. Where an execution of a death sentence is suspended under the condition described in (3) of the preceding Paragraph, the case shall be submitted to the Supreme People's Court for a revision of the judgment in accordance with the law.

Article 252 Before a death sentence is to be brought for execution, the people's court shall notify the people's procuratorate to send its personnel to the scene to supervise the execution.

A death sentence is executed by shooting, injection or other methods.

A death sentence may be executed in the execution yard or in a designated place of custody.

The adjudicating personnel instructing the execution shall verify the identity of the criminal, ask him/her whether there is any last word or letter, and then deliver him/her to the executioner for execution of the death sentence. Before the execution, if it is discovered that there might be a mistake, the execution shall be suspended and the matter shall be reported to the Supreme People's Court for an order.

Execution of a death sentence shall be announced in public, but not be exposed to the public.

After a death sentence has been executed, the court clerk at the site shall make a written record. The people's court which brought down the sentence shall report the execution of the death sentence to the Supreme People's Court.

After the execution of a death sentence, the people's court which brought down the sentence shall notify the family members of the criminal.

Article 253 When a criminal is delivered for the execution of a criminal penalty, the relevant legal documents shall be sent, within 10 days from the date on which the judgment becomes effective, to the public security organ or prison or other execution organ by the people's court which delivers the criminal for execution of the criminal penalty.

A criminal sentenced to death with a two-year suspension of execution or to life imprisonment or fixed-term imprisonment shall be brought by the public security organ to a prison for execution of the sentence. Where a criminal is sentenced to a fixed-term imprisonment and the remaining term of the sentence is less than three (3) months when he/she is delivered to serve his/her sentence, the sentence shall be executed in a detention centre instead. The sentences of criminal detention shall be executed by a public security organ.

Sentences of juvenile offenders shall be executed in a juvenile rehabilitation centre.

An execution organ shall bring a criminal into custody without delay and notify the family members of the criminal.

A criminal sentenced to fixed-term imprisonment or criminal detention shall be issued with a release certificate by the execution organ when the sentence is served.

Article 254 In one of the following situations, a criminal sentenced to fixed-term imprisonment or criminal detention may be allowed to serve his/her sentence temporarily outside prison:

(1) the criminal is seriously ill and needs to be released on parole for medical treatment;
(2) the criminal is pregnant or is breast-feeding her own baby; or
(3) the criminal is unable to manage his/her daily life, and the serving of his sentence outside prison temporarily would not cause harm to society.

Where a criminal sentenced to life-imprisonment falls within the provisions of Item (2) in the preceding Paragraph, the serving of the sentence may be executed temporarily outside prison.

If the release of a criminal on parole for medical treatment will endanger society, or if a criminal has made him/herself injured or disabled, the criminal shall not be released on parole for medical treatment.

Where a criminal is truly seriously ill and needs to be released on parole for medical treatment, the illness shall be diagnosed and certified by a hospital designated by the people's government at provincial level.

Before a criminal is transferred to prison, the decision on temporary execution of the sentence outside prison is to be made by the people's court that is to transfer the criminal to prison. After a criminal has been transferred to prison the matter of temporary execution of the sentence outside prison is to be proposed in writing by the prison or detention centre, and to be approved by the prison administration organ at provincial level or above, or by the public security organ at the level of city-with-districts or above.

Article 255 Where a prison or detention centre submits a written proposal on temporary execution of a sentence outside prison, it shall send a copy of the written proposal to the people's procuratorate. The people's procuratorate may present a written opinion to the organ that is to make the decision or give approval.

Article 256 The organ which has decided or approved the temporary execution of a sentence outside prison shall send a copy of its decision to the people's procuratorate. If the people's procuratorate is of the opinion that the decision on the temporary execution of the sentence outside prison is inappropriate, it shall, within one month from the date of the receipt of the copy, send its written opinion to the organ that has decided or approved the temporary execution of the sentence outside prison. The organ that has decided or approved the temporary execution of the sentence outside prison shall, after the receipt of the written opinion of the people's procuratorate, re-examine and verify its decision immediately.

Article 257 In any of the following situations the criminal serving his/her sentence outside prison shall be taken back to prison immediately:

(1) it is found that the conditions for temporary execution of a sentence outside prison are not met;
(2) there is serious violation of the provisions on the supervision and administration of the temporary execution of a sentence outside prison;
(3) when the conditions for temporary execution of a sentence outside prison no longer exist, the term of the criminal's sentence has not been completed.

Where the people's court decides that a criminal temporarily serving his/her sentence outside prison shall be taken back to prison, it shall make the decision and send the relevant legal documents to the public security organ, prison or other execution organs.

Where a criminal who does not meet the conditions for temporary execution of a sentence outside prison is granted such through illegal means such as bribery, etc., the period of sentence he/she has served outside prison is not to be included in the term of punishment. Where a criminal escapes when serving his/her sentence outside prison, the period during which he/she is on the run is not to be included in the term of punishment.

Where a criminal dies during the serving of a sentence outside prison, the execution organ shall notify the prison or detention centre without delay.

Article 258 Criminals sentenced to public surveillance, suspension of execution of their sentence, parole, or temporary execution of their sentence outside prison, are subject to community correction. The community correction execution organ is responsible for the execution.

Article 259 Where a criminal is sentenced to deprivation of political rights, his/her sentence shall be executed by a public security organ. When the term of sentence comes to an end, the execution organ shall notify, in writing, the criminal him/herself and the unit with which he/she works, or the basic local organisation in his/her residential place.

Article 260 Where a criminal sentenced to a fine fails to make the payment within the time limit, the people's court shall compel him/her to pay the fine. If there is true difficulty in paying the fine due to reasons of *force majeure*, the fine may be reduced or waived through an order.

Article 261 A judgment on confiscation of property, whether to be imposed as an additional penalty or an independent penalty, is to be executed by a people's court; where it is necessary, it may also be executed by a people's court in conjunction with a public security organ.

Article 262 Where a criminal, during the period of serving his/her sentence, commits a new crime or is found to have committed any other crime which was not known at the time of the making of the judgment, the case shall be transferred by the execution organ to the people's procuratorate for handling.

Where a criminal sentenced to public surveillance, criminal detention, fixed-term imprisonment or life imprisonment shows true repentance or performs meritorious acts during the period of serving the sentence, and therefore should be granted a reduced penalty or be released on parole, the execution organ shall submit a recommendation letter to the people's court for examination and verification and an order, and shall send a copy of the recommendation letter to the people's procuratorate. The people's procuratorate may send a written opinion to the people's court.

Article 263 Where a people's procuratorate is of the opinion that an order for reduction of a penalty or the granting of parole is inappropriate, it shall, within 20 days of the receipt of the copy of the order, send its written opinion regarding the correction to the people's court. The people's court shall, within one month of the receipt of the opinion for correction, form a new collegial panel to try the case and make a final order.

Article 264 In the course of execution of a sentence, if a prison or an execution organ of another kind considers that the judgment contains some mistake, or if the criminal files a petition, it shall submit the case to a people's procuratorate or the people's court which originally made the judgment for disposition.

Article 265 The people's procuratorates shall conduct supervision over execution organs regarding the legality of their activities in executing criminal penalties. Once an act of violation of law is found, they shall notify the execution organ concerned to make a correction.

Part V

Special Procedures

Chapter I

Litigation Procedures for Juvenile Criminal Cases

Article 266 For juvenile offenders the policy of educating, reforming via education and persuasion and rehabilitation is to be implemented, and the principle of education being essential and punishment being supplementary is to be upheld.

When handling juvenile offender cases, the people's courts, the people's procuratorates and the public security organs shall ensure that a juvenile's exercise of his/her litigation rights is protected and the juvenile receives legal assistance, and shall have the case handled by adjudicating personnel, procuratorial personnel and investigation personnel who understand the physical and psychological characteristics of juveniles.

Article 267 Where a juvenile criminal suspect or accused person has not appointed a defence counsel, the people's court, the people's procuratorate or the public security organ shall notify the legal aid organisation to assign a lawyer to provide defence for the juvenile.

Article 268 When handling a juvenile offender case, the people's court, the people's procuratorate and the public security organ may, in light of the circumstances, investigate the background, the reasons for the crime having been committed, and the custodianship, education, etc. of the juvenile suspect or accused person.

Article 269 The application of arrest measures for a juvenile criminal suspect or accused person shall be strictly limited. When a people's procuratorate conducts examination and approval of arrest and a people's court makes a decision on arrest, they shall interrogate the juvenile criminal suspect or accused person, and listen to the opinion of the defence lawyer.

Juveniles in custody, under arrest or serving a sentence shall be detained separately, administered separately and educated separately, from adults.

Article 270 In a juvenile criminal case, the statutory representative of the juvenile criminal suspect or accused person shall be notified to be present when an interrogation or a trial is being conducted. Where the notification cannot be delivered, or where the statutory representative is unable to attend or is a joint offender in the case, other adult relatives of the juvenile criminal suspect or accused person, representatives of the school which the juvenile criminal suspect or accused person attends, or the unit with which his/she works, and representatives of the basic local organisation or juvenile protection organisation in his/her residential place may also be notified to be present; such situations shall be recorded in the case file. The statutory representative present may exercise the litigation rights of the juvenile criminal suspect or accused person.

Where the statutory representative or other person/s present consider that the personnel handling the case have infringed upon the legitimate rights and interests of the juvenile during the interrogation or trial, they may express their opinion. The interrogation transcript and court transcript shall be handed over on the spot to the statutory representative or other person/s present to read, or shall be read out to them.

When a female juvenile criminal suspect is under interrogation, there shall be female personnel present.

In the trial of a juvenile criminal case, after the juvenile accused person has made his/her final statement, his/her statutory representative may make a supplementary statement.

The provisions of Paragraphs 1, 2 and 3 apply to where juvenile victims or witnesses are questioned.

Article 271 Where a juvenile is suspected of having committed a crime under Chapter 4, 5 and 6 of the Specific Provisions of the Criminal Law, where a criminal penalty of fixed term imprisonment of less than one year is likely to be imposed, the people's procuratorate may make a decision of conditional non-initiation of prosecution where conditions for prosecution are met but the juvenile has shown remorse. Before making the decision of conditional non-initiation of prosecution, the people's procuratorate shall hear opinions from the public security organ and the victim(s).

The provisions of Articles 175 and 176 of this Law apply to where the public security organ requests reconsideration or applies for a review of, or the victim files an appeal against, the decision of conditional non-initiation of prosecution.

Where the juvenile criminal suspect or his/her statutory representative objects to the people's procuratorate's decision of conditional non-initiation of prosecution, the people's procuratorate shall make a decision to initiate prosecution.

Article 272 During the probation period of conditional non-initiation of prosecution, the people's procuratorate shall supervise and observe the juvenile criminal suspect subject to conditional non-initiation of prosecution. The guardian of the juvenile criminal suspect shall increase discipline over and education of the juvenile criminal suspect, and shall cooperate with the people's procuratorate in its supervision and observation work.

The probation period for conditional non-initiation of prosecution is to be no less than six (6) months and no longer than one (1) year from the date on which the people's procuratorate makes the decision of conditional non-initiation of prosecution.

A juvenile criminal suspect subject to conditional non-initiation of prosecution shall abide by the following provisions:

(1) abide by laws and regulations, and obey the supervision;
(2) report his/her activities according to the provisions of the probation body;
(3) apply to the probation body for approval when wanting to leave the residential city or county, or move to another residential place; and
(4) accept rehabilitation and education as required by the probation body.

Article 273 Where a juvenile criminal suspect subject to conditional non-initiation of prosecution is found to be in one of the following situations during the probation period, the people's procuratorate shall cancel the conditional non-initiation of prosecution decision and initiate public prosecution:

(1) he/she has committed a new crime, or it is found that he/she has committed another crime that should have been prosecuted before the granting of conditional non-initiation of prosecution; and
(2) he/she has violated the public order administration provisions or the supervision and administration provisions of the probation body on conditional non-initiation of prosecution, and the circumstances are serious.

The people's procuratorate shall make a decision on non-initiation of prosecution if at the end of the probation period the juvenile criminal suspect subject to conditional non-initiation of prosecution has not met any of the above conditions during his/her probation period.

Article 274 No public hearing is to be conducted for cases where the accused person has not reached the age of 18 at the time of the trial. However, with the consent of the juvenile accused person and his/her statutory representative, the school which the juvenile accused person attends and the juvenile protection organisation may send representatives to be present.

Article 275 Where a criminal did not reach the age of 18 at the time of committing the crime and has been sentenced to a criminal penalty of fixed-term imprisonment of five (5) years or less, the relevant records of the crime shall be sealed and kept.

The records of a crime being sealed shall not be provided to any unit or individual, except where they are needed by judicial organs for the handling of the case or by relevant units for inquiry, in accordance with the State provisions. The units that conduct the inquiry according to the law shall maintain the confidentiality of the information in the sealed records.

Article 276 Cases involving juvenile crime, unless provided for in this Chapter, are to be handled in accordance with other provisions set forth in this Law.

Chapter II

Procedures for Reconciliation between the Parties in Public Prosecution Cases

Article 277 In the following public prosecution cases, where the criminal suspect or the accused person sincerely expresses his/her remorse and obtains the forgiveness of the victim through such means as offering compensation and an apology to the victim, and the victim voluntarily agrees to reconcile, the two parties may reconcile:

(1) cases in which the crime caused by a civil dispute involves a crime prescribed under Chapter IV or Chapter V of the Special Provisions of the Criminal Law and is punishable by a criminal penalty of fixed-term imprisonment of three (3) years or less;

(2) cases of criminal negligence which may attract a criminal penalty of fixed-term imprisonment of seven (7) years or less, except for crimes of dereliction of duty.

The procedures provided in this Chapter do not apply to cases where the criminal suspect or the accused person has committed an intentional crime in the past five (5) years.

Article 278 Where the two parties to the case reconcile, the public security organ, the people's procuratorate and the people's court shall listen to the opinions of the parties to the case and to other relevant persons, examine the voluntariness and legality of the reconciliation, and preside over the formulation of the reconciliation document.

Article 279 For cases where a reconciliation agreement is reached, the public security organ may recommend to the people's procuratorate to treat the case with leniency. The people's procuratorate may recommend to the people's court to treat the case with leniency, and may, where the criminal circumstances are minor and a criminal penalty is not necessary, decide not to initiate prosecution. The people's court may treat the accused person with leniency in accordance with the law.

Chapter III

Procedures for Confiscation of Illegal Gains in Cases Where the Criminal Suspect or the Accused Person Is On the Run or Dead

Article 280 In major criminal cases involving crimes of corruption, terrorism or other serious crimes, where the criminal suspect or the accused person is on the run and cannot be caught after one year of issuance of a circular order for arrest, or where the criminal suspect or the accused person dies, and his/her illegally obtained gains and other assets related the crime must be pursued for their return in accordance with the provisions of the Criminal Law, the people's procuratorate may apply to the people's court for confiscation of the illegal gains.

Where the public security organ is of the opinion that a situation prescribed in the preceding Paragraph exists, it shall produce an opinion letter of confiscation of illegal gains and send it to the people's procuratorate.

An application for confiscation of illegal gains shall contain evidence relevant to the facts of the crime and illegal gains, and list the types, quantity and location of the assets and their state of sealing, seizure and freezing.

The people's court may, where necessary, seal, seize and freeze the assets under application for confiscation.

Article 281 An application for confiscation of illegal gains is to be heard by a collegial panel formed by the intermediate people's court in the place of the crime or in the place of the residence of the criminal suspect or the accused person.

After accepting an application for confiscation of illegal gains, the people's court shall issue a public notice. The period for the public notice is six (6) months. Close relatives of the criminal suspect or the accused person and other interested parties have the right to apply to participate in the legal proceedings; they may also appoint litigation representatives to participate in the legal proceedings.

The people's court shall hear the application for confiscation of illegal gains after the period of the public notice ends. The people's court shall hold a hearing where interested parties participate in the legal proceedings.

Article 282 Where, after a hearing, the assets upon verification are found to be illegal gains or other assets related to the case, the people's court shall render an order on confiscation of the assets, except for those that shall be returned to the victim in accordance with the law; where the assets are found not to be those which shall be pursued for their return, the people's court shall render an order on rejection of the application and cancellation of the measures of sealing, seizure and freezing.

Close relatives of the criminal suspect or the accused person, or any interested party or the people's procuratorate may submit an appeal or protest against the order of a people's court made in accordance with the provisions of the preceding Paragraph.

Article 283 Where, during the adjudication, the criminal suspect or the accused person on-the-run has voluntarily surrendered or been caught, the people's court shall terminate the adjudication.

Where it is in fact a mistake to have the assets of the criminal suspect or the accused person confiscated, the assets shall be returned and compensation be made.

CHAPTER IV

PROCEDURES FOR COMPULSORY MEDICAL TREATMENT FOR MENTALLY ILL PERSONS WHO DO NOT BEAR CRIMINAL LIABILITY UNDER THE LAW

Article 284 A mentally ill person who commits violent acts that endanger public security or seriously harm the personal safety of citizens, and who has been examined and determined through legally prescribed procedures as being exempt from criminal liability, may, if he/she could continue to harm the society, be compelled to receive medical treatment.

Article 285 The decision to compel a mentally ill person to compulsory medical treatment is to be made by the people's court pursuant to the provisions in this Chapter.

Where a public security organ finds that a mentally ill person meets the conditions for compulsory medical treatment, it shall produce a compulsory medical treatment opinion letter and transfer it to the people's procuratorate. Where the people's procuratorate considers that the mentally ill person referred to by the public security organ or identified by itself in the examination for initiating prosecution meets the conditions for compulsory medical treatment, it shall submit a compulsory medical treatment application to the people's court. Where the people's court finds during the adjudication that the accused person meets the conditions for compulsory medical treatment, it may make the decision on compulsory medical treatment.

For a mentally ill person who commits violent acts, the public security organ may, before the people's court makes the decision on compulsory medical treatment, adopt temporary restriction measures of a protective nature.

Article 286 The people's court shall, after accepting an application for compulsory medical treatment, form a collegial panel to adjudicate the case.

In the adjudication of the case, the people's court shall notify the statutory representative of the person under application or the accused person to be present. Where the person under application or the accused person does not appoint a litigation representative, the people's court shall notify the legal aid organisation to assign a lawyer to provide legal assistance for that person.

Article 287 Where, after a hearing, the people's court finds that the person under the application for compulsory medical treatment or the accused person meets the conditions for compulsory medical treatment, it shall make a decision on compulsory medical treatment within one (1) month.

Where the person under the decision of compulsory medical treatment, the victim(s), their statutory representative or close relatives are dissatisfied with the decision on compulsory medical treatment, they may apply to the people's court at the next higher level for review.

Article 288 The medical institute carrying out compulsory medical treatment shall regularly examine and assess the condition of the person under compulsory medical treatment. Where the person is no longer a risk to the personal safety of others and compulsory medical treatment is no longer required, the medical institute shall produce a recommendation on the person's discharge in a timely manner, and report it to the people's court for approval.

The person under compulsory medical treatment and his/her close relatives have the right to apply for termination of compulsory medical treatment.

Article 289 The people's procuratorates conduct supervision over the compulsory medical treatment decisions and their enforcement.

Supplementary Provisions

Article 290 The security departments of the military forces exercise the powers of investigation of criminal cases occurring within the military forces.

Prisons conduct the investigation of criminal cases committed by criminals inside the prison.

The relevant provisions in this Law apply to criminal cases handled by the security departments of the military forces and prisons.

www.ingramcontent.com/pod-product-compliance
Lightning Source LLC
LaVergne TN
LVHW020651300926
849161LV00004B/891